P9-DMW-664

A WRITER'S RESOURCE

THIRD CANADIAN EDITION

Elaine P. Maimon
Governors State University

Janice H. Peritz
Queens College, CUNY

Melanie A. Rubens
*Seneca College of Applied Arts
and Technology*

McGraw-Hill
Ryerson

McGraw-Hill Ryerson

A Writer's Resource
Third Canadian Edition

Statistics Canada information is used with the permission of Statistics Canada. Users are forbidden to copy this material and/or redisseminate the data, in an original or modified form, for commercial purposes, without the expressed permission of Statistics Canada. Information on the availability of the wide range of data from Statistics Canada can be obtained from Statistics Canada's Regional Offices, its World Wide Web site at http://www.statcan.ca and its toll-free access number 1-800-263-1136.

The Internet addresses listed in the text were accurate at the time of publication. The inclusion of a website does not indicate an endorsement by the authors or McGraw-Hill Ryerson, and McGraw-Hill Ryerson does not guarantee the accuracy of information presented at these sites.

ISBN-13: 978-0-07-068584-0
ISBN-10: 0-07-068584-3

1 2 3 4 5 6 7 8 9 0 TCP 1 9 8 7 6 5 4 3 2

Printed and bound in Canada

Care has been taken to trace ownership of copyright material contained in this text; however, the publisher will welcome any information that enables it to rectify any reference or credit for subsequent editions.

Publisher: *Cara Yarzab*
Sponsoring Editor: *Karen Krahn*
Marketing Manager: *Margaret Janzen*
Developmental Editor: *Sara Braithwaite*
Supervising Editor: *Cathy Biribauer*
Editorial Associate: *Marina Seguin*
Photo/Permissions Researcher: *Danny Meldung / Photo Affairs, Inc.*
Copy Editor: *Ruth Bradley-St-Cyr*
Production Coordinator: *Lena Keating*
Cover and Inside Design: *Word & Image Design Studio Inc.*
Composition: *Bookman Typesetting Co. Inc.*
Cover Photo: © *Frans Lanting / Corbis*
Printer: *Transcontinental Printing Group*

Library and Archives Canada Cataloguing in Publication Data

Maimon, Elaine P.
   A writer's resource / Elaine P. Maimon, Janice H. Peritz, Melanie A. Rubens.
— 3rd Canadian ed.

Includes index.
ISBN 978-0-07-068584-0

   1. Report writing—Handbooks, manuals, etc.   2. English language—Grammar—Handbooks, manuals, etc.   3. English language—Rhetoric—Handbooks, manuals, etc.
I. Peritz, Janice   II. Rubens, Melanie, 1962-   III. Title.

PE1408.M3366 2012   808'.042   C2011-907003-0

PREFACE

Student writers need a handbook that...

...helps with the writing of a literary analysis for their literature course, a term paper for psychology, a case study for their management class, or a lab report for biology.

...navigates through a maze of online information.

...teaches how to analyze visual and print sources.

...provides a solid grammatical foundation in the context of editing a paper.

For this generation of tech-savvy writers, this mid-size handbook is *more* than a reference; it is a *resource*.

A Learning Resource: Critical thinking, reading, and writing are vital to a successful post-secondary career. *A Writer's Resource* devotes the first chapter to developing these skills. Reading and thinking critically lead to writing critically and presenting persuasive arguments.

A Writing Resource: Presenting writing as a process, the handbook demonstrates how to pre-write, draft, seek feedback from peers and educators, revise, and edit. Providing cross-discipline content and examples, *A Writer's Resource* shows how good writing is relevant to all disciplines.

A Researching Resource: Requiring students to think critically about each step of the research process, *A Writer's Resource* offers advice and guidelines for conducting primary research, evaluating sources, avoiding plagiarism, and more.

A Documenting Resource: Providing the most up-to-date coverage of the main documentation styles used by various disciplines—MLA, APA, and Chicago—*A Writer's Resource* is a practical tool for students throughout their academic careers. Model papers in Tabs 4, 5, and 6 demonstrate the correct usage of MLA, APA, and *Chicago* styles.

An Editing Resource: Editing for clarity is a necessary skill, and one that students often confuse with proofreading. *A Writer's Resource* provides a three-tier strategy: 1) Editing for global concerns of clarity and style; 2) Editing for grammar conventions; and 3) Editing for correctness—punctuation, mechanics, and spelling.

PEDAGOGY

Cross-Discipline Writing boxes provide relevant information for writing in different disciplines. Offering helpful material, such as interpretive assignments for different courses, as well as discipline-specific items, such as the function of passive voice in scientific and business writing, Cross-Discipline Writing boxes make this handbook useful throughout the academic career.

Tech Tips boxes offer easy-to-use tips for writing on computer, helping students take full advantage of available technology.

Writing Connections boxes, found in the Common Assignments section (Tab 2), alert students to a variety of real-world situations related to writing, helping writers understand how the skills they develop now will aid them in future careers.

Language Tips highlight grammatical information of value to all students. Additionally, the Focus on Language Index at the end of the text allows students to quickly locate useful information on grammar and language usage throughout the text.

FEATURES OF THE THIRD CANADIAN EDITION

Thoroughly revised and updated, the third Canadian edition of *A Writer's Resource*:

- **Showcases cross-disciplinary writing** from a variety of subject areas outside of the humanities to show differences in the writing process, such as task and audience analysis. This edition emphasizes some of the subtle differences in language and content when writing is prepared for a scientific or business audience.

- **Emphasizes academic writing** with an increase in third-person examples. The inclusion of scholarly examples in this edition provides appropriate models of the type of writing that students will produce in their academic careers.

- **Distinguishes between scholarly and non-scholarly sources** while providing more coverage about the importance and process of source evaluation. In a world where research can be conducted in just a few keystrokes, this handbook shows how to determine the credibility and reliability of various sources from print to electronic.

- **Provides relevant examples** to make the material more meaningful to the reader. Taken from current events, the examples not only provide a snapshot of Canada in time, they also serve as discussion points for learners.

- **Updates MLA and APA sections** to align them with the latest changes from the two associations. In addition to the specific formatting changes for each style, both sections now provide more detailed information about citing electronic sources, such as podcasts, virtual environments, blogs, wikis, and YouTube.

- **Expands the discussion on plagiarism** with the addition of material about co-authoring projects and peer review.

- **Uses photos and art** to illustrate rhetorical modes visually and to increase understanding of patterns of development while encouraging students to think of visuals as a natural part of the writing process.

- **Integrates Language Tips** that provide helpful grammatical information for all readers. While this advice is helpful particularly for those for whom English is a second, third, or fourth language, it is beneficial to *all* students.

SUPPLEMENTS

McGraw-Hill Connect™ is a web-based assignment and assessment platform that gives students the means to better connect with their coursework, with their instructors, and with important concepts needed for success now and in the future.

With Connect, instructors can deliver assignments, quizzes, and tests online and integrate grade reports easily with Learning Management Systems (LMS) such as WebCT and Blackboard. By choosing Connect, instructors provide their students with a powerful tool for improving academic performance and truly mastering course material. Connect allows students to practice important skills at their own pace and on their own schedule. Importantly, student assessment results and instructor feedback are all saved online—so students can continually review their progress and plot their course to success.

Connect English helps students improve their writing and grammar skills through comprehensive and reliable instruction, practice material, and more!

Talk to your iLearning Sales Specialist today!

SUPERIOR SERVICE

iLearning Sales Specialist

Your **Integrated Learning Sales Specialist** is a McGraw-Hill Ryerson representative who has the experience, product knowledge, training, and support to help you assess and integrate any of the products, technology, and services listed below into your course for optimum teaching and learning performance. Whether helping your students to improve their grades or putting your entire course online, your iLearning Sales Specialist is there to help you do it. Contact your iLearning Sales Specialist today to learn how to maximize all of McGraw-Hill Ryerson's resources.

Teaching and Learning Conference Series

The educational environment has changed tremendously in recent years, and McGraw-Hill Ryerson continues to be committed to helping you acquire the skills you need to succeed in this new milieu. Our innovative Teaching, Technology & Learning Conference Series brings faculty together from across Canada with 3M Teaching Excellence award winners to share teaching and learn best practices in a collaborative and stimulating environment. Pre-conference workshops on general topics, such as teaching large classes and technology integration, are also offered. We will also work with you at your own institution to customize workshops that best suit the needs of the faculty at your institution.

Create

McGraw-Hill's Create Online gives you access to the most abundant resource at your fingertips—literally. With a few mouse clicks, you can create customized learning tools simply and affordably. McGraw-Hill Ryerson has included many of our market-leading textbooks within Create Online for eBook and print customization as well as many licensed readings and cases. For more information, go to **www.mcgrawhillcreate.com**.

CourseSmart

CourseSmart brings together thousands of textbooks across hundreds of courses in an eTextbook format providing unique benefits to students and faculty. By purchasing an eTextbook, students can save up to 50 percent off the cost of a print textbook, reduce their impact on the environment, and gain access to powerful Web tools for learning including full text search, notes and highlighting, and email tools for sharing notes between classmates. For faculty, CourseSmart provides instant access to review and compare textbooks and course materials in their discipline area without the time, cost, and environmental impact of mailing print examination copies. For further details, contact your *i*Learning Sales Specialist or go to **www.coursesmart.com**.

ACKNOWLEDGMENTS

In memoriam patris.

The comments and recommendations provided by reviewers helped to develop and improve this third Canadian edition. Thank you to the following colleagues for their invaluable advice:

Heather Barfoot, *Niagara College*
Gretchen Huey Barnhill, *University of Lethbridge*
Gisele Baxter, *University of British Columbia*
Brad Bucknell, *University of Alberta*
Lucille Charlton, *Mount Royal University*
Julia Colella, *University of Windsor*
Bill Connor, *University of Alberta*
Roger Fowler, *University of Ottawa*
Kathleen Fraser, *University of Western Ontario*
Sandra Hagan, *Vancouver Island University*
Sally Hayward, *University of Lethbridge*
Pamela Heath, *Southern Alberta Institute of Technology Polytechnic*
Suzanne Hooke, *Fleming College*
Nancy MacIntosh, *University of Prince Edward Island*
Melanie Rabishaw, *Loyalist College*
Ron Srigley, *University of Prince Edward Island*
Lisa Stefaniak, *Fleming College*

One of the rewards of writing a book is to acknowledge the generosity of friends and family who have supported the effort from start to finish. For this third edition, I would like to thank FCE English faculty, colleagues, and student contributors for their invaluable input. I would especially like to thank my family: to my children, Mackenzie and Sydney, who tolerated my absence most mornings; to Frances and Gaye who were always there to make sure I had the time to write. In addition, I would like to recognize Karen Krahn and her team of extraordinary editors, particularly Sara Braithwaite, plus the designers, for their outstanding work on the third Canadian edition of *A Writer's Resource*.

Melanie A. Rubens
Seneca College of Applied Arts and Technology

1

WRITING AND DESIGNING PAPERS

1 Writing and Designing Papers

Reading, Thinking, Writing: The Critical Connection

Writing in response to what you have observed, read, or experienced is a way to transmit a personal perspective to others. Text messages, e-mail, letters, journals, blogs, editorials, and even academic papers provide a concrete "end product" confirming that the need to reflect, assess, and express is critical to the exchange of ideas.

The relationship between critical reading, thinking, and writing is mutually inclusive—each skill influences and shapes the others, providing greater opportunities for acquiring knowledge and then applying that knowledge in concrete, permanent ways. Critical readers, thinkers, and writers recognize that meanings and values are made, not found, so they pose pertinent questions, note significant features, examine relationships, and consider the credibility of what they read, see, and hear. The strategies in this chapter will help you read, think, and write critically.

1a   READING CRITICALLY.

Every text has a purpose, and, through close reading, critical readers clarify that purpose as they read. Identifying the main point and engaging actively in the content, readers then participate in an internal debate with the text as they read—questioning, examining, refuting, summarizing, and connecting important ideas.

1. Preview. Critical reading begins with previewing: a quick review of the author, publication information, title, headings, visuals, first and last paragraphs, and first sentences of the body paragraphs. Be skeptical: just because something is in print does not mean that it is true. Consider the following:

- **Author:** Who wrote this piece? What are the writer's credentials? Who is the writer's employer? What is the writer's occupation? Age? What do you know about his or her interests and values?
- **Context:** Where, when, and by whom was this piece of writing published? What are the facts of its publication?
  - **For a book:** Are you looking at the original publication, or is this a reprint from another source? What is the reputation of the publisher? When was the book published?

- **For an article in a periodical:** Look at the list of editors and their affiliations. What do you know about the journal, magazine, or newspaper in which this writing appears?

  - **For a Web page:** Who created the page? A Web page named for a political candidate, for example, may actually have been put on the Web by his or her opponents. (*See "Evaluating Internet Sources" on pp. 140–142.*)

- **Purpose:** What do the title and first and last paragraphs tell you about the purpose of the piece? Will the main purpose be to entertain, to teach, to persuade, or something else? Are there visuals in this piece? What do the visual aids suggest about the frame of reference for this work? What do the headings tell you?

- **Audience:** Whom do you suspect the writer is trying to entertain, teach, persuade, or influence?

2. Annotate. Annotate (add explanatory notes or comments) by underlining or circling words, phrases, and sentences as you read and by writing notes in the margin.

- Underline or circle words and phrases that capture the point of the text

- Record your reactions. Agree or disagree with the writer. Ask "Why?" or "How?"

Sounds more like idealism— and ideals are important.

Why would anyone divorce a sick spouse?

> Once upon a time I held these beliefs about divorce: that everyone who does it could have chosen not to do it. That it's a lazy way out of marital problems. That it selfishly puts personal happiness ahead of family integrity. Now I tremble for my (ignorance.) It's easy, in fortunate times, to forget about the ambush that could leave your head reeling: serious mental or physical illness, death in the family, abandonment, financial calamity, humiliation, violence, despair.
>
> —BARBARA KINGSOLVER, "Stone Soup"

- At important intervals, pause and put into your own words what the writer is saying:

Kingsolver used to believe that only selfish people got divorced; now she thinks that bad events may lead to divorce.

3. Summarize. A summary recounts (in your own words) someone else's ideas so that you can get a better understanding of what you have just read and then communicate those ideas to others. A good summary will help the reader to appreciate the meaning and function of the topic's component parts, creating a further opportunity to explore the relationship of those parts through analysis. But, summaries are not simply shortened versions of an original piece of writing; they identify the significant pieces of information needed for deeper understanding. Writing a clear and accurate summary of a complex text can be difficult. These suggestions may make that task a bit easier. To start, ask yourself the following questions after reading the text:

- Which ideas are most important? Why
- What is the relationship between these ideas?
- What do the main sections imply?

Once you have an idea of the main information, break it down further:

- Determine what information should actually be included or excluded.

- Determine how to best organize your information (a linear sequence of ideas is not always the most accurate). Consider other organizational principles—rank information from most/least important; most controversial; most applicable or relevant to the point.

- Provide depth rather than breadth (you can't explain or discuss every point in a short summary).

- Explain the "how" or "why" of a topic rather than just listing the "what."

Finally, develop the summary based on your preliminary examination of the topic:

- **Write down the text's main point**. Compose a sentence that identifies the text, the writer, what the writer does (reports, explores, analyzes, argues), and the most important point the writer makes about the topic.

- **Divide the text into sections.** To develop the main point, writers move from one subtopic to another or from the statement of an idea to the reasons, evidence, and examples that support it.

- **In one or two sentences, sum up what each of the text's sections says.** Compose your own topic sentence for each major section of the text.

- **Combine your sentence stating the writer's main point with the sentences summarizing each of the text's major sections.** Now you have a first draft. Read the draft to see if it makes sense. Add, remove, or change parts as needed.

4. Analyze. You analyze a subject by identifying its significant parts and examining how those parts are related to each other to make a whole. In a rhetorical analysis, the goal is to understand how a text or a speech conveys meaning and influences people. A visual analysis looks at how symbols (art, architecture, advertisements, dance, Web sites) communicate meaning and a literary analysis examines the elements of fiction and how they support interpretation of the texts. Ask and answer questions about the what, how, and why of a text:

- **Topic and point:** Identify what the text is about and the writer's main point. Usually, writers state the main point at the beginning and end of their text, often as a response to some question or issue the topic raises. Sometimes the point is signalled by such words as *in short, hence,* or *therefore.*

- **Writer's position and voice:** A writer's **position**—where he or she stands in relation to the audience and subject— involves his or her style, values, and way of establishing credibility. Does the writer seem to be speaking *at, to,* or *with* the audience? What about the writer's **voice**? How does the writer sound—like a reasonable judge, an enthusiastic preacher, a thoughtful teacher, or a reassuring friend?

- **Purpose:** To what extent is the writer's purpose informative? Interpretive? Argumentative?

- **Development of ideas:** What kind of support does the writer rely on to develop the main point? How is the topic organized? Does the writer define key terms? Tell relevant stories? Provide logical reasons? (*For more on ways of developing ideas, see Chapter 3, Drafting, pp. 27–42.*)

- **Appeals to emotion:** Does the text use any words, phrases, clichés, images, or examples that are emotionally charged? How much does the writer depend on emotional appeals to support his or her point?

- **Effect:** What is the text's effect on your images, ideas, beliefs, and actions?

5. Synthesize. People synthesize material every day. When you hear contrasting accounts of a party from two different sources, you assess the reliability and potential bias of each one; you select the information that is most pertinent to you; you evaluate the story that each one tells; and you finally create a composite, or synthesis, of what you think really went on. When you synthesize information from two or more texts, you follow the same process.

1b THINKING CRITICALLY.

Critical thinking is fundamental to all scholarly work and to active participation in the world around us. "Critical" is often understood to mean "finding fault" or "very important" (and therefore difficult to understand!). However, in the phrase *critical thinking*, the word *critical* refers to the discovery and acquisition of important information through objective, careful observation.

Critical thinkers write to communicate ideas to learn, to deepen understanding of concepts, and to clarify relationships between concepts. In other words, critical thinkers *use* writing as tool for learning ideas deeply and permanently.

Evaluating a text's argument is not always a simple exercise. Its purpose is more complex: to determine the text's promise, limitations, strengths, and weaknesses.

CROSS-DISCIPLINE **WRITING**

Mapping Your Topic

When you are analyzing a text within the framework of a particular discipline, you might begin your analysis by comparing the text you are studying with other texts written on the same topic but from different perspectives—from different places on the disciplinary map. For example, in a discussion about the housing crisis:

- **What issue might the topic raise for members of different disciplines?** For sociologists, the issue might be the human impact associated with the lack of affordable housing. For political scientists, the significant issue might be the funding debates between levels of government over housing.

- **How would members of different disciplines investigate the issues that interest them?** What data would sociologists or political scientists want? Where and how would they get the data?

- **What kinds of conclusions do members of different disciplines tend to expect and accept?** Sociologists expect and accept arguments about how people are affected by their living conditions, how groups within society are impacted by societal change, and what effects change has on society. Political scientists accept conclusions based on the analysis of government policy and procedures and the influence of laws, economics, and other political principles on the infrastructure.

1. Recognizing an argument. The word *argument,* when used in the context of critical thinking, does not mean a shouting match. In reasoned debate, inside and outside the classroom, an argument means a path of reasoning aimed at demonstrating the truth or falsehood of an assertion. The assertion must be arguable: it must be on an issue about which reasonable people can disagree.

For example, a journalism student writing for the school campus paper might make the following assertion:

> As Saturday's game illustrates, the Mustangs are on their way to winning the Queen's Cup.

2. Analyzing and evaluating an argument. There are a number of ways to analyze an argument and evaluate its effectiveness. Two common methods are (1) to concentrate on the type of reasoning the writer is using and (2) to question the logical relationship of a writer's claims, grounds, and warrants, using the Toulmin method (see page 9).

Type of reasoning Writers may use either inductive or deductive reasoning to make an argument. When writers use **inductive reasoning** (also known as "the **scientific method**"), they do not prove that the argument is true; instead they convince reasonable people that it is probable by presenting evidence (facts and statistics, anecdotes, and expert opinion). Investigators gather data from experiments, surveys, and careful observations and formulate hypotheses—arguments—to explain these data. They then test their hypotheses by collecting additional information. When writers use **deductive reasoning,** on the other hand, they make two or more assertions (called *premises*) and then draw a conclusion.

If the journalism student who is writing about the hockey team is reasoning inductively, she will present a number of facts—her evidence—and then draw the conclusion that seems probable:

FACT 1	With four games remaining, the Mustangs have a four-point lead over the second-place Thunderwolves.
FACT 2	The Mustangs' closest opponents, the Thunderwolves, have a combined record of 15 wins and 31 losses.
FACT 3	The Thunderwolves lost their final two games to opponents with lower overall points.
FACT 4	The Mustangs' last two games will be played at home, giving them the home-ice advantage.
CONCLUSION	The Mustangs are probably going to win the conference title.

A reader would evaluate this student's argument by judging the quality of her evidence, using the following criteria:

- **Is it accurate?** Make sure that any facts presented as evidence are correct.
- **Is it relevant?** Check to see if the evidence is clearly connected to the point being made.
- **Is it representative?** Make sure that the writer's conclusion is supported by evidence gathered from a sample that accurately reflects the larger population (for example, it has the same proportion of men and women, older and younger people, and so on). If the writer is using an example, make sure that the example is typical and not a unique situation.
- **Is it sufficient?** Evaluate whether there is enough evidence to satisfy questioning readers.

If the journalism student is using deductive reasoning, however, the reasonableness of her conclusion will depend on the accuracy of her premises.

PREMISE	Hockey teams with a two-game lead in their division in early February usually go on to win their conference.
PREMISE	As of February 11, the Mustangs have a two-game lead over their nearest opponent.
CONCLUSION	The Mustangs are probably on their way to winning the conference title.

A reader would evaluate this argument by deciding whether to accept the two premises. For example, a reader might question whether most hockey teams with two-game leads go on to win their conference.

In college and university, deductive reasoning predominates in philosophy and in other humanities disciplines. However, you should be alert to both types of reasoning in all your academic courses and in your life.

Toulmin method Philosopher Stephen Toulmin has developed another useful way to understand and implement logical thinking. His analysis of arguments is based on *claims* (assertions about a topic), *grounds* (reasons and evidence), and *warrants* (assumptions or principles that link the grounds to the claims). Consider the following sentence from an argument by a student in a Canadian literature class:

As *Survival* shows, Margaret Atwood presents survival (both literal and figurative) as the spirit of Canadian literature.

This example, like all logical arguments, has three facets:

- Logical arguments make a claim. A claim is the same thing as a point or a thesis; it is an assertion about a topic. It is important to remember that a thesis says something arguable about a topic. A weak thesis does not make a claim and therefore cannot be argued. (*For more on theses, see pp. 11–16 and Chapter 3, Drafting, pp. 27–42.*)

WEAK CLAIM   Atwood writes about survival.

STRONG
CLAIM
Atwood writes about survival as the physical, cultural, and spiritual struggle faced by many Canadians.

Evaluating claims:

- Are the terms in the claim clear and precise?
- Is the claim too absolute to be considered fair, or does it include qualifying words such as *might* or *possibly*?
- Is the claim merely a statement of fact or a statement with which few would argue?
- To what extent does the claim respond to a question or raise an issue of real concern to its audience (for example, the members of a discipline)?

- Logical arguments present grounds for the claim. Grounds consist of the reasons and evidence (facts, statistics, anecdotes, and expert opinion) that support the claim. In literary criticism, for example, a literary work often serves as the grounds for a claim. In the above claim "As *Survival* shows," etc., the book itself is the source of the grounds, the reasons, and the evidence for the writer's claim that Atwood's discussion presents literal and figurative survival as the spirit of Canadian literature.

Evaluating the grounds for a claim:

- To support his or her assertions, does the writer present data, cite statistics, quote authorities, or tell anecdotes (brief narratives)?
- Does the writer use different kinds of evidence, or does he or she rely on only one type?
- Are the writer's reasons and evidence relevant to the claim or are they off topic?
- Does the writer present enough evidence?
- What methods did the writer use to collect data? (*Also see pp. 14–15 for more on assessing evidence.*)

- Logical arguments depend on assumptions to link the grounds to the claim. When you analyze an argument, you should be aware of the unstated assumptions, or warrants, that underlie both the claim and the grounds that support it. For example, by selecting *Survival* to support the claim that "Atwood presents survival (both literal and figurative) as the spirit of Canadian literature," the writer assumes that in the text, the concept of survival can function as a symbol.

As you continue to read and write, look for unstated assumptions and bring them to the surface. Consider what the reader has to assume (take for granted) to accept the reasons and evidence offered in support of the claim. Be aware as well that hidden assumptions sometimes show **bias**: positive or negative inclinations that can manipulate unwary readers.

3. Recognizing common logical fallacies. Even expert logicians can drift off course in their enthusiasm to make a point. These errors in direction are called fallacies or mistakes in logic. Use the box on pages 12–13 to help you identify fallacies when you read and avoid them when you write.

1c WRITING CRITICALLY.

Sharpening your ability to think critically, objectively and to express your views effectively is the main purpose of post-secondary study. When you write critically, you gain a voice in the important discussions and major decisions of our society. Writing can make a difference.

Each writing situation will provide practice in addressing issues that are important in the larger community. Selecting a topic that you care about will motivate you to think matters through and to make cogent arguments. To make the most convincing case, though, you will have to go beyond personal emotions about an issue and will also have to empathize with potential readers who may disagree with you about the subject.

1. Find a topic worth writing about. Arguments occur in a context of debate and usually concern one or more of the following questions:

- What is true?
- What is good?
- What is to be done?

People seek answers to these questions, but they often disagree about which answers are best. To enter into the debate, you have to figure

Common Logical Fallacies

Non-sequitur: A conclusion that does not logically follow from the evidence presented or one that is based on irrelevant evidence.

> EXAMPLE Assistance to single mothers is provided by government agencies, thereby encouraging out-of-wedlock births. [Is single parenthood really motivated by government programs?]

Red herring: An argument that diverts attention from the true issue by concentrating on something irrelevant.

> EXAMPLE Atwood's book *Survival* is unsuccessful because it draws attention to the confusion around national identity in Canada. [Why can't a book that focuses on problems be successful? This statement is irrelevant.]

Bandwagon: An argument that depends on going along with the crowd, under the false assumption that truth can be determined by a popularity contest.

> EXAMPLE Everybody knows that Atwood exploits survival as a main theme in all her work. [Even if everyone "agrees," how does this make the premise/proposition true?]

Ad hominem: A personal attack on someone who disagrees with you rather than a reasoned attack on the person's argument.

> EXAMPLE The premier is a liar, so naturally he will oppose any change to the provincial funding formula. [Does the label "liar" have anything to do with the premier's policies? No, the criticism of the premier is simply a personal attack.]

Circular reasoning: An argument that restates the point rather than supporting it with reasonable evidence.

> EXAMPLE The wealthy should pay more taxes because taxes should be higher for people with higher incomes. [Why should wealthy people pay more taxes? The rest of the statement doesn't answer this question; it just restates the position.]

out what is at issue in these disagreements, where you stand on the issue, and why your position is reasonable.

Your purpose in presenting your position to others is not to win but to take part in the ongoing dialogue. As you present your

Begging the question: A form of circular reasoning that assumes the truth of a questionable opinion.

EXAMPLE   The prime minister's poor relationship with the military has weakened the armed forces. [Does the prime minister really have a poor relationship with the military?]

Hasty generalization: A conclusion based on inadequate evidence.

EXAMPLE   Temperatures across the United States and Canada last year exceeded the fifty-year average by two degrees, thus proving that global warming is a reality. [Is this evidence enough to prove this very broad conclusion?]

Biased language: Words with strong positive or negative overtones that are designed to sway opinion.

EXAMPLE   The opposition of the self-serving anti-poverty militants further increased the tensions between the street people and the police. [Does "self-serving" and "militants" fairly describe the anti-poverty protesters, or are the words meant to evoke negative reactions?]

Either/or fallacy: The idea that a complicated issue can be resolved by resorting to one of only two options when in reality there are additional choices.

EXAMPLE   Either the provincial government will raise taxes or our province's economy will suffer. [Are these really the only two possibilities?]

False analogy: The assumption that some similarities between two things indicate total similarity between the two.

EXAMPLE   Why should teachers complain about working more hours? Professional people often work longer hours without any apparent harm! [The assumption is that the type of work is the same and it should be evaluated by the same criteria.]

argument, keep in mind that reasonable people can see things differently. Acknowledge and respect the views of others. Negotiating differences should become part of your purpose.

2. Make a strong claim. Advancing a strong, debatable thesis on a topic of interest is key to writing a successful argument. Keep in mind, however, that writing itself is a tool for thinking through your position on a wide variety of issues. As you think, write, and learn about your topic, you will develop, clarify, and sometimes entirely change your views. Think of your writing as a "work in progress," evolving as you gain more knowledge about the topic.

If you write, "I feel that going green in Canada is possible," there is nothing to debate, because you are expressing an opinion—saying something about yourself rather than about the environment or the reasons why or how going green is addressed. But when the Suzuki Foundation in *Pricing Green: Saving Green* states that, "if Canada is to reduce its greenhouse gas emissions, then the introduction of a strong and consistent carbon price across the entire economy is necessary," several important concepts are introduced: a specific reference to a problem (greenhouse gases); the reasons why it is important (to reduce emissions); and, how it could be implemented without undue economic hardship (carbon pricing across the economy). (*For more on theses, see Chapter 3, Drafting, pp. 27–42*). Moving away from simply expressing an opinion to providing a well-crafted objective perspective will encourage readers to think more carefully about what you are saying.

3. Support and develop your claim with evidence. The intelligent selection and careful documentation of evidence—facts and statistics, anecdotes, and expert opinion—will support a credible case.

- Facts and statistics. Facts and statistics can be convincing support for a claim. Be aware, however, that people on different sides of an issue can interpret the same facts and statistics differently or can cite different facts and statistics to prove their point.

  The report *Pricing Carbon: Saving Green* claims that the introduction of carbon pricing into the Canadian economy will have little impact on the long-term gross domestic product.

  > According to the research [...], Canada's economy is expected to grow to a GDP of $1.79 trillion per year by the year 2020. The introduction of a carbon price is projected to slightly reduce this rate of GDP growth to $1.76 trillion—a difference of 1.9%. However, if the revenue that the government collects from carbon pricing is properly reintroduced, the projected decline in the rate of economic growth can be substantially reduced to 0.9%.

- **Anecdotes.** An anecdote is a brief narrative used as an illustration to support a claim. Stories appeal to the emotions as well as to the intellect and can be very effective in making an argument. Be especially careful to check anecdotes for logical fallacies (*see pp. 12–13*).

- **Expert opinion.** The views of authorities in a given field can also be powerful support for a claim. Make sure that the expert you cite has the proper credentials to comment on the issue about which you are writing.

In well-written arguments, reasoning often relies on research. As you find and read a variety of sources, you will clarify your claim and amass the evidence you need to support that claim. You will also want to demonstrate your credibility to readers by properly quoting and documenting the information you have gathered from your sources. (*See the guidelines for documenting sources in Tabs 4–6.*)

4. Appeal to your audience. You want your readers to see you as reasonable, ethical, and empathetic—qualities that promote communication among people who have differences. You display the quality of your thought, character, and feelings—what the ancient Greeks called logos, ethos, and pathos—by the way that you argue for what you believe.

Dominant in most sound arguments, these three main rhetorical styles are the basis of persuasive writing. For example, logos-driven documents represent most scholarly writing produced; ethos-driven writing relies strongly on reputation—of the writer or organization; and, pathos-based writing is often used to provoke an emotional reaction. To appeal to logos, ethos, or pathos, consider the following:

FOR LOGOS (LOGIC), USE	FOR ETHOS (ETHICS), USE	FOR PATHOS (EMOTION), USE
• Definitions • Quotations • Expert testimony • Facts and statistics • Denotative meaning • Factual and/or historical analogies • Theoretical, neutral, and/or abstract language	• Appropriate language based on audience and subject • Fair, balanced, and sincere presentation of ideas • Accurate and correct grammar/mechanics	• Vivid, concrete, and powerful language • Emotionally charged and figurative vocabulary • Connotative meaning • Emotional narratives

Giving reasons and supplying evidence for your position and arguing responsibly by avoiding fallacies establish your logos. (*For more on fallacies, see pp. 12–13.*) You also need to show that you are sincere (ethos) and that you care about your readers' feelings (pathos). For example, you might refer to a quality or belief you share with others, even those who disagree with you. Establishing common ground in this way will make readers more open to your argument.

- Do you share an interest in the same issue, topic, or field?
- Do you have overlapping goals or values?

When you read your argument to yourself or to peers, pay attention to how you are coming across. What would readers who have never met you think of you after reading what you have to say?

5. Consider opposing viewpoints. Don't ignore counterarguments—substantiated claims that challenge or refute your thesis. Instead, think critically about them, and try to refute or accommodate them. For example, you might present at least one counterargument and then refute it, perhaps by presenting evidence that shows why it is open to question. If you are unable to refute a counterargument, you can often accommodate it by qualifying your thesis with words such as likely, usually, most, or some. Another tactic is to make a more specific statement of the conditions for or exceptions to your thesis, such as, "If inflation continues, X" or "Until cloning is perfected, Y." These kinds of qualifications often appear in the conclusion of an argument, where it is appropriate to include a more subtle version of the paper's opening thesis.

6. Check for errors in your logic. Checking the logic of your own writing is probably the greatest challenge to your ability to read critically. It is essential to assess your argument objectively for errors in reasoning. Use the chart of Common Logical Fallacies on pages 12–13 to test your reasoning. Of course, nothing is more helpful than hearing and responding to your classmates' questions. Peer review is one of the best tools for developing critical thinking and writing skills. (*For advice on peer review, see Chapter 4, Revising, pp. 43–57.*)

Planning

2

A large part of learning involves writing papers that contribute to the ongoing conversation of educated people. The advice in this chapter will help you determine the writing requirements of a particular assignment and get you started on a first draft.

2a APPROACHING THE ASSIGNMENTS.

1. Write about a question. Whether you choose your topic or your topic is assigned, most topics must be narrowed. To arrive at a manageable topic, it helps to try to write about a question. To develop questions, consider the following plan:

- **I wonder:** Using the course content or the assignment as your point of departure, list concepts and issues that you wonder about.

- **They say:** Reviewing your class notes, course reading, online postings to discussion groups, and scholarly bibliographies, check to see what topics and issues others in the field say are important. Jot down relevant information, ideas, and issues.

- **I think:** Choosing an item or two that you have listed, determine your perspective on it, and consider what purposes you might fulfill by writing about it. Be curious. Connect your interests to the framework of the course.

The particular course you are taking defines a range of questions that are appropriate within a given discipline. Here are examples of the way your course would help define the questions you might ask if, for example, you were writing about Pierre Trudeau:

Canadian history: To what extent did the *Canadian Charter of Rights and Freedoms* change Canadian national identity?

Canadian politics: How did Trudeau's support of the "No" forces during the Quebec Referendum on Sovereignty Association affect his position on national bilingualism?

Canadian economics: Trudeau is blamed for increasing the national deficit by 1,200% during his years in power. What was the long-term impact on Canada?

2. Audience analysis. Who makes up your audience? Instructors are the primary readers for students' work, but they represent a larger group of readers who have an interest or a stake in the topic. An education professor, for example, reads and evaluates a paper as a representative of other students in the course, experts in educational policy, school board members, public school principals, and parents of school-age children, among others.

For most writers, understanding the intended audience is an important consideration in planning, writing, and reviewing a document. Good writers adjust their work to meet the needs, interests, and background of the target group of readers. However, an audience analysis can become rather complex when various factors are taken into consideration. For example,

- **Background—experience, knowledge, or expertise:** How much knowledge can you expect the target audience to have? How much detail are you, as the writer, expected to provide if some of the readers don't have the same background knowledge? Too little detail can frustrate readers without experience in your topic; likewise, too much detail can bore those to whom the subject is well known.

- **Interests and needs:** What do readers expect to read in your document? What don't they want to read? Knowing the readers' needs will help you determine the appropriate content for your document.

- **Mixed audience:** How do you provide content for more than one type of reader? Often, documents are accessed by mixed groups of readers (experts, novices, public), but it is sometimes difficult to balance the level of the writing. One option is to write for all your readers (which becomes complicated), or to present your document in sections, with headings specifying content. Readers can then choose what best suits their needs.

- **Variability within an audience:** What happens when the specific intended audience has varied levels of expertise? Writing for the least or most experienced can alienate a segment of the readers, so writing for the majority is often the best practice, using appendices and cross-references for those needing supplemental material.

- **Unknown audience:** How do you write a document when the audience is not known? Sometimes, it is not clear who will be reading your work, which makes it very difficult for a writer to make appropriate content and language choices. However, writers can overcome this dilemma by: 1) being neutral (to appeal to either side of an argument); 2) presenting sufficient, verifiable evidence; and 3) organizing material in a clear and logical way. These strategies are likely to hold the attention of most types of readers.

To start, here are some background questions to answer about your audience:

- What are the demographics of this audience? What is the education level, social status, occupation, gender, and ethnicity of a typical audience member?
- What common assumptions and differences of opinion do these readers bring to the issue?
- What images do they have, what ideas do they hold, and what actions do they support?
- What is your goal in writing for this audience? Do you want to intensify, clarify, complicate, or change their assumptions and opinions?

3. Task analysis. What kind of assignment are you doing? What is its purpose? Think beyond the simple statement, "I have to write an essay" or "I have a paper due." Are you expected to inform, interpret, or argue?

- **Informing:** writing to transmit knowledge. Terms like *classify, illustrate, report*, and *survey* are often associated with the task of informing.
- **Interpreting:** writing to produce understanding. Terms like *analyze, compare, explain,* and *reflect* are more likely to appear when the purpose is interpreting.
- **Arguing:** writing to state and negotiate matters of public debate. *Agree, assess, defend,* and *refute* go with the task of arguing.

Some terms, such as *comment, consider,* and *discuss,* do not point to a particular purpose, but many others do. If you are not clear about the kind of work you are expected to do, ask your professor.

4. Select the appropriate genre. Genre simply means kind of writing. Poems, stories, and plays are genres of literature, and they are unique. Different genres of writing predominate in different disciplines.

Sometimes an assignment will specify the kind of work, or genre, you are being asked to produce. For example, you may be asked to write a report (an informative genre), a comparative analysis (an interpretive genre), or a critique (an argumentative genre).

Some genres, like the case study, are common in a particular field such as sociology but not in all disciplines. Understanding the genre required is very important in successfully fulfilling an assignment. If you are supposed to be writing a description of a snake for a field guide, you will not be successful if you write a poem—even a very good poem—about a snake. (*See Tab 2: Common Assignments, pp. 73–122.*)

5. Use appropriate language. Understanding genre helps you make decisions about language. For the description of a snake in a field guide, you would use highly specific terminology, including some Latin and Greek words, to differentiate one type of snake from another. A poem would incorporate striking images, vivid words and phrases that evoke the senses, and other forms of language commonly used in literature.

6. Choose an appropriate voice. The concept of voice is difficult to grasp in a discussion of writing because we think of voice as something that we hear. But we also hear voices when we read, and we create voices when we write. The following two passages both deal with the death of a news anchor named Daniel McKay. Read both passages aloud, and listen to the different voices:

> Taylor originally planned her press conference on Thursday, but postponed it out of respect for Churchill news anchor Daniel McKay who died Wednesday morning after losing his 3-year battle with cancer.
>
> —J. G. BLACK, *The Chronicle*

> Daniel McKay would probably enjoy the network's plan to honour him with an on-air moment of silence. He was rarely ever quiet in the studio or anywhere else!
>
> —K. LINDER, *The Network Insider*

The first passage is written in an even tone that emphasizes factual reporting. The second passage is written in a poignant style that quietly and movingly celebrates McKay's life.

Different writing situations and assignments allow you to try out different voices. As a student, you will usually want to inspire trust in your readers by sounding informed, reasonable, and fair. Your **position**—where you stand in relation to your audience and your subject—is seldom that of an expert. Instead, you are writing as an educated person who is sharing what you have learned and what you think about it.

Readers tend to be most comfortable with an even tone of voice, a style that values the middle and avoids the extremes of the impersonal or the intimate, the long-winded or the curt, and the pretentious or the casual.

PRETENTIOUS	The epistolary mode of literary expression has assumed numerous distinctive guises since its original manifestation more than four thousand years ago in the cuneiform inscriptions of ancient Sumer.
CASUAL	Letters have been around for a really long time.
APPROPRIATE ACADEMIC VOICE	As Kany points out, epistolary writing has flourished ever since it first emerged among the Sumerians.

Writers also need to be aware of the levels of formality that still exist in some forms of written communications in spite of its uses in popular culture. For example, in virtual environments, the medium often causes confusion:

textspeak: hey! r u serious? i dont c ur point at all imho

In a text message, this type of communication is the norm; within an academic course online, this level of informality would not be acceptable, even though the topic may be the same. Clearly, the topic, purpose, and audience will also determine your approach

Read your work aloud to yourself or to classmates so that you can literally hear your voice. Do the tone and language suit the assignment's topic, purpose, and audience? (*For more about style, see Tab 7: Editing for Clarity.*)

2b EXPLORING YOUR IDEAS.

You explore new ideas when you are getting started on a project, when you are feeling stuck and when you are searching for something new to say. The following strategies will help you brainstorm and come up with ideas at any stage.

1. List. One way to brainstorm is to start with a topic and list the words, phrases, images, and ideas that come to mind. The key to brainstorming is to turn off your internal editor and just jot things down. Later, you can review this list, underline one or more key terms, and add or delete items. Here is a list a student produced on the topic of work:

Work—what is it?

Skilled/unskilled

Most jobs today in service industries

Work and retirement

My dad's retired, but has he stopped working?

If you never want to retire, is your job still considered work?

Jobs I have had: babysitter, camp counsellor, sales clerk, office
worker—I'd be happy to retire from those, especially the
salesclerk job

Standing all day

Do this, do that

Punch the clock

Do it over again and again

Difference between work and career

I want a career, not a job

Dress for success

High-powered lunches, late dinner

Travel

Making presentations

Pressure

Making decisions

Big house

Fast car

2. Cluster. Having something down in writing enables you to look for categories and connections. Clustering, sometimes called mapping, is a brainstorming technique that generates categories and connections from the beginning. To make an idea cluster, do the following:

- Write your topic in the centre of a piece of paper, and draw a circle around it.
- Surround the topic with subtopics that interest you. Circle each, and draw a line from it to the centre circle.
- Brainstorm more ideas. As you do so, connect each one to a subtopic already on the sheet, or make it a new subtopic of its own.

Working together as a group, the students in a composition course produced the following idea cluster on the topic of "work in Canada today" (see Figure 2.1):

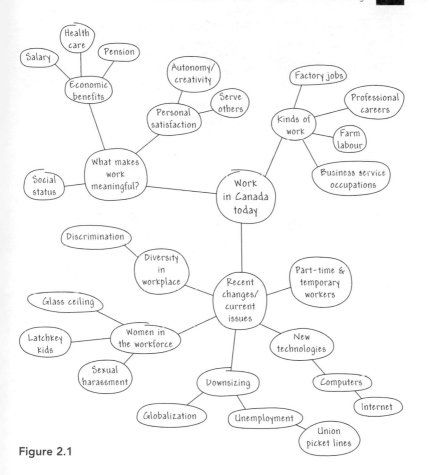

Figure 2.1

Another type of mapping—**concept mapping**—extends this strategy by diagramming the relationships among concepts rather than focusing on one central idea (see Figure 2.2). A concept map consists of graph nodes that are labelled and linked with directional arrows, arranged in a hierarchical pattern. The labelled links explain the relationship between the concepts (nodes).

3. Freewrite. When you feel blocked or unsure about what you think, try freewriting. Just write whatever occurs to you about a topic. If nothing comes to mind, then write "nothing comes to mind" until something else occurs to you. The trick is to keep pushing forward without stopping. Usually, you will discover some implicit point in

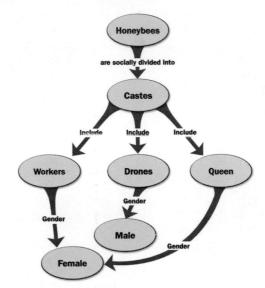

Figure 2.2

your seemingly random writing. The following is a student's freewriting on the topic of work:

> I want to talk about the difference between a job and work—between a job and a career. If you aren't paid, is it work? If it is, what's the difference between work and play? There are some things I would only do for money—like work as a waiter. But there are other things I would do even if I weren't paid—garden or ride my bike or play with kids. The trick is to find a career that would allow me to get paid for doing those things.

4. Question. Asking questions is a good way to explore a topic further. The journalist's five w's and an h (who? what? where? when? why? and how?) can help you find specific ideas and details. For example, a student group assigned to research and write a paper about some aspect of work came up with the following questions:

- In terms of age, gender, and ethnicity, who is working in the new cyberspace infotainment industry?
- What are the working conditions, benefits, and job security of those employed in the current Canadian service economy?
- Where are all the manufacturing jobs these days?
- When is it best for people to retire from jobs?

CROSS-DISCIPLINE WRITING

Different Questions Lead to Different Answers

Always consider what questions make the most sense in the context of the course you are taking. Scholars in different disciplines pose questions related to their fields.

- **Sociology:** A sociologist might ask questions about the ways management and workers interact in the high-tech workplace.
- **History:** A historian might ask how women's roles in the workplace have—or have not—changed since 1960.
- **Economics:** An economist might wonder what effect, if any, the North American Free Trade Agreement (NAFTA) has had on factory layoffs and closings in Canada.

- Why are so many Canadian businesses "downsizing"?
- How do people prepare themselves for career changes?

Other questioning techniques include the following:

- Looking at a topic dramatically, as an action (*what*) with actors (*who*), a scene (*where*), means (*how*), and purpose (*why*).
- Looking at a topic as a static thing—a particle—that has its own distinguishing features and parts, as a wave that changes over time, and as a field that operates as a system.

STATIC THING	What is work? Do the words work, job, and career mean the same thing to most people? How do we know when someone is not doing work? What is the opposite of work?
WAVE	How has work changed over time? Over the past 30 years, have there been significant shifts in the number and kinds of jobs available in Canada? Is the computer revolution likely to make a big difference in how business will work in the 21st century?
FIELD	Where does work fit into our lives? To what extent does a person's self-esteem depend on the job he or she has? What does work mean for a society in which most jobs are in the service and communication areas? How will the new global economy affect the quantity and quality of work in Canada?

For other useful examples of what and how to question, take note of the problems or questions your professor poses to get class discussion going. If you are using a textbook in your course, check out the study questions.

5. Review notes and annotations. If your assignment involves reading one or more texts or researching multiple sources, review your notes and annotations. If you are writing about something you have observed, review any notes or sketches you have made (see Figure 2.3). These immediate comments and reactions are your best sources for ideas. Look for patterns.

6. Browse in the library. Libraries are filled with ideas—and they can be a great inspiration when you need to come up with your own. Browse the bookshelves containing texts that relate to a topic of interest.

7. Search the Net. Exploring a subject on the World Wide Web is the electronic equivalent of browsing in the library. Type keywords related to your topic into a search engine such as Google, and visit several sites on the resulting list. (*See Tab 3: Researching, pp. 125–160.*)

Figure 2.3 **Sketching to record observations.** This student sketched a drawing of a photograph she planned to discuss in her paper. The sketch helped her to see elements and details of the photograph more clearly. © The McGraw-Hill Companies, Inc.

8. Exchange ideas. If you read the acknowledgments in books, you will see that writing is a social activity. Most authors thank family members, editors, librarians, and colleagues for help on work in progress. Likewise, you should welcome opportunities to talk about your writing with your classmates, friends, and family.

- Discuss your assignments in chat rooms and by exchanging e-mail, especially if your course has a class Web site.

- Seek out students who have taken the course in previous semesters and discuss with them their approaches to writing assignments.

- Most colleges and universities have writing centres that welcome students for discussions of work in progress.

Drafting

Planning, drafting, revising, and editing are not entirely separate activities. You will move back and forth as you plan, draft, revise, and edit, and you may circle back and go through the entire process again as you write. But even though the parts of the writing process are interconnected, make sure to give yourself enough time not only to draft, but also to revise and edit your work.

Think of drafting as an attempt to discover a beginning, a middle, and an end for what you have to say, but remember that a draft is preliminary. Avoid putting pressure on yourself to make it perfect the first time through.

3a DEVELOPING YOUR THESIS.

Your first goal in drafting is to develop a preliminary thesis—a **working thesis**—that fits your purpose, makes a difference to readers, and addresses a specific issue. A preliminary thesis is just that: preliminary. As you draft and revise your paper, you may change the thesis several times to make it stronger.

To start, begin with the answer to a question posed by your assignment. (*For more about questions, see Chapter 2, pp. 24–26.*) For example, an assignment in a political science class might ask you to defend or critique "The Great Divide," a report by economist Armine Yalnizyan on the increasing gap between the rich and the poor in

Canada. The question your thesis must answer is "Is Yalnizyan's position that social inequalities are increasing correct or incorrect?"

To create a strong thesis, you will need to think critically, developing a point of view based on reading course materials and doing research. Writing critically, then, begins with a clear, forceful thesis statement. Not all theses can be stated in one sentence, but all strong theses are suitable, significant, and specific. (*For more on strong theses, see Chapter 1, pp. 11–16.*)

1. Make sure your thesis is suitable. A suitable thesis fits the paper's main purpose. (*See Chapter 2, pp. 17–19.*) If you are asked to write a report of your research on the gap between rich and poor in Canada, for example, you should not try to argue a position. An argument will not fulfil the purpose of the assignment. All of the following theses are on the same topic, but each is for a paper with a different purpose:

THESIS TO INFORM	In terms of income and wealth, the gap between rich and poor has increased substantially during the past decade.
THESIS TO INTERPRET	The economic ideas Armine Yalnizyan expresses in "The Great Divide" are politically ambiguous.
THESIS TO ARGUE	Armine Yalnizyan's argument that the poor are getting poorer is a direct result of government cutbacks to social programs and services.

2. Make sure your thesis is significant. A significant thesis asserts something that could potentially make a difference in what readers know, understand, or believe. Chances are that what makes a difference to you will also make a difference to your readers. When you are looking for possible theses, be sure to challenge yourself to develop one that you care about.

It sometimes helps to think of the thesis as an answer to a question. In each of the following three examples, the topic of the thesis is in italics and the assertion about that topic is underlined.

QUESTION	What makes a photograph significant?
THESIS	*The significance of a photograph* depends on both its formal and its documentary features.
QUESTION	What did Alfred Stieglitz contribute to the art of photography?

THESIS	*Alfred Stieglitz's struggle to promote photography as an art* involved starting a journal, opening a gallery, and making common cause with avant-garde modernist artists.
QUESTION	Is Susan Sontag right that photography obstructs critical thinking?
THESIS	*Susan Sontag's critique of photography is* unconvincing, partly because it assumes that most people are visually unsophisticated and thoughtlessly voyeuristic.

3. Make sure your thesis is specific. Vague theses tend to be less significant than specific ones:

TOO VAGUE	The gap between rich and poor has increased, and that's bad. [What kind of "gap" is at issue? Who are these "rich and poor"? Why is the increase in the gap "bad"? What does "bad" mean in this context?]
SPECIFIC	Armine Yalnizyan's argument that the gap between rich and poor Canadians has increased despite economic growth is valid and should be accepted. Her assessment of the political choices that affected the growing disparity is well founded, focusing on two distinct periods in the 1990s—recession and recovery, which were crucial in creating the current dire situation for many Canadian families.

The working thesis in the second example is sufficiently specific. It names economic inequality as the general topic, identifies Armine Yalnizyan's argument as the particular issue, and offers valid reasons for accepting Yalnizyan's contention.

3b PREPARING AN OUTLINE.

An informal or a formal outline often helps you clarify your ideas and move forward with a draft. An informal outline can be as simple as your working thesis followed by a list of the supporting points you plan to include. Another type of outline is an informal do/say plan. To come up with such a plan, review your notes and other relevant material. Then write down your working thesis, and list what you will say for each of the following "do" categories: introduce; support and develop; conclude. Here is an example:

Working Thesis: Armine Yalnizyan is correct about the increasing gap between rich and poor Canadians.

1. **Introduce** the issue and my focus.
   - Use examples to show change in economic status:
   - In 1989, 30% of families registered an after-tax income of $35,038. By 1997, more than 37% of families found themselves in this income bracket" (CSJ). The poorest 10% of families fared the worst. In 1989, this group had an average after-tax income of less than $15,596. In 1997, their after-tax income had fallen to an average $13,806 (CSJ).
   - Identify the position ("The poor are getting poorer") and introduce Yalnizyan's report "The Great Divide." Summarize her argument.
   - State my thesis that there is an increasing gap between rich and poor Canadians.

2. **Support and develop** my thesis that Yalnizyan's position is correct.
   - Point out that Yalnizyan uses statistics that show significant socio-economic changes not only in lower income families, but also in those families in the middle and top income brackets.
   - Show that Yalnizyan has considered regional and provincial disparities in income, and that despite growth, inequality still exists.
   - Present Yalnizyan's position that government policy is accountable for the increasing economic gap.
   - Identify the importance of Yalnizyan's assertion about tax cuts not addressing the reality of Canada's poor.

3. **Conclude** that Yalnizyan provides specific evidence to support the position that inequality is a significant social problem in Canada.

In outlining his plan, this student has already begun drafting because as he works on the outline, he gets a clearer sense of what he thinks of Yalnizyan's argument. He starts writing sentences that he is likely to include in the first complete draft.

Occasionally, you may find it helpful to prepare a formal outline that classifies and divides the information you have gathered. (For some assignments, your instructor might require a formal outline.) Because the process of division always results in at least two parts, in a formal outline every I must have a II; every A, a B; and so on. In addition, items placed at the same level must be of the same kind; for example, if I is London, then II can be Toronto but not Cabbagetown (a Toronto neighbourhood) or Bay Street. Items at the same level should also be grammatically parallel. Here is the conventional format for a formal outline:

Topic/Thesis:

I. First subtopic or point

   A. First supporting idea

      1. First specific detail
      2. Second specific detail

   B. Second supporting idea

      1. First specific detail
      2. Second specific detail
      3. Third specific detail
         a. First part of specific detail
         b. Second part of specific detail

II. Second subtopic or point

   A. First supporting idea

      1. First specific detail
      2. Second specific detail

   B. Second supporting idea

      1. First specific detail
      2. Second specific detail

   C. Third supporting idea

3c DEVELOPING YOUR IDEAS.

When you develop ideas, you move your writing forward by giving it texture and depth. The following strategies are helpful ways to develop the ideas that support your thesis.

1. Narration. When you narrate, you tell a story. In other words, the goal of the narrative is to relate a chain of events that has a clearly stated purpose and that explains actions that occur in time. The following paragraph comes from a personal essay called "A Lifetime of Production":

> My father changed, too. He had come to that job feeling—as I do now—that everything was still possible. He had served in the air force during World War II. Then, while my mother worked as a secretary to support them, he earned a degree in business, studying at night and working odd jobs during the day. After graduation, he was offered a position managing the warehouse of a small printing company. He took it, though he has told me that he never planned to stay. It wasn't something he envisioned as his life's work. I try to imagine what it is like suddenly to look up from a stack of newly packaged paperbacks and discover that the job you started one December day has watched you age.

Notice that the writer begins with two sentences that state the topic and point of the narration. Then, using the past tense, she recounts in chronological sequence some key events that led to her father's taking a job in the printing company.

2. Description. To make an object, person, or activity vivid for your readers, describe it in concrete, specific words that appeal to the senses of sight, sound, taste, smell, and touch. The goal of descriptive writing is to capture a major point by creating a dominant impression for the readers. In the following example, a student describes her impression of a photograph.

> In the *Paratrooper* photograph, the rescuer's powerfully muscular arm is set firmly in the foreground and is so intensely illuminated that it appears lighter than the rest of his water-soaked body. The arm of the wounded man is also caught in the light. But it is oddly bent, as if to accentuate just how tightly—and painfully—these two bodies are intertwined. Here is a desperate yet loving embrace. Both soldiers are holding on to each other as if they were holding on to life—to the human reality of this moment with its illuminating hope. Togetherness supports that life-giving hope and ensures its life-sustaining strength.

The writer uses words and phrases that appeal to the reader's sense of sight ("powerfully muscular arm," "oddly bent"). Emotionally charged adjectives like "desperate," "loving," and "life-giving" give readers a clear sense of the writer's feelings about the subject. So, too, do the two "as if" constructions.

3. Classification. Classification is a useful way of grouping individual entities into identifiable categories. Classifying occurs in all academic disciplines and often appears with its complement—division, or breaking a whole entity into its parts.

Canadians drink over 7 billion cups of tea each year.

From the hills of Sri Lanka and India to the mountains and valleys of Kenya, tea is grown in some of the world's most exotic places. Three basic types of tea are produced and enjoyed worldwide: black, green and oolong teas. They all come from the *Camellia Sinensis* bush which in the wild can grow 90 feet and higher.

The tea types include:

1. **Black Tea:** Most commonly used in North American tea bags, black tea is made from leaves that have been fully oxidized, producing a hearty deep rich flavour in a coloured amber brew. It is the oxidation process, oxygen coming into contact with the enzymes in the tea leaf, that distinguishes black teas from green.

2. **Green Tea:** Most popular in Asia, green tea is not oxidized. It is withered, immediately steamed or heated to prevent oxidation and then rolled and dried. It is characterized by a delicate taste, light green colour and is very refreshing.

3. **Oolong Tea:** The name *oolong* literally translates as "Black Dragon" and is very popular in China. Oolong refers to partly oxidized leaves, combining the taste and colour qualities of black and green tea. Oolong teas are consumed without milk or sugar and are extremely flavourful and highly aromatic.

—Tea Council of Canada
<www.tea.ca>

To simplify the information, the writer first classifies tea into three main categories and then provides details that differentiate each type.

4. Definition. Define any concepts that the reader needs to understand to follow your ideas. Interpretations and arguments often depend on one or two key ideas that cannot be defined quickly and easily. In the following example, John Berger defines "image," a key idea in his televised lectures on the way we see things:

An image is a sight which has been recreated or reproduced. It is an appearance, or a set of appearances, which has been detached from the place and time in which it first made its appearance and preserved—for a few moments or centuries. Every image embodies a way of seeing. Even a photograph. For photographs are not, as is often assumed, a mechanical record.

Every time we look at a photograph, we are aware, however slightly, of the photographer selecting that sight from an infinity of other possible sights. This is true even in the most casual family snapshot. The photographer's way of seeing is reflected in his choice of subject.

—JOHN BERGER, *Ways of Seeing*

5. Illustration. No matter what your purpose and point may be, in order to appeal to readers you will have to show as well as tell. Detailed examples can make abstractions more concrete and generalizations more specific, as the following paragraph shows:

As Rubin explains, "for much of the Accord era, the ideal-typical family [. . .] was composed of a 'stay-at-home-mom,' a working father, and dependent children. He earned wages; she cooked, cleaned, cared for the home, managed the family's social life, and nurtured the family members" (97). Just such an arrangement characterized my grandmother's married life. My grandmother, who had four children, stayed at home with them, while her husband went off to work as a safety engineer. Sadly, when he died, she was left with nothing. She needed to support herself, yet had no work experience, no credit, and little education. But even though society frowned on her for seeking employment, my grandmother eventually found a clerical position—a low-level job with few perks.

6. Comparison and contrast. Comparison means exploring the similarities and differences among various items to prove a point or to support the thesis. When the term compare is used along with the term contrast, then compare is usually defined more narrowly as "to spell out key similarities." Contrast always means, "to itemize important differences."

In the following example, the student writer uses a **subject-by-subject** pattern to contrast the ideas of two social commentators, Jeremy Rifkin and George Will:

Rifkin and Will have different opinions about unemployment due to downsizing and the widening income gap between rich and poor. Rifkin sees both the decrease in employment and the increase in income disparity as evils that must be immediately dealt with lest society fall apart: "If no measures are taken to provide financial opportunities for millions of Americans in an era of diminishing jobs, then [. . .] violent crime is going to increase" (3). Will, on the other hand, seems to believe that both unemployment and income differences are necessary to the health of American society.

Will writes, "A society that chafes against stratification derived from disparities of talents will be a society that discourages individual talents" (92). Apparently, the society that Rifkin wants is just the kind of society that Will rejects.

—JACOB GROSSMAN, student paper

Notice that Grossman comments on Rifkin first and then turns to his second subject, George Will. To ensure paragraph unity, he begins with a topic sentence that mentions both subjects.

In the following paragraph, the student writer organizes her comparison **point by point** rather than subject by subject. Instead of saying everything about Smith's picture before commenting on the AP photo, the writer moves back and forth between the two images as she makes and supports two points: first, that the images differ in figure and scene, and second, that they are similar in theme.

Divided by an ocean, two photographers took pictures that at first glance seem absolutely different. W. Eugene Smith's well-known *Tomoko in the Bath* and the less well-known AP photo *A Paratrooper Works to Save the Life of a Buddy* portray distinctively different settings and people. Smith brings us into a darkened room where a Japanese woman is lovingly bathing her malformed child, while the AP staff photographer captures two soldiers on the battlefield, one intently performing CPR on his wounded friend. But even though the two images seem as different as women and men, peace and war, or life and death, both pictures figure something similar: a time of suffering. It is the early 1970s—a time when the hopes and dreams that modernity promoted are being exposed as deadly to human beings. Perhaps that is why the bodies in both pictures seem humbled. Grief pulls you down onto your knees. Terror impels you to crawl along the ground.

—ILONA BOUZOUKASHVILI, student paper

7. Analogy. An analogy compares topics that at first glance seem quite different. A well-chosen analogy can make new or technical information appear more commonplace and understandable:

The human eye provides a good starting point for learning how a camera works. The lens of the eye is like the *lens* of the camera. In both instruments the lens focuses an image of the surroundings on a *light-sensitive surface*—the *retina* of the eye and the *film* in the camera. In both, the light-sensitive material is protected within a light-tight container—the *eyeball* of the eye and the *body* of the camera. Both eye and camera have a mechanism for shutting off light passing through the lens to the interior of the container—the *lid* of the eye and the *shutter* of the camera. In both, the size of the lens opening, or *aperture,* is regulated by an *iris diaphragm.*

—MARVIN ROSEN, *Introduction to Photography*

8. Process. When you need to explain how to do something or show readers how something is done, you use process analysis, explaining each step in the process in chronological order, as in the following example:

To end our Hawan ritual of thanks, *aarti* is performed. First, my mother lights a piece of camphor in a metal plate called a *taree.* Holding the taree with her right hand, she moves the fire in a circular, clockwise movement in front of the altar. Next, she stands in front of my father and again moves the fiery *taree* in a circular, clockwise direction. After touching his feet and receiving his blessing, she attends to each of us children in turn, moving the fire in a clockwise direction before kissing us, one by one. When she is done, my father performs his *aarti* in a similar way and then my sister and I do ours. When everyone is done, we say some prayers and sit down.

—U. ROOPNARIAN, student paper

9. Cause and effect. Use this strategy when you need to trace the causes of some event or situation, to describe its effects, or both. In the following example, Norman Cousins explains the causes of the career-ending injuries that can plague professional athletes:

Professional athletes are sometimes severely disadvantaged by trainers whose job it is to keep them in action. The more famous the athlete, the greater the risk that he or she may be subjected to extreme medical measures when injury strikes. The star baseball pitcher whose arm is sore because of a torn muscle or tissue damage may need sustained rest more than anything else. But his team is battling for a place in the World Series; so the trainer or team doctor, called upon to work his magic, reaches for a strong dose of Butazolidine or other powerful pain suppressants. Presto, the pain disappears! The pitcher takes his place on the mound and does superbly. That could be the last game, however, in which he is able to throw a ball with full strength. The drugs didn't repair the torn muscle or cause the damaged tissue to heal. What they did was to mask the pain, enabling the pitcher to throw hard, further damaging the torn muscle. Little wonder that so many star athletes are cut down in their prime, more the victims of overzealous treatment of their injuries than of the injuries themselves.

—NORMAN COUSINS, "Pain Is Not the Ultimate Enemy"

3d WRITING PURPOSEFUL PARAGRAPHS THAT ARE UNIFIED, COHERENT, AND WELL DEVELOPED.

Readers expect a piece of writing to be divided into paragraphs that express thoughts or ideas relevant to the whole piece. Introductory and concluding paragraphs have special functions in a piece of writing, but all paragraphs should have sufficient development (level of detail), unity (a single, clear focus), and coherence (internal connections).

1. Introductions and conclusions. A paper's opening and ending paragraphs are especially important. You need to hook readers at the beginning and leave them with a strong final impression at the end.

The best way to get your reader's attention is to show why the topic matters. The opening of your paper should encourage the reader to share your view of the topic's importance. Here are some opening strategies:

- Tell a brief story related to the question your thesis answers.
- Begin with a relevant and attention-getting quotation.
- Begin with a paraphrase of a commonly held view that you immediately question.
- State a working hypothesis.
- Define a key term.
- Pose an important question.

For many types of papers, especially informative reports and arguments, your opening paragraph or paragraphs will include your thesis statement, usually at the beginning or near the end of the introduction. If your purpose is analytic, however, you may either include the thesis in your introduction or build up to your thesis, which you place near the end. Some types of writing, such as narratives, may not require an explicitly stated thesis if the main idea is clear without it.

Just as the opening makes a first impression and motivates the reader to continue reading, the closing makes a final impression and motivates the reader to think further. The purpose of the conclusion is to bring your paper to an interesting close. Do not merely repeat the main idea that you introduced at the beginning of the paper. Presumably, you have developed that idea throughout the paper. Your conclusion should remind readers of the paper's significance and satisfy those who might be asking, "So what?" Here are some common strategies for concluding a paper effectively:

- Refer to the story or quotation you used in your introduction.
- Answer the question you posed in your introduction.
- Summarize your main point.
- Call for some action on your reader's part.
- Present a powerful image or forceful example.
- Suggest some implications for the future.

2. Paragraph development. As you draft and revise your paper, ask yourself, does each paragraph provide enough detail? Although sometimes you will deliberately use a one- or two-sentence paragraph for stylistic emphasis, when paragraphs are short for no apparent stylistic reason, they may need to be developed more fully. Would more information make the point clearer? Perhaps a term should be defined. Do generalizations need to be supported with examples?

Note how this writer developed the draft of her introductory paragraph, adding details and examples to make her argument more clearly and effectively:

FIRST DRAFT

A 1913 advertisement for Shredded Wheat illustrates Kellner's claim that advertisements sell self-images. The ad suggests that serving Shredded Wheat will give women the same sense of accomplishment as gaining the right to vote.

REVISION

According to Kellner, "advertising is as concerned with selling lifestyles and socially desirable identities [. . .] as with selling the products themselves" (193). A 1913 ad for Shredded Wheat shows how the selling of self-images works. At first glance, this ad seems to be promoting the women's suffrage movement. In big, bold letters, "Votes for Women" is emblazoned across the top of the ad. But a closer look reveals that the ad is for Shredded Wheat cereal. Holding a piece of the cereal in her hand, a woman stands behind a large bowlful of

Shredded Wheat biscuits that is made to look like a voting box. The text claims that "every biscuit is a vote for health, happiness and domestic freedom." Like the rest of the advertisement, this claim suggests that serving Shredded Wheat will give women the same sense of accomplishment as gaining the right to vote.

—Holly Musetti, student paper, 2001

3. Paragraph unity. A unified paragraph has a single, clear focus. To check for unity, identify the paragraph's topic sentence. A topic sentence announces the paragraph's main point and usually appears at its beginning or end. Everything in the paragraph should be connected clearly and closely to the topic sentence.

Compare the first draft of the following paragraph with its revision, and note how the addition of a topic sentence (in bold in the revision) makes the paragraph more clearly focused and therefore easier for the writer to revise further. Note also that the writer deleted ideas that did not directly relate to the paragraph's main point (underlined in the first draft):

FIRST DRAFT

The city is plagued by problems with housing and homelessness. Groups came together at all levels of the government and public sectors. "By the 1990s, concerned citizens gathered to form the West Broadway Development Corporation for the purpose of inner-city revitalization" (Housing, 2005). Their goal was "creating better rental properties; increasing home ownership by providing 'affordable' ownership options; reducing transient population; increasing neighbourhood stability ..." (Housing, 2005). These ideas were unique, because they gave low-income families the chance to become homeowners. This is a major problem in the city. Families are not merely tenants of government housing but are able to become homeowners, which instils pride in them and in their neighbourhood. The problem in this setting starts when "affordable" housing is only affordable for some low-income families and families facing poverty have nowhere left to turn. "Low income is a reality in West Broadway where 75% of the households earn less than $20 000" (Housing, 2005). Simply put, the citizens the affordable housing programs were created for cannot afford to take part in those very programs.

REVISION

Similarly, Winnipeg began looking for more affordable housing options. Groups came together at all levels of the government and public sectors. "By the 1990s, concerned citizens gathered to form the West Broadway Development Corporation for the purpose of inner-city revitalization" (Housing, 2005). Their goal was "creating better rental properties; increasing home ownership by providing 'affordable' ownership options; reducing transient population; increasing neighbourhood stability …" (Housing, 2005). These ideas were unique, because they gave low-income families the chance to become homeowners. Families are not merely tenants of government housing but are able to become homeowners, which instils pride in them and in their neighbourhood. The problem in this setting starts when "affordable" housing is only affordable for some low-income families and families facing poverty have nowhere left to turn. "Low income is a reality in West Broadway where 75% of the households earn less than $20 000" (Housing, 2005). Simply put, the citizens the affordable housing programs were created for cannot afford to take part in those very programs.

—M. Thomas, student paper, 2005

4. Paragraph coherence. A coherent paragraph flows smoothly, with each sentence clearly related to the next. All of the sentences in a paragraph should be connected in ways that make the whole paragraph hold together. Use the following cues to strengthen coherence:

- Use pronouns and antecedents. In the following example, *it* refers back to uprooting families and connects the two sentences.

  Some cannot imagine *uprooting families* for a year or two and then having to do *it* all over again.

- Repeat key words.

  A photograph displays a unique *moment.* To capture that *moment...*

- Repeat sentence structures.

Because the former West Germany lived through a generation of prosperity, its people developed high expectations of material comfort. Because the former East Germany lived through a generation of deprivation, its people developed disdain for material values.

- Use synonyms, words that are close in meaning to words or phrases that have preceded them.

In the world of photography, critics *argue* for either a scientific or an artistic approach. This *controversy*...

- Use transitional words and phrases. Transitional expressions link one idea with another, thereby helping readers understand your logic. (*See the list of common transitional expressions in the box on p. 42.*) Use transitions to build logical bridges between paragraphs as well as between sentences.

Compare the following two paragraphs, the first version without transitions and the second, revised version with transitions (in bold type) that connect one thought to another:

FIRST DRAFT

The music industry in Canada has grown incredibly. Canadian Music Week, an industry conference and music festival, sees many of the big labels and buyers from the international music scene. "The CMW is a necessary and important venture for new or upcoming artists to showcase their talent in front of international buyers" (Foiré). It seems that in order for an artist or band to be really successful in the music industry, they need to look to multinational firms for promotion.

REVISION

Clearly, the music industry in Canada has grown incredibly. Canadian Music Week, an industry conference and music festival, sees many of the big labels and buyers from the international music scene. "The CMW is a necessary and important venture for new or upcoming artists to showcase their talent in front of international buyers" (Foiré). It seems, **however**, that in order for an artist or band to be really successful in the music industry, they need to look to multinational firms for promotion.

Transitional Expressions

To show relationships in space: above, adjacent to, against, alongside, around, at a distance from, at the . . . , below, beside, beyond, encircling, far off, forward, from the . . . , in front of, in the rear, inside, near the back, near the end, nearby, next to, on, over, surrounding, there, through the, to the left, to the right, up front

To show relationships in time: afterward, at last, before, earlier, first, former, formerly, immediately, in the first place, in the interval, in the meantime, in the next place, in the last place, later on, latter, meanwhile, next, now, often, once, previously, second, simultaneously, sometime later, subsequently, suddenly, then, therefore, third, today, tomorrow, until now, when, years ago, yesterday

To show something added to what has come before: again, also, and, and then, besides, further, furthermore, in addition, last, likewise, moreover, next, too

To give examples that intensify points: after all, as an example, certainly, clearly, for example, for instance, indeed, in fact, in truth, it is true, of course, specifically, that is

To show similarities: alike, in the same way, like, likewise, resembling, similarly

To show contrasts: after all, although, but, conversely, differ(s) from, difference, different, dissimilar, even though, granted, however, in contrast, in spite of, nevertheless, notwithstanding, on the contrary, on the other hand, otherwise, still, though, unlike, while this may be true, yet

To indicate cause and effect: accordingly, as a result, because, consequently, hence, since, then, therefore, thus

To conclude or summarize: finally, in brief, in conclusion, in other words, in short, in summary, that is, to summarize

3e USING ONLINE TOOLS FOR DRAFTING.

Nowadays, most writers use word processing to produce final, printed texts. Most computers come equipped with a word-processing program. Get to know whatever program you have, especially the various ways of setting up and saving files.

Most programs offer more than just word processing, however. They allow you to create Web pages; insert links to sites on the World Wide Web; include graphics; use templates and wizards to design documents; and count words, check spelling, track changes, and display and print foreign language fonts. Explore the many features of your word processing software to see how it can enhance your writing.

Revising

Drafting and revising are interdependent. As you draft, you will often review what you write and do some revision, but mostly you will be devoted, appropriately, to getting your words down on paper or into a computer file. Once you have a draft, you can revise in earnest. You will revise for substance—to clarify what you want to say—and for style—to say what you want to say as effectively as possible.

4a FOCUSING ON THE PURPOSE OF YOUR WRITING.

As you reread your paper and decide how to revise it, base your decisions on the purpose of your paper. Is your primary purpose to inform, to interpret, or to argue?

Clarity about your purpose is especially important when an assignment calls for interpretation. A description is not the same as an interpretation. With this principle in mind, Ilona Bouzoukashvili read over the first draft of her paper on the art of photography, a draft that included descriptions of several photographs. Here is her description of a photograph entitled *A Paratrooper Works to Save the Life of a Buddy*:

FIRST DRAFT

In *Paratrooper,* the surroundings are not entirely shown. For all we know, there could still be shelling or shooting in the area. One thing we see clearly is that the wounded soldier is lying on the muddy ground, yet his paratrooper buddy doesn't seem to mind. He leans over and tries to save his friend. Their clothes appear dirty and wet, which displays the ugliness of a war. One may even note how the paratrooper is almost crying; a part of his forehead is slightly wrinkled. His body as a whole is in a bent position.

Keeping her purpose in mind, the student asked herself which details in the paragraph were most significant—which ones could help her fulfill her interpretive purpose. She wanted to show her readers that even documentary photographs can be artistic. Her revision makes this interpretation clearer.

REVISION

Paratrooper subtly portrays the ugliness of war, not through a picture of shelling and shooting but through a close-up of war's devastating effects on the individual and on human relationships. Dirty, damp, and ugly, the photograph reflects the misery of war. The paratrooper is the rescuer, but he is bent over his wounded buddy as if he, too, is begging for help Bodies shown in both *Tomoko* and *Paratrooper* are either squatting or lying down. Grief and terror literally knock people over.

4b TESTING YOUR THESIS.

Understanding your purpose will help you test your thesis for clarity. Remember that a thesis makes an assertion about a topic. It links the *what* and the *why*. Is your thesis evident on the first page of your draft? Before readers get very far along, they expect an answer to the question, "What is the point of all this?" Not finding the point on the first page is a signal to revise, unless you are deliberately waiting until the end to reveal your thesis. (*For more on strong theses, see Chapter 3, pp. 27–29.*)

Most writers start with a working thesis, which often evolves into a more specific, complex assertion as ideas develop. One of the key challenges of revising is to compose a clear statement of this revised thesis. When she drafted the paper about compassion fatigue in nursing (*see Tab 5: APA Documentation Style, pp. 197–224*) Judith Applebaum stated her working thesis as follows:

WORKING THESIS

Nurses are subject to a great deal of stress in their jobs.

During the revision process, Applebaum realized that her working thesis was too weak to serve as the thesis of her final draft. A weak thesis is predictable: readers read it, agree (or disagree), and that's that. A strong thesis, on the other hand, stimulates thoughtful inquiry. Applebaum's revised thesis clearly identifies the purpose of the writing:

REVISED THESIS

Understanding the potential for development of compassion fatigue, and early intervention to prevent a full-blown symptomatology, can result in a healthier and happier work force, and, consequently, in better care provided for the clients.

When you need to identify or strengthen a thesis, it sometimes helps to compose a title for your paper. Applebaum's title, "Compassion Fatigue: Consequences for Health Care Professionals," which she decided on during the revising process, helped her see that her thesis needed to explain not only the causes of this problem, but also how to intervene effectively to avoid the problem starting at all.

Your thesis should evolve throughout the paper. Readers need to see a statement of the main idea on the first page, but they also expect a more complex or general statement near the end. After presenting much evidence to support her revised thesis, Applebaum concludes her paper by stating her thesis in a more general way:

> Investing in measures to decrease the incidence of this type of burnout among nursing staff (and, indeed, all caregivers) will definitely pay off—for institutions, clients, and the caregivers themselves.

4c   REVIEWING THE WHOLE PAPER AND ITS PARTS.

In a first draft, you would be wise to think broadly about the different parts of your paper and how you should order them. Does the paper have a beginning, a middle, and an end, with bridges between those parts? When you revise, however, you can design a structure that supports what you want to say more effectively.

One way to review your structure is by outlining the first draft. An outline makes clear the overall pattern of your thinking. Try listing the key points of your draft in sentence form; whenever possible, use sentences that actually appear in the draft. This kind of

Checklist

Revising Your Draft for Content and Organization

1. **Purpose:** Is my purpose for writing clear? If not, how can I revise to make my purpose apparent?
2. **Thesis:** Is my thesis clear and specific, and do I introduce it early in my draft? (If not, do I have a good reason for withholding it or not stating it at all?)
3. **Order:** Are my key points arranged effectively? Would another order support my thesis more successfully?
4. **Paragraphs:** Is each paragraph fully developed, unified, and coherent?

point-by-point outlining will allow you to see the logic (or lack of it) of your draft. Ask yourself if the key points are arranged effectively or if another arrangement would work better. The following structures are typical ways of organizing papers:

- An *explanatory structure* sets out the key parts of a topic.
- An *exploratory structure* begins with a question or problem and works step-by-step to discover an answer or a solution.
- An *argumentative structure* presents a set of linked reasons plus supporting evidence.

The structure you choose should be appropriate to the assignment, your purpose, and your thesis, and the paper's parts should develop your ideas in an orderly way. Examine each paragraph, asking yourself what role it plays—or should play—in the paper as a whole. Keeping this role in mind, check the paragraph for development, unity, and coherence—and consider how it contributes to the paper as a whole.

4d REVISING AND EDITING SENTENCES.

As you revise, you should consider not only the substance of what you have said, but also the style—the way you have said it.

1. Use an appropriate tone. For most academic papers, your tone should reflect seriousness about the subject matter and purpose, as well as respect for your readers. You express your seriousness by stating information and interpretations fairly, presenting reasonable arguments, and citing sources for your ideas. Unless you are writing a personal essay, the topic, not yourself or your feelings, should be the centre of attention. Be alert to your attitude. Writing with seriousness and authority does not mean talking down to readers. For example, the following sentence, as revised below, is informative without being condescending:

CONDESCENDING

As I already explained to you, the government's motion to extend Canada's mission in Afghanistan to 2011 is at risk.

REVISED

As previously mentioned, the government's motion to extend Canada's mission in Afghanistan to 2011 is at risk.

2. Vary your sentences. To capture and hold your readers' attention, your writing must be both clearly focused and interestingly varied. Vary sentence openings and sentence lengths, and use different kinds of sentences to add texture to your writing. For example, a student writing a personal essay about his father for an English composition class used a variety of sentence openings:

> *For me,* the time I spent watching my father develop and print his photographs was pure joy.
>
> *Remembering those days,* I began to look through the boxes of old photos.
>
> *Shocked to discover his secret life,* I felt deeply lonely, as if I didn't know my father after all.
>
> *The next day* I pretended nothing had happened.

Besides varying the openings of your sentences, vary their lengths, too. A volley of short, choppy sentences will probably distract readers from what you have to say, while an unbroken stream of long, complicated sentences is likely to dull their senses. In the example that follows, notice how the revised version connects ideas for readers and, consequently, is easier to read.

CHOPPY

> My father was a zealous photographer. He took pictures on every family outing. Often he spent the whole outing behind his camera. He went to his darkroom as soon as he got home. He usually developed his photos the same day he took them.

REVISED

> A zealous photographer, my father took pictures on every family outing, often spending the whole afternoon behind the camera and then hurrying straight to his darkroom to develop the pictures the very same day.

Short, direct sentences are usually more powerful when they introduce or follow a set of longer, more complex sentences. Notice how the student writer emphasizes his last sentence by making it short and simple, especially in comparison to the sentences that precede it.

> A few days later, I returned to college, and my dad and I didn't talk to each other for several weeks. Then one night I got a phone call from my mother, telling me, in an almost inaudible whisper and through the static of a bad connection, that she had some bad news. My father had died.

Just as too many short sentences can sound choppy, too many sentences strung together with coordinating words can make your work sound unfocused and monotonous. **Coordinating** conjunctions (*and, but, yet, or, nor, for, so*) combine equal ideas. You can often solve problems with too much coordination by subordinating one idea in your sentence to another, using **subordinating** conjunctions such as *after, although, as if, as soon as, because, even though, if, since, unless, until, when, whenever, where, wherever, while.*

UNFOCUSED

The cells were exposed to GA, but there was a lag period of eight hours, and then the enzyme was produced.

REVISED

After the cells were exposed to GA, there was a lag period of eight hours, and then the enzyme was produced.

Overuse of subordination, though, can also make it difficult for readers to see or remember your focus:

UNFOCUSED

Although both vertebral and wrist fractures cause deformity and impair movement, hip fractures, which are one of the most devastating consequences of osteoporosis, significantly increase the risk of death, since 12%–30% of patients with a hip fracture die within one year after the fracture, while the mortality rate climbs to 40% for the first two years post-fracture.

REVISED

Hip fractures are one of the most devastating consequences of osteoporosis. Although vertebral and wrist fractures cause deformity and impair movement, hip fractures significantly increase the risk of death. Within one year after a hip fracture, 12%–20% of the injured die. The mortality rate climbs to 40% after two years.

Cumulative sentences—simple sentences elaborated with accumulating details—are a powerful way of providing additional details while maintaining a clear focus. Notice how the student writer begins with a simple sentence (in italics) and then, after a comma, adds details through a succession of modifiers.

I was shocked, telling myself this wasn't real, trying to discover an explanation for the photos, photos that seemed to indicate a second wife, another family, a second home in an entirely different city, willing myself to believe that the evidence could be read to mean something else entirely.

(For more on sentence variety, see Chapter 25, pp. 248–251.)

3. Write direct sentences. More often than not, sentences beginning with *it is* or *there is* or *there are* (*it was* or *there was*)—called expletive constructions—are weak and indirect. Other indirect sentence structures based on the use of the passive form ("It was decided at the meeting that the company would not achieve its growth expectations") are standard in scientific, legal, and business writing. In most humanities and social science disciplines, however, a more direct (active) style ("The City Opera's rendition of *Don Giovanni* roars with drama") is preferred. Most computerized style checkers will highlight *it is* and *there is* or *there are* so that you can decide whether these phrases work. But using a clear subject and a vivid verb often makes a sentence more powerful.

WEAK	There are concerns about the proposed takeover of BCE.
REVISED	The proposed takeover of BCE has raised concerns.

(Also see Chapter 26, on wordy sentences, pp. 252–254.)

4. Choose precise words. Finding precisely the right word and putting that word in the best place is an important part of revision. In a sense, different disciplines and occupations have their own dialects that members of the community are expected to know and use. The word significant, for example, has a mathematical meaning for the statistician that it doesn't have for the literary critic. When taking courses in a discipline, you should use its terminology or dialect, not to impress the instructor but to be understood accurately. As you review your draft, look for general terms that might need to be made more specific.

TOO GENERAL	Foreign direct investment (FDI) in Germany will probably remain low because of several factors. [Factors is so general that it should signal you to get specific and answer the question, "What factors?"]
REVISED	Foreign direct investment (FDI) in Germany will probably remain low because of high labour costs, high taxation, and government regulation.

(For more on using exact language, see Chapter 28, pp. 260–264.)

A dictionary and a thesaurus are essential tools for choosing precise words. The dictionary gives a word's **denotations** (its exact definitions) and its **etymology** (its family history). In checking a definition in the dictionary, pay attention to the **parts of speech**, the different functions a word can have in a sentence. The same word can have a different meaning when its grammatical function changes. For example, the word light means one thing when it describes a "light" (noun) being turned on and something else when you note that a butterfly "lights" (verb) on a leaf. You will find both meanings in a dictionary, and you will have to choose the appropriate one. To check whether you have selected the appropriate meaning, try substituting the dictionary definition for the word. Does the sentence make sense?

A thesaurus provides synonyms, words with the same or nearly the same meaning. Just as siblings, even identical twins, differ from each other, so do words differ subtly from their synonyms. Because words have different **connotations**—that is, secondary or suggested meanings—some synonyms work in one context but not in another. Synonyms can have either positive or negative connotations. For example, in describing someone's manner of speaking, the word *direct* is usually positive, but *blunt* is not.

One student used both a thesaurus and a dictionary as aids in revising the following sentence:

DRAFT Pierre Trudeau had a special kind of power.

Dissatisfied with the precision of the word *power,* this writer checked a thesaurus and found the word *influence* listed as a synonym for *power* and the word *charisma* given as a special kind of influence:

THESAURUS EXAMPLE

172. INFLUENCE

1. nouns influence, influentiality; power 157, force, clout [informal], [...] prestige, [...] esteem, [...] leadership, charisma, magnetism, charm [...]

Going back to the dictionary, she found that *charisma* means a "divinely conferred" power and has an etymological connection with *charismatic,* a term used to describe ecstatic Christian experiences like speaking in tongues. *Charisma* was exactly the word she needed to convey both the spiritual and the popular sides of Trudeau:

DICTIONARY EXAMPLE

char·is·ma /kə'rızmə/ *noun* **1 a** the ability to inspire followers with devotion and enthusiasm. **b** an attractive aura; great charm. **2** (*pl.* **cha·ris·mata** /kə'rızmətə/) a divinely conferred power or talent. [ecclesiastical Latin from Greek *kharisma* from *kharis* favour, grace]

Both the dictionary and the thesaurus sometimes list **antonyms**: words that mean the opposite or nearly the opposite of a given word. But words are opposites only within a context of similarity. *Poor* is the opposite of *rich* when the context is wealth. *Light* is the opposite of *rich* when the context is food. In word choice, as in most of the decisions you make when revising, context makes all the difference. (*For more on the dictionary and the thesaurus, see Chapter 36, pp. 282–285.*)

5. Avoid biased language. Nonbiased language is inclusive, and achieving it requires thought as well as thoughtfulness. Because language reflects society, for good or ill, the English language has within it words and phrases that convey stereotypes, ideas about people that exclude, demean, ignore, or patronize them on the basis of gender, sexual preference, physical ability, race, religion, or country of origin. Effective writers are aware of language's power, and they choose to use that power to create a sense of community with readers.

- Use genderless nouns and pronouns. Using masculine pronouns and nouns to refer to both women and men usually sounds biased. Whenever possible, avoid using the pronouns he, him, his, and himself unless you are referring to a specific person. Using plural forms is often a good solution; so is revising a sentence to avoid masculine pronouns altogether. You can also use he or she or him or her, as long as you do not use them excessively or more than once in a sentence.

BIASED

Every student who wrote his name on the class list had to pay a copying fee in advance and pledge to attend every session.

REVISED AS PLURAL

Students who wrote *their* names on the class list had to pay a copying fee in advance and pledge to attend every session.

REVISED TO AVOID PRONOUNS

Every student who signed up for the class had to pay a copying fee in advance and pledge to attend every session.

REVISED WITH HIS OR HER

Every student who wrote *his or her* name on the class list had to pay a copying fee in advance and pledge to attend every session.

- Use parallel titles for women and men.

| BIASED | Sigmund Freud and Mrs. Brothers |
| REVISED | Dr. Freud and Dr. Brothers |

BIASED	men and ladies
REVISED	men and women or gentlemen and ladies
BIASED	Jane Austen, Mrs. Gaskell, and George Eliot described life in the provinces; Dickens described life in the city.
REVISED	Austen, Gaskell, and Eliot described life in the provinces; Dickens described life in the city.

or

> Jane Austen, Elizabeth Gaskell, and George Eliot described life in the provinces; Charles Dickens described life in the city. [First and last names are used for all.]

- Use terms that do not suggest gender for names of occupations and professions.

BIASED	The salesman gave an informative presentation.
REVISED	The sales representative gave an informative presentation.

(For more on unbiased language, see Chapter 27, pp. 257–260.)

Checklist

Revising Your Draft for Style

1. **Tone:** Is the tone I have used appropriate for my audience? Have I used any condescending language, or have I addressed the audience as equals?
2. **Sentence variety:** Are my sentences varied? Have I used too many short, choppy sentences or long, rambling ones?
3. **Direct sentences:** Are my sentences direct, or have I used too many constructions beginning with *There is (are)* or *It is*?
4. **Precise words:** Have I put the right words in the best places? Have I used any words that have the wrong connotation?
5. **Nonbiased language:** Have I used inclusive language, with parallel titles for men and women and occupation names that do not suggest gender? Have I avoided using the pronouns he, him, his, and himself to refer to anyone except a specific male? Have I eliminated any slang terms or clichés that can be considered racially discriminatory?

4e COLLABORATING WITH READERS ONLINE AND IN PRINT.

If you check the acknowledgments section in any book, you will see that writers consult with readers for comments on work in progress. Asking actual readers to comment on your draft is the best way to see your writing in a broader context. Computers may be the quintessential collaboration machines thanks to the ease with which electronic texts can move back and forth between them.

1. Write e-mail. When you work on papers with classmates, you can use e-mail in the following ways:

- To check out your understanding of the assignment
- To try out various topics
- To ask each other useful questions about ideas
- To share your freewriting, plan, or rough draft
- To respond to each other's ideas, including requests for clarification and additional information

2. Chat with each other about ideas. You can get together in a group to share ideas. You can use online chats or blog posts for this purpose (see Figure 4.1). A great deal of collaboration and communication is possible with e-mail, but other virtual spaces for interaction abound. Your instructor may include **chat** or virtual environment activities, where you work on assignments in small groups or visit and interact with other classes at other colleges or universities. Some people find that chatting in such virtual rooms, or synchronous spaces, prompts them to become more creative.

3. Try peer review. Peer review is a process that involves reading and critiquing your classmates' work while they review yours. Peer review is normally a supervised activity with very specific criteria:

- **Constructive feedback:** Think of the draft as a "work in progress" and offer honest, constructive suggestions for improvement. Be specific. Point out what you think needs revision: e.g., *Your conclusion has only one sentence. Shouldn't it be longer than that? You ended so suddenly;* or *You mentioned two points in your introduction, but in the body, you only discuss one. What happened to the second point?* Also, mention that you have noticed some grammar errors, but don't do the editing. Identify errors such as word order, spelling, or subject-verb agreement.

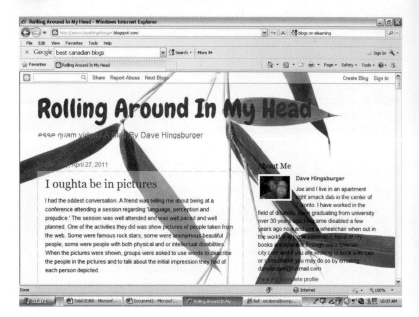

Figure 4.1

- **Academic honesty:** Sharing your material with others or having others review/edit your work can be viewed as plagiarism for several reasons. If your final product is significantly different in tone or style from your usual work or if you and your partner's final draft are too similar, then you risk censure by your school.

When you have a fairly solid draft to share, send it to your peer reviewers by e-mail (also print out a hard copy for yourself), or meet in person to exchange and read drafts. Consider including printouts of some of your peers' responses, if they arrive online, with your final draft so that your teacher knows you have taken the initiative to work with other writers. If you meet in person, ask your peer reviewers to write out their responses and then include these written responses with your final draft. Overall, the input from a peer review should provoke a critical review of your draft, which should help to strengthen your piece of writing.

Most readers genuinely want to be helpful. When sharing your drafts with your peers, help them give you the assistance you need by asking them specific questions. The best compliment they can pay you is to take your work seriously enough to make constructive suggestions. When you give them your draft, tell them the answers to the following questions:

- **What is your purpose?** Is your purpose mainly informative, interpretive, or argumentative? What do you want your readers to learn, to understand, or to believe?

- **How close is the project to being finished?** Your answer to this question helps readers understand where you are in the writing process and how best to assist you in taking the next step.

- **What steps do you plan to take to complete the project?** If readers know your plans, they can either question the direction you are taking or give you more specific advice, such as the titles of additional books or articles that you might consult.

Reading others' drafts will help you be a more objective reader of your own work, and comments from readers will help you see your own writing as others see it. As you gain more objectivity, you will become more adept at revising your work. In addition, the approaches that you see your classmates taking to the assignment will broaden your perspective and give you ideas for new directions in your own writing.

4. Use the writing centre. Many campuses maintain writing centres, staffed by tutors, that offer help for every stage of the writing process. The tutors can read and comment on drafts of your work; they can also help you find and correct problems with grammar, punctuation, and mechanics.

5. Use online writing labs or OWLs. Most OWLs present information about writing that you can access anytime, including lists of useful online resources. Some OWLs are staffed by tutors who support students working on specific writing assignments. OWLs with tutors can be useful in the following ways:

- You can submit a draft via e-mail for feedback. OWL tutors will return your work, often within forty-eight hours.

- OWLs may post your paper in a public access space where you will receive feedback from more than just one or two readers.

- You can read papers online and learn how others are handling writing issues.

You can learn more about what online writing labs have to offer by checking out the following Web sites:

- University of Ottawa's Writing Centre
  <www.uottawa.ca/academic/arts/writcent>
- University of British Columbia's Writing Centre
- Writing Labs and Writing Centres on the Web (visit almost fifty OWLs) <owl.english.purdue.edu/internet/owls/writing-labs.html>
- Wilfrid Laurier University Writing Resources
  <info.wlu.ca/writing/resources.shtml>

6. Respond to readers. Consider and evaluate your readers' suggestions, but remember that you are under no obligation to do what they say. Sometimes you will receive contradictory advice. One reader may like a particular sentence; a second reader may suggest that you eliminate the very same sentence. Is there common ground? Yes. Both readers stopped at that sentence. Ask yourself why—and if you want readers to pause there. You are the one who is ultimately responsible for your paper, so you need to make decisions that you are comfortable with.

7. Work with experts and instructors. In addition to sharing your work with peers in class or through e-mail or online chats, you can use e-mail to consult experts. Suppose, for example, that a friend at another school is an expert on the topic of your paper. You can use e-mail to interview that friend, and then include parts of the interview in your paper. As always, you must properly credit your source. (*See Tabs 4–6 on documentation styles.*)

You can also consult your instructor or other experts. Many students don't think to ask their instructor questions by e-mail. If your instructor is willing, you can quote from his or her response in your paper, along with a proper citation.

Your instructor's comments on an early draft are especially valuable. He or she will raise questions and make suggestions, but remember, it is not your instructor's job to tell you everything you need to do to get an "A" in the course. It is your responsibility to address the issues your instructor raises and to revise your work.

4f USING ONLINE TOOLS FOR REVISING.

Word-processing programs can make your text look beautiful, with a pleasing format and easy-to-read typeface. Even when a first draft looks finished, however, it is still a first draft. Be sure to check below the surface for problems in content, structure, and style. Move paragraphs around, add details, and delete irrelevant sentences. The computer makes these changes almost effortless. However, it is always a good idea to print out a copy of your draft, because a hard copy, unlike the computer screen, allows you to see the big picture—your paper as a whole.

Your word-processing program probably offers changes tracking. This feature is very useful, whether you are editing your own work or collaborating with other students on writing projects. "Track Changes" or "Revisions," which may be part of the "Tools" menu, allow you to edit writing while also maintaining the original text. Usually, strike-through marks or balloons show what you have deleted or replaced, and added text is coloured. Because you can still make out the original version of your text, you can judge whether a change has improved the paper and whether any vital information was lost when the change was made. If you change your mind, you can restore the deleted text. When collaborating with another writer, you should keep the original text intact while suggesting changes.

Another feature that may be included in the "File" menu is "Versions." When you are collaborating with other students on a paper, you can use the "Versions" feature to save and name various drafts of text. Too many versions can get confusing, though, so you should create versions only when your project requires it.

Whether you use special menu features or just the basic functions of a word-processing program, the computer allows you to save and compare several different versions of a piece of writing and decide which one works best. The following tips will make this process go smoothly.

1. Save your work. Always protect your creativity and hard-won drafts from power surges and other acts of technological treachery. Save often, and make backups.

2. Label revised drafts under different file names. Save successive versions of your paper under different file names: for example, Judith Applebaum could have saved drafts of her paper as Compassion1, Compassion2, Compassion3, and so on.

3. Print hard copies early and often. If you save and print the original, you can feel free to experiment.

5   Document Design

Like writing decisions, design decisions must be purposeful to be effective. As you plan your document, consider your purpose for writing, as well as the needs of your audience. If you are writing an informative paper for a psychology class, ask your instructor—your primary audience—which format he or she prefers and then follow that format. If you are writing a newsletter intended to persuade the citizens of your community to support a project, use design to draw attention to your most important points. Your goal is to enhance the content of your text, not just decorate it. Good design decisions should make it more understandable and informative.

5a   GETTING MARGINS, SPACING, TYPE, AND PAGE NUMBERS RIGHT.

The way you format a document determines how your text appears on the page—and how it affects readers. Here are a few basic guidelines for formatting academic papers:

- **First page:** The first page of your paper is often different from the other pages. In a short paper, less than five pages, page 1 contains a header with your name, your professor's name, your course and section number, and the date. If your paper exceeds five pages, page 1 is usually a title page.

- **Type:** Select a common typeface, or font, such as Courier, Times, or Bookman, and choose a 10- or 12-point size. Typefaces such as Arial and Eras Book are sometimes used for headings because of their simplicity. Many typefaces available on your computer are display fonts—Antique, *Calligrapher*, Old English, and others—and should be used rarely, if ever, in papers, on the screen, or in presentations.

TECH TIPS

Online Font Sources

To download new fonts or fonts you don't already have in your word processor, go to a site such as *Font Files* <www.fontfile.com>.

- **Margins:** Use 2.5-centimetre (one-inch) margins on all four sides of your text.

- **Margin justification:** Line up, or justify, the lines of your document along the left margin but not along the right margin. This procedure gives you a "ragged-right" margin, with lines ending unevenly on the right side, and enables you to avoid odd spacing between words.

- **Line spacing:** Double-space your paper unless you are instructed to do otherwise.

- **Page numbers:** Page numbers typically appear in the upper right-hand corner of all pages after the first.

5b THINKING INTENTIONALLY ABOUT DESIGN.

From straightforward academic papers to more elaborate documents such as reports, newsletters, or brochures, the same design principles apply.

1. Get to know your computer toolbar. The toolbars on your computer give you a range of options for editing, designing, and sharing your documents. There are a variety of toolbars available in the most widely used word-processing program, Microsoft Word. In the following example (Figure 5.1), the ribbon of toolbars, all stacked on each other using different tabs, is shown. The Home toolbar allows you to choose different typefaces: bold, italic, or underlined type, numbered or bulleted lists, and so on. (*See p. 62 for more help with these design options.*) The Insert toolbar allows you to insert boxes, photos, and clip art into your text; and the Review toolbar enables you to track changes, add comments, and even compare two different versions of a document.

Figure 5.1   The Ribbon of Toolbars in Microsoft Word.

CROSS-DISCIPLINE **WRITING**

Style Guides

The Modern Language Association (MLA) and the American Psychological Association (APA) have developed widely used guidelines for documentation and manuscript format. For more about the basic document styles recommended by MLA and by APA, see pages 164–194 and pages 197–224, respectively. For style guides in math, biology, chemistry, and other fields, see the online resources that accompany this textbook.

If you are using a word-processing program other than Microsoft Word, take some time to learn the different toolbars and formatting options available to you.

2. Use design to organize information. You can organize information visually and topically by grouping related items as closely together as your space allows. To help readers grasp the importance of each piece of information, use graphic accents such as boxes or indents, headings, spacing, and lists. For example, in this book, headings help group information, and italics and bold type draw readers' attention to particular words and phrases. These variations in text appearance can help readers scan, locate information, and dive in when they need to know more about a topic.

Decisions about typeface and type size can improve the readability of both print and online documents (or make them more difficult to read), as the following example illustrates:

AviationNow.com Insider—June 18
Headlines Direct from Paris Air Show

Updated News and Features from Global Aviation Event Available on AviationNow.com

Halifax, N.S., July 1, 2008—*Aviation Week's* AviationNow.com Insider—Daily Paris Extra newsletter announced the following headlines for June 18, 2008. The full text of the articles plus additional news items and features are available at AviationNow.com (www.AviationNow.com), a leading Internet portal serving the global aviation and aerospace industry. The Insider is written and produced onsite at the Paris Air Show by *Aviation Week's* multinational team of editors and reporters.

The first lines are in 12-point type, large enough to set the heading apart but not so large that it overwhelms the rest of the text. After a space, the next two lines are in a 10-point font, in bold italic type. The spacing and italics differentiate these lines, helping readers see that they explain the heading above. After the date line, in bold type, the title *Aviation Week* is italicized because it is the name of a periodical publication. Finally, the URL for AviationNow.com is underlined, a visual cue that this is a link to another Web site.

In the following example, visual cues are used to bring items together into a group as well as to highlight their singularity.

A heading in capital letters and 12-point type labels the group of headlines. Each headline then gets its own **bullet**, the ■ symbol.

TOP STORIES
- Murder at Midnight
- Taxes: Provincial and Federal
- Lightning Bugs: Unexpected Discovery
- Bird Brains: What Do They Tell Us about People?

---

3. Use design elements consistently. In design, simplicity, contrast, and consistency matter. If you emphasize an item by putting it in italic or bold type or in colour, or if you use a graphic accent such as a box to set it off, consider repeating this effect for similar items to give your document a unified look. Even a simple horizontal line can be a purposeful element in a long document when used consistently to help organize information.

4. Use restraint. If you use too many graphics, headings, bullets, boxes, or other elements in a document, you risk making it as "noisy" as a loud radio. Standard fonts have become standard because they are easy on the eye. Variations from these standard fonts jar the eye. Unusual typefaces are attention getting, but they lose their force when overused. Bold or italic type, underlining, or any other graphic effect should not continue for more than one sentence at a time.

Refrain from relying on bold and italics to emphasize ideas. Instead, use the structure of your text and your choice of words to let your readers know what is important. You should also be aware of certain conventions that govern the use of bold and italic type, especially in academic documents. Boldfaced words often signal that a glossary with key words and their definitions accompanies the text. Italics can be used instead of quotation marks to indicate that a word is being referred to as a word. They are also used for the titles of books and periodicals. (*See p. 172.*)

5c EMPHASIZING TEXT BY VARYING TYPE STYLE AND USING LISTS.

1. Bold, *italics*, and underlining. You can emphasize a word or phrase in your text by selecting it and clicking on a button on your toolbar to make it **bold**, *italicized*, or underlined.

2. ALL CAPS/SMALL CAPS. In general, you should avoid capitalizing entire words or phrases in your academic papers. This option should be used only for headlines in newsletters, brochures, and other non-academic documents. The "Caps Lock" key on your keyboard allows you to type words or phrases in capital letters. You can change your text to small caps by choosing "Font" in the "Format" menu and then clicking next to "Small Caps" (a checkmark will appear in the box). To turn small caps off, click on the "Small Caps" box a second time to remove the checkmark.

3. Lists. Numbered or bulleted lists help you cluster ideas. Because they stand out from your text visually, lists help readers see that ideas are related. For example, you can use a numbered list to display steps in a sequence, present checklists, or suggest recommendations for action.

Format your text as a numbered or bulleted list by choosing the option you want from the standard toolbar. Use parallel structure in your list, introduce it with a complete sentence followed by a colon, and put a period at the end of each entry if the entries are complete sentences. If they are not complete sentences, no punctuation is necessary.

5d ORGANIZING LONG PAPERS WITH HEADINGS.

Headings interrupt the text in short papers. In longer papers, though, they help you organize complex information.

Effective headings are short, descriptive, and, like lists, consistent in emphasis and parallel in grammatical structure. All of your headings in a paper might be in the form of questions, declarative or imperative sentences, or phrases beginning with *-ing* verbs. Note, for example, that each heading in this chapter starts with an *ing* verb telling you what to do: *getting, thinking, emphasizing, organizing, using,* and so on. This is parallel structure. (*For more on parallel structure, see Tab 7: Editing for Clarity, pp. 277–278.*)

Place and highlight headings consistently throughout your paper. For example, you might centre all first-level headings—which are like the main points in an outline—and put them in bold type. If you have second-level headings—your supporting points—you might align them at the left margin and underline them.

First-Level Heading

Second-Level Heading

5e USING VISUALS TO CLARIFY AND EXPLAIN A POINT.

Used judiciously, visuals such as tables, charts, and graphs provide clarity. Effective visuals are used for a specific purpose, not for decoration, and each type of visual illustrates some kinds of material better than others. For example, compare the table below and the line graph on page 65. Both present similar types of data, but do both have the same effect on you? Does one strike you as clearer or more powerful than the other?

Make your visuals simple and clear. If a chart is overloaded with information, separate it into several charts instead.

Because the inclusion of visual elements in papers is more accepted in some fields than in others, you may want to ask your instructor for advice before including a visual in your paper.

1. Tables. Tables are the easiest visuals to prepare. They are made up of rows and columns of cells; each cell presents an element of textual, numeric, or graphic information. Tables organize data for readers.

Consider this example taken from the Daily Commercial News Web site.

TABLE 1. Canadian provincial labour markets—April 2010

	Unemployment rate		Employment (000s)			
Province	April 2009	April 2010	April 2009	April 2010	Net change	% change
Newfoundland and Labrador	15.1%	15.0%	213.8	219.3	5.5	2.6%
Prince Edward Island	12.6%	9.5%	68.8	72.6	3.8	5.5%
Nova Scotia	9.2%	8.6%	449.4	453.8	4.4	1.0%
New Brunswick	8.8%	8.5%	364.7	367.3	2.6	0.7%
Québec	8.5%	7.9%	3,854.4	3,914.6	60.2	1.6%
Ontario	8.8%	8.8%	6,533.8	6,615.6	81.8	1.3%
Manitoba	4.6%	4.9%	603.9	619.0	15.1	2.5%
Saskatchewan	5.0%	5.2%	519.5	527.8	8.3	1.6%
Alberta	6.3%	7.4%	1,986.3	1,979.4	−6.9	−0.3%
British Columbia	7.6%	7.3%	2,253.6	2,302.6	49.0	2.2%
Canada	**8.1%**	**8.1%**	**16,848.1**	**17,071.9**	**223.8**	**1.3%**

Data source (seasonally adjusted figures): Statistics Canada
Table: Reed Construction Data—CanaData

TECH **TIPS**

Preparing Tables

You can usually create and edit tables in your word-processing program. If you use Microsoft Word, for example, the program allows you to size columns proportionally to avoid distorting their contents and to make them fit your text. Under the "Table" pull-down menu, select "Insert," then click on "Table." You will see a dialogue box. Choose "Autofit to contents" instead of "Fixed column width." As you create the table, the borders will automatically increase.

You can also create tables using database, spreadsheet, presentation, and Web-site-construction software.

2. Bar graphs. Perhaps because they are relatively easy to prepare and to read, bar graphs are quite common. These graphs show relationships and highlight comparisons between two or more variables. The following example compares the frequency of three kinds of activities during certain periods of the year.

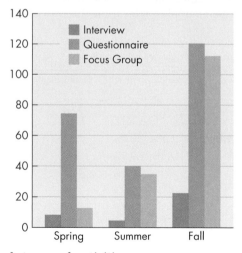

Figure 1.   Market research activities

3. Pie charts. For showing differences between parts in relation to a whole, use pie charts, which are circles divided into segments with each segment representing a piece of the whole. The segments must add up to approximately 100% of something. For another example, see the pie chart that follows:

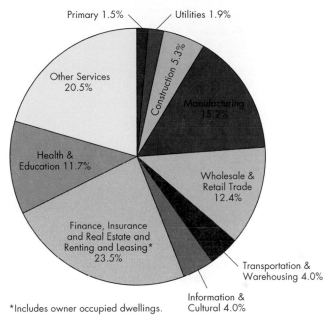

*Includes owner occupied dwellings.

Figure 2. Structure of the Ontario economy, 2009 percent share of GDP

Source: Statistics Canada and Ontario Ministry of Finance, 2011

4. Line graphs. Line graphs or charts are used to show changes over time or to show the relationship between two variables and are effective ways of comparing parallel sets of data:

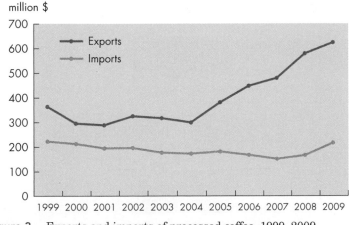

Figure 3. Exports and imports of processed coffee, 1999–2009

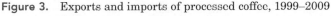
Source: Statistics Canada and Agriculture Canada.

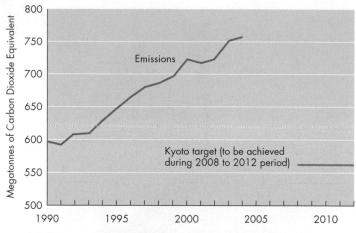

Figure 4. Kyoto targets for CO_2 emissions

Source: Statistics Canada website <www41.statcan.ca/2007/1762/grafx/htm/ceb1762_000_2-eng.htm>, Environment Canada, and Health Canada. *Data source:* Statistics Canada, Catalogue no. 16-251-XWE.

5. Diagrams. To show concepts, processes, or structures visually in writing, diagrams are often used. The following diagram, for example, shows the Appeal process in the Supreme Court of Canada.

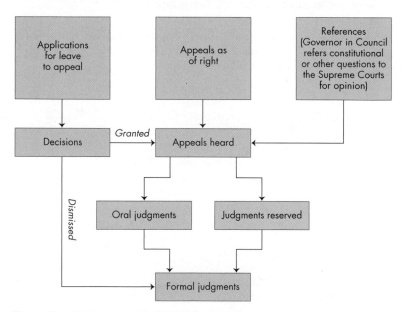

Figure 5. Supreme court of Canada appeal process

Source: The Supreme Court of Canada

Diagrams also provide powerful evidence when exploring the reasons behind events or the effects of those events. In this case, the fishbone (Ishikawa) diagram identifies root causes and overall effect(s). Although information like this seems self-explanatory, you will still need to analyze and interpret the data for your readers.

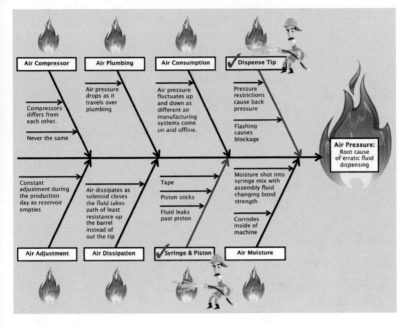

Figure 6. Root cause analysis of dispensing problems

Source: © 2011 Fishman Corporation Brand Imaging: Bergeron Creative Studios, Inc.

6. Photographs and illustrations. Photographs and illustrations can reinforce a point you are making in your text in ways that words cannot, showing readers what your subject actually looks like, or how it has been affected or changed. When you use photographs or illustrations, always credit your source, and be aware that most such items are protected by copyright. If you plan to use a photograph as part of a Web page, for example, you will usually need to obtain permission from the copyright holder.

Using photos can be a powerful way to reinforce a message or narrate events you discuss in your paper. Images like the one on page 68 help tell one of the many stories about Canadian forces working in Haiti after the January 2010 earthquake.

Visual details provide concrete examples of your ideas. This map illustrates the history of the borders and names of Canada's provinces and territories.

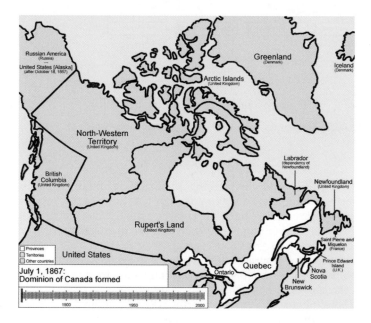

TECH **TIPS**

Reporting Data

If you are writing a lab report or any other report for which you have gathered data, consider including graphic representations of your data in your final report. (*See Tab 2: Common Assignments, pp. 73–122.*) Using a chart or graph to display the data lets you show rather than just tell your reader about your findings. The bar graph on page 64, for example, was created using the PowerPoint software program, which provides templates that allow you to create visual reports from "live" spreadsheets or databases.

To create a pie chart, just open a "blank presentation" in Power-Point. A group of different slide layouts will appear. Click on the pie chart, and you will see a premade slide with numbers already in the chart. Replace those numbers with your own by deleting the text in the little spreadsheet displayed along with the pie chart and typing in your own numbers. Re-label the categories, and you have your own spreadsheet graphic. A simple print screen of the full slide then allows you to paste that graphic into your text.

5f INTEGRATING VISUALS INTO DOCUMENTS EFFECTIVELY.

If you decide to use a table, chart, diagram, or clip art, keep this general advice in mind:

1. **Number tables and other figures** consecutively throughout your paper, and label them appropriately: Table 1, Table 2, and so on. Do not abbreviate *Table. Figure* may be abbreviated as *Fig.*

2. **Refer to the visual element in your text** before it appears, placing the visual as close as possible to the text in which you state why you are including it. If your project contains many or complex tables or other visuals, however, you may want to group them in an appendix. Always refer to a visual by its label—for example, "See Figure 1."

3. **Give each visual a title and caption** that clearly explains what the visual shows. A visual with its caption should be clear without the discussion in the text, and the discussion of the visual in the text should be clear without the visual itself.

4. **Include explanatory notes below the visuals**, and use the word *Note* followed by a colon to introduce explanations of the visual as a whole. If you want to explain a specific element within the visual, use a superscript *letter* (not a number) both after the specific element and before the note. This is essentially a footnote, but the explanation should appear directly beneath the graphic, not at the foot of the page or at the end of your paper. Do not use your word processor's "Insert/Footnote" command to create the footnote because the program will put the note in one of those two places.

5. **Credit sources for visuals.** If you use a visual element from a source, you need to credit the source. Use the word *Source,* followed by a colon and complete documentation of the source, including the author, title, publication information, and page number if applicable.

Note: The Modern Language Association (MLA) and the American Psychological Association (APA) provide guidelines for figure captions and crediting sources of visuals that differ from the previous guidelines. (*See Tab 4: MLA Documentation Style, p. 190, and Tab 5: APA Documentation Style, p. 216.*)

COMMON
ASSIGNMENTS

2 Common Assignments

2 Common Assignments

Most people are writers and use writing in their daily lives—students, however, use writing extensively as an expression of their learning. From case studies to literary analyses, writing is a concrete demonstration of ideas and opinions presented in a framework of academic objectivity. This section gives you tips on preparing the most common types of writing tasks and explains the distinctive features of each kind.

Informative Reports

6a UNDERSTANDING THE ASSIGNMENT.

Imagine a world where each person had to relearn everything from scratch, with no records of what others have learned. Fortunately, we have many sources of information to draw on, including informative reports. An **informative report** passes on what someone has learned about a topic or issue; it teaches.

Because a good way to reinforce learning is by teaching it to others, informative reports are often used. An informative report requires you to find out what is currently known about some specific topic and to present what you discover in a clear and unbiased way.

An informative report gives you a chance to do the following:

- Read more about an issue that interests you.
- Make sense of what you have read, heard, and seen.
- Teach others what you have learned.

Note: In some courses, a special kind of informative report called a *literature review* is required. Here the term *literature* refers to published research reports, not to poems and novels, and the term *review* means that you need to survey others' ideas, not evaluate them or argue for your opinion. A review presents an organized account of the current state of knowledge in a specific area that you and other researchers can use to develop new projects and directions for research.

6b SELECTING A TOPIC THAT INTERESTS YOU.

An informative report should be clear and reliable, but not dull. The major challenge of writing informative reports is engaging the reader's interest. Selecting a topic that interests you makes it more likely that your report will interest your readers.

Consider connecting what you are learning in one course with a topic you are studying in another course or with your personal experience. For example, one student, Den Birket, is a Junior A hockey player and has a stake in the "commodification" of professional athletes. For his topic, he decided to investigate the negative impact of this type of business practice on players and their teams *(Birket's paper begins on p. 77.)*

6c CONSIDERING WHAT YOUR READERS ALREADY KNOW.

Unless the writing task designates a different group, consider your classmates and your instructor to be the audience for your report. In other words, assume that your readers have some familiarity with the topic area, but that most of them do not have clear, specific knowledge of your particular topic *(For more on audience analysis, see Tab 1: Writing and Designing Papers, pp. 17–19)*.

6d DEVELOPING AN OBJECTIVE POSITION.

When writers have an objective position, they do not take sides. Instead, they present differing views fairly, without indicating a preference for one view over another. This commitment to objectivity gives an informative report its authority. Ideas and facts are presented methodically, and the emphasis is on the topic, not the writer. By contrast, when writers are subjective, they let readers know their view. Although a subjective point of view is appropriate for other types of writing, an informative report should come across as objective rather than subjective.

6e COMPOSING A THESIS THAT SUMMARIZES YOUR KNOWLEDGE OF THE TOPIC.

The thesis of an informative report is usually not controversial, even when the report is about a dispute. Because transmitting knowledge is the primary goal of an informative report, the thesis typically states an accepted generalization or reports the results of the writer's study.

Your thesis should also state the objective of your paper and forecast its content. Before you decide on a thesis, review the information you have collected and divide it up into categories, or subtopics.

Compose a thesis statement that summarizes—either generally or by category—what the information in your paper shows. (*For more on thesis statements, see Tab 1: Writing and Designing Papers, pp. 27–29.*)

In his paper about the commodification of professional athletes, Birket's thesis is a statement identifying the negative impact of commodification:

> The fact that professional athletes are treated as commodities has a negative impact in all professional sports. Some of these consequences show up as the lack of team unity and the inability of the fans to associate with the players on their favourite teams because of the constant changing in player personal and the lack of respect that they receive being by bought or sold to make or save money.

Notice how Birket forecasts the body of his paper. We expect to learn something about each of the two points presented in this statement of intent (thesis).

6f PROVIDING CONTEXT IN YOUR INTRODUCTION.

Informative reports usually begin with a relatively simple introduction to the topic and a straightforward statement of the thesis. To orient readers, the introduction may provide some relevant context or background, but writers of informative reports generally get to their topic as quickly as possible and keep it in the foreground. (*For more on introductions, see Tab 1: Writing and Designing Papers, pp. 37–38.*)

6g ORGANIZING YOUR PAPER FOR CLARITY BY CLASSIFYING AND DIVIDING INFORMATION.

Because you are explaining something in an informative report, clarity matters. Informative writers develop their ideas in an organized way, often by classifying and dividing information into categories, subtopics, or the stages of a process. (*For more on developing your ideas, see Tab 1: Writing and Designing Papers, pp. 31–37.*)

6h ILLUSTRATING KEY IDEAS WITH EXAMPLES.

Because clarity is so important to the success of an informative report, writers of these kinds of papers usually use specific examples to help readers understand their most important ideas. In his paper on the commodification of professional athletes, Birket devotes a lot

WRITING CONNECTIONS

Informative Reports

By writing reports in college or university, you prepare yourself for future professional and public occasions that will require you to pass on information to others. In many professions, writing informative announcements, manuals, and reports is part of the job:

- For a music appreciation textbook, a professor of music history writes a chapter explaining three distinctive characteristics of Renaissance music.
- In a published article, an anthropologist surveys and summarizes a large body of indigenous material on the hunting habits of the Inuit before government settlement.
- In a report for their colleagues, three physical therapists define what a critical pathway is, trace its development, and summarize the arguments for and against its use in patient care.
- For an encyclopedia of British women writers, a professor of literature briefly recounts the life and works of Eliza Fenwick, a recently rediscovered 18th-century author.
- In a journal for research biologists, two biochemists summarize the findings of more than two hundred recently published articles on defence mechanisms in plants.

of space to past and current examples that help to solidify his position on the subject. Examples make his paper interesting as well as educational. (*For more on using examples, see Tab 1: Writing and Designing Papers, p. 34.*)

6i DEFINING SPECIALIZED TERMS AND UNFAMILIAR ABBREVIATIONS.

Most informative reports include specialized terms that will probably not be familiar to most readers, or familiar terms that are being used in a specialized or an unfamiliar way. Writers of informative reports usually explain these terms with a synonym or a brief definition.

6j CONCLUDING BY ANSWERING "SO WHAT?"

Because informative writers want readers to remember what they have learned, they often try to conclude their reports with an image that suggests the information's value or a saying that sums it all up. The conclusion reminds readers of the topic and point that were first stated in the introduction and its straightforward thesis. It then answers the "So what?" question.

At the end of his paper on the commodification of professional athletes, Birket answers the "So what?" question with a prediction:

> With more and more emphasis on making money or buying a championship, athletes will be bought and sold according to the needs of the organization and in spite of their prior contribution or relationship to the team. It is a changed world in professional sports, one that revolves around money, and we are all just along for the ride.

(Also see information on conclusions in Tab 1: Writing and Designing Papers, pp. 37–38.)

6k STUDENT PAPER: INFORMATIVE REPORT.

In the paper that follows, Den Birket reports what he has learned about professional athletes who are "bought and sold" by their respective teams. As you read his report, notice how Birket provides a context for his topic, cites various sources, organizes the information, and illustrates his ideas with examples, all hallmarks of a clear, carefully developed paper. Besides being clear, informative reports are also expected to be objective. Do you think Birket's report meets this requirement?

Den Birket

Professor M. Rubens

EAC954CS

Athletes For Sale

The trading of professional athletes and contract negotia-
tions are an integral part of a sports team's success or failure.
However, in recent years, it has become more ruthless. Athletes
are more likely to be treated as commodities now—bought and
sold to the highest bidder. It is suggested that the Babe Ruth
incident in the early part of the century (where the Boston Red
Sox "sold" him to the New York Yankees for a lot of money
because Boston needed it to help pay off their debts) began the

Topic
introduced.

Examples
used to
establish
historic
context.

whole idea of treating professional athletes as commodities, rather than human beings. Former baseball and football star Bo Jackson, once discussed this matter on TSN's *For the Love of the Game*, where he argued that athletes are treated like "pieces of fruit" in a grocery stand. Indeed, when they are no longer

Thesis stated. of any use, they are "discarded like garbage" (Sports Ethics 1). The fact that professional athletes are treated as commodities has a negative impact in all professional sports. Some of these consequences show up as the lack of team unity and the inability of the fans to associate with the players on their favourite teams because of the constant changing in player personnel and the lack of respect that they receive by being bought or sold to make or save money.

Introduction to the first major point. In today's sporting world, with all the trades and contract discussions that transpire throughout the season, it is easy to understand the strain that it puts on the team's cohesion, togetherness, and overall team unity (Derson 87). Professional athletes insist that the importance of team unity is vital to the success of their team on the playing surface. However, the number of trades or contract incidents that go on during a season cause rifts and problems with team unity and affect overall team chemistry. Any championship team has to have a certain level of unity: problems in the dressing room, more often than not, spill over into game time. One situation more prevalent in recent years is the ongoing re-negotiation of player's contracts to

Acronym defined. deal with salary cap dilemmas. In the National Football League (NFL), players can be released at anytime, even if they are under contract. For example, Steve McNair, of the Tennessee Titans in the NFL was told to leave the team property in spite of his contract. The team states: "We have no choice but to protect the club and its future from the possibility of having a significant amount of our salary cap at risk in a single player should he sustain a major injury... This is entirely a risk management problem." ("McNair Asked to Leave..."). By dismissing McNair during the pre-season, the impact on the Titans was significant. Teammates wondered why the team told their star player to go home and not get ready for the upcoming season. McNair wondered whether his job was secure. The organization, as a whole, was unsettled.

Example of commodification and its impact on unity.

In other circumstances, players are "traded off" if they question or criticize the organization even if they are at the top of their game. Randy Moss of the NFL Vikings was sent to Los Angeles because of his constant attacks on his team's lack of investment into building a winning roster. He was always in the media saying that his owners were not doing enough to improve the team and that they were just saving money. "Tired of dealing with his distracting antics, the Vikings reportedly have agreed to trade Moss to the Oakland Raiders for linebacker Napoleon Harris, the No. 7 pick in April's draft and a later round pick ("Moss Frustrated..."). Because of the apparent lack of respect for players, they tend to switch teams more regularly causing disunity in the team because the roster is constantly changing. All this does is create a disassociation of players among the fans.

Fans suffer when they are not able to associate with players on the team because of the constant changing of faces. In the past, it was much more common to see athletes start and finish their careers with the same team; however, it is rarely the case now (Nordstrom 106). The business is to make money, which means cutting players or trading favourite players to either save money or make money.

A different perspective on the power of a professional sports organization over its roster.

The last statement introduces the second major point.

At the trade deadlines, for example, teams sell or trade players to the highest bidder if they think that the team is finished for the season. Known as a "salary dump" by some, it highlights the business practice of treating players like stocks and trading or selling them off to the highest bidder because the team does not want to have to pay the salary anymore. It is hard then for the fans to develop a sense of the players on the team. Many fans have turned to cheering for their team as a whole and not players as individuals (Brodie).

Third point implied here.

Many of these athletes do not want to be traded or to sign with a different team, but cannot control many of the aspects. It is simply a business for the organization. After a trade, stories emerge about how players find out about the change—they hear about it in the media. Without warning, players have to uproot their families, suddenly move to a new city, and start all over again. One of the most famous trades where the player was not informed involved Bobby Orr:

Long quotation offset as a separate passage.

> In 1976, Eagleson negotiated Orr's sale to the Chicago Black Hawks to Eagleson's close friend Bill Wirtz, even though Orr did not want to leave the Boston Bruins and Boston tried desperately to hold on to him. The Bruins even offered Orr an 18.5 percent ownership stake in the franchise, worth $16 million US by 1994. Eagleson never informed Orr of this offer, but instead lied to him and said that Boston did not want him. What kind of financial gain Eagleson made from this deal Conway does not know, though it likely was substantial (Sports Ethics 1).

Conclusion restates points and purpose.

The fact that players like Orr are disrespected, treated as "articles of commerce" and bought and sold is becoming more common in professional sports, and this has a negative impact on both the team and the individual athlete. As professional sport leagues are run more as businesses, athletes will continue to be traded and treated like commodities in the stock market. With more and more emphasis on making money or buying a championship, athletes will be bought and sold according to the needs of the organization and in spite of their prior contribution or relationship to the team. It is a changed world in professional sports, one that revolves around money, and we are all just along for the ride.

Works Cited

Brodie, Rob. "Trade Deadline Rush Started out as Dead Air."
Canoe Inc. 10 March 2006. Web. 3 April 2006.

Derson, J. T. "Sports Performance and Team Cohesiveness:
A Correlational Study." *International Journal of Sports
Behaviour* 22 (2008): 72–92. Print.

"McNair Asked to Leave Titans Camp." *TSN.ca.* 4 April 2006.
Web. 6 May 2006.

"Moss Frustrated with Frugal Vikings." *TSN.ca.* 25 February
2005. Web. 5 April 2006.

Nordstrom, E. *Psychology of Sports Fans.* Toronto: Ram
Publishing, 2008. Print.

"Receiver Eric Moulds Shuffled out of Buffalo; Agrees to Deal with
Houston." *Canoe.ca.* 4 April 2006. Web. 10 May 2006.

"Sports Ethics 1." Online posting. 5 April 2006. Let's Talk
Sports. Web. 30 June 2007.

"Works Cited" follows MLA style and begins on a new page. For more information on MLA Documentation Style, see Tab 4

The name of a book, journal, or Web site is italicized.

Interpretive Analyses

7

7a UNDERSTANDING THE ASSIGNMENT.

Interpretation is one of the key tasks of educated people. As the phrase "That's open to interpretation" suggests, searching for meaning does not involve looking for a single right answer. Instead, it involves figuring out a way of understanding that is meaningful to the writer and convincing to readers.

You will frequently get assignments that require you to explore the meaning of written documents, literary works, cultural artifacts, social situations, and natural events. When an assignment asks you to compare, explain, analyze, discuss, or do a reading of something, you are expected to study that subject closely, to figure out what it might mean.

Interpretive analyses, including comparative papers, encourage you to move beyond simple description and examine or compare particular items for a reason: to enhance your reader's understanding of people's conditions, actions, beliefs, or desires.

7b DISCOVERING AN ASPECT THAT IS MEANINGFUL TO YOU.

Although you will not include your personal reflections in the finished version of your interpretive analysis, your interpretation will have more energy if you take time to discover why the subject is meaningful to you. Think about your own experience while you read, listen, or observe. Connecting your own thoughts and experience to what you are studying can help you develop fresh interpretations.

7c DEVELOPING A CRITICAL POINT OF VIEW.

Interpretive analyses take your readers with you on an intellectual journey. You are saying, in effect, "Come, and think this through with me." Consequently, your position should be thoughtful, inquisitive, and open-minded. You are exploring the possible meaning of something. Usually it is wise to admit uncertainty, and sometimes it is good to qualify your interpretations with words like probably,

CROSS-DISCIPLINE **WRITING**

Interpretative Analyses across Disciplines

Students are often called upon to write interpretive analyses such as the following:

- A student in a literature course asserts that Flannery O'Connor's story "Everything That Rises Must Converge" can be understood as a character contest.
- A student majoring in music spells out the emotional implications of the tempo and harmonic progression in Schubert's *Der Atlas.*
- An economist demonstrates that, according to an econometric model of nine variables, deregulation has not decreased the level of airline safety.
- A social worker compares at-risk students from different neighbourhoods in urban settings.

may, and perhaps. Read your writing aloud, and as you listen to your words, ask yourself whether your position sounds as exploratory as it should. Keep in mind, though, that this type of analysis relies on objective (third person) perspective. While personal reflections are vital in the development of the ideas, the finished version should be free of subjective or personalized writing.

7d USING AN INTELLECTUAL FRAMEWORK.

To interpret your subject effectively, you will have to analyze it using a relevant perspective or an *intellectual framework*. An intellectual framework is a conceptual structure—a model for understanding—within which complex issues can be addressed. Sometimes, this framework will emerge from primary sources, structured around the commonalities of the resources themselves. Often, though, this framework will come from established models for analysis. For example, the basic elements of a work of fiction, such as plot, character, and setting, are often used to analyze stories. Sigmund Freud's theory of conscious and unconscious forces in conflict has been applied to various things, including people, poems, and historical periods. In his analysis of Flannery O'Connor's story "Everything That Rises Must Converge," Rajeev Bector uses sociologist Erving Goffman's ideas about "character contests" to interpret the conflict between a son and his mother. (*Bector's analysis begins on p. 87.*)

No matter what framework you use, analysis often entails taking something apart and then putting it back together by figuring out how the parts make up a meaningful whole. Because the goal of analysis is to create a meaningful interpretation, the writer needs to treat the whole as more than the sum of its parts and recognize that meaning is a complex problem with multiple solutions.

7e LISTING, COMPARING, QUESTIONING, AND CLASSIFYING TO DISCOVER YOUR THESIS.

To figure out a thesis, it is often useful to explore separate aspects of your subject. For example, if you are analyzing literature, you might consider the plot, the characters, the setting, and the tone before deciding to focus your thesis on how a character's personality drives the plot to its conclusion. If you were comparing two subjects, you would look for and list points of likeness and difference. Note that comparing is not just a way of presenting ideas; it is also a way of discovering ideas. What features do the items have—and not have—in common? Can you find subtle differences in aspects that at first seem alike? Subtle similarities in aspects that at first seem very different? Which do you find more interesting, the similarities or the differences? The answers to these questions might help you figure out your thesis.

As you work on discovering your thesis, try one or more of the following strategies:

- Take notes about what you see or read, and if it helps, write a summary. Look for interesting issues that emerge as you work on your summary and notes.

- Ask yourself questions about the subject you are analyzing, and write down any interesting answers. Imagine what kinds of questions might be asked about the artifact, document, or performance you are considering. In answering these questions, try to figure out the thesis you will present and support.

- Name the class of things to which the item you are analyzing belongs (for example, memoirs), and then identify important parts or aspects of that class (for example, scene, point of view, helpers, turning points).

7f DEVELOPING A FOCUSED AND PURPOSEFUL THESIS.

Because the subject of an interpretative analysis is usually complex, you cannot possibly write about all of its aspects. Each component part of a topic may have more than one meaning or perspective, which will increase exponentially the amount of writing you will have to do. Instead, focus your paper on one or two issues or questions that are key to understanding the subject. With these key elements in mind, you can then ask, "what does it mean" or interpret meaning in context of the issue. The whole point of an interpretive analysis is to provide a meaningful commentary about your subject. Focusing can help you resist the temptation to describe everything you see.

EXAMPLE

In O'Connor's short story, plot, setting, and characterization work together to reinforce the impression that racism is a complex and pervasive problem.

EXAMPLE

In the first section of Shubert's *Der Atlas,* both the tempo and the harmonic progression express the sorrow of the hero's eternal plight.

Although you want your point to be clear, you also want to make sure that your thesis anticipates the "So what?" question and sets up an interesting context for your interpretation. Unless you relate your specific thesis to some more general issue, idea, or problem, your interpretive analysis may seem pointless to readers. (*For more on developing your thesis, see Tab 1: Writing and Designing Papers, pp. 27–29.*)

7g WRITING A STRONG INTRODUCTION.

In interpretive analyses, it often takes more than one paragraph to do what an introduction needs to do:

- Identify the general issue, concept, or problem at stake. You can also present the intellectual framework that you are applying.
- Provide relevant background information.
- Name the specific item or items you will focus on in your analysis (or the items you will compare).
- State the thesis you will support and develop or the main question(s) your analysis will answer.

You need not do these things in the order listed. Sometimes it is a good idea to introduce the specific focus of your analysis before presenting either the issue or the background information. Just make sure that your introduction does the four things it needs to do, even though you may begin it with a provocative statement or a revealing example designed to capture your readers' attention. (*For more on introductions, see Tab 1: Writing and Designing Papers, pp. 37–38.*)

For example, the following is an introductory paragraph from a comparative report on the value of college and university education in Canada:

Compared to other OECD countries, Canada has the largest percentage of highly educated people in terms of postsecondary education. However, most of the Canadian students who choose to continue their education beyond high school enrol in community colleges rather than universities. Community colleges offer a more technically oriented education, where emphasis is given to practical job training rather than the more general curricula offered in universities. Almost 50% of the Canadian population aged between 25 to 64 years of age has a postsecondary

General issue: colleges vs. universities.

Relevant background information provided.

education (OECD). Canada stands apart not only because of the large population with postsecondary education, but also because it has the highest percentage (about 30%) of people attending non-university postsecondary education—called "community college" in Canada. One thing puzzling many economists is that, although highly educated, on average Canadians are

Thesis stated.   less productive than their American neighbours. The question naturally arising from this apparent lack of productivity is how effective college education really is for Canadians.

In this short paragraph, the writers have identified the general issue (postsecondary education) and the items to be compared (colleges and universities), and, in the last section, state their thesis.

7h PLANNING YOUR PAPER SO THAT EACH POINT SUPPORTS YOUR THESIS.

As with any paper, an interpretive analysis has three main parts: an introduction, a body, and a conclusion. After you pose a key question or state your thesis in the introduction, you need to work point by point, organizing the points to answer the question and support your interpretive thesis. From beginning to end, readers must be able to follow the train of thought in your interpretive analysis and see how each point you make is related to your thesis. (*For more on developing your ideas, see Tab 1: Writing and Designing Papers, pp. 31–37*). What is vital, however, is that all the elements in an interpretive analysis be *relevant* to the overall meaning or point of the paper. Adding extraneous detail that does not help to support your perspective will weaken the overall impact of your work.

For example, if Bector had simply described the events in Flannery O'Connor's "Everything That Rises Must Converge" or presented a random list of insights, his paper would not shed any light on what the story means. Instead, Bector ends his introduction with a compelling question about one character's motives:

QUESTION   But why would Julian want to hurt his mother, a woman already suffering from high blood pressure?

Bector answers this interpretive question in the body of his paper by pointing out and explaining three features of the character contest between mother and son.

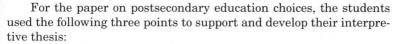

For the paper on postsecondary education choices, the students used the following three points to support and develop their interpretive thesis:

Thesis: The question naturally arising from this apparent lack of productivity is how effective college education really is for Canadians.

1. The writers provide facts about postsecondary education to establish a framework for the discussions.
2. Factual information about colleges and universities helps to clarify the differences in the two options.
3. The implied comparison in the thesis questions the viability of one educational choice over the other.

7i   CONCLUDING BY ANSWERING "SO WHAT?"

The conclusion of an interpretive analysis needs to do more than simply repeat the paper's thesis. It needs to answer the "So what?" question by saying why your thesis—as well as the analysis that supports and develops it—is relevant to the larger issue identified in the introduction. What does your interpretation reveal about that issue? *(For information about conclusions, see Tab 1: Writing and Designing Papers, pp. 37–38.)*

7j   STUDENT PAPER: INTERPRETIVE ANALYSIS.

In the following paper, Rajeev Bector uses Erving Goffman's ideas to analyze and interpret the actions of two characters in Flannery O'Connor's short story "Everything That Rises Must Converge." But what provoked Bector's interpretation in the first place is this question: How can we understand the mean way Julian and his mother treat each other? As he helps us better understand Julian and his mother, Bector raises the larger issue of racism. To what extent does Bector's interpretive analysis of O'Connor's story also illuminate the workings of racism in our society?

The Character Contest in Flannery O'Connor's

"Everything That Rises Must Converge"

Sociologist Erving Goffman believes that every social interaction establishes our identity and preserves our image, honour, and credibility in the hearts and minds of others. Social interactions, he says, are in essence "character contests" that occur not only in games and sports but also in our everyday dealings with strangers, peers, friends, and even family members. Goffman defines character contests as "disputes [that] are sought out and indulged in (often with glee) as a means of establishing where one's boundaries are" (29). Just such a contest occurs in Flannery O'Connor's short story "Everything That Rises Must Converge."

As they travel from home to the Y, Julian and his mother, Mrs. Chestny, engage in a character contest, a dispute we must understand in order to figure out the story's theme. Julian is so frustrated with his mother that he virtually "declare[s] war on her," "allow[s] no glimmer of sympathy to show on his face," and "imagine[s] various unlikely ways by which he could teach her a lesson" (O'Connor 185, 186). But why would Julian want to hurt his mother, a woman already suffering from high blood pressure?

Julian's conflict with Mrs. Chestny results from pent-up hostility and tension. As Goffman explains, character contests are a way of living that often leaves a "residue": "Every day in many ways we can try to score points and every day we can be shot down" (29). For many years, Julian has had to live under his racist mother's authority, and every time he protested her racist views, he was probably shot down because of his "radical ideas" and "lack of practical experience" (O'Connor 184). As a result, a residue of defeat and shame has accumulated that fuels a fire of rebellion against his mother. But even though Julian rebels against his mother's racist views, it doesn't mean that he isn't a racist himself. Julian doesn't realize that in his own way, he is as prejudiced as his mother. He makes it "a point" to sit next to blacks, in contrast to his mother, who purposely sits next to whites (182). They are two extremes, each biased, for if Julian were truly fair to all, he would not care whom he sat next to.

Key idea that provides intellectual framework.

Question posed.

Interpretation organized point-by-point—first point.

When we look at the situation from Mrs. Chestny's viewpoint, we realize that she must maintain her values and beliefs for two important reasons: to uphold her character as Julian's mother and to act out her prescribed role in society. Even if she finds Julian's arguments on race relations and integration valid and plausible, Mrs. Chestny must still refute them. If she didn't, she would lose face as Julian's mother—that image of herself as the one with authority. By preserving her self-image, Mrs. Chestny shows that she has what Goffman sees as key to "character": some quality that seems "essential and unchanging" (28).

"We" indicates thoughtful stance, not Bector's personal feelings.

Second point.

Besides upholding her character as Julian's mother, Mrs. Chestny wants to preserve the honour and dignity of her family tradition. Like an actor performing before an audience, she must play the role prescribed for her—the role of a white suprema-cist. But her situation is hopeless, for the role she must play fails to acknowledge the racial realities that have transformed her world. According to Goffman, when a "situation" is "hope-less," a character "can gamely give everything [. . .] and then go down bravely, or proudly, or insolently, or gracefully or with an ironic smile on his lips" (32). For Mrs. Chestny, being game means trying to preserve her honour and dignity as she goes down to physical defeat in the face of hopeless odds.

Third point.

Given the differences between Mrs. Chestny's and her son's values, as well as the oppressiveness of Mrs. Chestny's racist views, we can understand why Julian struggles to "teach" his mother "a lesson" (185) throughout the entire bus ride. Goffman would point out that "each individual is engaged in providing evidence to establish a definition of himself at the expense of what can remain for the other" (29). But in the end, neither character wins the contest. Julian's mother loses her sense of self when she is pushed to the ground by a "colored woman" wearing a hat identical to hers (187). Faced with his

Thesis.

mother's breakdown, Julian feels his own identity being over-whelmed by "the world of guilt and sorrow" (191).

For more
information
on Works
Cited pages,
see Tab 4

Works Cited

Goffman, Erving. "Character Contests." *Text Book: An Intro-duction to Literary Language.* Ed. Robert Scholes, Nancy Comley, and Gregory Ulmer. New York: St. Martin's, 1988. 27–33. Print.

O'Connor, Flannery. "Everything That Rises Must Converge." *Fiction.* Ed. R. S. Gwynn. 2nd ed. New York: Addison, 1998. 179–91. Print.

WRITING CONNECTIONS

Interpretive Analyses

You can find interpretive analyses in professional journals like *PMLA* (*Publications of the Modern Language Association*) as well as literary publications like *Grain* and *Lettres Québecois.* Take a look at some of these publications to see how your work connects with that of profes-sional scholars and critics.

- A cultural critic explores Québec poet Jean-Marc Desgent's vision of the contemporary world—its paradoxes and contradictions.
- Two geologists analyze photos of an arctic coastal plain taken from an airplane and infer that the effects of seismic exploration vary according to the type of vegetation.
- A musicologist compares the revised endings of two pieces by Beethoven to figure out what makes a work complete and finished.
- A philosopher reflects on personal identity as a complex and shifting concept by investigating how the ideas of the philosophers Descartes and Hume are alike and different.

Arguments

8a UNDERSTANDING THE ASSIGNMENT.

Reasoned positions matter more than opinions based on personal feelings, and writing arguments is a way to form reasoned positions. Bearing in mind that reasonable people can see things differently, always strive to write well-informed, thoughtful arguments, backed up with verifiable evidence or support.

When you write an argument paper, your purpose is not to win but to take part in a debate by stating and supporting your position on an issue. In addition to position papers, written arguments appear in various forms, including critiques, reviews, and proposals.

- **Critiques:** Critiques focus on answering the question "What is true?" Someone has taken a position on an issue, and the critique fairly summarizes that position before either refuting or defending it. Refutations use one of two basic strategies: either the presentation of contradictory evidence to show that the position is false or the exposure of inadequate reasoning to show that the position should not be considered true. Defences make use of three strategies: clarifying a position by explaining in more detail the author's key terms and reasoning; presenting new arguments to support the position; and showing that criticisms of the position are unreasonable or unconvincing.

- **Reviews:** Reviews focus on answering the question "What is good?" In a review, the writer evaluates an event, artifact, practice, or institution. Although the evaluation may begin with an everyday gut response—"I like it" or "I don't like it"—such initial opinions must be transformed into judgments. A judge in a court case thinks through a decision in light of legal principles. Likewise, judgments in reviews should be principled; that is, they should not be determined by personal taste or the mood of the moment but by commonly accepted criteria.

- **Proposals, or policy papers:** Proposals, sometimes called policy papers, focus on answering the question "What should be done?" They are designed to cause change in the world. Readers are not only asked to see the situation in a specific way, but they are also encouraged to act on that situation in a certain way.

8b FIGURING OUT WHAT IS AT ISSUE.

People argue about issues, not topics. Before you can take a position on a topic like the environment or child poverty, you must figure out what is at issue. Try turning your topic into a problem by asking questions about it. Are there indications that all is not as it should be? Have things always been this way, or have they changed for the worse? From what different perspectives—economic, social, political, cultural, medical, geographic—can problems be understood? Do people interested in the topic disagree about what is true, what is good, or what should be done?

Based on your answers to such questions, identify the issues your topic raises and decide which of these issues you think is most important, interesting, and appropriate for you to write about in response to your assignment.

8c DEVELOPING A BALANCED POINT OF VIEW THAT NEGOTIATES DIFFERENCES.

When writing arguments, you want your readers to respect your intelligence and trust your judgment. Conducting research on your issue can make you well informed; reading other people's views and thinking critically about them can enhance your thoughtfulness. Find out what others have to say about the issue, and make it part of your purpose to negotiate the differences between your position and theirs. Pay attention to the places where you disagree with other people's views, but also note what you have in common—topical interests, key questions, or underlying values. (*For more on appeals to your audience, see Tab 1: Writing and Designing Papers, pp. 15–16.*)

Always remember that two views on an issue can be similar yet not identical, or different yet not completely opposite. It is important to avoid language that may promote prejudice or fear. Also, misrepresentations of other people's ideas are as out of place in a thoughtful argument as are personal attacks on their character. You should write arguments to open minds, not slam doors shut.

Trying out different perspectives can also help you figure out where you stand on an issue. (*Also see the next section on stating your position.*) Argue with yourself. Make a list of the arguments for and against a specific position; then compare the lists and decide where you stand. Does one set of arguments seem stronger than the other? Do you want to change or qualify your initial position to make it more understandable, reasonable, or believable?

8d COMPOSING A THESIS THAT STATES YOUR POSITION.

A strong, debatable thesis on a topic of public interest is a key ingredient of an effective written argument. Without debate, there can be no argument and no reason to assert your position. Personal feelings and accepted facts are not debatable and therefore cannot serve as an argument's thesis.

PERSONAL FEELING, NOT A DEBATABLE THESIS

I feel that eating meat is fine.

ACCEPTED FACT, NOT A DEBATABLE THESIS

Many people continue to eat meat.

DEBATABLE THESIS

Because of scientific development and engineering, foods and supplements can provide an adequate amount of proteins and nutrition to promote a healthy lifestyle. This leaves no reason for humans to maintain a diet consisting of the flesh of animals. But is this rationalization enough? It is not that simplistic. Eating meat, for many people is a birthright.

In proposals and policy papers, the thesis presents a solution in terms of the writer's definition of the problem. The logic behind a thesis for a proposal can be stated like this:

Given these key variables and their underlying cause, one solution to the problem would be...

Because this kind of thesis is both complex and qualified, you will often need more than one sentence to state it clearly. You will also need numerous well-supported arguments to make it creditable. Readers will finally want to know that the proposed solution will not cause worse problems than it solves; they realize that policy papers and proposals call for actions, and actions have consequences.

8e USING REASONING TO SUPPORT AND DEVELOP YOUR THESIS.

A strong, debatable thesis needs to be supported and developed with sound reasoning. You can think of an argument as a dialogue between the writer and readers. A writer states a debatable thesis, and one reader wonders, "Why do you believe that?" Another reader wants to know, "But what about this factor?" A writer needs to antici- pate questions such as these and answer them by presenting claims (reasons) that are substantiated with evidence and by refuting oppos- ing views. (*For more on claims and evidence, see Tab 1: Writing and Designing Papers, pp. 8–11.*)

Usually, a well-developed argument paper includes more than one type of claim and one kind of evidence. Besides generalizations based on empirical data or statistics, it often includes authoritative claims based on the opinions of experts and ethical claims based on the application of principle. For example, in Pertman's paper about why humans continue to eat meat, he presents several different perspec- tives that support his argument. As you conduct research for your argument, note evidence—facts, examples, and expert testimony— that can be used to support each argument for or against your position.

In developing your argument, you should also pay attention to **counterarguments**, substantiated claims that do not support your position. Think critically about such claims and use one of the follow- ing strategies to consider the most important counterarguments:

- Qualify your thesis in light of the counterargument by includ- ing a word such as *most, some, usually,* and *likely.*

- Add to the thesis a statement of the conditions for or excep- tions to your position.

- Choose one or two counterarguments and plan to refute their truth or their importance in your paper.

8f CREATING AN OUTLINE, INCLUDING A LINKED SET OF REASONS.

Arguments are most effective when they present a chain—a linked set—of reasons, so it is a good idea to begin drafting by writing down your thesis and outlining the way you will support and develop it. Your outline should include the following parts:

- An introduction to the topic and the debatable issue.

- A thesis stating your position on the issue.

- A point-by-point account of the reasons for your position, including the evidence (facts, examples, authorities) you will use to substantiate each major claim.

- A fair presentation and refutation of one or two key counter- arguments to your thesis.

- A response to the "So what?" question. Why does your argument matter?

8g USING CRITIQUES FROM PEERS TO UNDERSTAND YOUR AUDIENCE.

Having peers review your work is especially important when you are writing arguments about debatable issues. You cannot assume that readers will agree with your position, so asking your peers to critique the content of your draft will give you valuable clues about your readers' likely reactions. As you revise your argument, try to incorporate what you have learned from your peers. You might use a "Some say, but I think" strategy to incorporate their objections to your thesis and show, as part of your argument, that you respect your audience and value dialogue.

8h EMPHASIZING COMMON GROUND IN THE INTRODUCTION.

You want your readers to listen to what you have to say, so make sure that when you present the topic and issue in your introduction, you

WRITING CONNECTIONS

Arguments

Arguments are a cornerstone of a free and open society. The opportunity to discuss and debate issues encourages critical and reasoned thinking, provides access to multiple points of view, and advances cultural openness. All fields of academic study value reason and welcome arguments such as the following:

- A moral philosopher argues that under certain circumstances, people have the right to die and, therefore, that liberal democracies should provide them with the means to exercise their right with dignity.

- The board of a national dietetic association publishes a position statement identifying obesity as a growing health problem that dieticians should be involved in preventing and treating.

- A political scientist critiques the idea that the prospects for Russian democracy depend on the country's economy, not on the quality of its political institutions.

- An art critic praises a museum's special exhibition of Canadian art treasures for its diversity and its thematic coherence.

- A sociologist proposes four policies that he claims will improve the quality of life and socio-economic prospects of people living in inner-city neighbourhoods.

establish some kind of common ground or shared concern with them. For example, in his essay on eating meat, Pertman presents the idea that it is a human necessity to consume meat products and provides the rationales to explain this position. If possible, you should return to that common ground at the end of your argument.

8i CONCLUDING BY RESTATING AND EMPHASIZING YOUR POSITION.

After presenting your reasoning in detail, conclude by restating your position. Arguments are always thesis-driven, so it is appropriate to remind readers of your thesis. The version of your thesis that you present in your conclusion should be more complex and qualified than the thesis statement you included in your introduction, to encourage readers to appreciate both your thoughtfulness and your argument's importance. In the end, readers may not agree with you, but they should know why the issue and your argument matter.

8j RE-EXAMINING YOUR REASONING.

After you have completed the first draft of your paper, take time to re-examine your reasoning. Ask yourself the following questions:

- Have I given a sufficient number of reasons to support my thesis, or should I add one or two more?
- Have I made any mistakes in logic? (*See the list of Common Logical Fallacies, Tab 1: Writing and Designing Papers, pp. 12–13.*)
- Have I clearly and adequately developed each claim presented in support of my thesis? Is the claim clear? Have I defined its key terms, illustrated its meaning, and explained its implications? Is my supporting evidence sufficient? Have I quoted or paraphrased from sources accurately and documented them properly? (*For more on quoting, paraphrasing, and documenting sources, see Tab 3: Researching, pp. 150–152, and Tabs 4–6.*)

8k STUDENT PAPER: ARGUMENT.

In the following position paper, Eyal Pertman argues that the practice of eating meat and the welfare of the animal can co-exist. How suitable, complex, and feasible do you think his solutions are?

Eyal Pertman

Professor Nakata

Humanities 234

26 April 2008

The Ethics of Eating Meat: A Carnivore's Digest

The practice of eating meat has arguably been a habit of humans for millennia. Meat had been a means of survival and nourishment. It was a necessity. Today, animal rights activists argue that it is no longer a necessity, but simply a luxury of superiority. Because of scientific development and engineering, foods and supplements can provide an adequate amount of proteins and nutrition to promote a healthy lifestyle. This leaves no reason for humans to maintain a diet consisting of the flesh of animals. But is this rationalization enough? It is not that simplistic. Eating meat, for many people is a birthright.

Topic introduced.

A general argument that supports the consumption of meat is that meat food is so "well-packaged" (Singer 95) that it separates meaning from the animal. This is to say, when meat is bought from the supermarket, the process by which the animal arrived at the store is hidden—all that is seen are nice neat packages of seasoned steak or chicken breasts. It is possible that if more people knew exactly what happened at factory farms where meat is processed, there would be more conversions to vegetarianism if not veganism. Still, there are those people who would continue to shish kebob, barbeque, or grill their flesh of choice regardless of how it got to their kitchens.

Issue introduced.

Counter-argument acknowledged.

A contemporary approach to help determine reasoning for eating meat is one that holds "rationale" as suspect. The post-modern view would dismiss an argument that holds humans to the systematic limits of reason. A major influential figure of post-modernism, Friedrich Nietzsche, a 19th century intellectual emphasizes that the motivating factors of humans largely included emotions, passions, and instincts (Spielvogel 674). This

Thesis stated.

means that reason alone does not create a perfect parallel to the multi-dimensional depths of the human mind.

First general argument.

This complexity creates a "realm" of sorts for humans into which animals cannot belong. In "Higher Animal: Duties to Sentient Life," Holmes Rolston III relates this difference to the development of culture. He refutes the vegetarian argument by arguing that our differences are relevant for consideration. He claims that "appealing to sentiment and logically attractive in its charitable egalitarianism, such argument fails to distinguish between nature and culture, between environmental ethics and inter human ethics" (Rolston 333). In essence, he argues that even though animals do suffer, it cannot be to the extent that humans do and therefore there is some sort of division. The intellectual world is a realm that separates humans from the animals. Rolston shows this as a relation to culture: "Because animals cannot enter culture, they do not suffer the affliction (a heightened, cognitively based pain, distinct from physical pain) that humans would if bred to be eaten" (Rolston 333). Writer Michael Pollan concurs by stating that "human pain counts for more than that of a mouse, since our pain is amplified by emotions like dread" (Pollan 499). Basically, there is a fundamental difference between humans and animals that takes away the equality factor argued by egalitarians. Animals are simply not cognitively aware enough to value life.

Presentation of one possible outcome.

Refutes the possibility of change.

The second argument introduces the dilemma of rational vs. instinctive thought when it comes to why people continue to eat meat.

An "animal rights" argument is that humans still eat meat because it is plainly a long-standing human tradition that has become force of habit. Though there are many conflicting views of the origin of eating meat, few deny that meat was at least at some point in history a necessity. Eating meat was a natural discourse for survival. Eating meat is *still* a necessity to an extent. The development of scientifically engineered foods and supplements now can make up for meat nutrition, implying that *all* people can become adjusted to these replacements. In theory, this may be true, but it does not come without the sacrifice of satisfaction to humans. For some, this does pose problems. For example, many people who reduce their meat and animal by-product intake are in danger of developing anemia:

> Anemia occurs when blood does not have enough red blood cells or when the blood does not have enough hemoglobin. Hemoglobin is the oxygen-carrying pigment found in red blood cells. *Anemia can be life-threatening*—one of the main causes—eating a vegan diet which excludes eggs, dairy products meat, and fish. (Healthscout)

Use of expert testimony to add validity to the point.

Some take to replacements easier than others but, in any case, each person would require a specific formulary diet to make up for the diet humans were naturally inclined to have. Often, when vegetables and soy are not enough, the only answer is genetically engineered pill substitutes. These pills may provide nutrition but do not satisfy the physical need to chew meat or close the hunger gap which the person may have to fill using unappealing or unappetizing nutritional supplements. The result is an aversion towards vegan style diets, pushing people to claim their superiority over animals in the natural world *for their own well-being*. To avoid suffering therefore, humans would be compelled to extract their nutrition from a lower rung of the natural order. In a vegan world, people who depend on direct meat protein would be considered outcasts or degenerates of society. In reference to Rolston's theory of cognitive (cultural) pain, this would take animal suffering and replace it with human suffering because people who are dependent on what is natural for their bodies would be shunned by society.

Details presenting the negative impact of eliminating meat from the human diet.

A traditional argument that cannot be so easily dismissed is the "right" of the natural food chain. "Humans in their eating habits follow nature; they can and ought to do so" (Rolston 334). Rolston reflects the natural tendencies of the human

Third point—uses differences introduced in the previous point to differentiate humans from animals further.

makeup. To deny humans the food to which they naturally are attracted, just as a lion inherently knows to kill and eat a zebra, is to deny humans their rights in the realm of nature.

Summarizes the positions of the two cited sources.

Acknowledgement of one of the main opposing arguments: the inhumane processing of meat products.

Position from the opposing side presented but refuted within the passage.

Reasons supporting why domestication through farming is a better means of species survival.

Details that refute the "habit" argument of eating meat.

Rationale for the continuation of a carnivorous diet.

So, at some point and to some extent it is defensible to eat meat. What cannot be refuted still is the suffering that animals go through before they reach our barbeques. As humans, we have obvious intellectual differences to animals. So while humans may have an innate tendency towards animal feasting, our emotional side causes an empathetic reconsideration. While not conclusive among all people, this is the general drive of animal activists. Emotionally, it is difficult to observe the pain inflicted on animals in factory farms. This is where it makes sense to find alternatives. Without compromising the natural rights of humans in the world order, animals should be allowed to live whatever days are required with as little suffering as possible. This conclusion is where moral thought derived from compassion requires us to become responsible for their well-being.

Michael Pollan, a journalist and professor in favour of eating meat, poses an argument on the fundamental existence of these animals. "Wouldn't life in the wild be worse for these animals?" (Pollan 498). Pollan argues that domesticated animals cannot survive in the wild; in fact, without us they wouldn't exist at all. So in a manner by farming these animals we are promoting the survival of their species.

There is no true way to expand and develop the human population without some sort of impact on nature. Mass civilization in fact opposes nature in order to maintain itself. Animals are soon pushed to extinction or become more domesticated and reliant on food from humans; whether it be on the farm or from the garbage people leave out at night. Even vegans can be charged with murder of animals as mass agriculture uses large machinery that turns the soil, murdering field mice and other animals that burrow in the fields (Pollan 503). Satisfying human demands rarely happens without consequence to nature.

Pollan goes on to describe a farm that does not use methods of factory farming. "Polyface Farm occupies 550 acres of rolling grassland and forest," which serves as a magnitude of roaming space for its animal inhabitants (Pollan 502). Concurring with Darwinian evolutionary theory, he points out that rather than being a show of dominance by humans, it is, in fact, a relationship of mutualism. He explains that domestication is a process by which groups of especially opportunistic species discovered through Darwinian trial and error that they were better off in an alliance with humans (Pollan 502). Though this argument has its weakness, it holds true that many animals were better off. Animals were protected from the dangers of the wilderness while they lived a relatively harmonious life on the farms. In turn, they fed the humans while protecting their own species. Since animals cannot comprehend death or contemplate "the end," farm life was a pretty good trade off.

Still enthusiasts would argue "the right to life" but Pollan points out that the surest way to kill a domesticated animal would be to release it to the wild. Every species must have an innate instinct or interest in survival determined in the theory of evolution. Farming offers that for many species which can no longer protect themselves in the wild. Furthermore, domestication of any kind helps species to survive. Modern day statistics show that while there are 50 million dogs in North America, their canine cousins—the wolves—have, in the wild, depleted to a mere 10 thousand (Pollan 502). In farms such as Polyface, the cows are allowed to graze comfortably, the chickens run free in the yard, and the pigs roll happily in mud (Polland 500). The animals live a better life than one in nature. In nature, death by a predator can be as excruciating (if not more) than a death at a factory farm. The open concept farms offer animals a life of contentment.

Supports the idea of change for the food processing industry.

Final position on animal welfare suggests that animal farming is a way to preserve various species.

People and animals can have a harmonious relationship if animal suffering can be minimized. Check the farm from which

Suggestions about how to reduce suffering and introduce changes to the food industry without impinging on the rights of meat eaters.

your grocery store buys or request this information from the grocer. Most supermarkets now support open concept farms and carry, at least, some supply of their goods. Pollan also suggests a glass wall approach. If more people were allowed to see what goes on in factory farms, then there could be two advantageous outcomes: some people would refuse to eat meat, so it would reduce the amount of livestock needed; and, because of the loss of business due to people seeing the atrocities, factory farms would be forced to amend their procedures to more humane methods in order to keep operating (Pollan 506). The meat industry is not inherently evil; it is just stuck in the competitive nature of capitalism.

Conclusion suggests that co-existence is the key to survival of all species.

The practice of eating meat may have become tainted, but is far from dead. Many farms like Polyface keep the welfare of the animal in mind while they continue to supply meat to carnivores worldwide. The role of society must now reverse the trend of factory farming for the more humane approach of the "traditional" farm. With a combination of engineered foods and meat, animals and humans could return to the harmonious co-existence that has helped all to survive.

For details on MLA Documentation Style, please see Tab 4

Works Cited

"Anemia." *HealthScout Network.* 21 April 2006. Web. 12 Feb 2007.

Pollan, Michael. "The Unnatural Idea of Animal Rights," *New York Times*, 12 Apr. 2002, 496–506. Print.

Rolston, Holmes III. "Higher Animals: Duties to Sentient Life," in *Taking Side: Clashing Views on Moral Issues*. Ed. Stephen Satris. 11th ed. Iowa: McGraw-Hill/Dushkin, 2007. 332–336. Print.

Spielvogel, Jackson J. *Western Civilization.* 5th ed. Belmont: Thompson-Wadsworth, 2003. Print.

Other Kinds of Assignments

9a PERSONAL ESSAYS.

Personal writing can be found in many places, including diaries and journals, but personal writing is not the same thing as a personal essay. The personal essay is one of the most literary kinds of writing. Like a poem, it feels significant—meaningful to readers and relevant to their lives. Like a play, it speaks to readers in a distinctive voice. Like a good story, it is both compelling and memorable.

1. Make connections between your experiences and those of your readers. When you write a personal essay, you are exploring your experiences, clarifying your values, and composing a public self. At one level, your purpose is to reveal something about who you are, how you got where you are now, and what you believe. The focus, however, does not need to be on you. You might write a personal essay about a tree in autumn or an athletic event, but whatever focus you choose, remember that your readers expect to learn more than the details of your experience. They expect to see the connections between your experience and their own.

2. Turn your essay into a conversation. Personal essayists often use the first person (I and we) to create an interpersonal relationship—a sense that the writer and reader are engaged in the open-ended give-and-take of conversation. How you appear in this conversation—shy, belligerent, or friendly, for example—will be determined by the details you include in your essay as well as the connotations of the words you use. Consider how Meghan Daum represents herself in relation to both computer-literate and computer-phobic readers in the following excerpt from her personal essay "Virtual Love," which appeared in a 1997 issue of the *New Yorker*:

> The kindness pouring forth from my computer screen was bizarrely exhilarating, and I logged off and thought about it for a few hours before writing back to express how flattered and "touched"—this was probably the first time I had ever used that word in earnest—I was by his message.
>
> I am not what most people would call a computer person. I have no interest in chat rooms, news groups, or most Web sites. I derive a palpable thrill from sticking a letter in the mail.

Besides Daum's conversational stance, notice the emotional effect of her remark on the word *touched* and her choice of words connoting excitement: *pouring forth, exhilarating,* and *palpable thrill.*

3. Structure your essay like a story. Typically, personal essays are centred around either actions or ideas. There are three common ways to narrate events and reflections:

- **Chronological sequence** uses an order determined by clock time; what happened first is presented first, followed by what happened second, then third, and so on.

- **Emphatic sequence** uses an order determined by the point you want to make; for emphasis, events and reflections are arranged either from least to most important or from most to least important.

- **Suspenseful sequence** uses an order determined by the emotional effect the writer wants the essay to have on the reader. To keep the reader hanging, the essay may begin in the middle of things with a puzzling event, then flash back or go forward to clear things up. Some essays may even begin with the end—with the insight achieved—and then flash back to recount how the writer came to that insight.

4. Make details tell your story. The story of an entire election campaign can be told in one sentence: "He was nominated; he ran; he lost." It is in the details that the story takes shape. No matter what you intend your essay to accomplish, the details you emphasize, the words you choose, and the characters you create all implicitly communicate the point of your essay. Often it is not even necessary to state your thesis. You can also control the pace of your essay through details. To emphasize the importance of a particular moment or reflection, you can provide numerous details that will slow the reader down. As an alternative, you can use details sparingly, a tactic that can surprise the reader, especially when the simple and direct sentences appear in a context filled with rich detail.

5. Connect your experience to a larger issue. To demonstrate the significance of a personal essay to its readers, writers usually connect their individual experience to a larger issue. Here, for example, are the closing lines of Daum's essay on "Virtual Love."

> The world had proved to be too cluttered and too fast for us, too polluted to allow the thing we'd attempted through technology ever to grow on the earth. PFSlider and I had joined the angry

WRITING CONNECTIONS

Personal Essays—Exposition

Personal essays are not only narratives based on subjective experience. They can also be expository (written to clarify, interpret, or examine an issue), where writers use observation and reflection as a way to bring personal meaning to distil general truths. Often, this type of work does not rely on external sources or research to support the main premise. Nowadays, it is not uncommon for people from all walks of life to use the short expository essay to learn about themselves and apply their experiences of the world to answer specific questions.

- Graham Murphy, a teacher, reflects on his own experience in the classroom to figure out what makes teachers successful.
- Sydney John uses observation to describe the differences between two cultural artifacts for her course.
- Carol Allen, a philosophy professor, uses Plato's allegory of the cave as a metaphor in Tea with Demons, her personal account of going mad and finding her way back.
- Oliver Sacks, a neurologist, writes about his experiences with people whose perceptual patterns are impaired and about what it means to be fully human.

and exhausted living. Even if we met on the street, we wouldn't recognize each other, our particular version of intimacy now obscured by the branches and bodies and falling debris that make up the physical world.

Notice how Daum relates the disappointment of her failed Internet romance with "PFSlider" to a larger social issue: the general contrast between cyberspace and material realities. Her point, however, is quite surprising; most people do not think of cyberspace as more "intimate"—or touching—than their everyday, earthy world of "branches and bodies."

Student Paper: Personal Essay. In this example, the student was required to compare two exhibits that included written symbols for her Linguistics/Anthropology class. Her comparison was based on careful observation of the artifacts and it used the information from the exhibits themselves to establish the historical context.

Sydney John

Professor Rogers

JAL 258Y

7 January 2010

The Tale of Two Exhibits

The Royal Ontario Museum houses many artifacts that are either etched, engraved, inscribed, painted, penned, or chiselled with symbols from the writing systems of different cultures. Two exhibits, *The Jade Book of the Heart Sutra* from China and *The Hunting Sword* from India are objects that bear no physical resemblance to each other except that they both proudly display inscriptions that glorify their individual scripts.

The ceremonial *Jade Book of the Heart Sutra* from the early Qing Dynasty (1644–1911) is comprised of ten 5" × 8" jade plaques inscribed with the Heart Sutra, scriptures central to Mahayana Buddhism. Each plaque is numbered in the lower right corner and the front and end pieces are adorned with Buddhist imagery. The characters have been etched into the jade then gold-filled. Writing during the Qing Dynasty was steeped in traditional ways; the characters were complex and were read vertically from the top right corner. The plaques were then read as a "book" from right to left.

The Hunting Sword from the predominantly Muslim Mughal Empire (early 18th century) by contrast, is functional rather than ceremonial. Commissioned for hunting, the straight blade weapon is made of steel, chiselled with hunting scenes all along the blade, and topped with a gilded gold-damascened hilt. On the blade near the hilt is an inscription in Arabic. Unlike the symmetry and size of the Chinese characters inscribed on the *Jade Book*, the Arabic inscription more closely resembles a calligraphic manuscript with its minutely spaced, elongated forms, which literally flow from right to left. Also, unlike the Chinese attention to spaces between characters, word boundaries in the Arabic inscription are very difficult to see.

What could a book and a sword have in common? Nothing. The only aspect shared by both objects is how their inscriptions typify the written symbols of their respective cultures: the exactness of classical Chinese characters and the fluid softness of Arabic letters.

9b RESEARCH ASSIGNMENT

The research paper or project is one of the most common academic writing assignments. Students are asked to collect information then evaluate, synthesize, and interpret it in response to a specific task. *Tab 3* contains detailed information about the process of writing research papers (pages 125–160).

9c LAB REPORTS IN THE EXPERIMENTAL SCIENCES.

Scientists use writing to help form hypotheses and plan new experiments as they observe, read, and write. When they work in the laboratory, they keep well-organized and detailed notebooks. They also write and publish lab reports, using a format that reflects the logic of scientific argument. In this way, they share their discoveries and enable other scientists to use their work.

As a student, you may be asked to demonstrate your scientific understanding by showing that you know how to perform and report an experiment designed to verify some well-established fact or principle. In advanced courses, you may get to design original experiments as well.

Lab reports usually include seven distinctive sections in the following order: Abstract, Introduction, Methods and Materials, Results, Discussion, Acknowledgments, and Literature Cited. Begin drafting the report, section by section, while your time in the lab is still fresh in your mind. Organize your writing as follows:

- Begin with the methods-and-materials and results sections.
- Next, draft your introduction and discussion sections, making sure your introduction includes a clearly stated hypothesis.
- Finally, prepare the literature cited section, the acknowledgments, and the abstract.

Follow the scientific conventions for abbreviations, symbols, and numbers. See if your textbook includes a list of acceptable abbreviations and symbols, or ask where you might find such a list. Use numerals rather than words for dates, time, pages, figures, tables, and standard units of measurement (for example, g/mL, percentages). Spell out numbers between one and nine that do not appear in a series of larger numbers.

1. Abstract. An abstract is a one-paragraph summary of what your lab report covers in much greater detail. Although usually written last, the abstract is the part that others will read first. Scientists often skim professional journals, reading nothing more than the titles and abstracts of articles. Abstracts generally use about 250 words to answer the following questions:

- What methods were used in the experiment?
- What variables were measured?
- What were the findings?
- What do the findings imply?

Summarizing your argument in an abstract is a good way to begin the revising process.

2. Introduction. The introduction gives readers the information they need to understand the focus and point of your lab report. State your topic, summarize prior research, and present your hypothesis.

As in the example that follows, you should use precise scientific terminology (*α-amylase*), spell out the key terms that you will later abbreviate (*gibberellic acid [GA]*), and whenever possible, prefer the active voice over the passive. (*For a discussion of active and passive voices, see Tab 7: Editing for Clarity, pp. 267–269.*) The present tense is used to state established knowledge ("the rye seed *produces*"), whereas past tense is used to summarize the work of prior researchers (for example, "Haberlandt *reported*"). The writer cites sources using a number system.

According to studies by Yomo,[2] Paleg,[3] and others,[1,4] barley seed embryos produce a gibberellic acid (GA) which stimulates the release of hydrolytic enzymes, especially α-amylase. It is evident that these enzymes break down the endosperm, thereby making stored energy sources available to the germinating plant. What is not evident, however, is how GA actually works on the molecular level to stimulate the production of hydrolytic enzymes. As several experiments[5–8] have documented, GA has an RNA-enhancing effect. Is this general enhancement of

RNA synthesis just a side effect of GA's action, or is it directly
involved in the stimulation of α-amylase?

The first sentence names both a general topic, barley seed embryos,
and a specific issue, GA's stimulation of hydrolytic enzymes. The last
sentence poses a question, one that prepares readers for the hypothesis by focusing their attention on the role enhanced RNA synthesis
plays in barley-seed germination.

3. Methods and materials. Experiments must be repeatable. The
purpose of the methods-and-materials section is to answer the how
and what questions in a way that enables other scientists to replicate
your work. Select the details that they will need to know to replicate
the experiment. Using the past tense, recount in chronological order
what was done with specific materials, as the following student did in
his lab report on α-amylase production in barley seeds:

> After incubating for 48 hours, the seeds were cut in half
> transversely. Five endosperm halves without embryos were
> placed in each of 14 small glass test tubes. Next, a solution
> with a GA_3 concentration ranging from 0 g/mL to 10^5 g/mL was
> added to each test tube.

Notice that the writer does not mention the time of day or the instru-
ment used to cut the seeds. These details do not influence the results
and therefore are not important variables. The student does describe
the range of GA concentrations because that is the key variable.

4. Results. In this section, your purpose is to tell your reader about
the results that are relevant to your hypothesis, especially those that
are statistically significant. Results may be relevant to your hypothesis even if they are different from what you expected. An experiment
does not need to confirm your hypothesis to be interesting.

To report what you have learned, you might provide a summarizing table or graph. For example, the graph below, which plots the
distance of a glider over a period of time, was used to summarize the
results of an engineering assignment. In this instance, a paper airplane was launched and the distance it travelled in a specific period
of time was measured. Each point on the graph represents the distance the glider travelled in consecutive tenths of a second from 0.1
second to 1.0 second. By reading the positions of the glider on the XY
plot (X equals time; Y equals position in centimetres), we can see that
the glider travelled a total distance of 98 centimetres in 1.0 second.

Every table and figure you include in a lab report must be
referred to in the body of your report. Do not repeat all the information in the display, but do point out and illustrate relevant patterns.

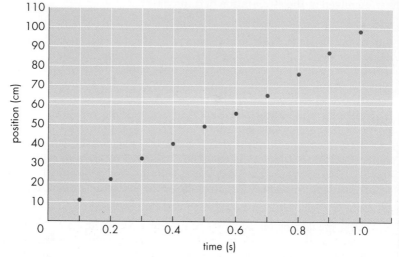

Figure 9.1 Data plot for position versus time in a glider flight

If you run statistical tests on your findings, be careful not to make the tests themselves the focus of your writing. In this section, you should emphasize the results of the tests, not the statistical procedures used to analyze the data. Refrain from interpreting why things happened the way they did. Interpretation belongs in the discussion section.

Note: Choose words carefully. Refer to an "increase," for example, as *marked* rather than as *significant*. Like the terms *correlated* and *random,* the term *significant* has a specific statistical meaning for scientists and should therefore be used in a lab report only when the appropriate statistical tests have been done.

5. Discussion. In your discussion section, you need to explain how and why your results do or do not confirm the hypothesis. Lab experiments produce results, not facts or laws. To transform results into accepted facts or laws, the scientific community depends on debate and consensus. In discussing your results, do the following:

- Interpret your major findings by explaining how and why each finding does or does not confirm the original hypothesis.

- Connect your research with prior scientific research. How and why do your findings and interpretations agree or disagree with the prior research summarized in your introduction?

- Look ahead to future research: where do scientists interested in this area seem to be going?

WRITING CONNECTIONS

Scientific Research

Research reports by professional scientists are published in journals such as Science, Current Directions in Psychological Science, and the American Journal of Physics. Take a look at one of these journals to see how your work relates to the work of professional scientists. Here are some examples of scientific research:

- A biochemist tests the hypothesis that THC (the major active ingredient in marijuana) acts as an estrogen (a female hormone).
- A mechanical engineer tests the hypothesis that 20 kilograms of force is sufficient to overcome the thermal contact resistance in the coupling joint of a mechanical switch designed for use on a rocket-borne telescope.
- A social psychologist tests the hypothesis that the more open-ended a question or task is, the more likely it is that an individual will behave in conformity with the will of a group.

6. Acknowledgments. You may have reason to include an acknowledgments section. In professional journals, most reports of experimental findings include a brief statement acknowledging those who assisted the author(s) during the research and writing process.

7. Literature cited. This section of your report should include a listing of all manuals, books, and journal articles you used during your research and writing process. Do not wait until the last minute to prepare this section, or you may find that you do not have time to get some missing piece of information. Use one of the citation formats developed by the Council of Science Editors (CSE style), unless another citation format is favoured by those working in the area of your research. If you are uncertain about which format to use, ask your professor for advice.

9d CASE STUDIES IN THE SOCIAL SCIENCES.

Social scientists are trained observers and recorders of the behaviour of individuals and groups, research that depends on writing. Accurate observations are essential starting points for a case study, and writing helps observers see more clearly and precisely.

1. Choose a topic that raises a question. In doing a case study, your purpose is to connect what you see and hear with issues and concepts in the social sciences. Choose a topic and turn it into a research question. Before engaging in your field research, write down your hypothesis—a tentative answer to your research question—as well as some categories of behaviour or other things to look for. Use your hypothesis as a starting point to develop a working thesis (one that will evolve as you research your topic) and consider the possible methods that you can use to obtain your data:

- For developmental psychology: study conflict resolution in children by observing a group of four-year-olds in a daycare centre.

- For sociology: study the role of the government in enforcing gender stereotypes by observing and interviewing women in the juvenile justice system.

- For anthropology: study the function of rituals in the formation of inner-city gangs by attending an initiation ceremony.

CROSS-DISCIPLINE WRITING

Case Studies

You will find case studies used in a number of social science disciplines.

- **In sociology:** You may be asked to draw on "insider" knowledge to describe and analyze a small group to which you have belonged or belong now. In this case, your study will address such issues as the group's norms and values, cultural characteristics, stratification and roles, initiation rites, and social control techniques. Your audience will be your professor, who will want to see how your observations reflect current theories on group norms.

- **In nursing:** A case study assignment may be an important part of your practicum in a local hospital. For a nursing class, you will note details of your care for a patient that corroborate or complicate what you have been taught to expect. Your audience is the supervising nurse, who is interested in your interactions with the patient.

- **In education:** As a student teacher in a classroom, you may closely observe and write about one student in the context of his or her socio-economic and family background. Your audience will be the co-operating teacher, who seeks greater insight into the behaviour of class members.

2. Assume an unbiased position. In a case study, you are presenting empirical findings, based on careful observation. Your position is that of an unbiased observer. Make a detailed and accurate record of what you observe, when, and how. Whenever you can, count or measure, and take down word for word what is said.

- **Count and measure.** Use frequency counts—the number of occurrences of specific, narrowly defined instances of behaviour. If you are observing a classroom, for example, you might count the number of teacher-directed questions asked by several children. If you are observing group counselling sessions for female parolees, as sociologist Lynne Haney did for a 1996 case study, you might count the number of women who attend.

- **Include direct quotations.** What the female parolees say to each other and to their female parole officer is essential information. Here is one female parole officer's comment on the subject of tattoos, from Haney's study: "Come on, girl, you'd be better than that. I'm teachin' you better. You ain't no wall to be graffitied on. What's next, you gonna tattoo his name on your brain?"

- **Avoid value-laden terms and unsupported generalizations.** Do not use words that will evoke emotion or broad statements that you cannot support. For example, in the article "Homeboys, Babies, Men in Suits," Haney writes, "I uncovered numerous institutions in the juvenile system, most of which were staffed by women." She provides evidence that juvenile institutions are staffed by women and does not use emotionally laden adjectives to describe either the juvenile system or the women working there.

    Note: Observe how Professor Haney uses *I* appropriately. The third person and the passive voice do not sound more objective or scholarly. If Haney had written that "numerous women-staffed institutions in the juvenile system were uncovered," her writing would sound stilted and unclear. Instead, she places herself, as a social scientist, in the midst of what she is studying.

3. Discover meaning in your data. Your case study is based on the notes you made during your observations. As you review this material, try to uncover connections, identify inconsistencies, and draw inferences. For example, ask yourself why a subject behaved in a specific way, and consider different explanations for the behaviour.

4. Present your findings in an organized way. There are two basic ways to present your findings in the body of a case study:

- **As stages of a process:** A student studying gang initiation organized her observations chronologically into appropriate stages. If you organize your study this way, be sure to transform the minute-by-minute history of your observations into a pattern with distinctive stages.

- **In analytic categories:** A student observing the behaviour of a preschool child used the following categories from the course textbook to present his findings: motor coordination, cognition, and socialization. In "Homeboys, Babies, Men in Suits," Haney uses quotes from the people she studied to organize her findings into two categories: "The Be-Your-Own Woman Rule" and "My Man Won't Do Me Like That."

Note: You will find it easier to organize the enormous amount of detail you gather for a case study if you develop stages or categories while you are making your observations. In your paper, be sure to illustrate your stages or categories with material drawn from your observations—with descriptions of people, places, and behaviour, as well as with telling quotations.

5. In your introduction, include a research review, a statement of your hypothesis, and a description of your methodology. The introduction presents the framework, background, and rationale for your study. Begin with the topic, and review related research, working your way to the specific question that your study addresses. Follow that with a statement of your hypothesis, accompanied by a description of your methodology: when and where you made your observations, and how you kept records.

6. In the conclusion, discuss your findings. The conclusion of your case study should answer the following three questions:

- Did you find what you expected?
- What do your findings show, or what is the bigger picture?
- Where should researchers working on your topic go now?

9e ESSAY EXAMS.

When you take an essay exam, you probably feel pressed for time and uninterested in the what, how, and why of the test. Still, if you spend some time thinking about what these tests expect you to do, you may feel less stress the next time you take one.

1. Understand your assignment. Your purpose in writing an essay exam is to demonstrate informed understanding. Because essay exams are designed to test your knowledge, not just your memory, working through possible questions is one of the best ways to study. Make up some essay questions that require you to:

- **Explain** what you have learned in a clear, well-organized way.
- **Apply** what you have learned to a new situation.
- **Interpret** the causes, effects, meanings, value, or potential of something.
- **Argue** for or against some controversial statement about what you have learned.

2. Prepare with the course and your instructor in mind. Consider the specific course as your writing context and the course's instructor as your audience. As you prepare for the exam, think about how your instructor approached and presented the course material.

- What questions or problems did your instructor explicitly or implicitly address?
- What frameworks did your instructor use to analyze topics?
- What key terms did your instructor repeatedly use during lectures and discussions?

3. Plan your time. During the exam period, time management is essential. Quickly look through the whole exam, and determine how much time you will spend on each part or question. Your instructor may give the point credit for each question or suggest the amount of time that should be spent on each part. You will want to move as quickly as possible through the short-answer questions that have lower point values so that you can spend the bulk of your time responding to the questions that are worth the greatest number of points.

4. Answer short identification questions by showing the significance of the information. The most common type of short-answer question is the identification question: Who or what is X? In answering questions of this sort, you need to present just enough information to show that you understand X's significance within the context of the course. For example, if you are asked to identify "Hagar" on a literature exam, don't just write "main character in Stone Angel." Instead, craft a sentence or two that identifies Hagar in the context of the story—a woman who turned to stone, trying to keep life from touching her.

5. Be tactical in responding to essay questions. When you are faced with an essay question, you may be inclined to start writing down everything you remember about the topic. Don't. Be tactical. Keep in mind that essay questions usually ask you to do something specific with a topic. Begin by determining precisely what you are being asked to do. Before you write anything, read the question—all of it—and circle key words.

> EXAMPLE   Explain two ways in which Picasso's Guernica evokes war's terrifying destructiveness.

To answer this question, you need to focus on two of the painting's features, such as colouring and composition, not on Picasso's life.

Sometimes you may be uncertain about what you are being asked to do, either because an essay question says too much or because it says too little. If a question includes more information or direction than necessary, try to isolate the root of the question—the main topic. If a question says too little, try to use the context of the course to give you clues. For example, "Discuss the power of the prime minister as well as the limits of that power" can be made more specific by applying the analytic terms used in class, such as the resources, methods, and conditions of the power of the PM's office. You should also consider asking the instructor for clarification.

6. Use the essay question to structure your response. You are unlikely to have time to make a complete outline before you begin writing. Whenever possible, use the question to structure your answer. Usually, you will be able to transform the question itself into the thesis of your answer. If you are asked to agree/disagree with the criticism of Pierre Trudeau during the October Crisis, you might begin with the following thesis:

> In the early 1970s, Pierre Trudeau was criticized for his handling of the October Crisis. Although his actions were considered radical, they served to end the crisis much sooner.

Take a minute or two to list evidence for each of your main points, and then write the essay.

7. Check your work. Leave a few minutes to read quickly through your completed answer, looking for words you might have omitted or key sentences that make no sense. Add the missing words, and rewrite the mixed-up sentences. If you double-space your work, you can cross out incorrect words and sentences to make corrections neatly above the original line of text.

9f ORAL PRESENTATIONS.

Oral presentations and written documents are quite different. When we write, we must imagine the presence of absent strangers. When we speak, the strangers are there, expecting us to connect with them right now. But thinking and working like a writer can help you prepare a speech that is appropriate, clear, and memorable.

1. Imagine the occasion and your audience. An oral presentation should suit the occasion. Who is likely to be there to listen to your speech? How and why have these people come together as an audience? Do they have significant demographic features in common, such as age, socio-cultural background, and profession? What are they expecting to hear: a business report, a sermon, an analysis of an issue, a toast to the bride and groom, or something else?

2. Decide on the purpose of your presentation. What does the audience already think about your topic? What contribution do you most want to make? Do you want to intensify your audience's commitment to what they already think, provide new and clarifying information, provoke more analysis and understanding of the issue, or change what the audience believes about something?

3. Make the focus and organization of your presentation explicit. Effective public speakers usually limit themselves to presenting a few clear-cut ideas. Select two or three ideas that you most want your audience to hear—and to remember. Make these ideas the focus of your presentation, and let your audience know what to expect by previewing the content of your presentation: "I intend to make three points about writing and learning."

Just as signs on the highway tell travellers where to go, signs in your presentation set the direction for your audience. In the sample preview, above, the phrase "to make three points" signals a topical organization. Of course, there are other common patterns, including chronological organization (*at first, later, in the end*), causal organization (*because of that, then this follows*), and problem-solution organization (*given the situation, then this set of proposals*). A question-answer format also works well, either as an overall strategy or as part of another organizational pattern.

4. Make your opening interesting. To get your listeners' attention, you need an interesting opener. Surprising statements, quotations, images, and anecdotes are all effective ways to begin.

5. Be direct. What your audience hears and remembers has as much to do with how you say your message as it does with what you say. For clarity, use a direct, simple style.

- Choose basic sentence structures.
- Repeat key terms.
- Pay attention to the rhythm of your speech.

Notice how applying these principles transforms the following written sentence into a group of sentences appropriate for oral presentation:

WRITTEN

Although the claim that writing increases student learning has yet to be substantiated by either an ample body or an exemplary piece of empirical research, advocates of writing across the curriculum persist in pressing the claim.

ORAL

The more students write, the more they learn. So say advocates of writing across the curriculum. But what evidence do we have that writing improves learning? Do we have lots of empirical research or even one really good study? The answer is, "Not yet."

6. Use visual aids. One way to make your focus explicit is by using visual aids. A computer projection of the points from your outline encourages your audience to make a few notes and discourages you from delivering—word for word—a boring, pre-packaged performance. Consider using slides, posters, objects, video clips, and music.

Presentation software such as PowerPoint can help you stay focused while you are speaking. The twelve PowerPoint slides on pages 120–121 offer advice on how to design effective slides for a presentation.

7. Make eye contact and keep your audience interested. To be an effective speaker, you need to make eye contact with your listeners to monitor their responses and adjust what you have to say accordingly. A written script can be a barrier; you can relate better to your audience if you speak from an outline. Write out only those parts of your presentation where precise wording counts, such as quotations. Telling a story during your oral presentation is another way to engage your listeners and keep their attention until the end.

For most occasions, it is inappropriate to write out the presentation then read it word for word. In some scholarly or formal settings, however, precise wording may be necessary, especially if your oral presentation is to be published or if your remarks will be quoted by others, including media representatives. Sometimes the setting for your presentation may be so formal or the audience may be so large that a script feels necessary. In such instances, do the following:

- Triple-space the typescript of your text.
- Avoid carrying sentences over from one page to another.
- Mark your manuscript for pauses, emphasis, and the pronunciation of proper names.
- Practise your delivery. It should take about seventy-five seconds to deliver one triple-spaced page of text.

8. Conclude in a memorable way. Your final comments will be the part of your speech that most members of your audience remember. Try to make your ending truly memorable: return to that surprising opener, play with the words of your opening quotation, look at the initial image from another angle, or reflect on the story you told.

9. Rehearse. Whether you are using an outline or a script, it takes a practised performer to deliver a memorable oral presentation. Practise with a clock, but be sure to leave yourself time to insert conversational gambits every now and then during the actual performance.

9g   COAUTHORED PROJECTS.

A project is coauthored when more than one person is responsible for producing it. As with any written work with more than one contributor, it is important that a discussion about authorship (assigning credit for intellectual work) occurs between the group members in consultation with the professor. Some issues that arise around coauthoring are intellectual property (who owns the material), writing ability, roles of the members, and production goals (the result). Scholarly success depends on a clear understanding of the responsibilities of each member of the collaborative team (*also, see Chapter 15 for a detailed discussion on plagiarism*).

In many fields, working collaboratively is essential. Coauthoring is more likely in data-driven disciplines like sociology or management theory than in the Humanities. Here are some suggestions to help you make the most of this challenge:

- Working with your partners, decide on some ground rules, including meeting times, deadlines, and ways of reconciling differences. Will the majority rule, or will some other principle prevail? Is there an interested and respected third party who can be consulted if the group's dynamics break down?

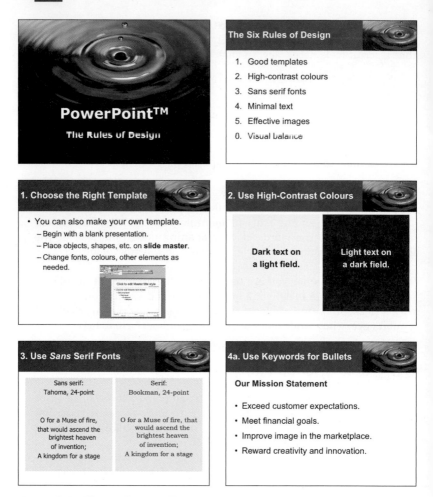

Figure 9.2 How to design effective slides for a presentation

- Divide the work fairly so that everyone has a part to contribute to the project. Keep in mind that each group member should do some researching, drafting, revising, and editing.

- In your personal journal, record, analyze, and evaluate the intellectual and interpersonal workings of the group as you see and experience them. If the group's dynamics begin to break down, seek the assistance of a third party.

- After each group member has completed his or her assigned part or subtopic, the whole group should weave the parts together to create a focused piece of writing with a consistent voice. This is the point where group members usually need to

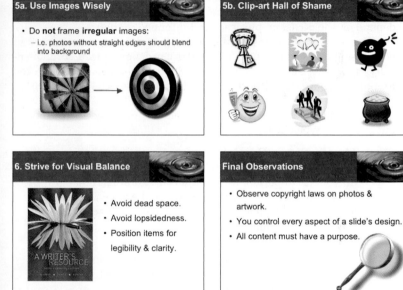

negotiate with one another. Tact is essential. Keep the goal of excellence in the forefront and all should go well.

Coauthoring online:
Computer networks make it easier for two or more writers to coauthor texts. With e-mail, you can preserve your individual contributions to the final paper and, if need be, share them with your instructor. You will also have a record of how the piece developed and how well you and your coauthor actually worked as a team. Blogs, discussion boards, personal Web sites, and synchronous communication can also be used to collaborate. Documents can be shared throughout the revision process and the changes tracked using that feature of many software programs.

9h   PORTFOLIOS.

From the Latin *portare* "to carry" and *foglio* "sheet of paper," the portfolio is a learning and assessment tool used in traditional and virtual environments that can promote changes in learner beliefs through critical reflection, ownership of learning, and active engagement. Portfolios are collections of "best" works, works-in-progress, self or peer assessments, and compilations of simple to complex elements of learning that become a purposeful collection that records a learner's efforts, progress, and achievement. The artifacts may focus on one conceptual area or they may span several areas over time. A portfolio assessment pays attention not only to the results, but also to the processes involved. The principles that guide selection and order depend on the occasion, purpose, and intended audience.

You should consider keeping an organized folder of your work in your discipline for later use. The folder can be organized chronologically, by field or subfield, or by issue. Successful job candidates often prepare well-organized portfolios of carefully selected materials to take with them to job interviews.

Different types of portfolios serve one or more specific purposes, but the main types include:

- **The Showcase Portfolio:** generally, this portfolio includes the semester-end (summative) collection of self-selected "best works." It supports multi-media contributions (photographs, video, and electronic records completed work). The showcase portfolio also includes written analyses, feedback, and reflections by the student upon the decision-making process(es) used to choose the work.

- **The Process Portfolio:** this collection of works documents phases of learning over time. Through the contributions, it can help to identify changes in learning like the progression of a skill: the levels of performance (from basic to advanced proficiency) and the strengths and weaknesses of the writer. It can show how students integrate specific knowledge or skills. Additionally, the process portfolio inevitably emphasizes students' reflection upon their learning process, including the use of journals, peer feedback, or other analytical tools.

- **The Evaluation Portfolio:** this portfolio is often used to record academic achievement—tests, scores, grades, and feedback on a variety of topics/subjects. It may also include criteria for evaluation as well as lists of learning goals. Examples of student work would demonstrate achievement and would parallel learning goals.

3

RESEARCHING

3

Researching

3 Researching

Understanding Research

10a BEING INFORMATION LITERATE.

Research is the active investigation into a topic to discover or extend knowledge. But locating information about a topic is only one component of an overall ability to *access, evaluate, and use* information effectively and competently. Information literacy is the cornerstone of successful research. To be information literate means to have:

- The ability to understand the form, format, and access methods of information *(see pages 125–127)*
- The ability to retrieve information efficiently
- The ability to assess information critically *(see pages 134–142)*
- The ability to apply information judiciously, correctly, and creatively *(see pages 143–156)*

10b UNDERSTANDING THE PURPOSE OF PRIMARY AND SECONDARY RESEARCH.

Primary research means working in a laboratory, in the field, or with an archive of raw data, original documents, and authentic artifacts to make firsthand discoveries. It often involves more than finding answers to questions in books and other printed material (secondary research). When you conduct primary research—examining authentic documents and original records, observing the world, and experimenting in the laboratory—you participate in the discovery of new knowledge. Primary research has also been greatly affected by technology. For example, in meteorology, weather databases are now available virtually in a format that both students and specialists can understand. Also, lab research, is being transformed by the development of dry or virtual labs—computer-based experimental arenas in which research is conducted through simulations.

Secondary research means looking to see what other people have learned and written. Knowing how to identify facts, interpretations, and evaluations is key to good secondary research:

- **Facts** are objective. Like body weight, facts can be measured, observed, or independently verified in some way.

- **Interpretations** spell out the implications of facts. Are you as thin as you are because of your genes or because you exercise every day? The answer to this question is an interpretation.

- **Evaluations** are debatable judgments about a set of facts or a situation. Attributing a person's thinness to genes is an interpretation, but the assertion that "one can never be too rich or too thin" is an evaluation.

Once you are up to date on the facts, interpretations, and evaluations in a particular area, you will be able to design a research project that adds to this knowledge. Usually, what you will add is your *perspective* on the sources you found and read:

- Given all that you have learned about the topic, what strikes you as important or interesting?

- What patterns do you see, or what connections can you make between one person's work and another's?

- Where is the research going, and what problems still need to be explored?

10c RECOGNIZING THE CONNECTION BETWEEN RESEARCH AND ACADEMIC WRITING.

In one way or another, research informs all academic writing. To get material for a personal essay, you have to search through your memory, reflect on events, and select a person, event, place, or other topic about which to write. When you write essay exams, you rely on what you have read and learned from textbooks and lectures.

But some assignments require more rigorous and systematic research than others. These **research project** assignments offer you a chance to go beyond your course texts—to find and read both classic and current material on a specific issue.

A paper based on research is not just a step-by-step account of your "search and find" mission. Nor is it a string of quotes from other writers or a set of summaries based on your sources. A researched paper constitutes your contribution to the ongoing discussion about a specific issue.

A research paper or project may seem overwhelming at first. But, if you break down the process into phases, and plan each phase carefully, you will be able to write a paper that will become your contribution to the academic community. This chapter and the five that follow it offer advice on completing each phase.

10d CHOOSING AN INTERESTING RESEARCH QUESTION TO GUIDE YOUR CRITICAL INQUIRY.

If you choose an interesting question to examine critically, your research is likely to be more meaningful and more motivating.

1. Choose a question with personal significance. Even though you are writing for a college or university assignment, you can still get personally involved in your work. Begin with the wording of the assignment, analyzing the project's required scope, purpose, and audience. Then browse through the course texts and your class notes, looking for a match between your interests and topics, issues, or problems in the subject area.

For example, suppose you have been assigned to write a report on a country's global economic prospects for a business course. If you have recently visited Mexico, you might find it interesting to explore that country's prospects.

2. Make your question specific. The more specific your question, the more your research will have direction and focus. To make a question more specific, use the "five w's and an h" strategy by asking about the *who, what, why, when, where,* and *how* of a topic (*see Tab 1: Writing and Designing Papers, pp. 24–26*).

After you have compiled a list of possible research questions, look through the list and choose one that is relatively specific or rewrite a

CROSS-DISCIPLINE **WRITING**

Typical Lines of Inquiry in Different Disciplines

Research topics and questions differ from one discipline to another, as the following examples show:

- **History:** Examine the events leading up to one of Canada's worst cases of institutional abuse—the Duplessis Orphans.
- **Psychology:** What were the long-term effects of the abuse suffered by the survivors?
- **Political science:** How did the scandal of Les Orphelines de Duplessis impact the Quebec government?
- **Sociology:** Which social institutions were named in this abuse case? How were they affected?

broad one to make it more specific and therefore answerable. For example, a student could rewrite the following broad question about institutional abuse to make it answerable:

TOO BROAD   What is institutional abuse?

ANSWERABLE   In terms of culpability, who is most responsible for the abuse suffered by the orphaned children of Quebec in the Duplessis era?

Create a Research Plan

Your research will be more productive if you take some time at the beginning to outline a plan for it. As a starting point, use the format below to help guide you through the process:

Project Planning

Activities include the following:

- Analyzing the assignment
- Deciding on a topic and a question
- Outlining a research plan

Research Phase I

Get a general overview of your topic by doing the following:

- Reading **reference works**
- Making a list of relevant **keywords**
- Compiling a **working bibliography** of print and online sources
- Sampling some of the items in your bibliography

Research Phase II

Most likely you will spend twice as much time in the second phase as you did in the first phase. Activities include the following:

- Locating, reading, and evaluating selected sources
- Taking notes
- Doing primary research

Research Phase III

Count on spending one-third to one-half of the available time working on the paper that grows out of your research:

- Drafting your paper
- Revising and editing your paper

3. Find a challenging question. To be interesting to you and to your readers, a research question must be challenging. If a question can be answered with a simple yes or no, a dictionary-like definition, or a textbook presentation of information, you should choose another question or rework the simple one to make it more challenging.

NOT CHALLENGING	Was the compensation paid to the Duplessis orphans adequate?
CHALLENGING	How can compensation for victims of abuse be determined fairly, based on their traumatic experiences?

4. Speculate about answers. Sometimes it can be useful to speculate on the answer to your research question so that you have a hypothesis to work with during the research process. But don't forget that a hypothesis is not the truth; it is a speculation that must be tested and revised through research. Keep an open mind as you work, and be aware of the assumptions embedded in your research question or hypothesis. Consider, for example, the following hypothesis:

HYPOTHESIS	With the trauma caused by this institutional sexual and physical abuse case, governments should be held accountable for the support of the survivors.

This hypothesis assumes that the government will acknowledge its involvement. But assumptions are always open to question. Researchers must be willing to adjust their ideas as they learn more about a topic.

Finding Print and Online Sources

Your research process will take place both in the library and on the Internet. Usually, a search for useful sources entails four activities:

- Using databases
- Locating appropriate material
- Collecting keywords from reference works
- Assessing the viability and credibility of material

11a CONSULTING VARIOUS KINDS OF SOURCES.

The sources you use will vary from one research project to another. It is always necessary, however, to consult more than one source and usually important to check out more than one kind of source.

Some sources, for example, are written for the public and are classified as popular or non-scholarly sources. Such publications include magazines like *Maclean's* or *L'actualité,* and books such as Daniel Goleman's *Emotional Intelligence,* a persuasive discussion on IQ and emotions. Other sources, classified as scholarly sources, report research findings. They include journals such as *Canadian Journal of History* and the *Canadian Journal for the Study of Adult Education,* and books such as Carl Bereiter's *Education and Mind in the Knowledge Age,* a work by an expert on knowledge building. The following chart identifies some of the differences between scholarly and non-scholarly sources:

SCHOLARLY SOURCES	NON-SCHOLARLY SOURCES
Articles are usually written by experts/ scholars in a discipline	May be written by professional writers/ journalists who may lack expertise in the subject
Audience includes academics, researchers, students	The audience is the general public and is less formal in tone and style
Publishers are usually professional organizations, associations, scholarly presses, or universities	Publishers are commercial businesses
Sources of information are always cited in bibliographies and/or footnotes	Sources of information are rarely cited
Text includes research results and specialized vocabulary	Text includes opinions or reports events
Generally, articles are text-based, with few pictures, ads, or graphics	Articles often include pictures and graphics
Authors and their institutional affiliation are always named	Authors may be anonymous

However, other non-scholarly sources like Internet/media sites, organizations/non-government organizations (NGOs) and government agencies may be recognized as legitimate resources in a research project. "Grey literature" is the term that describes documents and transient material published outside formal publication channels. These are some of the kinds of sources available to you:

- **General Reference Works**

    Encyclopedias, annuals, almanacs

    Computer databases, bibliographies, abstracts

- **Specialized Reference Works**
  Discipline-specific encyclopedias, almanacs, and dictionaries
- **Books and Electronic Texts**
- **Periodical Articles**
  Newspapers
  Magazines
  Scholarly and technical journals
  Internet
- **Web Sites**
- **Newsgroups, Listservs, and E-mail**
- **Virtual Environments**
  CVEs (collaborative virtual environments)
  MUVEs (multi-user virtual environments)
  Social networks
- **Pamphlets, Government Documents, Census Data**
- **Primary Sources**
  Original documents like literary works, art objects, performances, manuscripts, letters, and personal journals
  Museum collections; maps; photo, film, sound, and music archives
  Field notes, surveys, interviews
  Results of observation and lab experiments

11b USING THE LIBRARY.

Librarians are a good first resource. They know what is available at your library and how to get material on loan from other libraries. They can show you how to access the library's computerized book catalogue, periodical databases, and electronic resources and how to search their resources efficiently. Most school libraries list their reference works, books, and periodical holdings online, as shown in the Seneca example in Figure 11.1. Your library's Web site may also have links to important reference works available on the Internet.

Most libraries also provide **help sheets**. These discipline-specific documents list the location of relevant periodicals and non-circulating reference books, along with information about special databases, indexes, and sources of information on the Internet. Invaluable as time-savers, help sheets are a good way to start your research

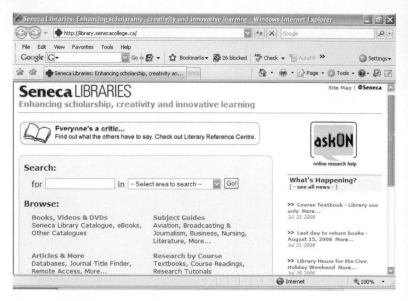

Figure 11.1 Library search engine.

inquiries and may be accessible online from the library's Web site or its online catalogue.

1. Reference works. Reference works provide an overview of a subject area. The information contained in general encyclopedias like *The Canadian Encyclopedia,* the *New Encyclopædia Britannica,* and *Collier's Encyclopedia* is less authoritative than the specialized knowledge found in discipline-specific encyclopedias, academic journals, and scholarly books. Start your research by consulting a general resource for your own information; for academic research, however, you will need to explore your topic in more scholarly sources. Often, the list of references at the end of general article can lead you to useful sources on your topic.

Reference books do not circulate; take notes or make photocopies of the pages you may need to consult later. Many libraries subscribe to services that provide access to online encyclopedias. Check your school library's home page for a link to reference materials like online encyclopedias.

Here is a list of some other kinds of reference materials available in print, on the Internet, or both:

ALMANACS *The Canadian Almanac in History*
Information Please Almanac
World Almanac

BIBLIOGRAPHIES	*Bibliographic Index* *Bibliography of Asian Studies* *MLA Bibliography*
BIOGRAPHIES	*Dictionary of Canadian Biography* *Dictionary of Philosophy* *Who's Who of Canadian Women* *Dictionary of National Biography* *Dictionary of Canadian Artists*
DICTIONARIES	*Canadian Oxford Dictionary* *Cambridge International Dictionary of English* *Oxford Dictionary of Quotations* *Gage Canadian Dictionary* *Dictionary of Literary Symbols* *Dictionary of Science* *Dictionary of Problem Words and Expressions*

2. Books. A search of the library's catalogue will provide you with a list composed mostly of books. The **call number** of each book will identify its location on the shelves.

Usually, online library catalogues can be searched by author, by title, by keyword, or by subject. Library databases may also be searched by keyword. As you consult reference works, spend some time collecting ten or more key terms associated with your topic and learning how those terms are related conceptually. If you only have one or two keywords, you may not get what you really need: a reasonable number of relevant sources.

If your school's library is part of a regional consortium, its online catalogue may list books available in affiliated libraries. A librarian can also get you books that are not in your school's library through an interlibrary loan process.

3. Periodicals. Newspapers, magazines, and scholarly journals that are published at regular intervals—daily, weekly, monthly, or quarterly— are classified as **periodicals**. Scholarly and technical journals, which publish articles written by experts and based on up-to-date research and information, are generally more reliable than articles written by journalists for popular newspapers and magazines. Although newspapers and magazines can provide useful background information, the writers are often not specialists in the field they are writing about, and occasionally they depend on sensationalism to attract attention. If you do not know which periodicals are considered important in a discipline you are studying, ask your instructor or librarian.

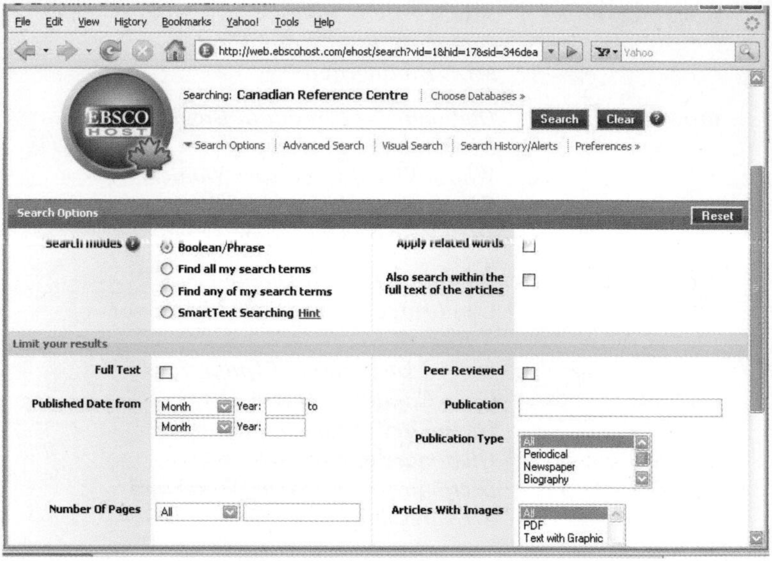

Figure 11.2   EBSCOhost periodical database.

Indexes. Articles published in periodicals are catalogued in general and specialized indexes, many of which are available in electronic formats, known as **databases**, as well as in print volumes shelved in the library's reference section. Many databases provide abstracts— short summaries of the works they list. Abstracts should not be mistaken for the full-text articles offered by such online subscription services as *InfoTrac* and *EBSCOhost*. If you are searching for articles that are more than twenty years old, you should use printed indexes. Otherwise, see what your library has available on CD-ROM or through an online subscription service. (*For help with search terms, see pp. 133–134 and 136–137.*) The list in the box on page 137 includes many of the most popular online indexes to periodical articles.

11c   EVALUATING PRINT SOURCES.

Just because something is in print does not make it true or relevant. How can you determine if a print source is likely to be both reliable and useful? Here are some questions to ask about any source you are considering:

Reliability

- **What information can you find about the writer's credentials?** Is the writer affiliated with a research institution dedicated to contributing to knowledge about an issue?

- **Who is the publisher?** University presses and academic publishers are considered more scholarly than the popular press because work published by them is usually based on research and subjected to rigorous peer review.

- **Does the source include a list of references?** Reliable research is always part of a conversation among specialists. To show familiarity with what other researchers have said about a topic, trustworthy writers cite a variety of sources and document their citations properly. Does this source do so? Does the source include a variety of citations?

- **Is there any indication that the writer has a particular point of view on your topic or that the writer is biased?** What kind of tone does the author use? Is the text objective or subjective? (*For more on evaluating a source's argument, see Tab 1: Writing and Designing Papers, pp. 3–6.*)

Relevance

- **Do the source's title and subtitle indicate that it addresses your specific research question?**

- **What is the publication date?** Is the material up to date (published within the past five years)? Or if you have a reason for working with older sources, is the publication date appropriate for your research?

- **Does the table of contents indicate that the source covers useful information?**

- **If the source is an article, does it have an abstract at the beginning? Is there a summary at the end?** An abstract or a summary presents the main points made in an article and can help you decide if a source is likely to be useful.

- **Does the work contain subheadings?** Skim the headings to see if they indicate that the source covers useful information.

- **If the source is a book, does it have an index?** Scan the index for keywords related to your topic to see how useful the book might be.

In academic research, relevance can be a complicated. Your sociology instructor will expect you to give special preference to sociological sources in a project on workplace organization. Your business management instructor will expect you to use material from that field in a project on the same topic. Relevance, then, can depend on the purpose, scope, and audience of the paper.

11d SEARCHING THE INTERNET.

The **Internet** is a global network of computers; it connects businesses, academic institutions, and individuals electronically. The easiest and most familiar way to gain access to the Internet is through the **World Wide Web**, which connects information by means of hypertext links. Besides providing access to online databases, reference works, and periodicals, the Internet can bring you closer to primary materials that were once difficult to examine firsthand. It can also put you in touch with a research community through e-mail, chat rooms, online class discussions, CVEs (collaborative virtual environments), MUVEs (multi-user virtual environments), discussion lists, and newsgroups.

As with any type of source you use, resources that you find on the Internet must be critically evaluated for their reliability. This step is especially important for information you find online, however, because anyone can publish on the Web, and unlike most books and articles, Web sites do not need to go through a rigorous process of peer review and evaluation before publication. (*For help with evaluating Internet resources critically, see pp. 140–142.*)

To get the most out of your Internet research, you need to learn how to use search engines and keywords to find useful Web sites, as well as how to gain access to and use other Internet resources such as discussion groups (listservs), usenet newsgroups, and virtual communities.

1. Search engines. To search for sources on the Internet, you type a keyword or phrase into a **search engine**, a software program that searches for Web sites that include your keyword and returns a list of potentially relevant sites. There are many search engines available, and because each covers a different group of Web sites and searches them in its own way, most researchers find it necessary to use more than one. (*See the box on p. 138 for a list of popular search engines.*)

Each search engine's home page provides a link to advice on using the search engine efficiently to get targeted results. Look for a link labelled "Search Help," "About Us," or something similar, and click on it to learn how a specific search engine can best serve your needs.

2. Keyword Internet searches. Besides learning more about the search engines you use, you need to know how to fine-tune your search process by adjusting your keyword or phrase. For example,

TECH **TIPS**

Some Online Databases

- **Academic Universe (Lexis-Nexis):** Updated daily, this online service provides full-text access to around 6,000 newspapers, professional publications, legal references, and parliamentary sources.
- **CBCA Business:** This database provides access to a broad range of Canadian business periodicals, including trade publications, academic journals, and professional publications.
- **EBSCOhost:** The Academic Search Premier service provides full-text coverage for more than 3,000 scholarly publications and indexes articles in all academic subject areas.
- **ERIC:** This database lists publications in the area of education.
- **E-STAT:** This database from Statistics Canada provides access to articles and statistical information about Canada and Canadians.
- **FirstSearch:** Offering a common interface for access to general databases such as NetFirst and WorldCat, this service also permits searches of such subject-specific bibliographic databases as ERIC, *Medline,* and the *MLA Bibliography.*
- **General Science Index:** As its name indicates, this index is general rather than specialized and is therefore most appropriate for beginning science students. It lists articles by biologists, chemists, and other scientists.
- **Humanities Index:** This index lists articles from journals in language and literature, history, philosophy, and similar areas.
- **JSTOR:** This electronic archive provides full-text access to scholarly journals in the humanities and social sciences.
- **MLA Bibliography:** Covering from 1963 to the present, the *MLA Bibliography* indexes more than 3,400 journals, essay collections, proceedings, and series published worldwide in the fields of modern languages, literature, literary criticism, linguistics, and folklore. Coverage includes all modern national literatures.
- **Periodical Abstracts:** This database indexes more than 1,500 general and academic journals covering business, current affairs, economics, literature, religion, psychology, and women's studies from 1986 to the present.
- **PsycInfo:** Sponsored by the American Psychological Association (APA), this database indexes and abstracts books, scholarly articles, technical reports, and dissertations in the area of psychology and related disciplines such as psychiatry, medicine, nursing, and education.
- **PubMed:** The National Library of Medicine publishes this database, which indexes and abstracts nine million journal articles in biomedicine and provides links to related databases.
- **Social Science Index:** This index lists articles from journals in such fields as economics, psychology, political science, and sociology.
- **Sociological Abstracts:** For researchers in the area of sociology and related disciplines, this database indexes and abstracts articles from more than 2,600 journals, as well as books, conference papers, and dissertations.

TECH **TIPS**

Popular Search Engines

Simple search engines, or *directories,* use hierarchical indexes created by people trained to categorize information. These directories are a good way to start your Internet research because they are easy to use and selective in the results they return.

- Google <www.google.ca>
- *Yahoo!* <www.yahoo.com>

For scholarly research, try Google Scholar <scholar.google.ca>
Standard search engines send "robots" or "spiders" to all points on the Web to return results. Using mathematical calculations, they inform you about the relevancy of each site to your search, putting the most relevant items at the top of the list.

- Lycos <www.lycos.com>
- FAST Search <www.altheweb.com>
- *Ask Jeeves* <www.ask.com>

Meta search engines return results by searching other search engines. They provide more sites than a simple search engine, but they are not as selective.

- *Dogpile* <www.dogpile.com>
- *MetaCrawler* <www.metacrawler.com>

Alternative search engines allow users to ask for information in different ways.

- *Northern Light* <www.northernlight.com>

a search query on the search engine AltaVista using the keywords "Canadian music" listed more than one million sites, a staggering number of links, or **hits**.

One approach to successful keyword searching is to start by defining your topic (Google's DEFINE feature—define: term—works well for this process) and scanning the top results for the base term and its synonyms. Collect brief notes (opinions, quotes, names) in a separate file for later use. Once you have completed this first step, you can then vary your keyword range to expand your potential list of resources.

You can further expand keyword searches by using various online tools: Google's Wonder Wheel; MetaGlossary.com; Reference.com; thefreedictionary.com (and other online dictionaries and thesauruses).

Also, tools like TwitScoop and SiteVolume are helpful in investigating trends and term popularity, using information from social networks for the analysis. The results can reveal different words or phrases related to your topic. Blog search engines are useful for more keyword options or check meme tracker (Techmeme, Megite) to identify to most current news and/or terms in blogs.

3. Online communication. In addition to providing information, the Internet also provides access to communities with common interests and varying levels of expertise on different subjects. Discussion lists (electronic mailing lists), usenet newsgroups, virtual environments (including social networking sites like Facebook) are the most common communities that can provide help with your research topics. They can help you in the following ways:

- You can get an idea for a paper by finding out what topics interest and concern people.

- You can learn what people think about almost any topic, from food to pop culture to sports to science.

- You can zero in on a very specific topic, such as sushi, a comic book character, a vintage TV show, a singer, or a scientific theory.

Social Networks are virtual environments made up of individual members connected by a mutual interest. Some sites like Facebook and MySpace are for general interest; others, like Academia.edu or LinkedIn are more focused. Such networks may provide information or a starting point for your research.

Discussion lists (electronic mailing lists) are networked e-mail conversations on particular topics that may be relevant to your research topic. Lists can be open (anyone can join) or closed (only certain people, such as members of a particular group, can join). If the list is open, you can subscribe by sending a message to a computer that has list-processing software installed on it.

Usenet newsgroups are one of the oldest features of the Internet. Like lists, newsgroups may exist on topics relevant to your research. You must subscribe to read postings. Unlike lists, newsgroups are posted to a *news server,* a computer that hosts the newsgroup and distributes postings to participating servers. Postings are not automatically distributed by e-mail.

Collaborative and multi-user virtual environments, known as CUVs and MUVEs (for example, Second Life or River City) are virtual spaces where participants interested in a topic meet and interact to create a world of objects, actions, and feelings. To join a CUV or MUVE, you need to apply to the manager for a password and character.

TECH **TIPS**

Discussion Lists

Check out the following Web sites for more information about discussion lists:

Harness E-mail: Mailing Lists <www.learnthenet.com/english/html/24mlists.htm>: Explains how discussion lists work.

Topica <www.topica.com>: Contains a searchable directory of 90,095 discussion lists.

Tile.net: The Reference to Internet Discussion and Information Lists <tile.net/lists>: Allows you to search for discussion lists by name, description, or domain.

TECH **TIPS**

Newsgroups

For more information about newsgroups, refer to these resources online:

Newsreaders.com <www.newsreaders.com/guide/news.html>: Explains why you would want a newsreader and how to use one.

Tile.net.news <tile.net>: A complete index to Internet usenet newsgroups. Browse by subject, hierarchy, or search. Provides links to newsgroup FAQs and use statistics.

Harley Hahn's Master List of Usenet Newsgroups <www.harley.com/usenet>: A master list of usenet newsgroups with descriptions. Search by category or keyword.

11e EVALUATING INTERNET SOURCES.

With print sources, you can have at least some confidence that the material has been filtered through editors and publishers. But the Internet is unfiltered. Anyone can create a web page that looks authoritative but contains misleading or even false information. When you use sources from the Internet for a paper or a presentation, one of your most important responsibilities is to analyze their reliability carefully and critically. You will find highly valuable, current, and relevant material online, but you must closely question every source you find before using it. Here are some points to keep in mind and guidelines to follow:

- **Authority and credibility:** Are the author and producer of the Web site identifiable? Does the author include biographical information? Is there any indication that the author has relevant expertise on the subject? Look for information about the individual or organization sponsoring the site; that can be an important indication of its reliability. The following extensions in the Web address, or uniform resource locator (URL), can help you determine the type of site (which often tells you something about its purpose):

  .com commercial (business)

  .net network

  .org nonprofit organization

  .gc Canadian government

  .ca (Canada)

  .on.ca provincial extension (Ontario)

  Canadian universities are often identified by the letter "u" in the name (e.g., queensu.ca or utoronto.ca).

  A tilde (~) followed by a name in a URL usually means the site is a personal home page not affiliated with any organization.

- **Purpose:** A site's purpose influences its presentation of information and its reliability. Is the site's main purpose to advocate a cause, advertise a product or service, provide factual information, present research results, provide news, share personal information, or offer entertainment?

- **Objectivity and reasonableness (bias):** Don't take the information that the site presents at face value. Look carefully at the purpose and tone of the text. Is there evidence of obvious bias? Clues that indicate a lack of reasonableness or bias include an intemperate tone, broad claims, exaggerated statements of significance, conflicts of interest, no recognition of opposing views, and strident attacks on opposing views. *(For more on evaluating a source's argument, see Tab 1: Writing and Designing Papers, pp. 3–6.)*

- **Relevance:** Is the information appropriate for your research? Consider the intended audience of the site, based on its purpose, content, tone, and style. Carefully consider the site's subject matter and the depth of its coverage of the subject.

- **Timeliness:** Is the information current enough for your needs, or is it outdated? Reliable sites usually post the date an item was published or loaded onto the Web or tell you when the information was last updated.

- **Context:** Finally, keep in mind that search engines retrieve individual Web pages out of context. Always try to return to the site's home page to determine the source of the information and to complete your citation.

NOTE: Websites that allow users to edit content (like Wikipedia) are not usually accepted as resources in academic work. Check with your professor before using such a site as a reference; better yet, use it as a starting point of your research for general information only. The most useful part of a wiki page is the list of sources after the article.

11f EVALUATING A SOURCE'S ARGUMENTS.

As you explore your sources, you should continue to assess their reliability. Does the writer of a piece appeal to your emotions, to your reason, or to both in a balanced way? Always ask yourself whether a particular writer is objective and fair-minded. Look for arguments that are qualified, supported with evidence, and well documented. Avoid relying on biased sources that appeal to emotions instead of rational thought or promote one-sided political or religious agendas. Critically analyze information sources by looking at the following components:

- **Audience:** Who is the intended audience (often a synopsis will identify some of this information)? Is the information appropriate for your needs (and level of current knowledge)?

- **Reasoning:** Is the information fact or opinion (facts can be verified)? Is it valid and well documented or does it remain unsupported by evidence? Are there errors or omissions in the information? Is the point of view unbiased, objective, or impartial or does it contain emotionally loaded terms? Does it differ radically from other sources in the same discipline (information that is almost contradictory from other experts in the field may require more critical analysis)?

- **Coverage:** Is it a primary or secondary source? Does it provide a comprehensive view of your topic or does it discuss it superficially?

- **Style:** Is the source well organized, clearly identifying and presenting points logically? Is it easy to read or follow? Is the argument repetitive?

Doing Research in the Archive, Field, and Lab

12a ADHERING TO ETHICAL PRINCIPLES WHEN DOING PRIMARY RESEARCH.

In the archive, field, or lab, you are working directly with something precious and immediate: an original record, a group of people, or special materials. Sometimes you will be the first person to see the significance of a document, to observe a particular pattern of behaviour, or to perform a new test in the lab. An ethical researcher shows respect for materials, experimental subjects, fellow researchers, and readers. Here are some guidelines to follow:

- Handle original documents and materials with great care, always leaving sources and data available for other researchers.
- Accurately report your sources and results.
- Follow the procedures mandated by your school and your field when working with human participants.

Research with human participants that you do as an undergraduate should also adhere to the following basic principles:

- **Confidentiality:** People who fill out surveys, participate in focus groups, or respond to interviews should be assured that their names will not be used without their permission.
- **Informed consent:** Before participating in an experiment, all participants must sign a statement affirming that they understand the general purpose of the research. Researchers agree that observations of crowds in a shopping mall or children in a classroom do not require informed consent, unless your observations intrude on the lives of the people you are observing.
- **Minimal risk:** Researchers must design experiments so that participants do not incur any risks greater than they do in everyday life.
- **Protection of vulnerable groups:** Researchers must be held strictly accountable for research done with participants in the following categories: the physically disabled, those who are mentally incompetent, minors, the elderly, and refugees.

Be fair when you refute the primary research or the views of others. Even if your purpose were to prove fellow researchers wrong, review their work and state their viewpoints in words that they themselves would recognize as accurate.

12b PREPARING YOURSELF FOR ARCHIVAL RESEARCH.

Archives are collections of specialized or rare books, manuscripts, and documents. They are accessible in libraries, other institutions, private collections, and on video- and audiotape. Your own attic may contain family archives—letters, diaries, and photograph collections that could have value to a researcher.

The more you know about your area of study, the more likely you will be to see the significance of an item in an archival collection. Reading about your topic in books, journals, and Internet documents will provide a framework for discovery and lead you to questions that can be answered only by consulting original materials in an archive.

Some archival collections are accessible through audio- and videotape as well as the Internet; others you must visit in person. (*See the box on p. 146.*) If you intend to do research in a rare-books library, you will need a letter of introduction, usually from your professor or your school librarian.

12c PLANNING YOUR FIELD RESEARCH CAREFULLY.

Field research involves recording observations, conducting interviews, or administering surveys. For the best results, you will need a strong research design and a plan for keeping accurate records.

1. Observe and write field notes. When you use direct observation, you need to keep careful records in order to gather the information you require. Here are some guidelines to follow:

- Be systematic and purposeful in your observations, but be alert to unexpected behaviour.
- Record what you see and hear as objectively as possible.
- Take more notes than you think you will ever need.
- When appropriate, categorize the types of behaviour you are looking for, and devise a system for counting instances of each type.

- When you have recorded data over a significant time, group your observations into categories for more careful study and discussion.

(For advice on conducting direct observations for a case study, see Tab 2: Common Assignments, pp. 111–114.)

2. Conduct interviews. Asking relevant questions of experts or people who are members of a population you are studying is a powerful research tool. Group interviews, called *focus groups,* are used in a number of fields, including marketing, education, and psychology. Interviews should be conducted in a relaxed atmosphere, but they are not simply conversations. To be useful as research tools, interviews require the following systematic preparation and implementation:

- Identify appropriate people for your interviews.
- Do background research, and plan your questions.
- Take careful notes, and if possible, tape-record the interview. (Be sure to obtain your subject's permission if you use audiotape.)
- Follow up on vague responses with questions that get at specific information.
- Politely probe inconsistencies and contradictions.
- Write thank-you notes to interviewees, and later send them copies of your report.

3. Take surveys. Conducted either orally from a script or in writing, **surveys** are made up of structured questions. Written surveys are called **questionnaires**. Survey research is complex; in fact, students in advanced social science courses spend a great deal of time studying the design and analysis of surveys. The following suggestions will help you prepare informal surveys:

- **Define your purpose.** Are you trying to gauge attitudes, learn about typical behaviours, or both?
- **Write clear directions and questions.** For example, if you are asking multiple-choice questions, make sure that you cover all possible options and that none of your options overlap.
- **Make sure that your questions are neutral,** that they do not suggest a preference for one answer over another.
- **Make the survey brief and easy to complete.** Most informal surveys should be no longer than one page (front and back).

TECH **TIPS**

Online Information about Archives

Here are some Internet sites that will help you find and understand a wide range of archival sources:

- *Images Canada* <imagescanada.ca/index-e.html>: This site offers search access to thousands of digital images of Canadian events, people, places, and things held by participating Canadian cultural institutions.

- *Library and Archives Canada* <www.collectionscanada.gc.ca/index-e.html>: This site results from the combined expertise of the former National Library of Canada and National Archives of Canada, whose objective is to offer easy access to important socio-historical and political documents and images that reflect Canadian culture.

- *CBC Archives* <archives.cbc.ca>: This site provides access to a selection of radio and television clips from the Archives of the Canadian Broadcasting Corporation.

- *Archives and Collections Society* <www.aandc.org>: This site lists thousands of archived maritime and nautical documents, books, images charts, and magazines.

- *Canadian Poetry Archive* <www.collectionscanada.ca/canvers>: This site lists selected digitized poems from over 100 early English- and French-language Canadian poets from the 19th and early 20th centuries.

- *Ontario Black History Society (OBHS) Archive* <www.blackhistorysociety.ca>: The OBHS provides access to a wide range of African-Canadian educational materials.

- *Canadian Association of Music Libraries, Archives, and Documentation Centres (CAML)* <www.yorku.ca/caml>: This is a professional association for librarians, archivists, and researchers in the field of music. Anyone interested in the organization and collection, preservation, and study of music, particularly music in Canada, is welcome to join.

12d KEEPING A NOTEBOOK WHEN DOING LAB RESEARCH.

All experimenters, from undergraduates to professional scientists, are required to keep careful records of their laboratory work. The purpose of these research records is to provide a complete and accurate account of the testing of a hypothesis in the controlled environment of the laboratory. In many courses, you will be required to use a lab manual for your notes. Whether or not you are using such a manual, the following guidelines will help you take accurate notes on your research.

1. Record immediate, on the spot, accurate notes on what happens in the lab. Write down as much detail as possible. Measure precisely; do not estimate. Identify major pieces of apparatus, unusual chemicals, and laboratory animals in enough detail so that, for example, a reader can determine the size or type of equipment you used (instead of "physiograph," write "physiograph, grass model 7b"). Use drawings, when appropriate, to illustrate complicated equipment setups. Include tables, when useful, to present results.

2. Follow a basic format. If you are working without a lab manual or if no standard format is provided, you will be expected to present your results in a format that allows you to communicate all the major features of an experiment. The five basic sections that must be included are title, purpose, materials and methods, results, and conclusions. (*For more advice on preparing a lab report, see Tab 2: Common Assignments, pp. 107–111.*)

3. Write in complete sentences, even if you are filling in answers to questions in a lab manual. Resist using shorthand to record your notes. Writing in complete sentences will ensure that you understand the concepts in the experiment. Complete sentences will provide a clear, unambiguous record of your procedures and results when you review it later. Notice the difference between the following two responses to a typical question in a lab manual:

Why is water readily polluted?

INCOMPLETE ANSWER   universal solvent

COMPLETE ANSWER   Water is a universal solvent. Consequently, many compounds, including pollutants,dissolve in water.

Highlight connections in your sentences by using the following transitions: *then, next, consequently, because,* and *therefore.* Cause-effect relationships are important to working scientists and should have similar importance in your lab notebook.

4. When necessary, revise and correct your laboratory notebook in visible ways. If you make a mistake in recording laboratory results, correct them as clearly as possible, either by erasing or by crossing out and rewriting on the original sheet. If you make an uncorrectable mistake in your lab notebook, do not tear the sheet out. Simply fold the sheet lengthwise and mark *omit* on the face side.

    If you need to add sheets to your notebook, paste them permanently to the appropriate pages. No matter how much preparation you do, unanticipated results often occur in the lab, and you may find yourself jotting down notes on a convenient piece of scrap paper or even a paper towel. Attach these notes to your laboratory notebook.

13 Working with Sources

Once you have a research question to answer, an idea about what the library and Internet have to offer, and some sense of the kinds of materials you need, you are ready to begin selecting and using sources.

13a MAINTAINING A WORKING BIBLIOGRAPHY.

As you research, compile a **working bibliography**—a list of those books, articles, pamphlets, Web sites, and other sources that seem most likely to help you answer your research question. It is essential to maintain an accurate and complete record of all sources you consult. For each source, record the following bibliographic information:

- Call number of book, reference work, or other print source; URL of each Web site (this refers to the actual Web address of the source, not the search string provided by the search engine)

  Web address: www.mcgrawhill.ca

  search string: www.google.ca/search?hl=en&q= McGraw-Hill+Ryerson&btnG=Google+ Search&meta=

- All authors, editors, and translators
- Title of chapter, article, or Web page
- Title of book, periodical, or Web site in which the chapter, article, or page appears
- For books, date of publication, place, and publisher as well as edition or volume numbers, if applicable
- For periodical articles, the date and edition or volume number, issue, and page numbers if applicable
- For a Web source, the date you consulted it

You can compile bibliographic information in a variety of ways:

1. Computer drives: If you are using a portable device (laptop, note/netbook or jump drive) you can save your researched materials directly to the drive for future access.

2. Printouts. In online searches, you may have the option of printing out the results or saving them to a portable device. On the printout or drive, be sure to note all relevant bibliographic information, including the database you used. If you rely on printouts to compile your working bibliography, you may want to use a highlighter to indicate those sources you actually plan to consult.

If possible, compile a list of sources and e-mail it to yourself, so you can keep your working bibliography in electronic form, printing out specific entries as you need them.

3. Photocopies. If you photocopy articles, essays, or pages of reference works from a print or a microform source, take time to note the bibliographic information on the photocopy. Spending a few extra minutes now can save you lots of time later.

13b TAKING NOTES ON YOUR SOURCES.

Taking notes increases learning and helps you to think through the answer to your research question. As you work, you can take notes on the information you glean from your sources by annotating photocopies of your source material or by noting useful quotations and ideas on paper, on cards, or in a computer file.

1. Annotation. One way to take notes is to annotate photocopied articles and printouts from online information services or Web sites. As you read, write the following notes directly on the page:

- On the first page, write down complete bibliographic information for the source (*see top of this page*).
- As you read, record your questions, reactions, and ideas in the margins.
- Comment in the margin on ideas that agree with or differ from those you have already learned about.
- Put important and difficult passages into your own words by paraphrasing or summarizing them in the margin. (*For help with paraphrasing and summarizing, see pp. 150–152.*)

- Use a highlighter to mark statements that are especially well expressed that you may want to quote; these are key to gaining an understanding of the issue.

When you are finished annotating the article or printout, use a research notebook to explore some of the comments, connections, and questions you recorded in the margins.

2. Separate notes. If you do not have photocopies to annotate, take notes on paper or a computer. Using a separate page for each idea you write down will make it easier to organize the material. Whatever method you use, be sure to record the source's bibliographic information as well as the specific page number for each idea.

It is important to enclose in quotation marks any exact words from a source. If you think that you may forget that the phrasing, as well as the idea, came from someone else, label the passage a "quote." Unless you think you might use a particular quotation in your paper, it is usually better to express the author's ideas in your own words by using a paraphrase or a summary.

When you **summarize**, you state the main point of a piece, condensing a few paragraphs into one sentence or a few pages into one paragraph. (*For guidelines on writing a summary, see Tab 1: Writing and Designing Papers, pp. 4–5.*)

When you **paraphrase**, you put someone else's statements into other words. Keep in mind that a paraphrase is not a word-for-word translation. Instead, you need to express the source's ideas *in your own way,* a way that will usually be shorter and less detailed than the original. Even though the sentences are yours, you must still give credit for the ideas to the original writer by citing his or her work properly. And if your paraphrase includes any exact phrasing from the source, put quotation marks around those phrases.

Paraphrasing is a valuable skill, but is often difficult to do well. For example, take a look at the following:

THE ORIGINAL PASSAGE

Basketball players often speak of having a "hot hand"—of being "in the zone" and feeling that they just can't miss. In recent years, however, a number of well-known scientists and statisticians (among them Stephen J. Gould and Thomas Gilovic) have argued that the hot hand is an illusion (similar to the illusion of being "hot" in poker or roulette). Studies of long-term shooting patterns, they claim, show that shooters are actually slightly *less likely* to make a shot if they have made their previous shot. Thus, contrary to what many players and fans believe, success does not breed success in basketball, and the hot hand is a myth.

— G. BASSHAM, W. IRWIN, H. NARDONE, & J. M. WALLACE,
Critical Thinking, A Student's Introduction, 3rd ed.

UNACCEPTABLE PARAPHRASE

"Being in the zone" and *"having a hot hand"* make basketball players feel that they can't miss. However, this feeling is an illusion according to some well-known scientists and statisticians. Accordingly, they claim that shooters are more likely to miss a shot if they have made the previous one. In my opinion, therefore, the "hot hand" theory is not real.

The paraphrase retains most of the original ideas as well as the original style. The writer has not acknowledged the original author and has personalized the passage ("In my opinion". . .) suggesting the ideas belong to him.

UNACCEPTABLE PARAPHRASE

In recent years, a number of well-known scientists and statisticians (among them Stephen J. Gould and Thomas Gilovic), have argued that having a "hot hand"—of being "in the zone" in basketball is an illusion. With the hot hand, players feel that they just can't miss but, in fact, they are actually slightly *less likely* to make a shot if they have made their previous shot according to studies of long-term shooting patterns. So, in spite of the common perception, the hot hand seems to be a myth.

This paraphrase contains most of the original author's ideas and several key phrases although they have been moved around or rephrased. The original author has not been acknowledged either.

UNACCEPTABLE PARAPHRASE

In *Critical Thinking* by Bassham et al. "success does not breed success in basketball, and the hot hand is a myth" (309). Basketball players often speak of feeling that they just can't miss—having a "hot hand." However, this is an illusion according to scientists. Their studies indicate that players are *less likely* to be successful if they have made their previous shot.

The writer does credit the original writer, but with only one of the ideas / phrases used. He also misrepresents what is said by omitting key information from the quotation.

ACCEPTABLE PARAPHRASE

In the book *Critical Thinking*, Bassham et al. speak about the negative correlation between making a basket and hitting the next shot. The authors believe the players are deceived by their recent successes on the court, wherein they have unrealistic expectations of future performance.

The writer has avoided using too many of the original key phrases, has condensed the content to the most relevant ideas, and clearly attributes them to the original author.

13c TAKING STOCK OF WHAT YOU HAVE LEARNED.

When you take stock, you assess the research you have done and synthesize what you have learned.

In academic writing, the credibility of your work depends on the relevance and reliability of your sources as well as the scope and depth of your reading and observation. A paper on Canadian music, for example, is unlikely to be credible if it relies on only one source of information. For lab reports, detailed observations are likely to be most important because they are the main kind of source that experimenters use when writing up their work.

As the context and kind of writing change, so too will the requirements for particular types and numbers of sources. Ask yourself the following questions about the sources you have consulted:

- Are your sources trustworthy? (*See Chapter 11, pp. 134–142, for more on evaluating sources.*)

- If you have started to develop a tentative answer to your research question, have your sources provided you with a sufficient number of facts, examples, and ideas to support that answer?

- Have you used sources that examine issues from several different perspectives?

It is also important to think about how the sources you have read relate to one another. Ask yourself when, how, and why your sources agree or disagree, and consider where you stand on the issues they raise. Did anything you read surprise or disturb you? Writing down your responses to such questions can help you clarify what you have learned from working with sources.

Writing the Paper

You have chosen a challenging research question and have located, read, and evaluated a variety of relevant sources. Now you need to come up with a thesis that will allow you to share what you have learned as well as your perspective on the issue.

14a PLANNING AND DRAFTING YOUR PAPER.

Begin planning by recalling the context and the purpose of your paper. If you have an assignment sheet, review it to see if the paper is supposed to be primarily informative, interpretive, or argumentative. Keep your purpose and context in mind as you decide on a position to support and develop.

1. Decide on a thesis. Consider the question that guided your research as well as other questions provoked by what you have learned during your research. Revise the wording of your question to make it intriguing as well as suitable (*see Chapter 10, pp. 127–129*). After you write down this question, compose an answer that you can use as your tentative thesis, as in the following example:

FOCAL QUESTION

What happens to Canadian performers as they become successful?

TENTATIVE ANSWER

To gain worldwide acclaim, Canadian performers are forced to rely on foreign-controlled promoters.

(*For more on devising a thesis, see Tab 1: Writing and Designing Papers, pp. 27–29.*)

2. Outline a plan for supporting and developing your thesis. Guided by your tentative thesis, outline a plan that uses your sources in a purposeful way. Decide on the kind of structure you will use to support your thesis—explanatory, exploratory, or argumentative—and develop your support by choosing facts, examples, and ideas drawn from a variety of sources. (S*ee Chapters 6–8 in Tab 2 for more on explanatory, exploratory, and argumentative structure.*). Choose your references wisely. There is no single rule that demands a specific amount of referenced material in a paper. Instead of quantity, focus on the quality of your source material: how does it help you to strengthen or support your position? Remember that external sources are meant to support your voice, not become it.

For an interpretative analysis on the state of Canadian music, an exploratory structure—which is organized around asking and answering a central question—seemed best:

- Provide background about the current success of Canadian performers.
- Introduce the problem about Canadian performers being promoted by foreign-controlled recording labels.
- State the question: What happens to these performers as they become more successful?
- Why do Canadian performers have to look outside their own country's music industry for international recognition?
- Conclude: Despite the worldwide success of Canadian performers, the Canadian music industry does not profit from their recognition.

To develop this outline, you would need to list supporting facts, examples, or ideas for each point. (*For more on developing an outline, see Tab 1: Writing and Designing Papers, pp. 29–31.*)

3. Write a draft. When you have a tentative thesis and a plan, you are ready to write a draft. Some writers plan to use a few pages to set up the context for the issue, but many others find that they can present their thesis or focal question at the end of an introductory paragraph or two.

As you write beyond the introduction, be prepared to re-examine and refine your position. Discovering interesting connections as well as new ways to express your ideas makes writing exciting. Such discoveries often occur when writers use what they have read in various sources to support and develop their ideas.

Make your conclusion memorable. Include an example or detail from the content to reinforce the intention or purpose of the paper, but avoid introducing a new topic.

Writers often do not come up with a conclusion until after the first draft, since at this stage they are still revising their introductions and body paragraphs. So it is important to be flexible when reviewing a first draft.

14b QUOTING AND PARAPHRASING BOTH PROPERLY AND EFFECTIVELY.

To support and develop your ideas, use quoted, paraphrased, or summarized material from sources. To do so properly and effectively, follow these guidelines.

1. Integrate quotations. Use quotations when a source's exact words are important to your point and make your writing more memorable, fair, or authoritative. Quotes should be short, enclosed in quotation marks, and well integrated into your sentence structure, as in the following example:

> The Task Force Report on the future of the Canadian music industry states, "Canadian firms earn about 90% of their revenue from selling Canadian-content recordings, while 88% of the revenues of foreign-controlled firms comes from selling recordings made from imported masters. Foreign firms have five times the revenue, 18 times the profit, ten times the long-term assets, and 16 times the contributed surplus and retained earnings of Canadian-controlled firms" (15).

2. Use brackets within quotations. Sentences that include quotations must make sense grammatically. Sometimes you may have to adjust a quotation to make it fit properly into your sentence. Use brackets to indicate any minor adjustments you have made. For example, here *my* has been changed to *his* to make the quotation fit better grammatically:

> Karen Bliss, a *Jam* columnist, says of Vancouver-based Kuba that "[his] goal was not to have one fast-forward song on the album" (1).

3. Use ellipses within quotations. Use ellipses to indicate that words have been omitted from the body of a quotation, but be sure that what you omit does not significantly alter the source's meaning. If you are using MLA style, it is acceptable to place the ellipsis points within square brackets. (*For more on using ellipses, see Tab 9: Editing for Correctness, pp. 383–385.*)

> As Marin states, "Ganz ... decided that he would do whatever he could to break down the racism ... in the jazz world" (69).

4. Use block format for longer quotations. Quotations longer than four lines should be used rarely. When they are used too frequently, long quotations tend to break up your text and make your reader impatient. If you include a longer quotation, put it in block format (*see Tab 9: Editing for Correctness, pp. 370–372*) and be especially careful to integrate it into your paper. Tell your readers why you want them to read the block quotation, and comment on it afterwards but make sure not to restate the comment itself.

5. Use signal phrases to introduce quotations and paraphrases. When you are integrating the thoughts or words of someone else into your writing, use a **signal phrase** that indicates whom you are quoting. Besides crediting others for their work, signal phrases can make ideas more interesting by giving them a human face. When a writer relies on the same signal phrase throughout a paper, readers quickly become bored. To keep things interesting, vary your signal phrases. Instead of using the verbs *says* and *writes* again and again, consider using *acknowledges, asserts, claims, concludes, emphasizes, explains, expresses, notes, points out, proves, reports, responds, shows,* or *suggests.*

14c AVOIDING PLAGIARISM AND COPYRIGHT INFRINGEMENT.

Writers need to remember that knowledge develops socially in a give-and-take process akin to conversation. In this kind of social situation, it is a matter of both personal integrity and academic honesty to acknowledge others, especially when you use their words or ideas. Writers who fail to acknowledge their sources correctly—either intentionally or inadvertently—commit **plagiarism**. And writers who unfairly use copyrighted material found on the World Wide Web or in print are legally liable for their acts.

1. Avoid plagiarism. To avoid plagiarism, adhere to these guidelines:

- Do not rely too much on one source, or you may easily slip into using that person's thoughts as your own.

- Keep accurate records while doing research and taking notes or you may lose track of where an idea came from. If you do not know where you got an idea or a piece of information, do not use it in your paper until you find out.

CROSS-DISCIPLINE **WRITING**

Using Data

Statistics—numerical data and methods of interpreting those data—are a critical part of research in many disciplines, particularly the social sciences. When providing statistics, always cite the source of the information.

EXAMPLE

Low income is a reality in West Broadway where 75% of the households earn less than $20,000 ("Housing Development," 2005).

- Choose an appropriate documentation style, and use it consistently and properly.

- When you take notes, be sure to put quotation marks around words, phrases, or sentences taken word for word from a source. If you use any of those words, phrases, or sentences when summarizing or paraphrasing the source, make sure to put them in quotation marks. Keep in mind that changing a word here and there while keeping a source's sentence structure or phrasing constitutes plagiarism, even if you credit the source for the ideas. (*See pp. 150–152 for examples of unacceptable paraphrases.*)

- Cite the source of all ideas, opinions, facts, and statistics that are not common knowledge.

"Common knowledge" though is sometimes difficult to determine. Some experts consider current events or geographic information to be common knowledge; others include folklore and slang. Information that readers in a field would know about from a wide range of general resources is considered common knowledge. In any case, you can evaluate information using the following criteria:

- Can the fact be found in numerous sources? Experts believe that if the information can be found in three or more reliable independent sources, then it could be considered common.

- Is it everywhere (available across disciplines)? Some facts may be well known within one discipline and sources written within that group may assume the information is commonly known. However, the same fact may need citing or referencing when it is sourced by non-experts or an audience outside a specific discipline.

- Can the fact be found in general reference source (i.e., a general knowledge encyclopedia)?

For example, in biology, the structure of DNA and the process of cell division or photosynthesis are considered common knowledge. A recent scientific discovery about genetics, however, would not be common knowledge, so you would need to cite the source of this information. The sequence of major historical events is considered common knowledge, but one historian's thoughts about the causes or impact of an event would need to be cited.

If it is unclear whether the information is common knowledge, assume that an idea is *not* and cite the source. Finally, when in doubt, check with your professor.

2. Use copyrighted materials fairly. All written materials, including student papers, letters, and e-mail, are covered by copyright, even if they do not bear an official copyright symbol. A copyright grants its owner exclusive rights to the use of a protected work, including reproducing, distributing, and displaying the work. The popularity of the Internet has led to increased concerns about the fair use of copyrighted material. Before you post your paper on the Web or produce a multimedia presentation that includes audio, video, and graphic elements copied from a Web site, make sure that you have used copyrighted material fairly.

The following four criteria are used to determine if copyrighted material has been used fairly:

- **What is the purpose of the use?** Educational, nonprofit, and personal use are more likely to be considered fair than commercial use.

- **What is the nature of the work being used?** In most cases, imaginative and unpublished materials can be used only if you have the permission of the copyright holder.

- **How much of the copyrighted work is being used?** If a writer uses a small portion of a text for academic purposes, this use is more likely to be considered fair than if he or she uses a whole work for commercial purposes.

- **What effect would this use have on the market for the original?** The use of a work is usually considered unfair if it would hurt sales of the original.

3. Document all your sources. Whenever you use information, ideas, or words from someone else's work, you must acknowledge that person. As noted on page 157, the only exception is for information that is common knowledge, such as the chemical composition of water or the names of all the Canadian provinces. When you tell readers

TECH **TIPS**

Using Sources Properly

Plagiarism: What It Is and How to Recognize and Avoid It
<www.mcgill.ca/library-assistance/plagiarism> is filled with tips from educators at McGill on how to recognize and avoid plagiarism.

Copyright and Fair Use
For in-depth information and discussion of copyright, check out The Copyright Board Canada <www.cb-cda.gc.ca>

what sources you have consulted, they can more readily understand your paper as well as the conversation you are participating in by writing it.

How sources are documented varies by field and discipline. Choose a documentation style that is appropriate for the particular course you are taking, and use it properly and consistently. If you are not sure which documentation style to use, ask your instructor. If you are required to use an alternative, discipline-specific documentation

CROSS-DISCIPLINE **WRITING**

Style Manuals for Specific Disciplines

SPECIFIC DISCIPLINE	POSSIBLE STYLE MANUAL
Chemistry	Dodd, Janet S., ed. *The ACS Style Guide: A Manual for Authors and Editors.* 2nd ed. Washington: American Chemical Society, 1997.
Geology	Bates, Robert L., Rex Buchanan, and Marla Adkins-Heljeson, eds. *Geowriting: A Guide to Writing, Editing, and Printing in Earth Science.* 5th ed. Alexandria: American Geological Institute, 1995.
Government	Garner, Diane L., and Diane H. Smith, eds. *The Complete Guide to Citing Government Information Resources: A Manual for Writers and Librarians.* Rev. ed. Bethesda: Congressional Information Service, 1993.
Law	*The Bluebook: A Uniform System of Citation.* 17th ed. Cambridge: Harvard Law Review Assn., 2000.
Journalism	Goldstein, Norm, ed. *Associated Press Stylebook and Libel Manual.* 35th ed. New York: Associated Press, 2000.
Linguistics	Linguistic Society of America. "LSA Style Sheet." *LSA Bulletin.* Published annually in the December issue.
Mathematics	American Mathematical Society. *AMS Author Handbook: General Instructions for Preparing Manuscripts.* Providence: AMS, 1997.
Medicine	Iverson, Cheryl, ed. *American Medical Association Manual of Style: A Guide for Authors and Editors.* 9th ed. Chicago: AMA, 1997.
Physics	American Institute of Physics. *Style Manual for Guidance in the Preparation of Papers.* 4th ed. New York: American Institute of Physics, 1990.
Political science	Lane, Michael K. *Style Manual for Political Science Papers.* Rev. ed. Washington: American Political Science Assn., 1993.

style, consult the list of possible manuals on page 159. Here are some of the most common documentation styles used in academic writing:

- **MLA (Modern Language Association) style** is often used for course papers in the arts and humanities, although some professors of music, religion, and philosophy prefer the *Chicago Manual of Style (Chicago)* format (*see below*), as do many historians. (*For MLA style, see pp. 164–194.*)

- **APA (American Psychological Association) style** is often used for written work in such social sciences as anthropology, psychology, and sociology as well as for course papers in such professional fields as education and business. (*See pp. 197–224.*)

- *Chicago (Chicago Manual of Style)* **style** is often used for course papers in history, communications, and business. (*See pp. 227–243.*)

- **CSE (Council of Science Editors) style** is typically used for written work in the natural sciences, math, and such technical fields as engineering, physical therapy, and computer science. (*Online*)

- **COS (Columbia Online Style)** provides the most in-depth guidance for documenting online sources and can be used with all types of documentation styles, including MLA, APA, *Chicago,* and CSE. (*Online*)

If your instructor asks you to use a documentation style other than MLA, APA, or *Chicago,* consult the appropriate discipline-specific manual. (*See p. 159.*)

4

MLA
DOCUMENTATION
STYLE

4 MLA Documentation Style

MLA STYLE: IN-TEXT CITATIONS: (CHAPTER 15)

MLA STYLE: LIST OF WORKS CITED (CHAPTER 16)

(*See pp. 166–170 for examples of in-text citations.*)

Academic papers include information, ideas, and quotations from external sources that help support an argument. When using external resources in scholarly work, it is important to identify the original author and the source of the material you have borrowed to make your point. Direct quotations, paraphrases, and summaries of other people's ideas must be accurately documented, regardless of the type of paper you are writing. (*For more on what to document, see Tab 3: Researching, pp. 156–159.*)

WHAT IS MLA?

The Modern Language Association (MLA) provides a style of documentation used in scholarly works. MLA publishes two writing guides: *The MLA Handbook for Writers of Research Papers* and the *MLA Style Manual and Guide to Scholarly Publishing.*

The guidelines presented here are based on the third edition of the *MLA Style Manual and Guide to Scholarly Publishing* (New York: MLA, 2008) and the seventh edition of the *MLA Handbook for Writers of Research Papers* (New York: MLA, 2009). MLA documentation style has two parts:

- In-text or "parenthetical" citations
- Works Cited page

In-text (parenthetical) citations and a works-cited page are mandatory. Endnotes (used to provide extra information to your reader) and a works-consulted page (used to identify sources you have read, but which you do not cite) are optional, depending on the criteria of the assignment.

MLA Style: In-Text Citations 15

MLA in-text citations require that you:

- **Provide the author's last name followed by the page number in the source**, for example: (Atwood 139). No "p." precedes the page number and there is no internal punctuation between the author's name and page number.

- **Provide only the page number, if the author's name has been incorporated into a signal phrase** such as "Atwood states..." For example:

  > Margaret Atwood states in the Introduction to *The Penelopiad* that she found two things profoundly "hysterical" in their strong demand for analysis and interpretation in Homer's *Odyssey*: Penelope's own life during Odysseus's absence and the hanging of the twelve maids in the original text (xiv).

- **Place the citation as close as possible to the material being cited** and before any punctuation marks that divide or end the sentence, such as commas, semicolons, or periods—except in a block quotation, where the citation comes after the period.

TECH **TIPS**

FAQs on MLA

For updates and responses to frequently asked questions (FAQs) about MLA documentation style, check out the MLA Web site at <www.mla.org>.

1. Author named in parentheses: Provide the name of the author in parentheses followed by a space and the page number from the source.

> While the multinational major labels—like SONY, Warner, and Universal—should be able to suck up the hit to their bottom line, some of Canada's smaller independent labels and distributors are bracing for the worst (Galloway 27).

Note that there is no comma between the author's name and the page number. If you cite two or more distinct pages, however, separate the numbers with a comma: (Galloway 27, 29).

2. Author named in text: You can use the last name only, unless two or more of your sources have the same last name.

> As Tagliamonte argues, "instant messaging is not the linguistic ruin of a generation" (27).

Note that the parenthetical page citation comes after the closing quotation mark but before the period.

3. Two or more works by the same author: If you use two or more works by the same author, you must identify which work you are citing, either in your sentence or in an abbreviated form in parentheses.

> "While foreign sales make up most of the revenue for Canadian bands, home-grown talent is starting to be recognized and valued in Canadian markets" (Melvin, *Canadian Music, Eh* 22).
> [**Or** (Melvin, *Canadian* 22).]

> In *Canadian Music, Eh*, Melvin reports, "While foreign sales make up most of the revenue for Canadian bands, home-grown talent is starting to be recognized and valued in Canadian markets" (22).

4. Two or more authors of the same work: If a source has up to three authors, you should name them all either in your text, as shown below, or in parentheses—(Allman and Michael 1).

TWO AUTHORS

According to Allman and Michael, artists whose careers were initially supported by FACTOR (Foundation to Assist Canadian Talent on Records) have gone on to become huge successes (1).

If the source has more than three authors, either list all the authors or give the first author's last name followed by "et al.," the abbreviation for the Latin phrase meaning "and others."

MORE THAN THREE AUTHORS

Changes in social regulations are bound to produce new forms of subjectivity (Henriques et al. 275).

5. Authors with the same last name: If two or more of your sources have the same last name, include the first initial of the author you are citing; if the first initial is also shared, use the full first name, as shown below.

Once the request has been initiated, it is up to the administration to determine the validity of that specific request (Sandra Noble 67).

6. Organization or group as author: To cite works by organized groups, government agencies, commissions, associations, or corporations, treat the organization as the author. If the organization's name is long, either put it in a signal phrase or use an abbreviated version of the name in the parentheses.

The Centre for Contemporary Cultural Studies claims that "there is nothing inherently concrete about historiography" (10).

Historiography deals with abstract issues (Centre 10).

7. Unknown author: When no author is given, you can cite a work by its title, using either the full title in a signal phrase or an abbreviated version in the parentheses. If you abbreviate the title, be sure to do so in a way that points clearly to the corresponding entry in your list of works cited.

"Canada Rocks" suggests more and more Canadian performers are attracting worldwide attention (45).

> More and more Canadian performers are attracting worldwide attention ("Canada Rocks" 45).

8. Entire work: When you want to acknowledge an entire work, such as a film, a concert, or a book, it is usually better to do so in your text, not in a parenthetical citation. Be sure to include the work in your list of works cited.

> Sarah Polley's film *Away From Her* is an adaptation of an Alice Munro short story.

9. Web site or other online electronic source: For online sources, MLA recommends using the guidelines already established for print sources. In addition, because Web sources are available in multiple forms and accessible in various ways, they can differ from version to version include the access date along with the publication information when citing electronic sources.

Like print, if you cannot find one of the main elements (like the author) of an online source, then identify the source by title, either in your text or in a parenthetical citation. Because most online sources do not have set page, section, or paragraph numbers, they must usually be cited as entire works.

> Canadian recording artists have taken the world by storm, but foreign-controlled firms are enjoying a large slice of the profit pie ("Canadian").

10. Electronic source with numbered paragraphs or screens instead of pages: Give the paragraph or screen number(s) after the author's name and a comma. To distinguish them from page numbers, use the abbreviation *par(s)* or the word *screen(s)*.

> Goodman understood how to balance the public's demand for pop with his own desire to push his players (Edgers, screen 1).

11. Electronic source with no page or paragraph numbers: When citing an online or print source without page, paragraph, or other reference numbers, try to work the author's name into your text instead of putting it in a parenthetical citation.

> Pacienza claims that "For many unknown acts, a trip to Canadian Music Week is a worthy investment since it attracts buyers from

Japan, Australia, France, Germany, the U.K. and, of course, the United States."

12. Multivolume work: When using and citing more than one volume of a multivolume source, include the volume number, followed by a colon, a space, and the page number.

> Murphy maintains that science fiction still lacks respect as a legitimate literary genre (2: 6).

However, if you consulted only one volume of a multivolume work, it is unnecessary to cite the volume number in the parenthetical reference. You should include it as part of the works-cited entry (*see p. 176*).

13. Literary works:

Novels and literary non-fiction books: Include the relevant page number, followed by a semicolon, a space, and the chapter number.

> Personal integrity and creative vision are prominent themes in Danowski's *Making Art* (122; ch. 13).

If the author is not named in your sentence, add the name in front of the page number: (Ellison 384; ch. 23).

Poems: Use line numbers, not page numbers.

> In "Senses Times Five," Frances Lilian asks "Can you see a sunset/Without seeing/the sun?" (lines 13–15). She strengthens this imagery with "Do you speak/of great things/to an empty room?" (17–19)

The word *lines* (not *l.* or *ll.*) is used in the first citation to establish what the numbers in parentheses refer to; subsequent citations need not use the word *lines*. (*See pp. 370–372 and 385–386 for more information about quoting poetry.*)

Plays and long, multi-section poems: Use division (act, scene, canto, book, part) and lines, not page numbers. In the following example, notice that Arabic numerals are used for act and scene divisions as well as for line numbers: (*Hamlet* 2.3.22–27). The same is true for citation of canto, verse, and lines in the following citation of Byron's *Don Juan:* (*DJ* 1.37.4–8).

14. The Bible: Cite material in the Bible by book, chapter, and verse, using an appropriate abbreviation when the name of the book is in the parentheses rather than in your sentence.

> As the Bible says, "The wise man knows there will be a time of
>
> judgment" (Eccles. 8.5).

Note that titles of biblical books are not italicized.

15. Indirect source: When you quote or paraphrase a quotation you found in someone else's work, put *qtd. in* (meaning "quoted in") before the name of your source.

> "Canada is very hot on the world music charts" (Dixon qtd. in
>
> Pacienza 1).

In your list of works cited, list only the work you consulted, in this case the indirect source by Pacienza.

16. Two or more sources in one citation: When you need to credit two or more sources for an idea, use a semicolon to separate the citations.

> "Canada is losing control of a cultural industry" (CAAMA 1;
>
> "Time" 9–13).

17. Work in an anthology: When citing a work in a collection, give the name of the specific work's author, not the name of the editor of the whole collection.

> In a tiny, grungy, antique store in Masset on the Queen Charlotte
>
> Islands, I found the mouse (Robinson 73).

Here, Robinson is cited as the source even though her work appears in a collection edited by Joy Gugeler.

18. E-mail, letter, personal interview: Cite by name the person you communicated with, using either a signal phrase or parentheses.

> In spite of huge changes in the record industry, multinational
>
> record companies sign most Canadian artists (Franklin).

In the works-cited list, you will need to identify the kind of communication and its date (*see pp. 181, 186, and 188*).

MLA Style: List of Works Cited

Besides in-text citations, MLA documentation style requires a works-cited page, where readers can find full bibliographic information about the sources you have used. The list of works cited should appear at the end of your paper, beginning on a new page entitled "Works Cited." Include only those sources you "cite" in your paper, unless your instructor also tells you to prepare a "Works Consulted" list, which identifies all the sources you "consulted," but not necessarily used in your paper.

16a GENERAL GUIDELINES FOR A LIST OF WORKS CITED IN MLA STYLE.

1. Begin on a new page.

2. Begin with the centred title "Works Cited" (omit the quotation marks)

3. Include an entry for every in-text citation.

4. Include author, title, and publication data for each entry, if available. Use a period to set off each of these elements from the others. Leave one space after the periods. *NB. The MLA Style Manual and the MLA Handbook call for the medium of the source cited (e.g., print, Web, PDF file) to be included in every entry. This information is generally found after the date of publication but before the access date of Web sources.*

5. Do not number the entries.

6. Put entries in alphabetical order by author's or editor's last name. (If the author is unknown, use the first word of the title, excluding the articles *a*, *an*, or *the*). Where available, use the author's or editor's full first name rather than just initials. If initials are used, there is a space between them (J. K. Rowling rather than J.K. Rowling).

7. Italicize titles of books and periodicals or use double quotation marks to identify articles within larger bodies of work.

8. Capitalize the first, the last, and all important words, including those that follow hyphens in compound terms, in all titles and subtitles. Do not capitalize articles,

prepositions, coordinating conjunctions, and the *to* in infinitives.

9. In the publication data, abbreviate publishers' names and months (*Dec.* rather than *December*; *Oxford UP* instead of *Oxford University Press*), and include the name of the city in which the publisher is located but not the province: *Toronto: McGraw-Hill Ryerson.* Abbreviating "university" to "u" and "press" to "p" applies to presses attached to universities, not presses in general.

10. For publishers' names, omit articles, business abbreviations (Co., Corp, Inc., Ltd.) and descriptors (Publishers, Press, House, etc.)

11. Do not use *p.*, *pp.*, or *page(s).* Numbers alone will do. When page spans over 100 have the same first digit, use only the last two digits of the second number: 243–47.

12. Use a hanging indent: Start the first line of each entry at the left margin, and indent all subsequent lines of the entry five spaces (about one-half inch or 1.25 centimetres on the computer).

13. Double-space within entries and between them.

In MLA, you italicize titles of works that were published as *separate items.*

a book	*Survival*
a play	*The Ecstasy of Rita Joe*
a scholarly journal	*CNIE*
a popular magazine	*Maclean's*
a newspaper	*Edmonton Journal*
a Web site	*Modern Language Association*
an online database	*LexisNexis Academic*
a film	*Les Invasions Barbares*
a DVD	*Puck Hogs*
a CD	*Famous Last Words* (Hedley)
a TV show	*Flashpoint*
a painting	*By the Lake* (A. Y. Jackson)
a sculpture	*Draped Reclining Woman* (Henry Moore)
a ballet	*Les Sylphides* (Chopin)
an opera	*Tosca* (Puccini)

For works too short to be published as separate items, use double quotations marks (" ") around the titles.

a short story	"Sans Souci"
a chapter in a book	"Educational Multimedia"
a scholarly journal article	"Meaningful, Interactive Distance Learning"
an encyclopedia article	"Poison"
a magazine article	"Write Right"
a newspaper article	"The Big Fix"
a dictionary definition	"Irony"
a lecture	"Hypertext in Virtual Space"
one episode of a TV show	"The Prosecutor" (an episode of *The Collector*)
one song on a CD	"Hit the Wall" (Brendan Canning)

16b BOOKS.

1. Book by one author: Italicize the book's title. Only the city, not the province or state, is included in the publication data.

> Moses, Daniel David. *The Exile Book of Native Canadian Fiction and Drama.* Toronto: Exile Editions, 2010. Print.

2. Two or more works by the same author(s): When you list more than one work by the same author, give the author's name in the first entry only. For subsequent works authored by that person, replace the name with three hyphens and a period. Multiple works by one author are alphabetized by title.

> Verity, Donna. *Case Studies in Human Resources Management.* Kingston: Corner Books, 2010. Print.

> ---. *Introduction to HRM.* Kingston: Corner Books 2008. Print.

3. Book by two or more authors: Name the two or three authors in the order in which they appear on the title page, putting the last name first for the first author only. When a work has more than three authors, you may use the abbreviation *et al.* (meaning "and others") to replace the names of all authors except the first.

> Murphy, Graham, Sandra Noble, and Melanie Rubens. *eLearning: The Process Explained.* Toronto: InHouse, 2009. Print.

Korymyla, Leonard, et al. *Calculus for Post Secondary Studies.*
Hamilton: Mountain, 2011. Print.

4. Organization or group as author: Consider as an organization any group, commission, association, or corporation whose members are not identified on the title page.

Centre for Contemporary Cultural Studies. *Making Histories:*
Studies in History Writing and Politics. London:
Hutchinson, 1982. Print.

5. Book by an editor or editors: If the title page lists an editor instead of an author, treat the editor as an author but put the abbreviation *ed.* after the name. Use the plural *eds.* when more than one editor is listed, and put only the first editor's name in reverse order.

Trebreve, Tina, ed. *Amore.* Toronto: Smith, 2011. Print.

6. Book with an author and an editor: Put the author and title first, followed by *Ed.* (meaning "edited by") and the name of the editor. However, if you cited something written by the editor rather than the author, see #10 below.

Cremattie, G. R. *Harper Year: What's Next?* Ed. F. R. Lilian.
London: Section A, 2012. Print.

7. Work in an anthology or chapter in an edited book: List the author and title of the selection, followed by the title of the anthology, the abbreviation *Ed.* for "edited by," the editor's name, publication data, and page numbers of the selection.

Baldwin, James. "Sonny's Blues." *The Broadview Anthology*
of Short Fiction. Eds. Julia Gaunce and Suzette Mayr.
Peterborough: Broadview, 2004. 148–168. Print.

8. Two or more items from one anthology: Include a complete entry for the anthology, beginning with the name of the editor(s). Each selection from the anthology that you are citing should have its own entry in the alphabetical list that includes only the author, title of the selection, editor, and page numbers.

Gaunce, Julia, and Suzette Mayr, eds. *The Broadview Anthology*
of Short Fiction. Peterborough: Broadview, 2004. Print.

Moore, Lorrie. "You're Ugly, Too." Gaunce and Mayr 276–290.

Print.

Robinson, Eden. "Queen of the North." Gaunce and Mayr

291–305. Print.

9. Signed article in a reference work: If an entry in an encyclopedia or dictionary is signed, cite the author's name, title of the entry (in quotation marks), title of the reference work (italicized), and publication information. If the entry is not signed, start with the title. (For well-known reference works, such as the *Encyclopædia Britannica,* the place and publisher can be omitted.)

Johal, R. D. "South Asian Diaspora in Fiction." *The New*

Dictionary of South Asian Literature. Vol. 6. Oakville:

Mosaic, 2012. 213–16. Print.

10. Preface, foreword, introduction, or afterword: When the writer of the part is different from the author of the book, use the word *By* after the book's title and cite the author's full name. If the writer of the part is the same as the author of the book, use only the author's last name after the word *By.*

Sharma, Petra. Foreword. *On the Side of the Angels.* By Marcel

Noyer. Montreal: Presse Egalité, 2012. iv–vi. Print.

Xiao, Ping. Introduction. *Vancouver.* By Xiao. Victoria:

WestCoast, 2009. 1–2. Print.

11. Translation: Cite the work under the author's name, not the translator's. The translator's name goes after the title, with the abbreviation *Trans.* (meaning "translated by").

Chu, Shun-Li, and Ping Xiao. *The Sun Still Sets in the East.* Trans.

J. S. Stowe. Vancouver: Douglas & McIntyre, 2011. Print.

12. Edition other than the first: If you are citing an edition other than the first, include the number of the edition: *2nd ed., 3rd ed.,* and so on. Place the number after the title, or if there is an editor, after that person's name.

Panassie, Hugues. *Piaf.* 2nd ed. New York: Knopf, 2003. Print.

13. Graphic narrative or illustrated book: In graphic narratives, the text and images are both equally important. For a work created by one person, format the works-cited entry like that of other non-periodical print publication.

> Akiro, Matsu. *Master Master.* Tokyo: Bungeishunju, 2009. Print.

For collaborative works, begin with the most relevant contributor (based on the focus of your research), followed by a label identifying his or her role.

> Declan, Cíaran. writer. *Candyland in Cyberspace.* Art by Vivienne
>
> Boutré. Vancouver: Anvil, 2009. Print.

In illustrated books, the works-cited format will depend on the function of the images within the body of work. For example, when illustrations complement a text (as in an illustrated version), the information about the illustrator appears *after the title* using the abbreviation "illus." ("Illustrated by"). If an editor or translator is also referenced, then put the names in the same order as the title page.

> Cordiega, Pau. *Exceptions to the Rules.* Trans. Trish Montera. Illus.
>
> Montse Gavalladá. Barcelona: Prensa Calle Dos, 2009. Print.

However, if you are referencing the illustrations and not the writer, start with the illustrator's name followed by *illus*, the title of the work, and then the author's name preceded by the word *By*.

> Gavalladá, Montse. illus. *Exceptions to the Rules.* By Pau
>
> Cordiega. Trans. Trish Montera. Barcelona: Prensa Calle
>
> Dos, 2009. Print.

14. The Bible: Give the version (italicized), the editor's name (if any), and the publication information.

> *New American Standard Bible*. La Habra: Lockman Foundation,
>
> 1995. Print.

15. Multivolume work: Your citation should indicate whether you used more than one volume of a multi-volume work. The first example indicates that the researcher used more than one volume of a three-volume work; the second shows that only the second volume of the work was used.

> Lissauer, Robert. *Lissauer's Encyclopedia of Popular Music in*
>
> *America*. 3 vols. New York: Facts on File, 1996. Print.

Lissauer, Robert. *Lissauer's Encyclopedia of Popular Music in America*. Vol. 2. New York: Facts on File, 1996. Print.

16. Book in a series: Put the name of the series and, if available on the title page, the number of the work at the end of the listing, after the medium of publication.

Uunglaut, Josiah A., ed. *Music from the Frozen North*. Fernie: Oolichan, 2009. Print. Contributions in Canadian Music Studies 128.

17. Republished book: Put the original date of publication, followed by a period, before the current publication data. In the following example, the writer cites a 2009 republication of a book that originally appeared in 1997.

Bender, Andrew. *Design Reality for Small Spaces*. 1997. Toronto: Key Porter, 2009. Print.

18. Title within a title: When a book's title contains the title of another book, do not italicize the second title. In the following example, the novel "Invisible Man" is not italicized.

O'Meally, Robert, ed. *New Essays on* Invisible Man. Cambridge: Cambridge UP, 1988. Print.

19. Unknown author: The citation begins with the title. In the list of works cited, alphabetize the citation by the first important word, not by articles like *A, An,* or *The*.

Webster's College Dictionary. New York: Random; New York: McGraw-Hill, 1991. Print.

Note that this entry includes both of the publishers listed on the dictionary's title page; they are separated by a semicolon.

16c PERIODICALS.

Periodicals are published at set intervals, usually four times a year for scholarly journals, monthly or weekly for magazines, and daily or weekly for newspapers. Between the author and the publication data are two titles: the title of the article, in quotation marks, and the title of the periodical, italicized.

20. Article in a journal paginated by volume: Many scholarly journals are published a few times each year and are then bound together into yearly volumes. When these journals are paginated by yearly volume, always include both the volume and issue number after the title. Give the year of publication in parentheses, followed by a colon, a space, the page numbers of the article, and medium. Place a period after the volume number and follow it with the issue number. In the example, the volume is 25 and the issue is number 4.

> Govan, Jennifer. "Adult Education in 21st Century Canada."
>
> *The Canadian Journal of Adult Education* 10.8 (2012):
>
> 713–30. Print.

21. Article in a journal paginated by issue: For scholarly journals paginated by issue, cite the issue number only.

> Lemieux, Thomas. "Newspeak Not so New." *Contemporary*
>
> *Literature* 4 (2010): 47–51. Print.

22. Article in a monthly/quarterly magazine: Provide the month and year, abbreviating the names of all months except May, June, and July.

> Bigge, Ryan. "Indie Won. Now What?" *Broken Pencil* Oct. 2010:
>
> 13–15. Print.

23. Article in a weekly magazine: Include the complete date of publication: day, month, and year.

> Madokku, Okinba. "Poems from Nigeria." *Voices* 6 Jan. 2011:
>
> 29–31. Print.

24. Signed article in a newspaper: Provide the day, the month, and the year. Omit any introductory article. If an edition is named on the masthead (the list of editors, etc. in a newspaper or magazine), specify the edition (*natl. ed.* or *late ed.,* for example) after the date and use a comma between the date and the edition. Whenever possible, give a section designation (*F* in the example) along with the page number. If the article appears on non-consecutive pages, put a plus (+) beside the first page number. Follow with the medium of publication.

> Coyle, Jim. "The Revolution Starts Here." *Toronto Star* 19 Feb.
>
> 2011: F1+. Print.

25. Unsigned article: The citation begins with the title and is alphabetized by the first word other than an article like *A, An,* or *The.*

"Canada, Oh No, Canada." *On Report* 2 Jan. 2011: 5. Print.

26. Review: Begin with the name of the reviewer and, if there is one, the title of the review. Add *Rev. of* (meaning "review of") and the title plus the author of the work being reviewed. Notice that the word *by* precedes the author's name.

Schmidtz, Androj. "Tradition vs. Innovation." Rev. of *Changing*

Assessment Tools in First Year Composition, by Gord

Roberts. *Teacher News* Aug. 2007: 12–18. Print.

27. Editorial: Treat editorials as articles, but add the word *Editorial* after the title. If the editorial is unsigned, begin with the title.

Shaw, Theodore M. "The Debate over Race Needs Minority

Students' Voices." Editorial. *Chronicle of Higher Education*

25 Feb. 2000: A72. Print.

16d OTHER PRINT SOURCES.

28. Government document: Either the name of the government and agency or the name of the author of the document comes first. If the government and agency name come first, follow the title of the document with the word *By* for a writer, *Ed.* for an editor, or *Comp.* for a compiler. Publication and medium information, abbreviated, comes last.

Canada. National Student Loan Service Centre. *Budget 2004:*

The Importance of Learning. Ottawa: Social Development

Canada, 2002. Print.

29. Pamphlet: Treat as you would a book. If the pamphlet has an author, list his or her name first; otherwise, begin with the title.

Hypertext and Text Speak. 2nd ed. Vancouver: ICBC, 2009. Print.

30. Conference proceedings: Cite as you would a book, but include information about the conference if it is not in the title.

Mendel, Arthur, Gustave Reese, and Gilbert Chase, eds. *Papers*

Read at the International Congress of Musicology held

at New York September 11th to 16th, 1939. New York:
Music Educators' National Conference for the American
Musicological Society, 1944. Print.

31. Published dissertation: Cite as you would a book, italicizing the
title and giving the place of publication, the publisher, and the year
of publication. After the title, add *Diss* for "dissertation," the name of
the institution, the year the dissertation was written, and medium.

> Fraser, Wilmot Alfred. *Jazzology: A Study of the Tradition in*
> *which Jazz Musicians Learn to Improvise.* Diss. U of
> Pennsylvania, 1983. Ann Arbor: UMI, 1987. Print.

32. Unpublished dissertation: Begin with the author's name, followed by the dissertation title in quotation marks, the abbreviation
Diss., the name of the institution, the year the dissertation was written, and medium.

> Murphy, Graham J. "Cy(ber)borgs and Netizens: (Re)Configuring
> the Post/Human Body in the Nodal Intersections of Scyber
> Fiction and Cyberspace." Diss. U of Alberta, 2002. Print.

33. Abstract of a dissertation: Use the format for an unpublished
dissertation. After the dissertation date, give the abbreviation *DA*
or *DAI* (for *Dissertation Abstracts* or *Dissertation Abstracts Interna-*
tional), then the volume number, the date of publication, the page
number, and medium.

> Quinn, Richard Allen. "Playing Together: Improvisation in
> Postwar American Literature and Culture." Diss. U of Iowa,
> 2000. *DAI* 61 (2001): 2305A. Print.

34. Published or broadcast interview: Name the person interviewed and give the title of the interview or the descriptive term
Interview, the by-line of the interviewer (if known and relevant), the
publication information, and medium.

> Peterson, Oscar. "An Interview with Oscar Peterson." Interview
> by Mike Hennessey. *Gallery* Sept. 1976: 34–40. Print.

35. Map or chart: Cite as you would a book with an unknown author.
Italicize the title of the map or chart, and add the word *Map* or *Chart*
following the title.

Rand McNally EasyFinder. Map. Toronto: Rand McNally Canada,
2011. Print.

36. Cartoon: Include the cartoonist's name, the title of the cartoon (if any) in quotation marks, the word *Cartoon*, the publication information, and medium.

Bradford, Jim. "Duty Can Exact a Terrible Price." Cartoon.
Canada Free Press Mar. 2005: 62. Print.

37. Advertisement: Name the item or organization being advertised, include the word *Advertisement*, indicate where the ad appeared, and give the medium.

Acting for the Senses. Advertisement. *Reality Check* 10 Mar.
2011: 67. Print.

38. Published letter: Treat like a work in an anthology, but include the date. Include the number, if one was assigned by the editor. If you use more than one letter from a published collection, follow the instructions for cross-referencing in #8.

Hughes, Langston. "To Arna Bontemps." 17 Jan. 1938.
Arna Bontemps–Langston Hughes Letters 1925–1967.
Ed. Charles H. Nichols. New York: Dodd, 1980. 27–28.
Print.

39. Personal letter: To cite a letter you received, start with the writer's name, followed by the descriptive phrase *Letter to the author*, the date, and then the form of the material (*TS* for typescript).

Goodman, Gene. Letter to the author. 15 Mar. 2011. TS.

To cite someone else's unpublished personal letter, see the guidelines in #40.

40. Manuscripts, typescripts, and material in archives: Give the author, a title or description of the material (*Letter*, *Notebook*), the date of composition, the form (*MS* if manuscript, *TS* if typescript), any identifying number, and the name and location of the institution housing the material.

Pierce, Lorne. Letter to Madge Macbeth. 21 Oct. 1939. TS. Box
3. Queen's University Archives, Kingston, ON.

16e   ELECTRONIC MEDIA.

The examples that follow are based on the updated guidelines for the citation of electronic sources in the (2008) *MLA Style Manual and Guide to Scholarly Publishing* and the (2009) *MLA Handbook for Writers of Research Papers*, seventh edition. As a rule, reference electronic sources in the same way as a fixed-media source; include all the same elements in the same order. As the MLA states, "Inclusion of URLs has proven to have limited value" (182). Only include a URL when the reader cannot locate the source without it or if your professor requires it.

Note: The Internet address for an electronic source is its uniform resource locator, or URL. The URL usually points you to the Web site or page; a DOI (*digital object identifier*) is an alphanumeric string that locates a specific article or document regardless of its location; and, the search string is an address created by the search engine to locate documents (*see Tab 5 for more details*). MLA style does not require the use of any of these; just note the format "Web" instead of "Print."

> URL: www.sanctiontext.ca

> DOI: Demain, Micheline. "Urban Youth." *Youth Studies Canada*
> 2.4 (2011): 19–31. doi:12.65398769876.76.5.007.

> Search String: http://www.google.com/search?sourceid=
> navclient&aq=t&ie=UTF-8&rlz=1T4SUNA_enCA765
> AA287&q=sanction+text

If you are providing a URL or a DOI in your citation, give it immediately following the date of access and enclose it in angle brackets, followed by a period. If you need to divide the URL between lines, divide it after a slash. Do not insert a hyphen in either address.

> Campbell, Sandra. "A Girl in a Book": Writing Marjorie Pickthall
> and Lorne Pierce. *Canadian Poetry* 39 (Fall/Winter 1996).
> Web. 12 Aug. 2011. <www.canadianpoetry.ca/cpjrn/
> vol39/girl_in_a_book.htm>.

41. Online scholarly project:

Entire Web site: Begin with the title (italicized) of the source, followed by the name of the editor (if any) and the electronic publication data, which includes, if relevant, the version number, the date of publication or update, the name of the sponsoring institution (if any), and the medium (Web). End with the date you used the project.

> *William Ransom Hogan Archive of New Orleans Jazz.* Ed. Bruce
>> Boyd Raeburn. 30 May 2000. Tulane. Web. 6 June 2000.

Part of a Web site: When citing one part, document, or page of a project, add the author (if known) and the title of the part in quotation marks. If the author is unknown, start with the title of the part in quotation marks.

> Raeburn, Bruce Boyd. "An Introduction to New Orleans Jazz."
>> *William Ransom Hogan Archive of New Orleans Jazz.* Ed.
>> Bruce Boyd Raeburn. 29 May 2000. Tulane U. Web.
>> 21 June 2000.

42. Professional or personal Web site: Name the person responsible for the site, the title of the site (italicized), the name of the associated institution or organization (if any), medium (Web), and date of access. If no title is available, use a descriptive term such as "Home page" (without italics or quotation marks).

> Fortier, Monique. *MusicPage.* Web. 12 Apr. 2009.

> Rubens, Melanie. Survey of Canadian Literature. Course
>> homepage. Jan.–Apr. 2010. Dept. of English–FCE. Seneca
>> College. Web. 12 June 2010.

If you are citing a home page for a course, substitute the name of the course for the title of the site, but do not underline or italicize it.

TECH **TIPS**

URL Addresses

Some popular word-processing programs such as Microsoft Word automatically turn all URLs into hyperlinks. The MLA recommends disabling this automatic hyperlinking before you print your document. To turn this feature off, go to "Tools"/"AutoCorrect"/"AutoFormat as You Type" and remove the checkmark next to "Internet and network paths with hyperlinks." Another way to do this is to right-click on each link and select "Remove Hyperlink."

43. Online book:

Entire book: Cite as for print books, including author; title (italicized); editor, translator, or compiler (if any); and publication data for the print version. Add, if available, the name of the database or project, date of electronic publication, sponsoring organization, medium (Web), and date of access.

> Morgan, Harry. *Cognitive Styles and Classroom Learning.*
>
> Westport: Praeger Publishing, 1997. *Questia.com.* 13
>
> Sept. 2004. Web. 27 Oct. 2005.

Work in an online book: If you use part of an online book, add the title of the part after the author and put it in quotation marks, unless the part cited is an introduction, foreword, preface, or afterword.

> Sandburg, Carl. "Chicago." *Chicago Poems.* New York: Holt,
>
> 1916. *Bartleby.com.* Aug. 1999. Web. 14 June 2000.

44. Article in an online periodical: Many newspapers, magazines, and scholarly journals are now available online. When citing a work from an online periodical, provide as much of the following information as is available: the writer's name; title of the work in quotation marks or a descriptive term (for example, *Editorial*); the name of the periodical, italicized; volume, issue, or other identifying number; publication date; total pages, paragraphs, or sections, if numbered; medium (Web); and date of access.

> "Bulletin Board; Louis Armstrong Centenary." *New York Times on*
>
> *the Web* 7 Nov. 2001. Web. 10 Dec. 2001.

> Kieran, Julie. "The Canadian Context: Monolingual Education in
>
> an 'Officially" Multilingual Country." *The Reading Matrix*
>
> 11.1 (2011). 16–33. Web. 10 Feb. 2011.

45. CD-ROM: Works on CD-ROM are usually cited like books or parts of books, but the term *CD-ROM* and the name of the vendor, if different from the publisher, are added before the publication data.

> "Music." *Microsoft Bookshelf 2000.* CD-ROM. Redmond:
>
> Microsoft, 1998.

46. Work from a library or personal subscription service: For material that you accessed through a library subscription service such as *Ebsco*, *InfoTrac*, and *Lexis-Nexis*, add the following to your citation: the name of the online service used; the medium (Web); and the date of access.

> Portian, David L. "Learning in a Virtual World: Why not all will
>
> succeed." *Adult Learning* 5 (2008): n. pag. *Expanded*
>
> *Academic ASAP. InfoTrac.* Web. 14 Feb 2009.

If you used a personal subscription service such as America Online, and you retrieved information by using a keyword or a topic path, identify the online service, the date accessed, and either the keyword used or the path taken. Use a colon after the capitalized words "Keyword" or "Path," and use semicolons to separate topics in the path.

> "Jazz." *Concise Columbia Electronic Encyclopedia.* 3rd ed. 1994.
>
> *America Online.* Web. 21 Apr. 2000. Path: Research
>
> and Learn; Encyclopedia; Columbia Concise; Louis
>
> Armstrong; Jazz.

47. Online posting: Begin with the author and (in quotation marks) the title or subject line; the words *Online posting*, without quotation marks or italics, follow. End with the posting date, the list or group name, the medium (Web); and the date of access. Include the e-mail address of the list's moderator if no URL is available.

> Grober, Cate. "Tarot for the Uninitiated." Online posting. 17 Mar.
>
> 2011. Holistic Healers. Web. 17 April 2011.

48. Blogs, Pods, and Wikis: Weblogs, Podcasts, and Wikipedia articles are generally documented using electronic-citation format. Basic entries normally include the contributor's name (if applicable), the title in double quotation marks, date of upload or last modification, type of upload or identifying label, publisher of the contribution, date posted, the medium (Web), and the date accessed. There is a certain amount of flexibility when sourcing these types of sites as not all the elements will be easily accessible or appear in the same consistent order in a list of Works Cited.

> Attes, J. K. "Bluetooth? BluRay?" 11 Mar. 2011. Weblog entry.
>
> Web. 21 Mar. 2011.
>
> "Memes." 10 Jan 2011. Podcast. *Webinar Inc.* Web. 5 Mar 2011.
>
> "Robert Hunter (journalist)." Wikipedia, The Free Encyclopedia. 16
>
> Jan. 2008. Wikimedia Foundation, Inc. Web. 26 Feb. 2008.

49. Synchronous communication: Include a description and the date of the event, the title of the forum, the medium (Web), and the date of access. If relevant, the speaker's name can begin the citation.

> Curran, Stuart, and Harry Rusche. Discussion: Plenary Log
>
> 6. Third Annual Graduate Student Conference in
>
> Romanticism. 20 Apr. 1996. Prometheus Unplugged:
>
> Emory MOO. Web. 4 Jan. 1999.

50. E-mail: Include the author; the subject line (if any), in quotation marks; the descriptive term *Message* plus the name of the recipient; the date of the message; and the medium of delivery.

> Banwait, Harjinder. "Re: Corrupt computer files." Message to
>
> Melanie Rubens. 3 December 2010. E-mail.

51. Online graphic, audio, video, or digital file: Base the form of your citation on the most closely related print or non-print model. When possible, include the creator's name, the title or description of the source, the title of the larger work in which the source appears (italicized), the publication data, the medium (Web), and the date of access.

> Greenpeace Canada. "Polluter Harmony: Pete and Janet's Story!"
>
> *YouTube*. 12 Feb. 2011. Web. 21 Feb. 2011.

For digital files, instead of the date of access, include the digital file format, followed by the word *file*.

> Canadian Centre for Policy Alternatives. *Our Schools/Our Selves*.
>
> Ottawa: CCPA, 2009. PDF file.

52. Computer software: Provide the author's or editor's name, if available, the medium, title (italicized), the version number, and the publication information, including place of publication, publisher, and date. If you downloaded the software from the Internet, replace the publication information with the medium (Web), and the date of access.

> *AllWrite! 2.1 with Online Handbook*. CD-ROM. Vers. 2.1. New
>
> York: McGraw-Hill, 2003.

16f   AUDIOVISUAL AND OTHER NON-PRINT SOURCES.

53. Film or videotape: Begin with the title (italicized). For a film, cite the director and the lead actors or narrator (*Perf.* or *Narr.*), followed by the distributor, year, and medium consulted. For a videotape or DVD, add the medium (*Videocassette* or *DVD*) before the name of the distributor.

> *Artists and Models.* Dir. Raoul Walsh. Perf. Louis Armstrong,
>
> Martha Raye, and Connie Boswell. Paramount Pictures,
>
> 1937. Film.

54. TV or radio program: Start with the episode title (in quotation marks), followed by the program title (italicized), the name of the series (if any), the name of the network, the city, the broadcast date, and the medium of reception.

> "Laughter and Lyrics." *New Voices.* CDFM, Dartmouth. 3 May
>
> 2009. Radio.

55. Sound recording: The entry starts with the composer, conductor, or performer, depending on your focus. Include the following information: the song or piece's title, if any (in quotation marks); the work's title (italicized); the artist(s), if not already mentioned; the manufacturer; the date of release; and the medium.

> Arcade Fire. "City With No Children." *The Suburbs.* Merge (US);
>
> Mercury (UK), 2010. CD.

56. Musical composition: Include only the composer and title, unless you are referring to a published score. Published scores are treated like books except that the date of composition appears after the title. Note that the titles of instrumental pieces are italicized only when they are known by name, not just by form and number, or when the reference is to a published score.

> Schaefer, Hal. *Hearing and Seeing is Believing.*

> Haydn, Franz Josef. Symphony No. 94 in G Major.

> Haydn, Franz Josef. *"Surprise" Symphony No. 94 in G Major.*
>
> 1791. Ed. H. C. Robbins Landon. Salzburg: Haydn-Mozart,
>
> 1965. Print.

57. Artwork: Provide the artist's name, the title of the artwork (italicized), the medium of composition, and the institution or private collection and city in which the artwork can be found.

> Hatt, Shari. *Untitled (Quitlcy).* Photograph. Canadian Museum of
>
> Contemporary Photography, Ottawa.

If you used a photograph of a work of art from a book, treat it like a work in an anthology (see #7), but italicize the titles of both the work and the book and include the institution or collection and city where the work can be found.

58. Unpublished interview: Begin with the person interviewed, followed by *Personal interview* (if you conducted the interview personally) and the date of the interview. (*See #34 for a published interview.*)

> Verity, Donna. Personal interview. 10 June 2011.

59. Lecture or speech: To cite an oral presentation, give the speaker's name, the title (in quotation marks), the name of the forum or sponsor, the location, the date, and the form of delivery.

> Haarkonsen, Juri. "The Ethics of Combustion." PK Centre
>
> for Environmental Studies, Morristown. 12 Apr. 2011.
>
> Address.

60. Performance. To cite a play, opera, ballet, or concert, begin with the title; followed by the authors (*By*); pertinent information about the live performance, such as the director (*Dir.*) and major performers; the site; the city; the performance date, and the medium (Performance).

> *The Secret Garden*. By Frances Hodgson Burnett. Dir. Anna
>
> Linstrum. The Royal Alexandra Theatre, Toronto. 17 Feb.
>
> 2011. Performance.

17 MLA Style: Notes— Footnotes and Endnotes

Notes are used to cite multiple sources for borrowed material or to give readers supplemental information. Their purpose is to avoid distracting readers with an overly long parenthetical citation or an interesting but not directly relevant idea. You can also use notes to acknowledge people who helped you with research and writing. Notes can be formatted either as footnotes at the bottom of a manuscript page or as endnotes on a separate page (titled "Notes") before the works-cited list. Identify each note with a superscript Arabic number in the text.

TEXT

When citing electronic sources, make sure to include as much information as possible.[1]

NOTE

[1] Boskya 22. In addition to the traditional models of assessment at the college level, newer, more progressive "virtual" options are becoming more accepted.

MLA Style: Paper Format

The following guidelines will help you prepare your research paper in the format recommended by the *MLA Style Manual and Guide to Scholarly Publishing*. For an example of a research paper that has been prepared using MLA style, see pp. 190–194.

61. Materials. Before printing your paper, make sure that you have a backup of your final draft somewhere besides your hard disk. Use a high-quality printer and good, white 8½-by-11-inch (216-by-279 millimetres) paper. Choose a standard 10- or 12-point font such as Courier, Times, or Bookman. Join the printed pages with a paper clip, not a staple, and do not use a folder or binder unless you have been told to do so by your instructor.

62. Heading and title. No separate title page is needed. In the upper left-hand corner of the first page, one inch (2.5 centimetres) from the top and side, type on separate, double-spaced lines your name, your instructor's name, the course number, and the date. Double-space between the date and the paper's title and the title and the first line of text, as well as throughout your paper. The title should be centred and properly capitalized (*see p. 171*). Do not italicize the title or put it in quotation marks or bold type.

63. Margins and spacing. Use one-inch (2.5-centimetre) margins all around, except for the right-hand top corner, where the page number goes. Your right margin should be ragged (not "justified," or even).

Double-space lines throughout the paper, including in quotations, notes, and the works-cited list. Indent the first word of each paragraph one-half inch (1.25 centimetres) from the left margin using the tab key. For block quotations, indent one inch (2.5 centimetres) from the left (two tabs or use the ruler to change the margin).

64. Page numbers. Put your last name and the page number in the upper right-hand corner of the page, one-half inch (1.25 centimetres) from the top and flush with the right margin.

65. Visuals. Place visuals (tables, charts, graphs, and images) close to the place in your text where you refer to them. Label and number tables consecutively (*Table 1, Table 2*) and give each one an explanatory caption or title; put this information above the table. The term *Figure* (abbreviated *Fig.*) is used to label all other kinds of visuals, except for musical illustrations, which are labelled *Example* (abbreviated *Ex.*). Place figure or example titles or captions below the visual. Below all visuals, cite the source of the material and provide explanatory notes as needed. *(For more on using visuals effectively, see Chapter 5: Document Design, pp. 58–70.)*

19 Student Paper in MLA Style

As a first-year college student, Melissa Thomas wrote the following paper for her Canadian studies course. Prior to writing the paper, Melissa had very little information about the Canadian music business. For this paper, she used government and industry resources.

½″ (1.25 cm)

1″ (2.5 cm)

Melissa Thomas

Professor Dineson

CAN609

10 May 2011

Canadian, eh? Not Really

1″ (2.5 cm)   Canada has increasingly drawn attention to itself through the success and development of its musicians. Canadians cherish homegrown talent and delight in the success of their own.

Superstars such as Céline Dion and Michael Bublé, internationally acclaimed bands like Sum 41 and the Barenaked Ladies have achieved superstar status inside and outside of the country.

Recording stars from Canada have taken their place on the world stage, but foreign-controlled corporations are reaping the benefits of Canadian music success ("Canadian in Name Only").

Unfortunately, as more of the world takes notice, Canadian performers still have to rely on non-Canadian distributors to promote their product.

Clearly, the music industry in Canada has grown incredibly.

Canadian Music Week, an industry conference and music festival, sees many of the big labels and buyers from the international music scene. "The CMW is a necessary and important venture for new or upcoming artists to showcase their talent in front of international buyers" (Foiré). It seems, however, that in order for an artist or band to be really successful in the music industry, they need to look to multinational firms for promotion.

The Canadian sound recording industry is dominated by six multinational firms (Warner, Sony, Polygram, BMG, EMI and MCA)—known collectively as the majors. They

Thomas 2

are vertically integrated and dominate the distribution of sound recordings in Canada. They also capture 80% to 90% of the Canadian market, with independent Canadian-owned companies capturing the remainder— 16% in the early nineties. Independent labels in Quebec capture 31% of that market, compared with about 10% for independents in the rest of Canada. (Chater and Robertson 56, 87)

Canada can produce high-end artists; it has always "had a pool of creative musical artists of the first order. Many Canadian lyricists, composers, musicians and performers have acquired an enviable national and international reputation, and have distinguished themselves in every genre of music" (Chater and Robertson 92). The sound recording industry, however, has suffered from neglect. One of the major issues is funding. The government decided to discontinue the FACTOR (Foundation to Assist Canadian Talent on Records) funding program. Graham Henderson, president of the Canadian Recording Industry Association, is encouraging Ottawa to renew the music fund. "Federal funding of the independent music community has directly lead to phenomenal success stories for decades. Artists whose careers were helped at the beginning by FACTOR have gone on to sell millions" (qtd. in Allman and Michael). The independent labels believe that the lack of government policy has resulted in a loss of major Canadian artists, contributing to the weakening of their companies. These companies, which continue to develop a diverse range of new Canadian talent, say that their financial capacity to do so has been increasingly compromised and that the lack of policy is affecting efforts to strengthen

Major problem identified.

Acronym explained.

In-text citation: Source quoted from a source.

Thomas 3

their firms (Kravits 33; Desfevre 81). Direct financial support
is vital for indie labels, and, without it recording opportunities
for emerging Canadian talent will be significantly diminished
(Pershar 10). Even established performers who started on the
indie circuit have had to sign with a major label in order to gain
worldwide recognition (Cameron 12).

In-text citation: Magazine article author named.

It is unfortunate that artists cannot stay with Canadian
labels and gain international favour. Despite Canada's "success
on the world charts" (Foiré), it will lose control of a cultural
industry without a stronger infrastructure that nurtures homegrown recording talent.

Impact and conclusion.

Works Cited

Allman, Catherine, and Kendra Michael. "The Canadian
Recording Industry Calls for Federal Support to Music
Industry: Renewal of Canadian Music Fund and Revision
of Copyright Act." *The Canadian Recording Industry
Association*. 24 Nov. 2004: n. pag. Web. 23 Mar. 2011.

Cameron, Sheena. "What is 'Canadian' about Canadian Music?"
Nuance Nov. 2010: 12–14. Print.

"Canadian in Name Only." *Music, eh?* 10 Jan, 2010: n. pag.
Web. 1 Apr. 2011.

Chater, Brian, and Brian Robertson. Department of Canadian
Heritage. *A Time for Action: Report of the Task Force on
the Future of the Canadian Music Industry*. Ottawa. 26
Feb. 2011. Web. 24 Mar. 2011.

Desfevre, Gilbert. "Economics of Canadian Cultural Artifacts."
Canadian Economic Review 2 (2009): 80–89. Print.

Thomas 4

Foiré, Didier. "CMW—A Must for New Bands." *La Musicologie.*
10 Feb. 2009: n. pag. Web. 25 Mar. 2011.

Kravits, C. D. "Canadian Business in Crisis." *Journal of New
Canadian Business* 10 (2009): 30–42. Print.

Pershar, Tyron. "Indie Music Needs Money." *Underground* ♫
Aug. 2010: 3–9. Print.

5

APA
DOCUMENTATION
STYLE

APA Documentation Style

APA STYLE: IN-TEXT CITATIONS: (CHAPTER 20)

APA STYLE: REFERENCES: (CHAPTER 21)

Instructors of social science and professional courses in psychology, sociology, political science, communications, education, and business usually prefer a documentation style that emphasizes the author and the year of publication, in part because the style makes it easy to tell if the sources cited are current.

WHAT IS THE AMERICAN PSYCHOLOGICAL ASSOCIATION?

The American Psychological Association (APA)—the largest psychological organization in the world—has developed a widely used version of the author-date style. It helps writers prepare and present scientific data, and it contains special sections on how to construct tables, how to present statistics, and how to cite scientific references. APA is most often consulted by students in behavioural and social sciences, education, social work, nursing, and business.

The information in Chapters 21–23 is based on the sixth edition of its *Publication Manual* (Washington, DC: APA, 2010).

APA documentation style has two mandatory parts:

- In text citations
- List of references

20 APA Style: In-Text Citations

When you use ideas, information, or words from a source, APA in-text citation format requires that you do the following:

- **Identify the author(s) of the source**, either in the sentence or in a parenthetical citation.

- **Indicate the year of publication of the source** following the author's name. The year goes in parentheses by itself if the author is named in the sentence. If the author is not named in the sentence, use the author's last name, then a comma, then the year in a parenthetical citation.

- **Include a page reference for a quotation or a specific piece of information.** Put a *p.* before the page number. If the author is named in the text, the page number appears in the parenthetical citation following the borrowed material. Page numbers are not necessary when you are summarizing the source as a whole or paraphrasing an idea found throughout a work. (*For more on summary, paraphrase, and quotation, see Tab 3: Researching, pp. 150–152.*)

TECH **TIPS**

FAQs on APA Style

For updates to the APA documentation system, check the APA-sponsored Web site at <www.apastyle.org>.

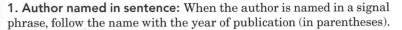

1. Author named in sentence: When the author is named in a signal phrase, follow the name with the year of publication (in parentheses).

> According to Verity (2010), communities of practice serve not
> only academics, but corporates as well.

2. Author named in parentheses: If you do not name the source's author in your sentence, then you must include the name in the parentheses, followed by the date and, if you are quoting directly or presenting a specific piece of information, the page number. The name, date, and page number are separated by commas.

> "It is the quality of the parenting, not the age of the parent that
> counts" (Harishana, 2011, p. 25).

3. Two to five authors: If a source has five or fewer authors, name all of them the first time you cite the source.

> As Singh, Naipour, and Johal (2012) suggest, "South Asian
> literature in English provides access to the region's historical and
> rich cultural heritage" (p. 112).

If you put the names of the authors in parentheses, use an ampersand (&) instead of *and*.

> "South Asian literature in English provides access to the region's
> historical and rich cultural heritage" (Singh, Naipour, & Johal,
> 2012, p. 112).

After the first time you cite a work by three or more authors, use the first author's name plus *et al.* Always use both names when citing a work by two authors.

> In addition, South Asian literature in English offers readers a
> look at the impact of modernization on regions in various stages
> of development (Singh et al., 2012, p. 114).

4. Six or more authors: In all in-text citations of a work by six or more authors, give the first author's name plus *et al.* In the reference list, however, list the first six authors' names, followed by *et al.* for all others.

> As Michaux et al. (2009) have stated, using scaffolding as a
> way to support at-risk youth has proven successful in many
> difficult cases.

5. Organization or group as author: Treat the organization or group as the author and spell out its name the first time the source is cited. If the organization is well known, you may use an abbreviation thereafter.

> The Environmental Safety Watch (2012) laments the extinction of so many plant and animal species.

> The Centre for Linguistic Diversity (2012) argues that any type of writing, even textspeak, furthers communication skills.

> Public service announcements are used to inform and direct people to specific programs (Social Development Canada [SDC], 2010).

In subsequent citations, as long as you are sure that readers will know what the abbreviation stands for, only the abbreviation and the date need to be given: (SDC, 2010).

6. Unknown author: When no author or editor is listed for a work, use the first one or two important words of the title. Use quotation marks for titles of articles or chapters and italics for titles of books or reports.

> Social networking has become "the single most important communication tool in recent history" ("TechToday," 2011, p. 64).

> Eco-literature or writing about nature in the 21st century is considered the "newest way to draw attention to the plight of our environment" ("Green Literature," 2009, p. 45).

7. Two or more authors with the same last name: If the authors of two or more sources have the same last name, always include the appropriate first initial, even when the year of publication differs.

> M. Sullivan (2011) states that all the equipment has been tested and found to comply with the limits for a Class B digital device.

8. Two or more sources cited at one time: When you are indebted to two or more sources for an idea, cite the authors in the order in which they appear in the list of references. Separate the two sources with a semicolon.

> Crises in the Middle East continue to affect the oil supply lines to the West (Faisir, 2011; "Oil Intl," 2012).

9. E-mail, letters, and conversations: To cite information received from unpublished forms of personal communication, such as conversations, letters, notes, and e-mail messages, give the source's initials and last name, and provide as precise a date as possible.

> According to G. Murphy (personal communication, March 4, 2011), cyberfiction is not to be considered the same as science fiction.

Note: Because readers do not have access to them, you should not include personal communications—e-mail, notes, and letters—in your reference list.

10. Indirect source: When referring to a source that you know only from reading another source, use the phrase *as cited in*, followed by the author of the source you actually read and its year of publication.

> A study by Seema (as cited in Singnurkar et al., 2011, p. 56) found that some South Asian literature is more accessible than others, dependent often on domestic publishing opportunities.

Note: The work by Seema would not be included in the reference list, but the work by Singnurkar et al. would.

11. Classical works: If a source has no publication date, cite in-text the author's name—or, if this is not available, the title—followed by a comma and *n.d.* for "no date." When the date of publication is not applicable (as in very old works), cite the year of translation used, preceded by *trans.*

> (I Ching, trans. 1951)

12. Electronic source: Cite an electronic source the same way you would a print source, with the author's last name and the publication date. If the document is a pdf (portable document format) file with stable page numbers, cite the page number as you would a print source. If the source has paragraph numbers instead of page numbers, use para. or ¶ instead of *p.* when citing a specific part of the source.

> According to Strangis (2012), Wealth Strategies Inc. will force CorporateClass into bankruptcy by the next quarter (para. 2).

Note: If the specific part lacks any kind of page or paragraph numbering, cite the heading and the number of the paragraph under that heading where the information can be found. If you cannot find the name of the author, or if the author is an organization, follow the appropriate guidelines for print sources (*see items #5 and #6 above*). If you cannot determine the date, use the abbreviation *n.d.* in its place: (Wilson, n.d.).

21 APA Style: References

APA documentation style requires a list of references where readers can find complete bibliographical information about the sources referred to in your paper. The list of references should appear at the end of your paper, beginning on a new page entitled "References."

21a GENERAL GUIDELINES FOR A LIST OF REFERENCES IN APA STYLE.

1. Begin on a new page.

2. Begin with the centred title References.

3. Include a reference for every in-text citation.

4. Put references in alphabetical order by author's last name.

5. Give the last name and initial(s) for each author. If there is more than one initial, use a space between them (J. K. Rowling rather than J.K. Rowling).

6. Put the publication year in parentheses following the author or authors' names.

7. Capitalize only the first word and proper nouns in titles. Also, capitalize the first word of the subtitle following the colon (even if it is *A*, *An*, or *The*).

8. Use italics for titles of books but not articles. Do not enclose titles of articles in quotation marks.

9. Include the city and publisher for books. You should always list the city and province/state using the two letter postal abbreviation without periods (Vancouver, BC). For internationally famous cities outside of North America (Beijing, Johannesburg, London, Tokyo, Paris, Mexico City, Berlin, etc.) no province/state is necessary.

10. Provide the name of the publisher, including the names of associations, university presses, and corporations. Do not

include terms like *Publishers, Co.,* or *Inc.,* but retain the words *Books* or *Press[es].*

11. Include the periodical name and volume number (both in italics) as well as the page numbers for a periodical article.

12. Separate the author's or authors' names, date (in parentheses), title, and publication information with periods.

13. Use a hanging indent. Begin the first line of each entry flush left, and use the ruler function (you can format the entire page at once) to create a hanging indent for all subsequent lines of an entry one-half inch (1.25 cm).

14. Double-space within and between entries.

21b BOOKS.

1. Book with one author:

> Davies, J. (2012). *In praise of suffering: The psychology and anthropology of emotional discontent.* London: Routledge.

2. Book with two or more authors:

> Nuunagulak, G., Brancé, M., & Dreuillet, J. (2009). *For sale: The great white north.* Yellowknife, NT: Northern Press.

> Yuk, K., & Hakem, K. (2011). *ReCrossing the bridge.* Fredericton, NB: Goose Lane.

3. Organization or group as author: To credit a subdivision like "Economics Department," put its name after the name of the parent organization. When the publisher is the same as the author, use the word "Author" instead of repeating the organization's name as the publisher.

> Centre for Linguistic Diversity. (2008). *Textspeak as the new standard.* Toronto, ON: Author.

4. Two or more works by the same author: List the works in publication order, the earliest first.

> Bryant, B. R. (2010). *The Canadian East Coast.* St. John's, NF: Breakwater Books.

> Bryant, B. R. (2011). *East Coast waterways.* St. John's, NF: Breakwater Books.

If the works were published in the same year, put them in alphabetical order by title and add a letter (*a, b, c*) to the year so that you can distinguish each entry in your in-text citations (*see item #15 below for an example related to periodicals*).

5. Book with editor(s): Add (*Ed.*) or (*Eds.*) after the name. If a book lists an author and an editor, treat the editor like a translator (*see item #7*).

> Damianno, D. D. (Ed.). (2011). *Privatization of Canada.*
>
> Vancouver, BC: Benton Institute.

6. Selection in an edited book or anthology: The selection's author, year of publication, and title come first, followed by the word *In* and information about the edited book. Note that the page numbers of the selection go in parentheses after the book's title.

> Sonnerson, K. J. (2009). The shifting reality of urban Canadian
>
> youth. In F. Gallagher (Ed.), *Canada at the crossroads* (pp.
>
> 66–89). Montreal, QC: McGill-Queen's University Press.

7. Translation: After the title of the translation, put the name(s) of the translator(s) in parentheses, followed by the abbreviation *Trans.*

> Brasseau-Crian, D., & Chanteau, F. (2012). *The downing of flight*
>
> *27* (G. LeFevre, Trans.). Montreal, QC: Baraka Books.

> Montero-Diez, A. (2009). *Gaudi's Barcelona* (G. Diego, Trans.).
>
> Vancouver, BC: Talon Books.

8. Article in a reference work: Some encyclopedias and similar reference works name the authors of individual selections. Begin with the author's name, if given. If no author is given, begin with the title of the selection.

> Uphadya, V. (2009). Biological reactants in non-evasive
>
> procedures. In *Biological Review* (Vol. 3, pp. 23–30).
>
> Thousand Oaks, CA: SAGE Publications.

9. Unknown author or editor: Start with the title. When alphabetizing, use the first important word of the title (excluding articles such as *The, A,* or *An*).

> *Home, sweet home.* (2009). Vancouver, BC: Rocky Mountain
>
> Books.

10. Edition other than the first: After the title, put the edition number in parentheses, followed by a period.

> Leung, J. (2009). *Nowhere to go—nowhere to live* (2nd ed.).
>
> Toronto, ON: James Lorimer.

11. One volume of a multivolume work: If the specific volume used has its own title, put it before the title of the whole work. Note that no period separates the parenthetical volume number and the title that precedes it.

> Lombard, S. (Ed.). (2008). The Danson decisions and
>
> amendments. In *The history of federal dangerous offender*
>
> *legislation and related laws: Criminal law in Canada* (Vol.
>
> 4). Whitby, ON: McGraw-Hill Ryerson.

12. Republished book:

> Le Bon, G. (1960). *The crowd: A study of the popular mind.* New
>
> York, NY: Viking. (Original work published 1895).

Note: In-text citations should give both years: "As Le Bon (1895/1960) pointed out..."

21c PERIODICALS.

13. Article in a journal paginated by volume: Do not put the article title in quotation marks, and do not use *pp.* before the page numbers. Italicize the title of the periodical and the volume number.

> Cooper, N. (2009). Policy and practice in Canadian social work.
>
> *Sociology Today, 12,* 27–35.

14. Article in a journal paginated by issue: Include the issue number (in parentheses). Notice that the issue number is not italicized as part of the journal's title.

> Blau, S., & Briggs, C. A. (2011). The role of forensic
>
> anthropology in Disaster Victim Identification (DVI).
>
> *Forensic Science International, 205*(1), 29–35.

15. Two or more works in one year by the same author: Alphabetize the works by title, and attach a letter to each entry's year of publication, beginning with *a,* then *b,* and so on. In-text citations must use the letter as well as the year so that readers know exactly which work is being cited.

> Bargello, M. (2010a). *Unemployment in first world countries? An overview* (Discussion Paper No. 299). Lyon, France: World Economic Institute.

> Bargello, M. (2010b). Impact of unemployment in developed countries. *Journal of Social Economics, 34*(5), 12–27.

Note: Also see #22 below, which explains the format for a report or working paper.

16. Article in a magazine: After the year, add the month for magazines published monthly or the month and day for magazines published weekly. Note that the volume number is also included, as it is for journals.

> Buttigieg, H. (2011, February). An organized you, a better you. *Home Décor and Renovations, 7*(2), 24.

17. Article in a newspaper: Use *p.* or *pp.* with the section and page number. List all page numbers, separated by commas, if the article appears on discontinuous pages: pp. C1, C4, C6. If there is no identified author, begin with the title of the article.

> Friesen, J. (2011, February 25). Canadian-born visible minorities earn less. *The Globe and Mail*, p. A2.

18. Editorial or letter to the editor: In brackets, add to the title a phrase describing the form of the source.

> Harvington, H. (2012, March 20). Not so visible minorities [Editorial]. *The SEA News,* Sec. 2, p. 6.

19. Unsigned article: Begin the entry with the title, and alphabetize it by the first important word (excluding articles such as *The, A,* or *An*).

> Year of the thousand cuts. (2010, June 16). *The Economic Times*, p. 34.

> Open source software. (2009, January 4). *Digital Concepts Magazine*, p. 90.

20. Review:

Browski, B. (2009). Science and the urban classroom. [Review
of the book *Science education in Canada; What it does not
teach,* by G. D. Kinnell]. *Current Review, 59,* 30–32.

Note: If the review is untitled, use the bracketed description in place
of a title.

21d OTHER PRINT AND AUDIOVISUAL SOURCES.

21. Government document: When no author is listed, use the government agency as the author.

Foreign Affairs and International Trade Canada (DFAIT). (2012).
Crises in the Middle East: Report to Canadians. Ottawa,
ON: Author.

22. Report or working paper: If the issuing agency numbered the
report, include that number in parentheses after the title.

Bargello, M. (2010a). *Unemployment in first world countries? An
overview* (Discussion Paper No. 299). Lyon, France: World
Economic Institute.

Note: For reports from a deposit service like the *Educational
Resources Information Center (ERIC),* put the document number in
parentheses at the end of the entry.

23. Conference presentation: Treat published conference presentations as a selection in a book (*see #6*), as a periodical article (*#13 or
#14*), or as a report (*#22*), whichever applies. For unpublished conference presentations, including poster sessions, provide the author, the
year and month of the conference, the title of the presentation, and
information on the presentation's form, forum, and place.

Sakoya, I. (2009, March). *First Nations funding in crises.* Paper
presented at the Second Annual Conference of Aboriginal
Peoples of Canada, Ottawa, ON.

Carter, J. (2009, March). *First Nations of Canada: An analysis
of economic prospects.* Poster session presented at the

Second Annual Conference of Aboriginal Peoples of
Canada, Ottawa, ON.

24. Unpublished dissertation or dissertation abstract: Canadian theses are available through Library and Archives Canada (LAC) at <nlc-bnc.ca/thesescanada/index-e.html>.

Barentsen, G. (1999). Where is the anti-nowhere league?
English romanticism and punk structure. (Unpublished
doctoral dissertation). York University.

25. Film, videotape, and recording: Begin with the cited person's name and, if appropriate, a parenthetical notation of his or her role. After the title, identify the medium in brackets, followed by the country and name of the distributor.

JRDN (2010). Like magic. On *IAMJRDN* [CD]. Toronto, ON:
Kuya Productions.

Taborrok, N. (Producer), & Sobol, J. (Director). (2010). *The
beginner guide to endings* [Motion Picture]. Toronto, ON:
Darius Films.

Junior Inc. (Producer). (2012). *Computer concepts and
unassumed algorithms* [DVD]. Available from
https://www.junior.net/videos/ccua

26. Television program: When citing a single episode, treat the scriptwriter as the author and the producer as the editor of the series.

White, K. (Writer), & De Lint, R. (Director) (2011). View to a
nursing home [Television series episode]. In D. Lesiuk
(Producer), *InSecurity*. Regina, SK: CBC.

When citing a whole series or specific news broadcast, name the producer as author.

White, K., Thompson, V., & De Lint, R. (Producers). (2011).
InSecurity. Regina, SK: CBC.

Bourgeon, R. (Executive Producer). (2010, July 1). *Les promesses*
[Television broadcast]. Montreal, QC: Private Broadcast.

27. Personal Communication: APA Style considers personal communication to include private letters, memos, personal interviews, some electronic communication, and telephone conversations. Since some of this type of communication is not recoverable (there is no permanent record of it), it is not included in the reference list. Instead, it is cited in text only.

> (F. S. Greenwood, personal communication, May 10, 2011).

21e ELECTRONIC MEDIA.

Referencing electronic media can be difficult because not all Internet sites include the information needed to locate the source accurately. As a rule, reference electronic media in the same way as a fixed-media source; include all the same elements in the same order then provide as much of the electronic retrieval information necessary to locate the specific document or page.

Evaluating the validity of online sources can be equally as challenging. Electronic publishing is not regulated by the same rules as traditional print media, which makes locating information like copyright or the author's name more difficult. Understanding the component parts of the *uniform resource locator* (URL or Internet address) will help you critically evaluate the source:

Figure 21.1 Components of a Uniform Resource Locator (URL).

- *Protocol* identifies the method by which a Web browser or Internet software exchanges data with a server. The most common protocols are *http* (hypertext transfer protocol), *https* (hypertext transfer protocol secure), and *ftp* (file transfer protocol).

- *Domain name* identifies the server on which the files reside. It is often the home page address of an organization.

- *Domain name extension* helps to determine the type of organization from which your information has come. It can identify an institution, an organization, a government, or a commercial site. It can also include provincial or country codes.

Because the Internet is dynamic, electronic documents are consistently moved, relocated, or restructured, resulting in broken hyperlinks. To overcome this problem, e-publishers are now assigning *digital object identifiers* (DOI) to scholarly articles and documents. A DOI is an identification system for eContent and is comprised of a unique alphanumeric string to identify a piece of intellectual property on a digital network, regardless of its current location.

28. Journal articles:

Article with a DOI: No database name or URL is required because the DOI functions as an identifier and a link to the content.

> Smith, M. (2011). Multiple property models of lexical categories.
>
> *Linguistics, 49*(1), 1–51. doi:10.1515/LING.2011.001

Article without a DOI:

> Zachery, J. (2012). Grey literature and academic publishing.
>
> *Tech Trends, 4*(5), 75–89. Retrieved from https://
>
> www.techtrends.edu.ca/ejournal/article/70/open

Note: If there is no DOI assigned and the reference was retrieved online, provide the URL of the home page.

Note: To cite an electronic version of an article from a print journal, use the standard format for a periodical article (*see #13*) and add *[Electronic version]* after the article title.

29. Electronic books:

> Danziger, E. A. (n.d.). *Diary of a teenage carnivore.* Available
>
> from http://www.ebooks.com/viewitem/asp?itemID=39

When the URL leads to information about how to obtain the source (rather than the source itself), use "Available from" instead of "Retrieved from."

30. Reference material:

Online dictionary:

> Paradigm. (n.d.). In *Merriam-Webster's online dictionary.*
>
> Retrieved April 6, 2011 from http://www.m-w.com/
>
> dictionary/

Online encyclopedia:

> Persaud, R. (2011). Giftedness explained. In *The Gifted in Canada*. Retrieved February 2, 2012 from http:// plato.xta.edu

Note: If the date of the latest update is not clear, include the retrieval date.

Note: Provide the home or index page URL for reference works.

Online handbook:

> Hypertext vs. Hypermind. (2011). In L. Hopertyn & J. Helwit (Eds.). *The new manual for digital linguistics online.* Retrieved March 3, 2011 from http://www.nmdigling.org/ htdt/index.shtml

Wiki:

> Julian Assange. (2011, February 27). In *Wikipedia, The free encyclopedia.* Retrieved March 2, 2011 from http:// en.wikipedia.org/wiki/Julian_Assange

31. Curriculum and course material:

Lecture notes:

> Noble, S. (2010). *Lecture 4: Politics in Canada.* Retrieved from Seneca College of Applied Arts & Technology Web site: http://bbol.senecac.on.ca/fce/lecturenotes.cfm

Curriculum guide:

> Minsky, J. (2010). Compassion fatigue: A review. Retrieved from Public Health Agency of Canada Web site: http:// www.phac-aspc.gc.ca/ compfatigue/html

32. Computer software:

> *AllWrite! 2.1 with Online Handbook.* (2003). [Computer software]. New York, NY: McGraw-Hill.

33. Grey literature: Grey (or gray) literature is commonly defined as documentary/scientific material issued by government, academics, business and industry in all formats, but is not commercially published. Grey literature is produced by government departments, corporations, advocacy groups, research institutes, for-profit and non-profit organizations, and trade groups. It targets the public as well as scholars and provides accessible and broad-based information.

Types of grey literature include:

Annual reports:

Bronridge. (2011). *Annual review and summary statements 2006.* Retrieved from http://www.bronridge.com/ar2011/ pdfs/summary_reports_2011.pdf

Public service announcements:

National Advisory Board on Mental Health (Producer). (2007). *Teen depression: The real deal* [Video file]. Retrieved from https://www.nabmh.gc/depress/PSARealDeal.html

Presentation slides:

Edquivst, J. (2010). *Northern peoples* [PowerPoint slides]. Retrieved from http://www.senecac.on.ca/~edquivst/ digest.html

Technical reports:

Taamiquit, J., Gorjivna, D., & Kalamquit, W. (2011). *High risk northern communities: Results from the 2010 National Survey* (Report No. 2011–231). Retrieved from the National Centre of Environmental Assessments: http://ncea-caen.ed.gc/pubs2011/ 2011231.pdf

Newsletter articles:

Grynshod, B. (2010, Spring). Writing across curriculum. *OnScene: Newsletter of the Language Institute, 4*(1). Retrieved from http://cpi.edu/onscene/docs/Newletter/ newsletter0034/Spring 2010.pdf

34. Online communities:

Messages posted to online forums, discussion groups, or newsgroups:

PowerPlay. (2011, June 6). Value added microeconomics. [Msg
4]. Message posted to alt.society.economic-dev message
board, archived at http://www.remarq.com/read/9755/
qSZ61SoC-vwH#LR

Note: If the author's full name is not available, use the screen name and provide the exact date of the posting. The subject line of the message or "thread" follows the date. Include an identifier in brackets after the title. Do not use italics for title.

Message posted to an electronic mailing list:

Quintero, J. (2010, December 17). Gradebook confusion [Msg
574839]. Message posted to PowerSchool Users Group
mailing list, archived at http://tech.groups.yahoo.com/
group/PSUG/message/574839

Weblog:

Lian, C. (2010, July 25). Health Canada's debacle part
VI. Message posted to http://bmimedical.blogspot.
com/2010/07/health-canadas-debacle-part-iii.html

Video Weblog:

Greenpeace Canada. (2007, April 12). Shame Canada! [Video file].
Video posted to http://youtube.com/watch?v=N192b7dg_h4

Newspaper article:

Kuitenbrouwer, P. (2011, February 26). A giant game of tag. *The
National Post.* Retrieved from http://news.nationalpost.com/
2011/02/26/peter-kuitenbrouwer-a-giant-game-of-tag/

Podcast:

DeVries, T. (Producer). (2011, August 1). *First of a kind* [Audio
podcast]. Podcast retrieved from http://www.originfirst
radio.com/

35. Web sites:

> Petrucci, K. (June 21, 2011). A simple guide to creating
>
> Facebook promotions. In *SocialMediaToday*. Retrieved
>
> June 28, 2011 from http://socialmediatoday.com/

36. Electronic Images: The basic format for citing an electronic image depends on how much information is available. Many web images do not have an author, title, or date, so you might have to look for this missing information by clicking the image or checking links under the image.

Basic Format:

> Butress, K. (photographer). (2011). *Autumn leaves and trees*
>
> [Photograph], Retrieved May 12, 2011 from http://world
>
> photos.com/buttress2011/pnum145352.htm

Basic Format (no author):

> Peonies in bloom [Photograph]. (2011). Retrieved April 22,
>
> 2011 from: http://www.dver.org/pe/bloom31/10.htm

Basic format (no author, title, or date):

> [Untitled photograph of Los Cabos]. Retrieved November 12,
>
> 2010 from: http://syd.fr.net/nm54/beach/beach4.htm

21f APA FOOTNOTES.

APA discourages the use of explanatory content notes to supplement the ideas in a paper, but they are an option. If you decide it is necessary to include a few content notes, double-space the notes on a separate page with the centred title "Footnotes." Indent the first line of each note half an inch with all lines after the first flush with the left margin (use the ruler tool for this). Most word processors have an automatic function to add footnotes (see the "References" menu in Word), which is useful, as the note number is automatically tied to its correct footnote. If you move text around, the notes renumber automatically.

APA Style: Paper Format

The following guidelines will help you prepare your research paper in the format recommended by the *Publication Manual of the American Psychological Association,* sixth edition. For an example of a research paper that has been prepared using APA style, see pp. 216–224.

Materials. Before printing your paper, make sure that you have a backup of your final draft somewhere besides your hard disk. Use a high-quality printer and good white 8½-by-11-inch paper (about 216 by 279 mm). Choose a standard 12-point font such as Times New Roman or Bookman. Do not justify your text or hyphenate words at the right margin; it should be ragged.

Title page. The title page includes title, running head, author's name (by-line), and institutional affiliation (for professional papers an author's note is also included). Make the first page of your paper the title page and start the numbering at 1. The running head (an abbreviated title—50 characters or less including spaces and punctuation) appears flush left in uppercase letters at the top of all pages in the paper. Centre the title between the left and right margins in the upper half of the page, and put your name a few lines below the title. Instructors may also want you to include the course number and title, the instructor's name, and the date (*See p. 217 for an example*).

Margins and spacing. Use one-inch (2.5-centimetre) margins all around, except for the right-hand top corner, where the page number goes.

Double-space your text throughout the paper, including in the abstract, within any notes, and in the list of references. Indent the first word of each paragraph one-half inch (one tab).

For quotations of more than forty words, use block format and indent half an inch from the left margin. Double-space the quoted lines.

Page numbers and abbreviated titles. All pages, including the title page, should have a number preceded by a short (one- or two-word) version of your title. Put this information in the upper right-hand corner of each page, about one-half inch (1.25 cm) from the top.

Abstract. Instructors sometimes require an abstract—a 75-to-100-word summary of your paper's thesis, major points or lines of development, and conclusions. The abstract appears on its own numbered page, entitled "Abstract," and is placed right after the title page. (*For more on abstracts, see Tab 2: Common Assignments, p. 108.*)

Headings. Although headings are not required, most instructors of social science and professional courses welcome them. The primary headings should be centred, and all key words in the heading should be capitalized. Do not use a heading for your introduction. You can also use secondary headings if you need them; they should be italicized and flush left.

Visuals. Place visuals (tables, charts, graphs, and images) close to where you refer to them. Label each visual as a table or a figure, and number each kind consecutively ("Table 1," "Table 2"). You will also need to provide an informative caption for each visual. Cite the source of the material, preceded by the word *Note* and a period, and provide explanatory notes as needed.

23 Student Paper in APA Style

Judith Applebaum researched and wrote the following paper on compassion fatigue for a course in her nursing program. Because some of the most relevant information comes from "front-line" sources, Judith consulted an expert in the field (Kargach) and included the information provided with an in-text citation. Since this paper was meant to be reviewed by people in the health care profession, some of the medical terminology has not been defined.

COMPASSION FATIGUE 1

Compassion Fatigue: Consequences for

Health Care Professionals

Judith Applebaum

Athabasca University

Abstract

Compassion fatigue, a type of burnout experienced by many in service professions, can be detrimental to an individual's overall mental and physical health. The resulting exhaustion can have a significant impact on job performance and professionalism as well as personal relationships. Focusing on healthcare workers, this paper will discuss the implications of compassion fatigue on professional and personal behaviours as well as how early intervention can prevent it, resulting in mutually beneficial improved job performance for the worker and his or her clients.

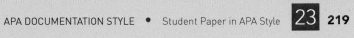

½" (1.25 cm)

Compassion Fatigue   1" (2.5 cm)   3

Compassion Fatigue: Consequences for

Health Care Professionals

" (2.5 cm)   Compassion fatigue—believed to come from the "profes-

sional liability of caring too much"—is a form of burnout that if

left unattended has the potential to lead to the development of

Secondary Post Traumatic Stress Disorder. Compassion fatigue is

characterized by physical and psychological exhaustion resulting

from excessive professional demands (Altholz, Dziegielewski, &

Leon, 1999). These demands together with the coexisting stress-

ors of daily life can result in the depletion of available personal

resources. Understanding the potential for development of this

concept, and early intervention to prevent a full-blown symptom-

atology, can result in a healthier and happier work force, and,

consequently, in better care provided for the clients.

The concept of compassion fatigue has been around since

1992. It appeared as a term in a nursing magazine in relation

to nurses who were worn out by the daily hospital emergen-

cies (Figley, 2000). Compassion fatigue may manifest itself

differently in each person; however, it carries some common

characteristics as noted among health professionals. Figley

identified five major symptoms associated with compassion

fatigue in 1995:

1) Decreased concern for the client

2) Decrease in positive feelings or empathy for the client

3) Physical and emotional exhaustion

4) Decreased job satisfaction

5) Feelings of hopelessness related to the job and spilling

over into other areas of the individual's life.

Full title repeated on first page only.

Introduces topic and key question.

Short thesis, answers question.

Notice the use of medical terminology.

Provides background to establish context for the information.

Points are set off in a numbered list for emphasis.

Compassion Fatigue   4

Identifies
some of the
causes related
to this topic.

If left untreated, compassion fatigue may eventually lead to absenteeism, apathy towards one's job, and unhappiness with life in general. In the most severe cases, it could lead to the development of Secondary Traumatic Stress Disorder. The phenomenon of compassion fatigue is not unique to nurses. It can develop among any direct service workers. Compassion fatigue appears to be presently "flourishing" (Gilley & Pfifferling, 2000) among family physicians, due to increased demands of today's health care. Physicians see more patients and do more administrative work around their client's care, while also trying to keep up with numerous new developments in medicine. Many of them find themselves in an endless spiral of burnout that pulls them down slowly (Gilley & Pfifferling, 2000).

Another area where compassion fatigue concept is documented is in a perioperative setting. Perioperative nurses, especially those working in trauma centres, experience more exposure to major traumatic events in their practice (Figley, 2000). The psychological reaction of nurses providing trauma care was compared to the responses of those individuals who experienced trauma first hand. Being exposed to the results of traumatic events that nurses themselves did not witness, they were not always able to achieve a desired outcome in their care of the casualties. This resulted in the development of compassion fatigue (Altholz et al., 1999). Other groups at risk of developing this type of burnout are police officers, firefighters, social workers, and personal caregivers. Teachers, paramedics, and air traffic controllers could be included as well.

APA in-text
citation:
Author, date.

Working with chronically ill patients or a newly diagnosed disease and dealing with the related issues of mortality and decline in health significantly increases the risk of developing compassion fatigue. Nurses become more attuned to these issues regarding themselves and their loved ones. As nurses become sensitive to the changes and reactions of their clients to the aging process, counter-transferral occurs (Altholz et al., 1999). Feelings of one's own aging and mortality may interfere with care provided and lead to compassion fatigue.

For example, if the nurse takes care of her own aging parents as well as the elderly clients at work, the nurse may start to experience feelings similar to those of the people in her care—and start to relate these feelings to her personal experience instead of the client's (Altholz et al., 1999). Figley (2002) called these phenomena of over-identifying with the clients "emotion contagion." Figley, as quoted in Altholz et al. (1999), says that the more the worker identifies the client's situation as her own, the greater the chances of the helping professional experiencing emotion similar to the older person and/or their family. Stated simply: "The greater the degree to which the helper has unsolved trauma and the longer the exposure to the suffering of the clients the greater the possibility of compassion fatigue" (Altholz et al., 1999). Several factors can contribute to the development of compassion fatigue in nurses working with the elderly. These can be both external—coming from the system nurses work in—and internal—coming from the client issues and the nurse's personal issues. Some of the external factors are:

    1)   Serving clients who suffer from chronic illness, both physical and mental. Those illnesses may be combined in the elderly population.

Compassion Fatigue   6

2) The labour-intensive nature of the helping
   relationship.

3) Lack of services and pressure to cut costs in
   today's health care system (Altholz et al., 1999).

Besides the external factors, there are also internal factors
associated with the nurses themselves (Altholz et al., 1999).

1) Emphatic ability. Ironically, the more empathetic
   the nurses are, the higher their risk of developing
   compassion fatigue (Figley, 2000)

2) Degree of satisfaction in one's work. Feeling that
   the services provided are not sufficient and/or did not
   bring the desired outcome may result in feelings of
   inadequacy as a nurse.

3) Taking care of the one's own aging parents or dealing
   with serious illness in one's family.

It is crucial that individuals who work in the health field
build support through interpersonal relationships with other
professionals. In addition, the health care providers must ensure
that they are:

- mentally healthy to begin with
- interact in positive and professional ways with
  colleagues
- stay flexible and be ready for the unexpected
- learn what resources and people within the community
  to whom they can make referrals
- be mindful of the influence of non-verbal actions that
  lend support to those in need, from giving them tissues
  to offering them symbols of comfort

Compassion Fatigue   7

- take care of themselves through physical exercise, keeping a journal, eating properly, and debriefing regularly (Thompson, 2003)

The potential for burnout and the development of compassion fatigue in working in healthcare cannot be entirely eliminated but there are ways to reduce the impact of this distressing phenomenon. Most important is the education of future and current nurses. Nurses need to be familiar with signs and symptoms of compassion fatigue in order to be able to identify the problem in its early stages. The development of this type of a burnout should not be viewed as failure to provide adequate care but rather as a signal to address the issues (Kargach, personal communication, April 2005).

Because this type of resource is not recoverable, it only appears in-text and not on the References list.

Compassion fatigue needs to be discussed in work places via in-services as a part of stress management education. The caregivers need to be educated in the unique needs of the patient and in setting realistic goals for care. One of the ways in which a workplace can be made more supportive to caregivers in risk of developing compassion fatigue is by providing many opportunities for nurses to share their thoughts and feelings. In this way, nurses can draw upon each other's strength and resources in order to cope with the stressors that may lead to compassion fatigue.

Last but not least, it is crucial that nurses learn to take care of themselves. Taking time out to pursue personal interests—be they social (such as time with friends), physical (such as exercise), spiritual, or any other activity which helps the caregiver relax and regenerate—may well be the recipe to ward off compassion fatigue.

Compassion Fatigue   8

    Although compassion fatigue is a relatively new concept, it is indeed a serious enough concern (especially in such high-risk areas as geriatrics emergency) to merit both serious consideration and prevention measures. The lack of education concerning the concept may lead to the development of full-blown fatigue syndrome. Therefore, early intervention through the education of nurses—both new and experienced—is imperative to the prevention of compassion fatigue. Investing in measures to decrease the incidence of this type of burnout among nursing staff (and, indeed, all caregivers) will definitely pay off—for institutions, clients, and the caregivers themselves.

References

Altholz, J. A., Dziegielewski, S. F., & Leon, A. M. (1999). Compassion fatigue: Considerations for working with the elderly. *Journal of Gerontological Social Work, 32*(1), 43–59.

Figley, C. R. (2000). *Compassion fatigue: An introduction.* Retrieved from http://www.giftfromwithin.org/html/cmpfatig.html

Gilley, K., & Pfifferling, J. H. (2000). Overcoming compassion fatigue. *Family Practice Management, 7*(4), 39–47.

Thompson, R. (2003). Compassion fatigue: The professional liability for caring too much. Public Entity Risk Institute. Retrieved from https://www.riskinstitute.org

6

CHICAGO
DOCUMENTATION
STYLE

6 Chicago Documentation Style

DIRECTORY OF CHICAGO STYLE

There are many documentation styles besides MLA (*see Tab 4*) and APA (*see Tab 5*). In this section, we cover *Chicago Manual* style. Please see online for two other styles developed by the Council of Science Editors (CSE), and the Columbia Online Style (COS). You can also learn about other style types by consulting the list of style manuals on page 159. If you are not sure which style to use, ask your instructor.

Chicago Documentation Style 24

The note and bibliography documentation style presented in the sixteenth edition of *The Chicago Manual of Style* (Chicago: University of Chicago Press, 2010) is used in many disciplines, including history, art, philosophy, business, and communications. The *Chicago* style has three parts:

- Numbered in-text citations
- Numbered footnotes or endnotes
- A bibliography of works consulted

TECH **TIPS**

FAQs on Chicago Style

For updates and answers to frequently asked questions (FAQs), go to the *Chicago Manual*'s Web site at <www.chicagomanualofstyle.org/home.html> and click on "Chicago Manual of Style FAQ."

The first two parts are necessary; the third is optional, unless your instructor requires it. (*Chicago* also has an alternative author-date system that is similar to APA style.) For more information on *Chicago* style, consult the *Manual of Style* or *A Manual for Writers of Term Papers, Theses, and Dissertations*, sixth edition, by Kate L. Turabian (Chicago: University of Chicago Press, 1996).

Deciding which documentation style to use. Always check with your instructor if you are not sure which documentation style to use. Each of the styles presented in this book is academically sound, and any one of several styles could provide the guidance you need to document your sources. The style choice is often guided by the discipline or the preference of the professor.

24a CHICAGO STYLE: IN-TEXT CITATIONS AND NOTES.

Information referenced from an external source is identified by a superscript number in the text [1] at the end of the borrowed material. These superscript numbers are placed after all punctuation marks except for the dash.

> As Kristakis points out, multinational major labels are better
>
> able to withstand economic changes in the music industry than
>
> smaller, indie labels.[1]

Each in-text superscript number must have a corresponding note either at the foot of the page or at the end of the text. Footnotes begin with the number and are single-spaced, with a double space between notes. If you are using the "footnote/endnote" function, keep in mind that this feature automatically formats the numbers both in the text and in the note.

TECH **TIPS**

Superscript Numbers

To find the superscript option in your computer's word-processing program, click on "Format" on your tool bar and then choose "Font." Superscript is one of many font options. In Word, the superscript function may also appear on your screen as the "x^2" button.

If you are using endnotes instead of footnotes, they should begin after the last page of your text on a new numbered page entitled "Notes." Endnotes are also single-spaced, with a double space between them.

The first time a source is cited in either a footnote or an endnote, include a full citation. Subsequent citations require only the author's last name and a page number.

FIRST REFERENCE TO A SOURCE

1. Carmen Bialys, *Holism* (Vancouver: Ronsdale Press, 2011), 127.

ENTRY FOR A SOURCE ALREADY CITED

6. Bialys, 127.

24b CHICAGO STYLE: BIBLIOGRAPHY.

Some instructors require a separate list of works cited or of works consulted. If you are asked to provide a works cited list, then use a separate, numbered page with the title "Works Cited." If the list is supposed to include works consulted as well as cited, then title it "Bibliography."

General Guidelines for a Bibliography or a Works Cited List in Chicago Style

1. Begin on a new page.
2. Begin with the centred title Works Cited if you are including only works referred to in your paper. Use the title "Bibliography" if you are including every work you consulted.
3. List sources alphabetically by author's (or editor's) last name.
4. Capitalize the first and last words in titles as well as all important words and the first word of the subtitle (following the colon) even if it is *A*, *An*, or *The*.
5. Use a hanging indent: indent all lines except the first of each entry one-half inch (1.25 cm) using the ruler function.
6. Use periods between author and title as well as between title and publication data.
7. Single-space each entry; double-space between entries.

24c SAMPLE CHICAGO-STYLE NOTES AND BIBLIOGRAPHY ENTRIES.

Books

1. Book by one author:

NOTE

1. Anosh Irani, *The Song of Kahunsha* (Toronto: Doubleday, 2007), 23.

BIBLIOGRAPHY

Irani, Anosh. *The Song of Kahunsha*. Toronto: Doubleday, 2007.

2. Multiple works by the same author: After providing complete information in the first footnote, include only a shortened version of the title with the author's last name and the page number in any subsequent footnote. In the bibliography, list entries in either alphabetical order by title or chronological order from earliest to latest. After the first listing, replace the author's name with three M-dashes (in Word, found in the symbols list on the insert menu).

NOTE

7. Irani, *Song of Kahunsha,* 276.

12. Irani, *Cripple and His Talisman,* 78.

BIBLIOGRAPHY

Irani, Anosh. *The Song of Kahunsha*. Toronto: Doubleday, 2007.

———. *The Cripple and His Talisman*. Vancouver: Raincoast Books, 2005.

3. Book by two or more authors: In notes, you can name up to three authors. When there are three authors, put a comma after the first name and a comma plus *and* after the second.

NOTE

2. Don Tapscott and Anthony D. Williams, *Wikinomics: How Mass Collaboration Changes Everything* (New York: Portfolio, 2008), 47.

BIBLIOGRAPHY

Tapscott, Don, and Anthony D. Williams, *Wikinomics: How Mass Collaboration Changes Everything.* New York: Portfolio, 2008.

When more than three authors are listed on the title page, use *et al.* after the first author's name in the note.

NOTE

3. Jacinta Fuentes et al., *Psychopathologies in Hispanic Immigrant Women* (Toronto: University of Toronto Press, 2009), 467.

BIBLIOGRAPHY

Fuentes, Jacinta, Marisol DeSousa, Pilar Xavier, and Veena Serapia. *Psychopathologies in Hispanic Immigrant Women.* Toronto: University of Toronto Press, 2009.

Notice that *et al.* is not used in bibliography entries, even when a book has more than three authors.

4. Book by an author and an editor or a translator: Put the author's name first and add the editor's (*ed.*) or translator's (*trans.*) name after the title.

NOTE

4. Jay Grosman, *Everyday Math,* ed. P. Chan (Vancouver: Pacific Educational Press, 2010), 47.

BIBLIOGRAPHY

Grosman, Jay. *Everyday Math.* Edited by P. Chan. Vancouver: Pacific Educational Press, 2010.

BIBLIOGRAPHY

Montero, P. *Barcelona in Transition.* Translated by Jordi Conterrá. Barcelona: Prensa Catalana, 2011.

5. Book with editor(s):

NOTE

5. Marianne Patrine, ed., *Channels of Discourse.* (Black Point, NS: Fernwood Publishing, 2012), 123.

BIBLIOGRAPHY

Patrine, Marianne, ed., *Channels of Discourse*. Black Point, NS: Fernwood Publishing, 2012.

6. Organization or group as author (and publisher):

NOTE

6. Canadian Race Relations Foundation (CRRF), *Silence is Acceptance* (Toronto: CRRF, 2009), 45.

BIBLIOGRAPHY

Canadian Race Relations Foundation (CRRF). *Silence is Acceptance*. Toronto: CRRF, 2009.

7. Work in an anthology or part of an edited book: Begin with the author and title of the specific work or part.

NOTE

7. James Baldwin, "Sonny's Blues," in *The Broadview Anthology of Short Fiction*, eds. Julia Gaunce and Suzette Mayr (Peterborough: Broadview Press, 2004), 148.

NOTE

8. David Suzuki, foreword to *Water: The Essence of Life*, by Mark Niemeyer (London: Duncan Baird, 2008), vii.

BIBLIOGRAPHY

Baldwin, James. "Sonny's Blues." *The Broadview Anthology of Short Fiction*, eds. Julia Gaunce and Suzette Mayr, 148. Peterborough: Broadview Press, 2004.

BIBLIOGRAPHY

Suzuki, David. Foreword to *Water: The Essence of Life*, by Mark Niemeyer. London: Duncan Baird, 2008.

In notes, the descriptive terms *foreword, introduction, preface,* and *afterword* are not capitalized. In bibliography entries, these descriptive terms are capitalized.

8. Article in an encyclopedia or a dictionary: For well-known reference works, publication data can be omitted from a note, but the edition or copyright date should be included. There is no need to include page numbers for entries in reference works that are arranged alphabetically; the abbreviation *s.v.* (*sub verbum*, meaning "under the word") plus the entry's title can be used instead.

NOTE

9. S. P. Meryn, "First World War Nursing," in *The Canadian Encyclopedia* (Toronto: Historica-Dominion Institute, 2009).

NOTE

10. *Encyclopedia Britannica,* 15th ed., s.v. "English."

Reference works are not listed in the bibliography unless they are unusual or crucial to your paper.

BIBLIOGRAPHY

Meryn, S. P. "First World War Nursing," in *The Canadian Encyclopedia.* Toronto: Historica-Dominion Institute, 2009.

9. The Bible: Abbreviate the name of the book, and use Arabic numbers for chapter and verse. Name the version of the Bible cited only if it matters, and do not include the Bible in your bibliography.

NOTE

11. Eccles. 8:5 Jerusalem Bible.

10. Edition other than the first: Include the number of the edition after the title or, if there is an editor, after that person's name.

NOTE

12. E. Portos, *Refuse to Be,* 2nd Canadian ed. (Toronto: Dundurn Press, 2012), 56.

BIBLIOGRAPHY

Portos, E. *Refuse to Be.* 2nd Canadian ed. Toronto: Dundurn Press, 2012.

11. Multivolume work: Put the volume number, followed by a colon, before the page number.

NOTE

13. David Sloly, *Virtual Space* (Ottawa: University of Ottawa Press, 2011), 6:30–34.

BIBLIOGRAPHY

Sloly, David. *Virtual Space.* Vol. 6. Ottawa: University of Ottawa
Press, 2011.

12. Work in a series: Include the name of the series as well as the
book's series number.

NOTE

14. Deanne deMuette, ed., *Voices of Acadia,* Contributions
in French Canadian Studies, no. 12 (Sydney, NS: Cape Breton
University Press, 2009), 6.

BIBLIOGRAPHY

deMuette, Deanne, ed., *Voices of Acadia.* Contributions in
French Canadian Studies, no. 12. Sydney, NS: Cape Breton
University Press, 2009.

13. Unknown author: Cite anonymous works by title and alphabetize them by the first word, ignoring *A, An,* or *The.*

NOTE

15. *The British Album* (London: John Bell, 1790), 2:43–47.

BIBLIOGRAPHY

The British Album. Vol. 2. London: John Bell, 1790.

Periodicals

14. Article in a journal paginated by volume: Many scholarly
journals are issued a few times each year, and the issues are bound
together to make yearly volumes. When journals are paginated by
yearly volume, your citation should include the following: author, title
of article in quotation marks, title of journal, volume number and
year, page number(s).

NOTE

16. Lilian Frances, "Rules are Meant to be Broken,"
Journal of Language History 14 (2012): 34.

BIBLIOGRAPHY

Frances, Lilian. "Rules are Meant to be Broken." *Journal of
Language History* 14 (2012): 34–35.

15. Article in a journal paginated by issue: If the periodical is paginated by issue rather than by volume, add the issue number, preceded by the abbreviation *no.*

NOTE

17. Sumeet Dang, "Intellectual Property Rights," *Legal Issues* 2, no. 1 (2012): 19.

BIBLIOGRAPHY

Dang, Sumeet. "Intellectual Property Rights." *Legal Issues* 2, no. 1 (2012): 19–28.

16. Article in a magazine: Identify magazines by week (if available) and month of publication.

NOTE

18. Natasha Morris, "Sanctuary," *Pagan Practice,* December 2011, 12–15.

BIBLIOGRAPHY

Morris, Natasha. "Sanctuary." *Pagan Practice,* December 2011: 12–15.

If the article cited does not appear on consecutive pages, do not put any page numbers in the bibliography entry. You can give specific pages in the note, however.

NOTE

19. Tasmin Jarvik, "Going Green?" Ideas, 7 August 2009, 45, 47.

BIBLIOGRAPHY

Jarvik, Tasmin. "Going Green?" *Ideas,* 7 August 2009.

17. Article in a newspaper:

NOTE

20. Dave Deibert, "Grand Prix showdown has MMA world abuzz," *The Montreal Gazette,* 19 February 2011, S1.

BIBLIOGRAPHY

Deibert, Dave. "Grand Prix showdown has MMA world abuzz." *The Montreal Gazette,* 19 February 2011: S1.

Other Sources

18. Review:

NOTE

21. Payton Seimers, "Canadian performers—Virtual stars," review of *Canadian Music Strong and Free*, by Terry Lynne, *Musicbox*, January 2010, 27.

BIBLIOGRAPHY

Seimers, Payton. "Canadian performers—Virtual stars." Review of *Canadian Music Strong and Free*, by Terry Lynne. *Musicbox*, January 2012: 26–31.

19. Interview: Start with the name of the person interviewed, and note the non-print medium (tape recording, video). Only interviews accessible to your readers are listed in the bibliography.

NOTE

22. Oscar Peterson, "An Interview with Oscar Peterson," interview by Mike Hennessey, *Gallery*, September 1976, 35.

BIBLIOGRAPHY

Peterson, Oscar. "An Interview with Oscar Peterson." Interview by Mike Hennessey. *Gallery*, September 1976: 34–40.

20. Government document: If it is not already obvious in your text, name the country first.

NOTE

23. National Student Loan Service Centre, *Budget 2004: The Importance of Learning* (Ottawa: Social Development Canada, 2002).

BIBLIOGRAPHY

Canada. National Student Loan Service Centre. *Budget 2004: The Importance of Learning*. Ottawa: Social Development Canada, 2002.

21. Unpublished dissertation or document: Include a description of the document as well as information about where it is available.

NOTE

24. Graham J. Murphy, "Cy(ber)borgs and Netizens: (Re) Configuring the Post/Human Body in the Nodal Intersections of ScyberFiction and Cyberspace" (Ph.D. diss., University of Alberta, 2002).

BIBLIOGRAPHY

Murphy, Graham J. "Cy(ber)borgs and Netizens: (Re)Configuring the Post/Human Body in the Nodal Intersections of ScyberFiction and Cyberspace." Ph.D. diss., University of Alberta, 2002.

22. Musical score or composition: Treat a published score as a book, and include it in the bibliography.

NOTE

25. Franz Josef Haydn, *Symphony No. 94 in G Major,* ed. H. C. Robbins Landon (Salzburg: Haydn-Mozart Press, 1965), 22.

BIBLIOGRAPHY

Haydn, Franz Josef. *Symphony No. 94 in G Major.* Edited by H. C. Robbins Landon. Salzburg: Haydn-Mozart Press, 1965.

For a musical composition, give the composer's name, followed by the title of the work. Put the title in italics unless it names an instrumental work known only by its form, number, and key.

NOTE

26. Oscar Peterson, *God Bless the Child.*

NOTE

27. Franz Josef Haydn, Symphony no. 94 in G Major.

23. Film or video:

NOTE

28. *Incendies,* dir. Denis Villeneuve (Canada: TS Productions, Micro Scope, 2010), feature film.

BIBLIOGRAPHY

Incendies. Directed by Denis Villeneuve. Canada: TS Productions, Micro Scope, 2010.

24. Sound recording: Begin with the composer or other person responsible for the content.

NOTE

> 29. Neil Young, *The Riverboat,* Reprise Records, 2008.

BIBLIOGRAPHY

Young, Neil. *The Riverboat.* Reprise Records, 2008.

25. Artwork: Begin with the artist's name, and include both the name and location of the institution holding the work. Works of art are usually not included in the bibliography.

NOTE

> 30. Harry Palmer, *Oscar Peterson*, photograph, 1984, Canadian Museum of Contemporary Photography, Ottawa.

26. Performance: Begin with the author, director, or performer—whoever is most relevant to your study.

NOTE

> 31. Terrence McNally, Lynn Athrens, and Stephen Flaherty, *Ragtime,* dir. Frank Galati, Ford Performing Arts Center, New York, 11 November 1998.

BIBLIOGRAPHY

McNally, Terrence, Lynn Athrens, and Stephen Flaherty. *Ragtime.* Directed by Frank Galati. Ford Performing Arts Center, New York, 11 November 1998.

27. CD-ROM:

NOTE

> 32. *Microsoft Bookshelf 2000*, s.v. "Gould, Glenn" [CD-ROM] (Redmond, WA: Microsoft, 1998).

BIBLIOGRAPHY

Microsoft Bookshelf 2000. "Gould, Glenn." CD-ROM. Redmond,
WA: Microsoft, 1998.

Online Sources

Chicago style (16th ed.) includes a comprehensive set of guidelines
for citing online sources. Add the URL or DOI (if available) wherever
possible to direct the reader to the resource.

28. Online book or periodical article:

NOTE

33. Elise Firestone, *Don't Tell, Don't Tell,* (Halifax: IndieBooks,
2011), doi: 10.2323/intxt:bnb/748294738291832.002.94827.

NOTE

34. Diane Lankowsky, "On the Effects of Computer-
assisted Guidance for High Risk College Students," *Canadian
School Counsellor* 5, no. 6 (2009): 6–9, https://snca.bc/csc/
issues/lankowsky.html.

BIBLIOGRAPHY

Firestone, Elise. *Don't Tell, Don't Tell.* Halifax: IndieBooks, 2011.
doi:10.2323/intxt:bnb/748294738291832.002.94827.

BIBLIOGRAPHY

Lankowsky, Diane. "On the Effects of Computer-assisted
Guidance for High Risk College Students." *Canadian
School Counsellor* 5, no. 6 (2009). https://snca.bc/csc/
issues/ lankowsky.html.

29. Online database, Web site, or blog: Identify as many of the
following items as you can: author, title, publication data, including
publication type and date of revision/modification or access.

NOTE

35. Shari Soloman and Natalia Bruskaya, "Funding
Post-Secondary Education for Immigrant Women," *Canadian
Educator*, July 1, 2011, LexisNexis Academic.

NOTE

36. Julian Assange's Facebook fan page, accessed March 1, 2010, http://www.facebook.com/#!/pages/Julian-Assange/135936113104134.

BIBLIOGRAPHY

Cohen, D. "Statistical Power Analysis for the Sciences." In *Review for Cognitive and Behavioural Sciences*. Gen Psyc. 10, no. 3. (2010). https://www.archgenpsyc/~cohen/poweranalysis.html.

BIBLIOGRAPHY

Cellucci, Clare. Music Fans (blog). http://www.musicfansblog.com.

24d SAMPLE FROM A STUDENT PAPER IN CHICAGO STYLE.

The following excerpt from Melissa Thomas's paper on Canadian music has been put into Chicago style so that you can see how citation numbers, endnotes, and bibliography work together. *(Melissa's entire paper, in MLA style, can be found on pp. 191–194.)*

Chicago style allows you the option of including a title page. If you do provide a title page, count it as page 1, but do not include the number on the page. Put page numbers in the upper right-hand corner of the remaining pages, except for the pages with the titles "Notes" and "Bibliography" or "Works Cited"; on these pages, the number should be centred at the bottom of the page.

2

Canadian, eh? Not Really

Canada has increasingly drawn attention to itself through the success and development of its musicians. Canadians cherish homegrown talent and delight in the success of their own.

3

Superstars such as Céline Dion and Michael Bublé, internationally acclaimed bands like Sum 41 and the Barenaked Ladies have achieved superstar status inside and outside of the country. Recording stars from Canada have taken their place on the world stage, but foreign-controlled corporations are reaping the benefits of Canadian music success.[1] Unfortunately, as more of the world takes notice, Canadian performers still have to rely on non-Canadian distributors to promote their product.

Clearly, the music industry in Canada has grown incredibly. Canadian Music Week, an industry conference and music festival, sees many of the big labels and buyers from the international music scene. "The CMW is a necessary and important venture for new or upcoming artists to showcase their talent in front of international buyers."[2] It seems, however, that in order for an artist or band to be really successful in the music industry, they need to look to multinational firms for promotion. The domestic recording infrastructure therefore needs to be realigned given the monopoly of non-Canadian companies:

> The Canadian sound recording industry is dominated by six multinational firms (Warner, Sony, Polygram, BMG, EMI and MCA)—known collectively as the majors. They are vertically integrated and dominate the distribution of sound recordings in Canada. They also capture 80% to 90% of the Canadian market, with independent Canadian-owned companies capturing the remainder—16% in the early nineties. Independent labels in Quebec capture 31% of that market, compared with about 10% for independents in the rest of Canada.[3]

Notes

1. "Canadian in Name Only," *Music, eh?* accessed April 5, 2010, http://www.musiceh.com

2. Didier Foiré, "CMW—A Must for New Bands," *La Musicologie,* February 10, 2009, accessed March 25, 2011. http://www.lamusic.com/cmw/articles098987.htm.

3. Brian Chater and Brian Robertson, Ottawa: Department of Canadian Heritage, *A Time for Action: Report of the Task Force on the Future of the Canadian Music Industry,* February 26, 2011, accessed March 24, 2011, http://www.music publishercanada.ca/2011/02/26/a-time-for-action-report-of-the-task-force-on-the-future-of-the-canadian-music-industry/.

Bibliography

Allman, Catherine, and Kendra Michael. "The Canadian Recording Industry Calls for Federal Support to Music Industry: Renewal of Canadian Music Fund and Revision of Copyright Act." *The Canadian Recording Industry Association.* November 24, 2004. Accessed March 23, 2011. http://www.cria.ca/news/241104_n.php.

Barris, Alex. *Making Music: Profiles from a Century of Canadian Music.* Toronto: HarperCollins Canada, 2003.

Canadian in Name Only." *Music, eh?* January 10, 2010. Accessed April 1, 2011. http://www.statcan.ca/Daily/English/030620/d030620e.htm.

Chater, Brian, and Brian Robertson. Ottawa: Department of Canadian Heritage. *A Time for Action: Report of the Task Force on the Future of the Canadian Music Industry.* February 26, 2011. Accessed March 24, 2011. http://www.musicpublishercanada.ca/2011/02/26/a-time-for-action-report-of-the-task-force-on-the-future-of-the-canadian-music-industry/.

Foiré, Didier. "CMW—A Must for New Bands." *La Musicologie.* February 10, 2009. Accessed March 25, 2011. http://www.lamusic.com/cmw/articles098987.htm.

Kallman, Helmut, ed. *Encyclopedia of Music in Canada.* Toronto: University of Toronto Press, 1981.

Writer includes *all* sources she consulted, not just those she cited in the body of her paper.

7

EDITING
FOR CLARITY

Editing can be a creative process. Sometimes being creative means focusing on the sentence as a whole and asking whether the parts fit together well. At other times, it means assessing your word choice within a bigger passage to see if you are meeting your audience's needs. Editing tends to take place after major revisions or first drafts, but modifications can take place as you write. To start editing, ask yourself the following questions:

- Are the focus, flow, and intent of the sentences clear, or are some sentences ineffective? (*See Chapter 25, Sentence Variety, p. 248.*)

- Are all sentences concise? Are any overloaded in ways that make them difficult to read and understand? (*See Chapter 26,*

Wordy Sentences, p. 252 and Chapter 32, Coordination and Subordination, p. 272.)

- Are all sentences complete? Are any necessary words missing from compounds or comparisons? (*See Chapter 29, Missing Words, p. 265.*)

- Do the parts of each sentence fit together in a way that makes sense, or is the sentence mixed up? (*See Chapter 31, Mixed Constructions, p. 269.*)

- Do the key parts of each sentence fit together well, or is there a mismatch in person, number, or grammatical structure? (*See Chapters 33 and 34, Confusing Shifts, p. 275, and Faulty Parallelism, p. 277.*)

- Are the parts of each sentence clearly and closely connected, or are some modifiers separated from what they modify? (*See Chapter 35, Misplaced and Dangling Modifiers, p. 279.*)

- Are the verbs used in each sentence active rather than passive, or is there too much reliance on the various forms of the verb "to be"? (*See Chapter 30 Active Verbs, p. 267.*)

- Are the words used in each sentence appropriate and accurate, or are some biased, overspecialized, vague, or clichéd? (*See Chapters 27–28 Appropriate Language, p. 254, Exact Language, p. 260; Chapters 36–37, The Dictionary and the Thesaurus, p. 282, and Glossary of Usage, p. 286.*)

25   Sentence Variety

Writers can enliven their prose while maintaining their focus by using a variety of sentence patterns. Varying your sentence structure helps you keep your readers interested.

25a   VARYING YOUR SENTENCE OPENINGS.

Try opening some of your sentences in a different way, by moving a modifier to the beginning. The modifier may be a single word, a phrase, or a clause.

Eventually,
➤ Armstrong's innovations ~~eventually~~ became the standard.

In at least two instances, the
➤ ~~The~~ smoke detectors failed. ~~in at least two instances.~~
   ^   ^

After Glaser became his manager,
➤ Armstrong no longer had to worry about business. ~~after Glaser~~
   ^   ^

   ~~became his manager.~~

A **participial phrase** begins with an -*ing* verb (*driving*) or a past participle (*moved, driven*) and is used as an adjective. You can move it to the beginning of a sentence for variety, but if you move it, make sure that the phrase describes the explicit subject of the sentence or you will end up with a dangling modifier. (*See pp. 279–281.*)

Pushing the other children aside,
➤ Joseph, ~~pushing the other children aside,~~ demanded that the
   ^

   teacher give him a cookie first.

Stunned by the stock market crash, many
➤ ~~Many~~ brokers, ~~stunned by the stock market crash,~~ committed
   ^

   suicide.

25b   VARYING YOUR SENTENCE LENGTH AND STRUCTURE.

Short, simple sentences will keep your readers alert, but only if they occur in a context that also includes longer, complex sentences.

As you edit your work, check to see if you have overused one kind of sentence structure. Are all or most of the sentences short and simple? If so, use subordination to combine some of the short sentences into longer, complex sentences. (*See p. 273.*) But if all or most of your sentences are long and complex, put at least one of your ideas into a short, simple sentence. Your goal is to achieve a good mix. For example,

DRAFT   I saw the accident. It was bad. I called 911. Some people were trying to do first aid. I forgot all my first aid training. The paramedics came quickly. The paramedics did CPR. Then they rushed the person away in the ambulance.

REVISED   I saw a bad accident and called 911. Some people were trying to do first aid but I had forgotten all my training. The paramedics came quickly and started CPR, and then they rushed the person away in the ambulance.

(For more information on sentence types, see Tab 10: Basic Grammar Review, pp. 443–444. For more on sentence variety, see Tab 1: Writing and Designing Papers, pp. 46–53.)

25c INCLUDING A FEW CUMULATIVE AND PERIODIC SENTENCES.

Cumulative sentences add a series of descriptive participial or absolute phrases to the basic subject-plus-verb pattern, making your writing more forceful and detailed. *(See Tab 10: Basic Grammar Review, pp. 438–443 for more on participial and absolute phrases.)* The following example, with the participial phrases underlined, illustrates the force a cumulative sentence can have.

➤ **The motorcycle spun out of control, <u>plunging down the ravine</u>,**

  <u>crashing through a fence</u>, and <u>coming to rest at last on its side</u>.

Besides making your writing more forceful, cumulative sentences can also be used to add details, as the following example shows.

➤ **Wollstonecraft headed for France, <u>her soul determined to be</u>**

  <u>free</u>, <u>her mind committed to reason</u>, <u>her heart longing for love</u>.

Another way to increase the force of your writing is to use a few periodic sentences. In a **periodic sentence,** the key word, phrase, or idea appears at the end, precisely where readers are most likely to remember it.

WEAK	"Fire" is one word that you should definitely not yell in a crowded theatre.
FORCEFUL	One word that you should definitely not yell in a crowded theatre is "Fire."

25d TRYING AN OCCASIONAL INVERSION, RHETORICAL QUESTION, OR EXCLAMATION.

Most of the sentences you write will be declarative, designed to make statements and follow the normal sentence pattern of subject + verb + object. Occasionally, though, you might try using an inverted sentence pattern or another sentence type, such as a rhetorical question or an exclamation. *(For more on sentence types, see Tab 10: Basic Grammar Review, pp. 443–444.)*

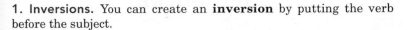

1. Inversions. You can create an **inversion** by putting the verb before the subject.

➤ **Characteristic of Crohn's disease are early satiety (feeling fuller earlier than normal) and stomach pain.**

Because many inversions sound odd, they should be used infrequently and carefully.

2. Rhetorical questions. To get your readers to participate more actively in your work, you can ask a question. Because you do not expect your audience to answer you, this kind of question is called a **rhetorical question**.

➤ **Teenagers go through a rough few years trying to discover their own place in the world. Is it any wonder that this is a time of conflict with their parents?**

Rhetorical questions are attention-getting devices that work best in the middle or at the end of a long, complicated passage. Sometimes they can also help you make a transition from one topic to another. Avoid using them more than a few times in a paper, however, and never begin an essay with a broad rhetorical question, such as "Why should we study *The Stone Angel*?" or "How did Katimavik begin?" Such openings sound canned and may lead readers to suspect that the writer could not be bothered to think of something better.

3. Exclamations. In academic writing, exclamations are rare, perhaps because they seem rather adolescent. If you decide to use one for special effect, be sure that you want to express strong emotion about the idea and can do so without losing credibility with your readers.

➤ **Wordsworth completed the twelve-book *Prelude* in 1805, after seven years of hard work. Instead of publishing his masterpiece, however, he devoted himself to revising it—for 45 years! The poem, in a thirteen-book version, was finally published in 1850, after he had died.**

26 Wordy Sentences

A sentence does not have to be short and simple to be concise. Instead, every word in it must count, especially when the subject matter is complex or technical.

26a ELIMINATING REDUNDANCIES.

Redundancies are meaningless repetitions that result in wordiness. Be on the lookout for such commonplace redundancies as *first and foremost, full and complete, final result, past history, mix together, join together, round in shape, blue in colour,* and *refer back.*

➤ Students living ~~in close proximity~~ in the dorms need to cooperate ~~together if they want~~ to live in harmony.

Sometimes, modifiers such as *very, rather,* and *really* and intensifiers such as *absolutely, definitely,* and *incredibly* do not add meaning to a sentence but are simply redundant and can be deleted.

➤ The ending ~~definitely~~ shocked us ~~very much.~~

26b AVOIDING UNNECESSARY REPETITION.

Although repetition is sometimes used for emphasis, unnecessary repetitions weaken sentences and should be removed.

➤ The children enjoyed playing online games more than ~~they enjoyed~~ watching television.

26c FINDING CONCISE ALTERNATIVES.

Make your sentences more concise by replacing wordy phrases with appropriate one-word alternatives.

➤ *Tests must now*
~~It is necessary at this point in time that tests~~ be run ~~for the~~
 to measure
~~purpose of measuring~~ the switch's strength.

Wordy Phrases	Concise Alternatives
at this point in time	now
in this day and age	nowadays, today
at that point in time	then
in the not-too-distant future	soon
in close proximity to	near
is necessary that	must
is able to	can
has the ability to	can
has the capacity to	can
due to the fact that	because
for the reason that	because
in spite of the fact that	although
in the event that	if
in order to	to
for the purpose(s) of	to

26d MAKING YOUR SENTENCES STRAIGHTFORWARD.

Concise sentences are direct; they get to the point quickly and clearly. To make a sentence more direct, eliminate expletive constructions like *there is, there are*, and *it is* and replace the static verbs *to be* and *to have* with active verbs.

ROUNDABOUT

There are many new software programs that display and test new designs; these tools help engineers and architects in their work.

STRAIGHTFORWARD

Many new software programs display and test new designs; these tools help engineers and architects in their work.

Eliminating the expletive *there are. . .* and the word *that* makes the main subject of the sentence—*software programs*—clearer. To find the action in the sentence, ask what *software programs* do here; they *display and test*. Do the same for the sentence's other subject, *tools*, by asking what they do: *tools . . . help*.

26e REDUCING CLAUSES AND PHRASES.

For conciseness and clarity, simplify your sentence structure by turning modifying clauses into phrases.

➤ The film *Where the Truth Lies*, which was directed by Atom Egoyan, was criticized for its explicit content.

Also look for opportunities to reduce phrases to single words.

➤ Egoyan's film *Where the Truth Lies* was criticized for its explicit content.

27 Appropriate Language

Language is appropriate when it fits your topic, purpose, and audience. But what is "fitting"? One way you can develop a sense of audience is through reading. Whether you are preparing to write about literature or natural science or history, take some time to read how writers in the field have handled your topic.

27a AVOIDING SLANG, REGIONAL EXPRESSIONS, AND NON-STANDARD ENGLISH IN ACADEMIC WRITING.

Slang, regional sayings, and non-standard English appear often in conversation but rarely in scholarly writing—unless that writing is reporting conversation.

Slang words change frequently. (Remember *awesome*?) They are popular mostly with the young, even though some journalists may occasionally use such terms as *homey* as slang for "a close friend or fellow gang member" (according to *Webster's College Dictionary*) rather than its standard meaning of "suggesting home; cosy" (according to the *Canadian Oxford Dictionary*). In academic papers, slang terms and the hip tone that goes with them should be avoided.

> SLANG   In *Heart of Darkness*, we hear a lot about a *dude* named Kurtz, but we don't see the *guy* much.
>
> REVISED   In *Heart of Darkness*, Marlow, the narrator, talks almost continually about Kurtz, but we meet Kurtz himself only at the end.

Like slang, regional and non-standard expressions such as *eh?* and *don't be doing that* work fine in conversation, but do not translate well into formal academic writing. In universities and colleges, professions, and businesses, the dominant dialect is standard written English, the language this book focuses on. Most of your instructors will expect you to write in this dialect, unless you have a good reason not to.

27b USING AN APPROPRIATE LEVEL OF FORMALITY.

Academic writing assignments usually call for a style that avoids the extremes of the stuffy and the casual, the pretentious and the chatty. Some people consider this middle style formal, perhaps because it adheres to the grammatical and mechanical rules of standard written English more than the style of a personal letter or a journal does. Others, however, think that the middle style is informal, perhaps because it is more direct than formal treatises and scholarly papers usually are. Both perspectives are probably true; the point is that as a college or university writer, you will need to find and revise passages that veer to one extreme or the other.

> **PRETENTIOUS**   Romantic lovers are characterized by a preoccupation with a deliberately restricted set of qualities in the love object that are viewed as means to some ideal end.
>
> **REVISED**   People in love see what they want to see, usually by idealizing the beloved.

CROSS-DISCIPLINE **WRITING**

Discourse Communities

People who share certain interests, knowledge, and customary ways of communicating constitute a **discourse community**. Members of the discourse community of hockey fans, for example, talk and write about *goals against average, home ice advantage,* and *slap shots*, terms that are probably unfamiliar to people outside the community. Each of us belongs to several discourse communities, in and out of school. Historians, literary critics, economists, astronomers, pilots, surgeons, lovers of fishing, and thousands of others have their own discourse communities. The more familiar you are with a discourse community, the more you will know about the language appropriate in that community.

27c AVOIDING JARGON.

When specialists communicate with each other, they often use technical language that can sound incomprehensible to non-specialists. Such language is appropriate in many contexts and has a place in academic writing. Without it, no one could write a lab report, an economic analysis, or a philosophical argument. Technical language becomes a problem, however, when it is used as jargon.

Jargon is the inappropriate use of specialized or technical language. Technical language becomes jargon when it does not fit a writer's purpose and audience. If you want to be understood, you should not use discourse appropriate for specialists when writing for a general audience. Jargon puts people off, making them feel like outsiders.

As you edit, look for jargon and revise any you find.

JARGON	To evaluate employees, *360-degree feedback* offers a fuller picture than *downward feedback*.
REVISED	To evaluate employees, feedback from colleagues, subordinates, and customers, as well as from a person's boss, offers a fuller picture than feedback just from the boss.
	Or
	Feedback from colleagues, subordinates, and customers, as well as from a person's boss, offers a fuller picture than feedback just from the boss when performing employee evaluations (In this second version, there is also a voice shift in the subordinate sentence.)

If you need to use a few technical terms when writing for non-specialists, be sure to define them.

➤ **Armstrong's innovative singing style featured "scat," a technique that combines "nonsense syllables [with] improvised melodies" (Robinson 425).**

27d AVOIDING MOST EUPHEMISMS AND ALL DOUBLESPEAK.

Although most writers strive to be clear and direct, euphemisms and doublespeak have another goal: to cover up the truth. **Euphemisms** substitute nice-sounding words like *correctional facility* and *passing away* for such harsh realities as *prison* and *death*. On some occasions, a euphemism like *passing away* may serve a useful purpose; for example, you may wish to avoid upsetting a grieving person. Usually, however, words should not be used to evade or deceive.

Doublespeak is another word for deceit. Its purpose is not to prevent hurt feelings but to confuse or mislead readers. As the following example shows, bureaucrats sometimes use doublespeak to obscure facts and evade responsibility.

➤ **Pursuant to the environmental protection regulations**

enforcement policy of the Ministry of Natural Resources,

special management area land use permit issuance procedures

have been instituted.

Although it is difficult to figure out what is being said here, we can surmise that the Ministry is issuing permits for the use of lands designated as "special management areas." What are these "special management areas"? In reality, they are ecologically fragile lands that the government had decided to protect against development. Now the Ministry is telling firms that want to develop those lands to go ahead and do so but to secure a permit first. In other words, the Ministry's "policy" is to ignore regulations established to protect the environment.

27e REMOVING BIASED OR SEXIST LANGUAGE.

1. Recognize biased language. Words can wound. Ethnic and religious groups, people with disabilities, gay men and lesbians, and workers in some occupations often object to the way people talk and write about them. Always review your writing to see if it is unintentionally biased. Be on the lookout for subtle stereotypes that demean, ignore, or patronize people because of gender, race, religion, national origin, ethnicity, physical ability, sexual orientation, occupation, or any other human condition. Revise for inclusiveness.

For example, do not assume that Mormons have large families.

       The   a   Mormon family with

➤ ~~Although the~~ Browns are ~~Mormons, there are only~~ two children.

~~in the family.~~

In addition, remember that a positive stereotype is still a stereotype.

                                            We

➤ ~~Because Asian students are whizzes at math, we~~ all wanted

    math whizzes

    ~~them~~ in our study group.

CROSS-DISCIPLINE WRITING

Biased Language

When writing on topics in history and the social sciences, take special care not to use terms like *underprivileged* or *culturally deprived*. The American Psychological Association recommends this test. substitute your own group for the group you are discussing. If you are offended by the resulting statement, revise your comments to eliminate bias.

2. Recognize sexist language. Sexist language demeans or stereotypes women and men, but women are usually the explicit targets. For example, many labels and clichés imply that women are not as able or as mature as men. Consider the meaning of words and phrases like *the weaker sex, the fair sex, the little woman, [acting like a] girl, gal, broad, dame, my better half, working mother, housewife, poetess,* and *coed.*

3. Avoid stereotypes. Avoiding bias means more than simply not using derogatory words and slurs. It also means avoiding subtle stereotypes.

For example, not all heads of state are or have been men. Secretaries can be either women or men.

BIASED	Wives of firemen spend lots of time worrying about their husbands.
REVISED	Spouses of firefighters spend lots of time worrying about their partners.
BIASED	We advertised for a new secretary because we needed another girl in the office.
REVISED	We advertised for a new secretary because we had too much work for the staff on hand.

(For additional examples, see Tab 1: Writing and Designing Papers, pp. 51–52.)

4. Avoid the generic he. Traditionally, the pronoun *he* has been used to represent either gender. Today, however, unless a group consists only of men, the use of *he* to represent everyone in the group offends many people.

BIASED	Everybody had his way.
REVISED	We all had our way.

5. Revise sexist language. Review your writing to see if it is unintentionally biased. As you revise, follow these simple principles.

- Replace terms that indicate gender with their genderless equivalents:

Gendered Terms	Genderless Terms
chairman	chair, chairperson
forefathers	ancestors
man, mankind	people, humans
man-made	artificial, manufactured
policeman	police officer
spokesman	spokesperson

- Do not make unnecessary references to or overemphasize a woman's marital status, relationship to children, or appearance. Refer to men and women in parallel ways: *ladies and gentlemen* [not *ladies and men*], *men and women, husband and wife*.

BIASED   D. H. Lawrence and Mrs. Woolf met, but Lawrence did not like the Bloomsbury circle that revolved around Virginia.

REVISED   D. H. Lawrence and Virginia Woolf met, but Lawrence did not like the Bloomsbury circle that revolved around Woolf.

- Whenever possible, replace the masculine pronouns *he, him, his,* and *himself* when they are being used generically to refer to both women and men. One satisfactory way to replace masculine pronouns is to use the plural.

BIASED   It's every man for himself.

REVISED   All of us have to save ourselves.

Some writers alternate *he* and *she, him* and *her.* This strategy may be effective in some writing situations, but switching back and forth can also be distracting. The constructions *his or her* and *he or she* are acceptable, as long as they are not used excessively or more than once in a sentence.

AWKWARD   Each student in the psychology class was to choose a different book according to *his or her* interests, to read the book overnight, to do without *his or her* normal sleep, to write a short summary of what *he or she* had read, and then to see if *he or she* dreamed about the book the following night.

REVISED Every student was to choose a book, read it overnight, do without sleep, write a short summary of the book the next morning, and then see if *he or she* dreamed about the book the following night.

The construction *his/her* and the unpronounceable *s/he* are not acceptable in academic writing.

Note: Using the neuter impersonal pronoun *one* can sometimes help you avoid masculine pronouns. *One* can make your writing sound stuffy, though, so it is usually better to try another option.

STUFFY *One* must not play the radio too loud if *one* wants good relations with *one's* neighbours.

REVISED Those who want good relations with their neighbours must not play the radio too loud.

(For more on editing to avoid the generic use of he, him, his, or himself, see Tab 8: Editing for Grammar, p. 331.)

28 Exact Language

To convey meaning clearly, you not only need to put words in the right order, but you also need to choose the right words. As you revise, be on the lookout for problems with diction: Is your choice of words as precise as it should be?

28a CHOOSING WORDS WITH SUITABLE CONNOTATIONS.

Words have primary (or explicit) meanings, called denotations, and secondary (or implicit) meanings, called connotations. Connotations come from the feelings and images people associate with a word, so they influence what readers understand a writer to be saying. Consider, for example, the following three statements:

Murdock *ignored* the no-smoking rule.

Murdock *disobeyed* the no-smoking rule.

Murdock *flouted* the no-smoking rule.

Even though the three sentences depict the same event, each sentence describes Murdock's action somewhat differently. If Murdock *ignored* the rule, it may simply have been because he did not know or care about it. If he *disobeyed* the rule, he must have known about it and consciously decided not to follow it, but what if he *flouted* the rule? Well, then there was probably a look of disdain on his face as he made sure that others would see him ostentatiously puffing away at a cigarette.

As you revise, consider replacing any word whose connotations do not exactly fit what you want to say.

> *demand*
> The nurses' union should ~~request~~ that the hospital amend its
> pension plan.

If you cannot think of a more suitable word, consult a print or an online thesaurus (see p. 285) for *synonyms,* words with similar meanings. Keep in mind, however, that most words have connotations that allow them to work in some contexts, but not in others. To find out more about a synonym's connotations, look the word up in a dictionary.

28b INCLUDING SPECIFIC AND CONCRETE WORDS.

In addition to general and abstract terms, clear writers use specific and concrete words.

General words name broad categories of things, such as *trees, books, politicians,* or *students.* **Specific words** name particular kinds of things or items, such as *pines, Victorian novels, Conservatives,* or *college students.*

Abstract words name qualities and ideas that do not have physical properties, such as *charity, beauty, hope,* or *radical.* **Concrete words** name things we can sense by touch, taste, smell, hearing, and sight, such as *velvet, vinegar, smoke, screech,* or *bicycle.*

By creating images that appeal to the senses, specific and concrete words can help make your writing more precise.

VAGUE   The trees were affected by the bad weather.

PRECISE   The small pines shook in the gale.

As you edit, make sure that you have developed your ideas with specific and concrete details. Also check for overused, vague terms— such as *factor, thing, good, nice,* and *interesting*—and replace them with more specific and concrete alternatives.

> *many challenging projects.*
➤ **The engineers were given ~~lots of interesting things to do.~~**
                                                    ^

28c USING STANDARD IDIOMS.

Idioms are habitual ways of expressing ideas, and they usually cannot be translated from one language to another. In fact, sometimes they cannot be transferred from one region to another within a country.

As customary forms of expression, idioms are not always logical. Often they involve selecting the right preposition. We are not capable *to* but capable *of*; we do not go *with* the car but *in* the car or simply *by* car; we do not abide *with* a rule but *by* a rule. If you are not sure which preposition to use, look up the main word in a dictionary.

Some verbs, called **phrasal verbs,** include a preposition to make their meaning complete. These verbs often have an idiomatic meaning that changes significantly when the attached preposition changes.

Henry *made up* with Gloria.

Henry *made off* with Gloria.

Henry *made out* with Gloria.

(For more on correct idiom, see pp. 428–429.)

28d AVOIDING CLICHÉS.

A cliché is an overworked expression. The moment we read the first word or two of a cliché, we know how it will end. If someone says, "She was as mad as a ___," we expect the next word(s) to be *hornet, wet hen,* or *lion with a thorn in his paw.* We have heard these expressions so often that they no longer create vivid pictures in our imaginations. It is usually best to rephrase a cliché as simply as you can in plain language.

CLICHÉ	Brenda decided that she had *an ace up her sleeve* since her parents were already friends with her professor.
BETTER	Brenda decided that she had a *definite advantage* since her parents were already friends with her professor.

The list that follows gives some common clichés to avoid.

Common Clichés

acid test

agony of suspense

beat a hasty retreat

beyond the shadow of a doubt

blind as a bat

blue as the sky

brave as a lion

brutal murder

calm, cool, and collected

cold, hard facts

crazy as a loon

dead as a doornail

deep, dark secret

depths of despair

doomed to disappointment

every dog has his day

face the music

few and far between

flat as a pancake

give 110 percent

green with envy

heart of gold

heave a sigh of relief

hit the nail on the head

in this day and age

ladder of success

last but not least

live from hand to mouth

the other side of the coin

paint the town red

pale as a ghost

pass the buck

pick and choose

poor but honest

poor but proud

pretty as a picture

proud possessor

quick as a flash

rise and shine

rise to the occasion

sadder but wiser

shoulder to the wheel

sink or swim

smart as a whip

sneaking suspicion

sober as a judge

straight and narrow

tempest in a teapot

tired but happy

tried and true

untimely death

walking the line

white as a ghost

white as a sheet

worth its weight in gold

28e CREATING SUITABLE FIGURES OF SPEECH.

Figures of speech make writing vivid, most often by using a comparison to supplement the literal meaning of words. A **simile** is a comparison that contains the word *like* or *as*.

➤ He was as private about his artwork as a packrat is about hiding his loot.

A **metaphor** is an implied comparison. It treats one thing or action, such as a critic's review, as if it were something else, in this case, an extreme method of clearing land.

➤ **The critic's slash-and-burn review devastated the cast.**

Because it is compressed, a metaphor is often more forceful than a simile.

Comparisons can make your prose more vivid, but only if they suit your subject and purpose. Be especially careful not to mix metaphors; if you use two or more comparisons together, make sure they are compatible. Not only does the following sentence mix three incompatible figures (a mineral, running, and a ship), but two of the three are also unsuitable (running a race, boarding a ship).

MIXED   His presentation of the plan was so *crystal clear* that in a *burst of speed* we decided *to come aboard.*

REVISED   His clear presentation immediately convinced us to support the plan.

28f AVOIDING MISUSE OF WORDS.

As your vocabulary grows, you can expect to make some mistakes in your use of new terms and unfamiliar words. You can reduce such mistakes by consulting a dictionary whenever you include an unfamiliar word in your writing.

exhibited
➤ **The municipal council exuded numerous vices, including greed**
conflict of interest.   ^
and conflicted interest.
^

Also, check your textbooks for glossaries that can help you use new terms properly.

Missing Words

29

When editing, make sure you have not omitted any words the reader needs to understand the meaning of your sentence.

29a ADDING WORDS TO MAKE COMPOUND STRUCTURES COMPLETE AND CLEAR.

For conciseness, words can sometimes be omitted from compound structures. In the following example, the second *is* can be omitted because the verb in the first part of the compound structure is also *is: His anger is extreme and his behaviour violent.*

    Do not leave out part of a compound structure unless both parts of the compound are the same, however.

>   *with*
> **The detectives neither cooperated ^ nor listened to the crown**
>
> **attorney.**

29b INCLUDING *THAT* WHEN IT IS NEEDED FOR CLARITY.

The subordinator *that* should be omitted only when the clause it introduces is short and the sentence's meaning is clear: *Jann Arden sings the kind of songs many women love.* Usually, *that* should be included.

>   *that*
> **The lawyer argued ^ his client was not guilty by reason of**
>
> **insanity.**

29c MAKING COMPARISONS CLEAR.

To be clear, comparisons must be complete. If you have just said "Peanut butter sandwiches are boring," you can say immediately afterward "Curried chicken sandwiches are more interesting," but you cannot say in isolation "Curried chicken sandwiches are more interesting." You need to name who or what completes the comparison.

    Check comparisons to make sure your meaning is clear. In the following example, does the writer mean that she loved her grandmother more than her sister did—or more than she loved her sister? To clarify, add the missing words.

did
➤ I loved my grandmother more than my sister.
 ^

I loved
➤ I loved my grandmother more than my sister.

When you use *as* to compare people or things, be sure to use it twice:

as
➤ Chan's car was temperamental as a rattlesnake.
 ^

Include *other* or *else* to indicate that people or things belong to the group with which the subject is being compared.

➤ At the 2011 Genie Awards, *Barney's Version* won seven awards,

more than any *other* English language film, but *Incendie*, a

French-Canadian film, won eight awards.

➤ Professor Koonig wrote more books than anyone *else* in the

department.

Use a possessive form when comparing attributes or possessions.

WEAK	Plato's philosophy is easier to read than *that of Aristotle*.
BETTER	Plato's philosophy is easier to read than *Aristotle's*.

Keep in mind that complex comparisons may require more than one addition to be completely clear.

than Budzik's book
➤ Fyfe's book is longer, but her account of the war is more
 ^   *Budzik's account.*
interesting than ~~Budzik's~~.
 ^

29d ADDING ARTICLES (*A, AN, THE*) WHERE NECESSARY.

In English, omitting an article usually makes an expression sound odd, unless the omission occurs in a series of nouns.

➤ A dog that bites should be kept on *a* leash.

➤ He gave me *the* books he liked best.

➤ Ruth's library cubicle contained a water bottle, bag of cookies, and coffee mug, but no actual books.

Note: If the articles in a series are not the same, each one must be included.

➤ Ruth's library cubicle contained an empty water bottle, *a* bag of *a* cookies, and coffee mug, but no actual books.

(For more information about the use of articles, consult Tab 10: Basic Grammar Review, pp. 418–419.)

Active Verbs

30

Active verbs are more direct and forceful than forms of the *be* verb (*am, are, is, was, were, been, being*) or passive-voice constructions. As you edit your work for clarity, pay attention to verb choice. The more active verbs you use, the stronger and clearer your writing will be.

30a CONSIDERING ALTERNATIVES TO SOME *BE* VERBS.

Although it is not a strong verb, *be* does a lot of work in English. As a linking verb, a form of *be* can connect a subject with an informative adjective or noun complement.

➤ Canada *is* ready to win another medal in paralympic sailing.

➤ Decent health care *is* a necessity, not a luxury.

As a helping verb, a form of *be* can work with a present participle to indicate an ongoing action.

➤ Macbeth *was* returning from battle when he met the three witches.

Be verbs are so useful, in fact, that they *are* easily overworked. Watch for weak, roundabout sentences containing *be* verbs, and consider replacing those verbs with active verbs.

➤ The mayor's refusal to meet with our representatives ~~is a~~

        demonstrates

    ~~demonstration of~~ his lack of respect for us, as well as for the

               ^

    environment.

30b   PREFERRING THE ACTIVE VOICE.

Verbs can be in the active or passive voice. In the **active voice**, the subject of the sentence acts; in the **passive voice**, the subject is acted upon.

ACTIVE	The House of Commons finally passed the back-to-work legislation.
PASSIVE	The back-to-work legislation was finally passed by the House of Commons.

The passive voice downplays the actors as well as the action, so much so that the actors are often left out of the sentence.

PASSIVE	The back-to-work legislation was finally passed.

Unless you have a good reason to use the passive voice, prefer the active voice. It is more forceful, and readers usually want to know who or what does the acting.

PASSIVE	Polluting chemicals were dumped into the river.
ACTIVE	Industrial Products Corporation dumped polluting chemicals into the river.

When the *recipient* of the action is more important than the *doer* of the action, however, the passive voice is the more appropriate choice.

➤ After her heart attack, my mother was taken to the hospital.

Mother and the fact that she was taken to the hospital are more important than who took her to the hospital.

As most verbs have two voices (active and passive), try to be consistent with your choice, especially when the subject remains the same.

                                   They favoured violet,

➤ The Impressionist painters hated black. ~~Violet,~~ green, blue, pink,

                                        ^

    and red. ~~were favoured by them.~~

      ^

CROSS-DISCIPLINE **WRITING**

Passive Voice

The passive voice is often used in scientific reports to keep the focus on the experiment and its results rather than on the experimenters:

➤ **After the bacteria were isolated, they were treated carefully with nicotine and were observed to stop reproducing.**

The passive voice also appears in some forms of business writing, such as memos, when it is important to deliver information impersonally and objectively.

➤ **After a year of dismal sales, deep cuts and massive layoffs have been deemed necessary.**

Mixed Constructions

31

When a sentence's parts do not fit together either grammatically or logically, a mixed construction results. Mixed constructions confuse readers and must be revised to make meaning clear.

31a UNTANGLING MIXED-UP SENTENCE STRUCTURES.

Mixed-up sentences occur when writers start a sentence one way and then change grammatical direction. The following sentence begins with a prepositional phrase (a phrase introduced by a preposition such as *at, by, for, in,* or *of*) and then, midway through, tries to make that phrase into the subject. A prepositional phrase cannot be the subject of a sentence, however.

MIXED-UP SENTENCE   For family members who enjoy one another's company often decide on a vacation spot together.

Eliminating the preposition *for* makes it clear that *family members* is the subject of the verb *decide*.

REVISED SENTENCE   Family members who enjoy one another's company often decide on a vacation spot together.

In the following sentence, the dependent clause *when a Curanderos is consulted* cannot serve as the subject of the sentence.

MIXED-UP SENTENCE   In Mexican culture, when a Curanderos is consulted can address spiritual or physical illness.

The revision transforms the dependent clause into an independent clause with a subject and predicate (a complete verb) that make sense together.

REVISED SENTENCE   In Mexican culture, a Curanderos can be consulted for spiritual or physical illness.

Sometimes you may have to separate your ideas into more than one sentence to clarify the point you are trying to make.

MIXED-UP SENTENCE   In a publicly traded biotech company like Biopharma is, a few people have the decision making power rather than a company like Bioking, which is ruled by its founder.

This writer is trying to do two things at one time: to contrast Biopharma and Bioking and to define the difference between a publicly traded company and a private one. By using two sentences instead of one, the writer makes both ideas clear.

REVISED SENTENCES   Biopharma is a publicly traded company where many people share decision-making power. In contrast, Bioking is a privately held company, run exclusively by its founder.

31b MAKING SURE PREDICATES FIT THEIR SUBJECTS.

A **predicate** is the complete verb along with any words that modify it, any objects or complements, and any words that modify them. A predicate must match a sentence's subject both logically and grammatically. When it does not, the result is faulty predication.

FAULTY PREDICATION

The best kind of education for me would be a university with both a school of music and a school of government.

A university is an institution, not a type of education, so the sentence needs revision.

REVISED SENTENCE

A university with both a school of music and a school of government would be best for me.

Avoid using the phrases *is where, is when,* and *the reason . . . is because.* These phrases may sound logical, but they usually result in faulty predication.

FAULTY PREDICATION

Photosynthesis is where carbon dioxide, water, and chlorophyll interact in the presence of sunlight to form carbohydrates.

Photosynthesis is not a place, so *is where* is illogical. Also, to be grammatically correct, the linking verb *is* needs to be followed by a **subject complement**—a word or word group that specifies or describes the subject.

REVISED SENTENCE

Photosynthesis is the production of carbohydrates from the interaction of carbon dioxide, water, and chlorophyll in the presence of sunlight.

Although *is because* may seem logical, it creates an adverb clause following the linking verb rather than the required subject complement.

FAULTY PREDICATION

The reason the joint did not hold is because the coupling bolt broke.

To fix this kind of faulty predication, turn the adverb clause into a noun clause by changing *because* to *that,* or change the subject of the sentence.

REVISED SENTENCES

➤ The reason the joint did not hold is ~~because~~ that the coupling

  bolt broke.

  or

➤ ~~The reason~~ The joint did not hold ~~is~~ because the coupling

  bolt broke.

32 Coordination and Subordination

Coordination and subordination allow you to combine and develop your ideas in ways that readers can easily follow and understand, but coordination and subordination frequently cause problems for writers.

Use coordination to express equal ideas. Coordination gives two or more ideas equal weight. To coordinate parts within a sentence, join them with a coordinating conjunction (*and, but, or, for, nor, yet,* or *so*). To coordinate two or more sentences, use a comma plus a coordinating conjunction, or insert a semicolon.

➤ The auditorium was huge, *and* the acoustics were terrible.

➤ The professor bellowed loudly, *but* no one in the back could hear him.

➤ Jones did not agree with her position on health care; *nevertheless*, he supported her campaign for office.

Note: When a semicolon is used to coordinate two sentences, it is often followed by a conjunctive adverb such as *moreover, nevertheless, however, therefore,* or *subsequently.* (For more on conjunctive adverbs, see Tab 10: Basic Grammar Review, p. 432.)

Use subordination to express unequal ideas. Subordination makes one idea depend on another and is therefore used to combine ideas that are not of equal importance. The main idea is expressed in an independent clause, and the secondary ideas are expressed in subordinate clauses or phrases. Subordinate clauses start with a relative pronoun (*who, whom, that, which, whoever, whomever, whose*) or a subordinating conjunction such as *after, although, because, if, since, when,* and *where.*

➤ The blue liquid, *which will be added to the beaker later,* must be kept at room temperature.

➤ Marie Curie discovered radium and polonium and was awarded the Nobel Prize in Chemistry in 1911, *although she never understood the true dangers of radiation until much later.*

➤ *After accepting the second offer,* **Jaspal submitted his**

resignation.

Keep in mind that subordinate clauses used alone (without an independent clause) are considered fragments. *(For more information on sentence fragments, see Tab 8, Editing for Grammar, pp. 229–304.)*

Note: Commas often set off subordinate ideas, especially when the subordinate clause or phrase opens the sentence. *(For more on using commas, see Tab 9: Editing for Correctness, pp. 347–358.)*

32a COMBINING SHORT, CHOPPY SENTENCES.

Short sentences are easy to read, but several of them in a row can become so monotonous that meaning gets lost.

> CHOPPY   My cousin Priti is not an accountant. But she does my taxes every year. She suggests various deductions. These deductions reduce my tax bill considerably.

You can use subordination to combine a series of short, choppy sentences to form a longer, more meaningful sentence. Put the idea you want to emphasize in the main clause, and use subordinate clauses and phrases to include the other ideas. In the following revision, the main clause is underlined.

> REVISED   Even though she is not an accountant, <u>my cousin Priti does my taxes every year</u>, suggesting various deductions that reduce my tax bill considerably.

If a series of short sentences includes two major ideas of equal importance, use coordination for the two major ideas and subordinate the secondary information. The following revision shows that Smith's and Johnson's opinions are equally important. The information about bilingual education is of secondary interest.

> CHOPPY   Bilingual education is designed for children. The native language of these children is not English. Smith supports expanding bilingual education. Johnson does not support expanding bilingual education.

> REVISED   Smith supports bilingual education for children whose native language is not English; Johnson, however, does not support bilingual education.

32b   USING SUBORDINATION FOR IDEAS OF UNEQUAL IMPORTANCE.

Coordination should be used only when two or more ideas deserve equal emphasis: *Smith supports bilingual education, but Johnson does not.* Subordination, not coordination, should be used to indicate that information is of secondary importance and to show its logical relation to the main idea.

➤   *When the*
  ~~The~~ rain started, ~~and~~ someone put the cake away.

➤   The fourth set of needs to be met, ~~are~~ esteem needs, ~~and they~~
  includes
  ~~include~~ the need for success, self-respect, and prestige.

32c   AVOIDING SUBORDINATION OF MAJOR IDEAS.

Major ideas belong in main clauses, not in subordinate clauses or phrases where readers are unlikely to give them the attention they deserve. The writer revised the following sentence because the subject of the paper was definitions of literacy, not who values literacy.

INEFFECTIVE SUBORDINATION	Literacy, which has been defined as the ability to talk intelligently about many topics, is highly valued by businesspeople as well as academics.
REVISION	Highly valued by businesspeople as well as academics, literacy has been defined as the ability to talk intelligently about many topics.

32d   AVOIDING EXCESSIVE SUBORDINATION.

When a sentence seems overloaded, try separating it into two or more sentences.

OVERLOADED	Professors who expect a great deal from their students may be doing the students a favour but should be aware that their student evaluations may suffer as a result, which unfortunately can affect their job prospects, so it makes you wonder if expecting nothing might be a better alternative.

REVISED   Professors who expect a great deal from their students may be doing the students a favour. They should be aware, however, that their student evaluations may suffer as a result, which unfortunately can affect their job prospects. It makes you wonder if expecting nothing might be a better alternative.

Confusing Shifts

When you are editing, look for jarring shifts in point of view, tense, mood, or voice that may confuse readers. Shifts can also occur in number, voice, and tense (*see 36a and 36b for examples*).

33a MAKING YOUR POINT OF VIEW CONSISTENT IN PERSON AND NUMBER.

A writer has three points of view to choose from. First person (*I* or *we*) emphasizes the writer and is used in personal writing. Second person (*you*) focuses attention on the readers and is used to give them orders, directions, or advice. Third person (*he, she, it, one,* or *they*) is topic-oriented and therefore prevalent in academic writing. Choose one point of view and use it consistently.

Writers sometimes make jarring shifts in person when they compose generalizations. For example, the writer of the following sentence initially shifted from the third person (*students*) to the second person (*you*), a common kind of confusing shift.

➤ **Students should have no trouble getting the courses they want if**
    they
    ~~you~~ **log onto the registration website at 6 a.m.**

Note: When making a general statement about what people should or should not do, use the third person, not the second person.

Confusing shifts in number occur when writers switch from singular to plural or plural to singular for no apparent reason. When you correct such shifts, you should usually choose the plural to avoid using *his* or *her* or introducing gender bias. (*See Tab 8: Editing for Grammar, p. 331.*)

➤ ~~A person is~~ often assumed to know what they are doing even

People are

when they have no idea.

33b KEEPING YOUR VERB TENSES CONSISTENT.

Verb tenses show the time of an action in relation to other actions. Writers are expected to choose a time frame for their work—present, past, or future—and use it consistently, changing tense only when the meaning requires it.

Confusing shifts in time from past to present may occur when you are narrating events that are still vivid in your mind.

➤ The wind was blowing one hundred twenty kilometres an hour

was *fell*

when suddenly there ~~is~~ a big crash, and a tree ~~falls~~ into the

living room.

You may also introduce inconsistencies when you are using the present perfect tense, perhaps because the past participle causes you to slip from present tense to past tense.

CROSS-DISCIPLINE **WRITING**

Present Tense and Literary Works

By convention, the present tense is used to write about the content of literary works. When you write about literary characters and events, be careful not to shift out of the present tense as you move from one sentence to another.

➤ David Copperfield observes other people with a fine and

sympathetic eye. He describes villains such as Mr. Murdstone

and heroes such as Mr. Micawber in unforgettable detail. But

is

Copperfield ~~was~~ not himself an especially interesting person

➤ **She has admired many strange buildings at the university but**
    thinks   *looks*
~~thought~~ that the new Science Centre ~~looked~~ completely out

of place.

33c   AVOIDING UNNECESSARY SHIFTS IN MOOD

Besides tense, verbs in a sentence also have a mood and a voice. There are three basic moods: the **indicative**, used to state or question facts, acts, and opinions; the **imperative**, used to give commands or advice; and the **subjunctive**, used to express wishes, conjectures, and hypothetical conditions. Unnecessary shifts in mood can confuse and distract your readers. Be on the lookout for shifts between the indicative and the subjunctive.

    could go
➤ **If he ~~goes~~ to the University of Waterloo, he would take computer**

science.

Faulty Parallelism

34

Parallel constructions enhance clarity by presenting equally important ideas in the same grammatical form.

➤ **The Collaboration Accord of 2005, an agreement between the**

Government of Canada and the Franco-Manitoban community,

provides a framework *to ensure* long-term funding to the

Francophone community, *to increase* services available in

French, and *to develop* the products and services that originate

in the Francophone community.

When you notice that items in a series or paired ideas do not have the same grammatical form, correct them by making them parallel.

34a   MAKING ITEMS IN A SERIES PARALLEL.

A list or series of equally important items should be parallel in grammatical structure. To make the series in the following sentence parallel, the writer changed *working* to *work* so that it matches *receive* and *are*.

➤   The Government classifies people as employed if they receive

     payment for any kind of labour, are temporarily absent from
                              work
     their jobs, or ~~working~~ at least fifteen hours as unpaid labourers
                   ^

     in a family business.

In the next example, the writer changed a noun to an adjective. Notice that the writer also decided to repeat the word *too* to make the sentence more forceful and memorable.

                                       too
➤   My sister obviously thought that I was too young, ignorant, and
                                           ^
   too troublesome.
   ~~a troublemaker.~~
       ^

34b   MAKING PAIRED IDEAS PARALLEL.

Paired ideas are connected with a coordinating conjunction (*and, but, or, nor, for, so, yet*), a correlative conjunction (*not only . . . but also, both . . . and, either . . . or, neither . . . nor*), or a comparative expression (*as much as, more than, less than*). Paired ideas must have parallel grammatical form.

                     both   *challenge their students.*
➤   Successful teachers must inspire ~~students~~ and ~~challenging them~~
                        ^   ^

     ~~is also important.~~
                               winning
➤   I dreamed not only of getting the girl but also of the gold medal.
                                         ^

                                 to compromise.
➤   The student union preferred to fight rather than ~~compromising.~~
                                             ^

Misplaced and Dangling Modifiers

35

For a sentence to make sense, its parts must be arranged appropriately. When a modifying word, phrase, or clause is misplaced or dangling, readers get confused.

35a PUTTING MODIFIERS CLOSE TO THE WORDS THEY MODIFY.

For clarity, modifiers should come immediately before or after the words they modify. In the following sentence, the clause *after the police arrested them* modifies *protesters,* not *property.* Putting the clause before the word it modifies makes it clear that if any property destruction occurred, it occurred before—not after—the arrest.

➤ *After the police had arrested them, the*
   ~~The~~ G-20 protesters were charged with vandalism and
   ^

   destroying public property. ~~after the police had arrested them.~~

Like adverbial clauses, prepositional phrases used as adverbs are easy to misplace. The following sentence was revised to make it clear that the hikers were watching the storm from the porch:

➤ *From the cabin's porch, the*
   ~~The~~ hikers watched the storm gathering force. ~~from the cabin's~~
   ^   ^

   ~~porch.~~

35b CLARIFYING AMBIGUOUS MODIFIERS.

Because adverbs can modify what precedes or what follows them, it is important to make sure that the adverbs you use are not ambiguously placed. In the following sentence, what is vehement, the objection or the argument? Changing the position of *vehemently* eliminates this ambiguity.

➤   *vehemently*
   Doctors who objected to this diagnosis ~~vehemently~~ argued that
                          ^

   the patient's life was never endangered.

Problems often occur with limiting modifiers such as *only, even, almost, nearly,* and *just.* When you edit, check every sentence that includes one of these modifiers. In the following sentence, does the writer mean that vegetarian dishes are the only dishes served at dinner or that dinner is the only time when vegetarian dishes are available? Editing clears up the ambiguity.

AMBIGUOUS   The restaurant *only offers* vegetarian dishes for dinner.

REVISED   The restaurant *offers only* vegetarian dishes for dinner.

Or

The restaurant *offers* vegetarian dishes *only* at dinner.

35c MOVING DISRUPTIVE MODIFIERS.

When you separate grammatical elements that belong together with a lengthy modifying phrase or clause, the resulting sentence can be difficult to read. In the following sentence, the phrase beginning with *despite* initially came between the subject and verb, disrupting the flow of the sentence. With the modifying phrase at the beginning of the sentence, the edited version restores the connection between subject and verb.

Despite their similar conceptions of the self,

➤ **Descartes and Hume, ~~despite their similar conceptions of the self,~~ deal with the issue of personal identity in different ways.**

35d AVOIDING SPLIT INFINITIVES.

An **infinitive** couples the word *to* with the present tense of a verb. In a **split infinitive,** one or more words intervene between *to* and the verb form. Avoid separating the parts of an infinitive with a modifier unless keeping them together results in an awkward or ambiguous construction.

In the following example, the modifier *successfully* should be moved. The modifier *carefully* should probably stay where it is, however, even though it splits the infinitive *to assess. Carefully* needs to be close to the verb it modifies, and putting it after *assess* would cause ambiguity because readers might think it modifies *projected economic benefits.*

➤ To ~~successfully~~ complete this assignment ^*successfully,*^ students have to carefully assess projected economic benefits in relation to potential social problems.

35e FIXING DANGLING MODIFIERS.

A **dangling modifier** is a descriptive phrase that implies an actor different from the sentence's subject. When readers try to connect the modifying phrase with the subject, the results may be humorous as well as confusing. The following sentence, for example, describes a *crowded beach* as *swimming.*

DANGLING   *Swimming toward the boat on the horizon,* the
MODIFIER   crowded beach felt as if it were miles away.

To fix a dangling modifier, its implied actor must be explicitly named, either as the subject of the sentence or in the modifier itself.

REVISED   Swimming toward the boat on the horizon, *I* felt
                 as if the crowded beach were miles away.

                 Or

                 As *I swam* toward the boat on the horizon, the
                 crowded beach seemed miles away.

Note that simply moving a dangling modifier won't fix the problem. To make the meaning clear, the implied actor in the modifying phrase must be made explicit.

DANGLING   *After struggling for weeks in the wilderness,* the
MODIFIER   town pleased them mightily.

Moving the dangling modifier to the end of the sentence won't change its unintended meaning, which is that the town had been struggling in the wilderness for weeks.

REVISED   After struggling for weeks in the wilderness, *they*
                 were pleased to come upon the town.

                 Or

                 After *they had struggled* for weeks in the
                 wilderness, the town was a pleasing sight.

36 The Dictionary and the Thesaurus

A dictionary and a thesaurus are essential tools for all writers. You should also find out about specialized dictionaries for the subject area of your field of study.

36a USING THE DICTIONARY AS A HABIT.

A standard dictionary—such as the *Oxford Canadian Dictionary* or the *Gage Canadian Concise Dictionary*—contains 140,000 to 180,000 entries. Along with words and their definitions, most dictionaries provide additional information such as the correct spellings of important place names, the official names of countries with their areas and populations, and the names of capital cities. Biographical entries give birth and death years and enough information to explain each person's importance to society. Many dictionaries also include lists of abbreviations and symbols, names and locations of colleges and universities, titles and correct forms of address, and conversion tables for weights and measures.

All dictionaries include guides to their use, usually in the front. The guides explain the terms and abbreviations that appear in the entries as well as special notations such as *slang, non-standard, and vulgar.*

An entry from the *Canadian Oxford Dictionary* follows. The labels point to the kinds of information discussed in the following sections.

Phonetic symbols showing pronunciation.

Word endings and grammatical abbreviations.

Dictionary entry.

com · pare • *verb* 1 *transitive* (usu. foll. by *to*) express similarities in; liken (*compared the landscape to a painting*). **2 *transitive*** (often foll. by *to, with*) estimate the similarity or dissimilarity of; assess the relation between (*compared radio with television; that lacks quality compared to this*). ¶ In current use *to* and *with* are generally interchangeable, but *with* often implies a greater element of formal analysis, as in *compared my account with yours*. **3 *intransitive*** (often foll. by *with*) bear comparison (*compares favourably with the rest*). **4 *intransitive*** (often foll. by *with*) be equal or equivalent to. **5 *transitive*** Grammar form the comparative and superlative degrees of (an adjective or an adverb). • *noun* literary comparison (*beyond compare; has no compare*).

Definitions a transitive verb (v.t.).

Definitions an intransit verb (v.i.).

Definition as a noun (*n.*).

□ **compare notes** exchange ideas or opinions. [Old French *comparer* from Latin *comparare* (as COM-, *parare* from *par* equal)]

Etymology.

Figure 36.1 Definition from the *Canadian Oxford Dictionary* for "compare."

1. Spelling, word division, and pronunciation. Entries in a dictionary are listed in alphabetical order according to their standard spelling. In the *Canadian Oxford Dictionary,* the verb *compare* is entered as **com·pare.** The dot separates the word into its two syllables. If you had to divide the word *compare* at the end of a line, you would place the hyphen where the dot appears.

Phonetic symbols in parentheses following the entry show its correct pronunciation; explanations of these symbols appear on the bottom of each right-hand page in some dictionaries. The second syllable of *compare* receives the greater stress when you pronounce the word correctly: you say "comPARE." In this dictionary, an accent mark (´) appears after the syllable that receives the primary stress.

Plurals of nouns are usually not given if they are formed by adding an *s,* unless the word is foreign (*gondolas, dashikis*). Irregular plurals—such as *children* for *child*—are noted.

Note: Some dictionaries list alternative spellings, always giving the preferred spelling first or placing the full entry under the preferred spelling only.

2. Word endings and grammatical labels. Dictionaries can also provide other information. The abbreviation *v.* immediately after the pronunciation would tell you that *compare* is most frequently used as a verb. The suffix *-pared* would show the simple past and past participle form of the verb; the present participle form, *-paring,* indicates that *compare* drops the final *e* when *-ing* is added. The *n.* indicates that *compare* can sometimes function as a noun, as in the phrase *beyond compare.*

Here is a list of common abbreviations for grammatical terms:

adj.	adjective	*prep.*	preposition
adv.	adverb	*pron.*	pronoun
conj.	conjunction	*sing.*	singular
interj.	interjection	*v.*	verb
n.	noun	*v.i.*	intransitive verb
pl.	plural	*v.t.*	transitive verb
poss.	possessive		

3. Definitions, word origins, and usage. In the sample entry, the definition begins with the words ***verb* 1 *transitive,*** which indicates that the first meaning relates to *compare* as a transitive verb. A little farther down in the entry, **3 *intransitive*** introduces a definition of *compare* as an intransitive verb. Next, after ■ ***noun*** comes the definition of *compare* as a noun. Finally, a special meaning not included in

CROSS-DISCIPLINE **WRITING**

Dictionaries

In the library's reference section, you can usually find numerous specialized dictionaries such as biographical and geographical dictionaries; foreign-language dictionaries; dictionaries of first lines of poems and of famous quotations; dictionaries of legal and medical terms; and dictionaries of philosophy, sociology, engineering, and other disciplines. These dictionaries can help you write an essay or simply expand your knowledge of various subjects. Ask the reference librarian to help you locate a useful specialized dictionary for your topic or field.

the previous definitions is given: □ *compare notes* means "exchange ideas or opinions," not to sit down and see how two sets of notes are alike and different.

Included in most dictionary entries is an etymology—a brief history of the word—set off in brackets. There we see earlier words from which compare is derived: the Old French word *comparer*, which came from the Latin *comparare*. Etymological information can be useful to writers who need to define a word for their readers.

A usage note concludes some main entries in the dictionary. In the sample entry, the usage notes are included with the definitions, such as rules for using *compare to* or *compare with*.

4. Tips for using a [print] dictionary.

- **Use the guide words.** At the top of each dictionary page are guide words (usually in bold type) that tell you the first and last words on the page. Because all the entries are in alphabetical order, you can locate the word you are seeking by looking for guide words that would appear before and after your word in an alphabetical listing.

- **Try alternate spellings.** If you cannot find a word on the first try, think of another way to spell it.

- **Use the pronunciation key.** The letters and symbols that indicate each word's pronunciation are explained in a separate section at the front or back of a dictionary. In some dictionaries, they are also summarized at the bottom of each right-hand page of entries. Pronouncing new words aloud will help you learn them.

- **Pay attention to the parts of speech in a definition.** The same word can have different meanings depending on how it is used in a sentence—that is, its part of speech.

- **Always test the meaning you find.** To check whether you have selected the correct word, substitute the meaning for the word in your sentence and see if the sentence makes sense.

36b CONSULTING A THESAURUS FOR WORDS THAT HAVE SIMILAR MEANINGS.

The word *thesaurus* in Latin means "treasury" or "collection." A thesaurus is a dictionary of synonyms. Several kinds of thesauruses are available, many called *Roget's* after Peter Mark Roget (pronounced roZHAY), who published the first one in 1852. Today, thesauruses are included in most word-processing software packages.

Most writers find a thesaurus a pleasure to use, but you need to be cautious when using one. Consider the connotations as well as the denotations of the words you find in the thesaurus.

Tips for using a thesaurus.

- Use a thesaurus to find a more precise word, not a fancier one.

- Know how the words in your thesaurus are arranged. In *Roget's International Thesaurus,* the words are listed in numbered categories, and you need to use the index in the back to find the word whose synonyms you seek. In other thesauruses, the words are arranged in simple alphabetical order like a dictionary. Usually, an online thesaurus will provide synonyms for words that you highlight in your text.

- Never use an unfamiliar synonym that you pick up from a thesaurus without first looking it up in the dictionary. Otherwise, your sentence may be unintentionally humorous or incomprehensible.

- Treat the replacement word carefully in your sentence. Make sure that your replacement has appropriate connotations as well as the correct denotation.

37   Glossary of Usage

Although the meanings of some words change over time, clear communication is enhanced when change takes place slowly and meanings remain relatively constant. The following words and expressions are often confused (such as *advice* and *advise*), misused (such as *etc.*), or considered non-standard (such as *could of*). Consulting this list will help you use words more precisely.

a, an Use *a* with a word that begins with a consonant sound: *a cat, a dog, a one-sided argument, a house.* Use *an* with a word that begins with a vowel sound: *an apple, an X-ray, an honour.*

accept, except *Accept* is a verb meaning "to receive willingly": *Please accept my apologies. Except* is a preposition meaning "but": *Everyone except Julie saw the film.*

adapt, adopt *Adapt* means "to adjust or become accustomed to": *They adapted to the customs of their new country. Adopt* means "to take as one's own": *We adopted a puppy.*

advice, advise *Advice* is a noun; *advise* is a verb: *I took his advice and deeply regretted it. I advise you to disregard it, too.*

affect, effect As a verb, *affect* means "to influence": *Inflation affects our sense of security.* As a noun, *affect* means "a feeling or an emotion": *To study affect, psychologists probe the unconscious.* As a noun, *effect* means "result": *Inflation is one of the many effects of war.* As a verb, *effect* means "to make or accomplish": *Inflation has effected many changes in the way we spend money.*

agree to, agree with *Agree to* means "consent to"; *agree with* means "be in accord with": *They will agree to a peace treaty, even though they do not agree with each other on all points.*

ain't A slang contraction for *is not, am not,* or *are not, ain't* should not be used in formal writing or speech.

all/all of, more/more of, some/some of Except before some pronouns, the "of" in these constructions can usually be eliminated. *All France rejoiced. Some students cut class.* But: *All of us wish you well.*

all ready, already *All ready* means "fully prepared." *Already* means "previously." *We were all ready to go out when we discovered that Jack had already ordered a pizza.*

all right, alright The spelling *alright* is an alternative, but many educated readers still think it is incorrect in standard written English. *He told me it was all right to miss class tomorrow.*

all together, altogether *All together* expresses unity or common location. *Altogether* means "completely," often in a tone of ironic understatement. *At the NRA convention, it was altogether startling to see so many guns set out all together on one table.*

allude, elude, refer to   *Allude* means "to refer indirectly": *He alluded to his miserable adolescence. Elude* means "to avoid" or "to escape from": *She eluded the police for nearly two days.* Do not use *allude* to mean "to refer directly": *The teacher referred* [not *alluded*] *to page 468 in the text.*

almost, most   *Almost* means "nearly." *Most* means "the greater part of." Do not use *most* when you mean *almost. He wrote to me about almost* [not *most*] *everything he did. He told his mother about most things he did.*

a lot   *A lot* is always two words. Do not use *alot.*

A.M., AM, a.m.   These abbreviations mean "before noon" when used with numbers: 6 A.M., 6 a.m. Be consistent in the form you choose, and do not use the abbreviations as a synonym for *morning: In the morning* [not *a.m.*]*, the train is full.*

among, between   Generally, use *among* with three or more nouns, *between* with two. *The distance between Kingston and Montreal is 290 kilometres. The desire to quit smoking is common among those who have smoked for a long time.*

amoral, immoral   *Amoral* means "neither moral nor immoral" and "not caring about moral judgments." *Immoral* means "morally wrong." *Unlike such amoral natural disasters as earthquakes and hurricanes, war is intentionally violent and therefore immoral.*

amount, number   Use *amount* for quantities you cannot count; use *number* for quantities you can count. *The amount of oil left underground in the United States is a matter of dispute, but the number of oil companies losing money is tiny.*

an   *See* a, an.

anxious, eager   *Anxious* means "fearful": *I am anxious before a test. Eager* signals strong interest or desire: *I am eager to be done with that exam.*

anymore, any more   *not anymore* means "no longer." *Not any more* means "no more." Both are used in negative contexts. *I do not enjoy dancing anymore. I do not want any more peanut butter.*

anyone/any one, anybody/any body, everyone/every one, everybody/every body   *Anyone, anybody, everyone,* and *everybody* are indefinite pronouns: *Anybody can make a mistake.* When the pronoun *one* or the noun *body* is modified by the adjective *any* or *every,* the words should be separated by a space: *A good mystery writer accounts for every body that turns up in the story.*

as   Do not use *as* as a synonym for *since, when,* or *because. I told him he should visit Alcatraz since* [not *as*] *he was going to San Francisco. When* [not *as*] *I complained about the meal, the cook said he did not like to eat there himself. Because* [not *as*] *we asked her nicely, our teacher decided to cancel the exam.*

as, like   In formal writing, avoid the use of *like* as a conjunction: *He sneezed as if* [not *like*] *he had a cold. Like* is perfectly acceptable as a preposition that introduces a comparison: *She handled the reins like an expert.*

at Avoid the use of *at* to complete the notion of *where:* not *Where is Michael at?* but *Where is Michael?*

awful, awfully Use *awful* and *awfully* to convey the emotion of terror or wonder (awe-full): *The vampire flew out the window with an awful shriek.* In writing, do not use *awful* to mean "bad" or *awfully* to mean "very" or "extremely."

awhile, a while *Awhile* is an adverb: *Stay awhile with me. A while* is an article and a noun. Always use *a while* after a preposition: *Many authors are unable to write anything else for a while after they publish their first novel.*

being as, being that Do not use *being as* or *being that* as synonyms for *since* or *because. Because* [not *being as*] *the mountain was there, we had to climb it.*

belief, believe *Belief* is a noun meaning "conviction"; *believe* is a verb meaning "to have confidence in the truth of." *Her belief that lying was often justified made it hard for us to believe her story.*

beside, besides *Beside* is a preposition meaning "next to" or "apart from": *The ski slope was beside the lodge. She was beside herself with joy. Besides* is both a preposition and an adverb meaning "in addition to" or "except for": *Besides a bicycle, he will need a tent and a pack.*

between, among *See* among, between.

better Avoid using *better* in expressions of quantity: *Crossing the continent by train took more than* [not *better than*] *four days.*

bring, take Use *bring* when an object is being moved toward you, *take* when it is being moved away: *Please bring me a new disk and take the old one home with you.*

but that, but what In expressions of doubt, avoid writing *but that* or *but what* when you mean *that: I have no doubt that* [not *but that*] *you can learn to write well.*

can, may *Can* refers to ability; *may* refers to possibility or permission. *I see that you can rollerblade without crashing into people, but nevertheless you may not rollerblade on the promenade.*

can't hardly This double negative is ungrammatical and self-contradictory. *I can* [not *can't*] *hardly understand algebra. I can't understand algebra.*

capital, capitol *Capital* refers to a city; *capitol* refers to a building where lawmakers meet. *Protesters travelled to the U.S. state capital to converge on the capitol steps. Capital* also refers to wealth or resources.

censor, censure *Censor* means "to remove or suppress material." *Censure* means "to reprimand formally." *The Chinese government has been censured by Amnesty International for censoring newspapers.*

cite, sight, site The verb *cite* means "to quote or mention": *Be sure to cite all your sources in your bibliography.* As a noun, the word *sight* means "view": *It was love at first sight. Site* is a noun meaning "a particular place": locations on the Internet are referred to as *sites.*

compare to, compare with Use *compare to* to point out similarities between two unlike things: *She compared his singing to the croaking of a* *wounded frog.* Use *compare with* for differences or likenesses between two similar things: *Compare Shakespeare's* Antony and Cleopatra *with Dryden's* All for Love.

complement, compliment *Complement* means "something that goes well with something else": *I consider sauerkraut the perfect complement to sausages. Compliment* means "praise": *She received many compliments on her thesis.*

conscience, conscious The noun *conscience* means "a sense of right and wrong": *His conscience bothered him.* The adjective *conscious* means "awake" or "aware": *I was conscious of a presence in the room.*

continual, continuous *Continual* means "repeated regularly and frequently": *She continually checked her computer for new e-mail. Continuous* means "extended or prolonged without interruption": *The car alarm made a continuous wail in the night.*

could of, should of, would of Avoid these ungrammatical forms of *could have, should have,* and *would have.*

criteria, criterion *Criteria* is the plural form of the Latin word *criterion,* meaning "standard of judgment." *The criteria are not very strict. The most important criterion is whether you can do the work.*

data *Data* is the plural form of the Latin word *datum,* meaning "fact." Although *data* is often used informally as a singular noun, in writing, treat *data* as a plural noun: *The data indicate that recycling has gained popularity.*

differ from, differ with *Differ from* expresses a lack of similarity; *differ with* expresses disagreement. *The ancient Greeks differed less from the Persians than we often think. Aristotle differed with Plato on some important issues.*

different from, different than The correct idiom is *different from* and is used in comparison to something else. Avoid *different than. The east coast of Florida is very different from the west coast.*

discreet, discrete *Discreet* means "tactful" or "prudent." *Discrete* means "separate" or "distinct." *What's a discreet way of telling them that these are two discrete issues?*

disinterested, uninterested *Disinterested* means "impartial": *We expect members of a jury to be disinterested. Uninterested* means "indifferent" or "unconcerned": *Most people today are uninterested in alchemy.*

don't, doesn't *Don't* is the contraction for *do not* and is used with *I, you, we, they,* and plural nouns. *Doesn't* is the contraction for *does not* and is used with *he, she, it,* and singular nouns. *You don't know what you're talking about. He doesn't know what you're talking about either.*

due to, because of *Due to* is an overworked and often confusing expression when it is used for *because of.* Use *due to* only in expressions of time in infinitive constructions after the verb "is" or in other contexts where the meaning is "scheduled." *The plane is due to arrive in one hour. He is due to receive a promotion this year.*

each and every Use one of these words or the other but not both. *Every cow came in at feeding time. Each one had to be watered.*

each other, one another Use *each other* in sentences involving two subjects and *one another* in sentences involving more than two. *Husbands and wives should help each other. Classmates should share ideas with one another.*

eager, anxious *See* anxious, eager.

effect, affect *See* affect, effect.

e.g., i.e. The abbreviation *e.g.* stands for the Latin words meaning "for example." The abbreviation *i.e.* stands for the Latin for "that is." *Come as soon as you can, i.e., today or tomorrow. Bring fruit with you, e.g., apples and peaches.* In formal writing, replace the abbreviations with the English words: *Keats wrote many different kinds of lyrics, for example, odes, sonnets, and songs.*

either, neither Both *either* and *neither* are singular: *Neither of the two boys has played the game. Either of the two girls is willing to show you the way home. Either* has an intensive use that *neither* does not, and when it is used as an intensive, *either* is always negative: *She told him she would not go either.* (For *either . . . or* and *neither . . . nor* constructions, see page 278.)

elicit, illicit The verb *elicit* means "to draw out." The adjective *illicit* means "unlawful." *The detective was unable to elicit any information about other illicit activity.*

elude, allude *See* allude, elude, refer to.

emigrate, immigrate *Emigrate* means "to move away from one's country": *My grandfather emigrated from Greece to Canada in 1945. Immigrate* means "to move to another country and settle there": *Grandpa immigrated to Canada from Greece in 1945.*

eminent, imminent, immanent *Eminent* means "celebrated" or "well known": *Many eminent Victorians were melancholy and disturbed. Imminent* means "about to happen" or "about to come": *In August 1939, many Europeans sensed that war was imminent. Immanent* refers to something invisible but dwelling throughout the world: *Medieval Christians believed that God's power was immanent through the universe.*

etc. The abbreviation *etc.* stands for the Latin *et cetera,* meaning "and others" or "and other things." Because *and* is included in the abbreviation, do not write *and etc.* In a series, a comma comes before *etc.,* just as it would before the coordinating conjunction that closes a series: *He brought string, wax, paper, etc.* In most college writing, it is better to end a series of examples with a final example or the words *and so on.*

everybody/every body, everyone/every one *See* anyone/any one. . .

except, accept *See* accept, except.

expect, suppose *Expect* means "to hope" or "to anticipate": *I expect a good grade on my final paper. Suppose* means "to presume": *I suppose you did not win the lottery on Saturday.*

explicit, implicit *Explicit* means "stated outright." *Implicit* means "implied, unstated." *Her explicit instructions were to go to the party without her, but the implicit message she conveyed was disapproval.*

farther, further   *Farther* describes geographical distances: *Six kilometres farther on is a hotel. Further* means "in addition" when geography is not involved: *He said further that he didn't like my attitude.*

fewer, less   *Fewer* refers to items that can be counted individually; *less* refers to general amounts. *Fewer people signed up for indoor soccer this year than last. Your argument has less substance than you think.*

first, firstly   *Firstly* is common in British English but not in Canada and the United States. *First, second, third* are the accepted forms.

flaunt, flout   *Flaunt* means "to wave" or "to show publicly" with a delight tinged with pride and even arrogance: *He flaunted his wealth by wearing overalls lined with mink. Flout* means "to scorn" or "to defy," especially in a public way, seemingly without concern for the consequences: *She flouted the traffic laws by running through red lights.*

former, latter   *Former* refers to the first and *latter* to the second of two things mentioned previously: *Mario and Alice are both good cooks; the former is fonder of Chinese cooking, the latter of Mexican.*

further, farther   *See* farther, further.

get   In formal writing, avoid colloquial uses of *get*, as in *get with it, get it all together, get-up-and-go, get it,* and *that gets me.*

good, well   *Good* is an adjective and should not be used in place of the adverb *well. He felt good about doing well on the exam.*

half, a half, half a   Write *half, a half,* or *half a* but not *half of, a half a,* or *a half of. Half the clerical staff went out on strike. I want a half-dozen eggs to throw at the actors. Half a loaf is better than none, unless you are on a diet.*

hanged, hung   People are *hanged* by the neck until dead. Pictures and all other things that can be suspended are *hung.*

hopefully   *Hopefully* means "with hope." It is often misused to mean "it is hoped." *We waited hopefully for our ship to come in* [not *Hopefully, our ship will come in*].

i.e., e.g.   *See* e.g., i.e.

if . . . then   Avoid using these words in tandem. Redundant: *If I get my licence, then I can drive a cab.* Better: *If I get my licence, I can drive a cab. Once I get my licence, I can drive a cab.*

illicit, elicit   *See* elicit, illicit.

imminent, immanent   *See* eminent, imminent, immanent.

immigrate, emigrate   *See* emigrate, immigrate.

immoral, amoral   *See* amoral, immoral.

implicit, explicit   *See* explicit, implicit.

imply, infer   *Imply* means "to suggest something without stating it directly": *By putting his fingers in his ears, he implied that she should stop singing. Infer* means "to draw a conclusion from evidence": *When she dozed off in the middle of his declaration of eternal love, he inferred that she did not feel the same way about him.*

in, in to, into *In* refers to a location inside something: *Charles kept a snake in his room. In to* refers to motion with a purpose: *The resident manager came in to capture it. Into* refers to movement from outside to inside or from separation to contact: *The snake escaped by crawling into a drain. The manager ran into the wall, and Charles got into big trouble.*

incredible, incredulous The *incredible* cannot be believed; the *incredulous* do not believe. Stories and events may be *incredible*; people are *incredulous*. *Nancy told an incredible story of being abducted by a UFO over the weekend. We were all incredulous.*

infer, imply *See* imply, infer.

inside of, outside of The "of" is unnecessary in these phrases: *He was outside the house.*

ironically *Ironically* means "contrary to what was or might have been expected." It should not be confused with *surprisingly,* which means "unexpected," or with *coincidentally,* which means "occurring at the same time or place." *Ironically, his fast ball lost speed after his arm healed.*

irregardless This construction is a double negative because both the prefix *ir-* and the suffix *-less* are negatives. Use *regardless* instead.

it's, its *It's* is a contraction, usually for *it is* but sometimes for *it has: It's often been said that English is a difficult language to learn. Its* is a possessive pronoun: *The dog sat down and scratched its fleas.*

kind, kinds *Kind* is singular: *This kind of house is easy to build. Kinds* is plural and should be used only to indicate more than one kind: *These three kinds of toys are better than those two kinds.*

lay, lie *Lay* means "to place." Its main forms are *lay, laid,* and *laid.* It generally has a direct object, specifying what has been placed: *She laid her book on the steps and left it there. Lie* means "to recline" and does not take a direct object. Its main forms are *lie, lay,* and *lain: She often lay awake at night.*

less, fewer *See* fewer, less.

like, as *See* as, like.

literally *Literally* means "actually" or "exactly as written": *Literally thousands gathered along the parade route.* Do not use *literally* as an intensive adverb when it can be misleading or even ridiculous, as here: *His blood literally boiled.*

loose, lose *Loose* is an adjective that means "not securely attached." *Lose* is a verb that means "to misplace." *Better tighten that loose screw before you lose the whole structure.*

may, can *See* can, may.

maybe, may be *Maybe* is an adverb meaning "perhaps": *Maybe he can get a summer job as a lifeguard. May be* is a verb phrase meaning "is possible": *It may be that I can get a job as a lifeguard, too.*

moral, morale *Moral* means "lesson," especially a lesson about standards of behaviour or the nature of life: *The moral of the story is do not drink and drive. Morale* means "attitude" or "mental condition": *Office morale dropped sharply after the dean was arrested.*

more/more of   *See* all/all of . . .

more important, more importantly   The correct idiom is *more important,* not *more importantly.*

most, almost   *See* almost, most.

myself (himself, herself, etc.)   Pronouns ending with *-self* refer to or intensify other words: *Jack hurt himself. Standing in the doorway was the man himself.* When you are unsure whether to use *I* or *me, she* or *her, he* or *him* in a compound subject or object, you may be tempted to substitute one of the *-self* pronouns. Don't do it. *The quarrel was between her and me* [not *myself*]. *(Also see Problems with Pronouns beginning on p. 329 in Tab 8.)*

neither, either   *See* either, neither.

nohow, nowheres   These words are non-standard for *anyway, in no way, in any way, in any place,* and *in no place.* Do not use them in formal writing.

number, amount   *See* amount, number.

off of   Omit the *of*: *She took the painting off the wall.*

one another, each other   *See* each other, one another.

outside of, inside of   *See* inside of, outside of.

plus   Avoid using *plus* as a substitute for *and: He had to walk the dog, do the dishes, empty the garbage, and* [not *plus*] *write a term paper.*

practicable, practical   *Practicable* is an adjective applied to things that can be done: *A space program that would land human beings on Mars is now practicable. Practical* means "sensible": *Many people do not think such a journey is practical.*

precede, proceed   *Precede* means "come before"; *proceed* means "go forward." *Despite the heavy snows that preceded us, we managed to proceed up the hiking trail.*

previous to, prior to   Avoid these wordy and somewhat pompous substitutions for *before.*

principal, principle   *Principal* is an adjective meaning "most important" or a noun meaning "the head of an organization" or "a sum of money": *Our principal objections to the school's principal are that he is a liar and a cheat. Principle* is a noun meaning "a basic standard or law": *We believe in the principles of honesty and fair play.*

proceed, precede   *See* precede, proceed.

quote, quotation   *To quote* means to repeat a passage or refer to something as proof. *He was able to quote several situations of negative behaviour. She quoted the professor.* On the other hand, *quotation* is the noun that refers to the passage or expression being cited. *He used several long quotations from the book to support his argument.*

raise, rise   *Raise* means "to lift or cause to move upward." It takes a direct object—someone raises something: *I raised the windows in the classroom. Rise* means "to go upward." It does not take a direct object—something rises by itself: *We watched the balloon rise to the ceiling.*

real, really Do not use the word *real* or *really* when you mean *very*: *The cake was very* [not *real* or *really*] *good.*

reason . . . is because This is a redundant expression. Use either *the reason is that* or *because*: *The reason he fell on the ice is that he cannot skate. He fell on the ice because he cannot skate.*

refer to *See* allude, elude, refer to.

relation, relationship *Relation* describes a connection between things: *There is a relation between smoking and lung cancer. Relationship* describes a connection between people: *The brothers have always had a close relationship.*

respectfully, respectively *Respectfully* means "with respect": *Treat your partners respectfully. Respectively* means "in the given order": *The three Williams she referred to were Shakespeare, Wordsworth, and Yeats, respectively.*

rise, raise *See* raise, rise.

set, sit *Set* is usually a transitive verb meaning "to establish" or "to place." It takes a direct object, and its principal parts are *set, set,* and *set: DiMaggio set the standard of excellence in fielding. She set the box down in the corner. Sit* is usually intransitive, meaning "to place oneself in a sitting position." Its principal parts are *sit, sat,* and *sat: The dog sat on command.*

shall, will *Shall* was once the standard first-person future form of the verb *to be* when a simple statement of fact was intended: *I shall be twenty-one on my next birthday.* Today, most writers use *will* in the ordinary future tense for the first person: *I will celebrate my birthday by throwing a big party. Shall* is still used in questions. *Shall we dance?*

should of, could of *See* could of, should of, would of.

site, sight, cite *See* cite, sight, site.

some Avoid using the adjective *some* in place of the adverb *somewhat*: *He felt somewhat* [not *some*] *better after a good night's sleep.*

some of *See* all/all of . . .

somewheres Use *somewhere* or *someplace* instead.

stationary, stationery *Stationary* means "standing still": *I worked out on my stationary bicycle. Stationery* is writing paper: *That stationery smells like a rose garden.*

suppose, expect *See* expect, suppose.

sure Avoid confusing the adjective *sure* with the adverb *surely*: *The dress she wore to the party was surely bizarre.*

sure and, sure to *Sure and* is often used colloquially. In formal writing, *sure to* is preferred: *Be sure to* [not *be sure and*] *get to the wedding on time.*

take, bring *See* bring, take.

that, which Many writers use *that* for restrictive (that is, essential) clauses and *which* for non-restrictive (that is, non-essential) clauses. *The bull that escaped from the ring ran through my china shop, which was located in the square. (Also see Commas, pp. 347–359, in Tab 9.)*

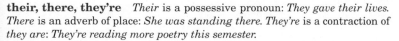

their, there, they're   *Their* is a possessive pronoun: *They gave their lives.* *There* is an adverb of place: *She was standing there.* *They're* is a contraction of *they are*: *They're reading more poetry this semester.*

then/than   The mandatory retirement age is higher *than* it was *then*.

this here, these here, that there, them there   When writing, avoid these non-standard forms.

to, too, two   *To* is a preposition; *too* is an adverb; *two* is a number. *The two of us got lost too many times on our way to his house.*

try and, try to   *Try to* is the standard form: *Try to* [not *try and*] *understand.*

uninterested, disinterested   *See* disinterested, uninterested.

use, utilize   *Utilize* seldom says more than *use,* and the simpler term is almost always better: *We must learn how to use the computer's zip drive.*

verbally, orally   To say something *orally* is to say it aloud: *We agreed orally to share credit for the work, but when I asked her to confirm it in writing, she refused.* To say something *verbally* is to use words: *His eyes flashed anger, but he did not express his feelings verbally.*

wait for, wait on   People *wait for* those who are late; they *wait on* tables.

weather, whether   The noun *weather* refers to the atmosphere: *She worried that the weather would not clear up in time for the victory celebration. Whether* is a conjunction referring to a choice between alternatives: *I can't decide whether to go now or next week.*

well, good   *See* good, well.

which, who, whose   *Which* is used for things, *who* and *whose* for people. *My fountain pen, which I had lost last week, was found by a child who had never seen one before, whose whole life had been spent with ballpoint pens.*

whether, weather   *See* weather, whether.

will, shall   *See* shall, will.

would of   *See* could of, should of, would of.

your, you're   *Your* is a possessive pronoun: *Is that your new car? You're* is a contraction of *you are*: *You're a lucky guy.*

8

EDITING
FOR GRAMMAR

8 Editing for Grammar

When you edit, your purpose is to make your sentences clearer and stronger. One way to improve your writing is to edit for common grammatical problems, but it is sometimes difficult to "see" grammatical problems in your own work. To overcome this difficulty, focus on each sentence in turn and look for problems that may confuse or distract readers. Ask yourself the following questions:

- Does each sentence include a subject, a complete verb, and an independent clause? (*See Chapter 38, Sentence Fragments, below.*)

- Does any sentence seem like two or more sentences jammed together without a break? If a sentence has more than one independent clause, are those clauses joined in an acceptable way? (*See Chapter 39, Comma Splices and Run-on Sentences, p. 304.*)

- Do the key parts of each sentence fit together well, or are the subjects and verbs mismatched in person and number? (*See Chapter 40, Subject-Verb Agreement, p. 308.*)

- Is the time frame of events represented accurately and consistently, or are there problems with verb form, tense, and sequence? (*See Chapter 41, Problems with Verbs, p. 316.*)

- Do the pronouns in every sentence clearly refer to a specific noun or pronoun and agree with the nouns or pronouns they replace? (*See Chapter 42, Problems with Pronouns, p. 329.*)

- Does the form of each modifier match its function in the sentence? (*See Chapter 43, Problems with Adjectives and Adverbs, p. 338.*)

Sentence Fragments 38

A complete sentence is a group of words that contains a subject and verb. It also must express a complete thought. As you edit, look for unintentional sentence fragments.

Learn how to identify sentence fragments. Does the following example contain two complete sentences?

POSSIBLE   Pool hustlers deceive their opponents in many ways.

FRAGMENT   For example, deliberately putting so much spin on the ball that it jumps out of the intended pocket.

A complete sentence meets all three of the following requirements:

- **A sentence names a *subject*,** the who or what that the sentence is about. To locate a sentence's subject, find the verb and ask the *who* or *what* question about it. In the first group (example above), *who* or *what deceive*s opponents? The answer is *Pool hustlers,* the subject of the first sentence. In the second group, *who* or *what* is *putting spin on the ball?* The word group does not provide an answer, but it does provide an answer to the question *who or what jumps?* The answer is *it* (the ball).

- **A sentence has a complete *verb* that indicates tense, person, and number.** In the first group, *deceive* is the third-person plural form of the verb in the present tense and is a complete verb. In the second group, however, *putting* is not a complete verb; instead, it is a verbal, a word derived from a verb. (*For more on verbals, see pp. 302 and 325.*)

- **A sentence includes at least one independent *clause*.** An independent clause has a subject and a complete verb. In the example, the first group, which has a subject and a complete verb, is an independent clause. Even though the second group includes the subject-plus-verb combination *it jumps,* the combination is preceded by the subordinating word *that,* so the clause cannot be considered independent. The phrase that precedes it, *deliberately putting so much spin on the ball,* does not include a subject and a complete verb.

In the example, the first group meets all three requirements and is a complete sentence. Although the second group has a subject and a complete verb, they are part of a dependent clause that begins with the subordinating word *that.* Because the second group does not have an independent clause with a subject and a complete verb, it is not a complete sentence.

Intentional fragments. Advertisers often use attention-getting fragments: "Got Milk?" "Nothing but Net." "Because you're worth it." You may want to use a sentence fragment for stylistic reasons, but you should avoid these types of "grabber" phrases in formal academic writing. Advertising and academic writing have different contexts, purposes, and writing parameters. In formal writing, standard English is the expected norm in most post-secondary work. For that reason, avoid using deliberate sentence fragments.

Repair sentence fragments in one of two ways. You can fix unintentional fragments in one of two ways: either transform them into sentences or attach them to a nearby independent clause. Consider the following examples.

➤ **Pool hustlers deceive their opponents in many ways.**
 they
 For example, deliberately ~~putting~~ so much spin on the ball
 ^
 that it jumps out of the intended pocket.

➤ **Pool hustlers deceive their opponents in many ways/,**
 ^
 for example, by
 ~~For example~~, deliberately putting so much spin on the ball
 ^
 that it jumps out of the intended pocket.

38a DEPENDENT CLAUSES AS FRAGMENTS.

Fragments often begin with a subordinating word such as *although, because, even though, since, so that, whenever,* or *whereas.* Usually, a fragment that begins with a subordinating word can be attached to a nearby independent clause.

➤ **On the questionnaire, none of the thirty-three subjects indicated**
 any concern about the amount or kind of fruit the institution
 even
 served/, ~~Even~~ though all of them identified diet as an important
 ^
 issue for those with diabetes.

As the next example shows, however, it is sometimes better to transform such a fragment into a complete sentence by deleting the subordinating word.

➤ **The solidarity of our health team was undermined in two ways.**
 Participants
 ~~When participants~~ either disagreed about triage priorities or
 ^
 advocated significantly different treatment strategies.

38b PHRASES AS FRAGMENTS.

Unintentional fragments come in a variety of forms. Often they are **phrases**, word groups that lack a subject or a complete verb or both and usually function as modifiers or nouns. Phrase fragments frequently begin with **verbals**—words derived from verbs, such as *putting* or *to put*. Here is an example of a phrase fragment that begins with an *-ing* verbal.

> FRAGMENT   That summer, we had the time of our lives.
> Playing outside from morning until night.

One way to fix this fragment is to transform it into an independent clause with its own subject and verb:

➤ **That summer, we had the time of our lives. We played outside**

   from morning until night.

Notice that all of the *-ing* verbals in the fragment need to be changed to keep the phrases in the new sentence parallel. (*For more on parallelism, see Tab 7: Editing for Clarity, pp. 227–228.*)

Another way to fix the problem is to attach the fragment to the part of the previous sentence that it modifies (in this case, the *time of our lives*):

➤ **That summer, we had the time of our lives/, playing outside from**

   morning until night.

Phrase fragments can also begin with one-word prepositions such as *as, at, by, for, from, in, of, on,* or *to*. To correct these types of fragments, it is usually easiest to attach them to a nearby sentence.

➤ **Impressionist painters often depicted their subjects in everyday**
                    at
   situations/, a restaurant, perhaps, or by the seashore.

38c OTHER TYPES OF FRAGMENTS.

Phrase fragments don't always begin with subordinating words, verbals, or one-word prepositions. Other word groups that can also cause problems include word groups that start with transitions or with words that introduce examples, appositives, lists, and compound predicates.

1. Watch for word groups that start with transitions. As the following example shows, some fragments start with two- or three-word prepositions that function as transitions, such as *as well as, as* *compared with, except for, in addition to, in contrast with, in spite of,* and *instead of.*

➤ **For the past sixty-five years, growth in the town of Beaver Creek**

as

has been both steep and steady/, As compared with the growth
^

in Moose Pond, which declined significantly.

2. Watch for words and phrases that introduce examples. It is always a good idea to check word groups beginning with *for example, like, specifically, including,* or *such as.* When you spot one of these words or phrases, make sure that the word group it introduces is a complete sentence.

➤ **Elizabeth I of England faced many dangers as a princess. For**

she fell

example, falling out of favour with her sister, Queen Mary, and
^

was

being imprisoned in the Tower of London.
^

including

➤ **In my English class, we had to read many books/, Including**
^

Hey Nostradamus! **by Douglas Coupland.**

3. Watch for appositives. An **appositive** is a noun or noun phrase that renames a noun or pronoun.

the

➤ **We visited the home of Lucy Maud Montgomery/, The author of**
^

Anne of Green Gables.

4. Watch for fragments that consist of lists. Usually, you can connect a list to the preceding sentence using a colon. If you want to emphasize the list, consider using a dash instead.

➤ **The engineer's performance can be described in three words/:**
^

w

Weak, uninspired, and deeply flawed.

5. Watch for fragments that are parts of compound predicates. A compound predicate is made up of at least two verbs as well as their objects and modifiers, connected by a coordinating conjunction such as *and, but,* or *or.* The parts of a compound predicate have the same subject and should be together in one sentence.

and

➤ **The firefighters gathered back at the fire hall/, And reassembled**
^

their equipment in preparation for the next call.

39 Comma Splices and Run-on Sentences

A **comma splice** is a sentence with at least two independent clauses joined by only a comma.

> COMMA
> SPLICE
> Dogs that compete in the annual dog show are already champions, they have each won at least one dog show before arriving at this competition.

A **run-on sentence**, sometimes called a **fused sentence**, does not even have a comma between the independent clauses, making it difficult for readers to tell where one clause ends and the next clause begins.

> RUN-ON
> From time to time, new breeds enter the ring the Border Collie is a recent addition to the show.

Learn how to identify comma splices and run-on sentences. Comma splices and run-ons often occur when clauses are linked with a transitional expression such as *as a result, for example, in addition, in other words, on the contrary* or a conjunctive adverb such as *however, consequently, moreover, nevertheless.* (*See p. 306 for a list of familiar conjunctive adverbs and transitional expressions.*)

> COMMA
> SPLICE
> Louis Riel led the Métis Rebellion in 1885, he was considered both a hero and a madman.

> RUN-ON
> Most nurses complied with the new policy however a few refused to do so.

(*For help punctuating a sentence that links clauses with a transitional expression or conjunctive adverb, see Tab 9: Editing for Correctness, pp. 360–361.*)

Run-ons may also occur when a sentence's second clause either specifies or explains its first clause.

> RUN-ON
> The economy changed in 2008 corporate bankruptcies increased by 40 percent.

To find comma splices and run-ons, begin by checking those sentences that include transitional expressions or conjunctive adverbs. If a comma precedes one of these words or phrases, you may have found a comma splice. If no punctuation precedes one of them, you may have found a run-on sentence. Check the word groups that precede and follow the conjunctive adverb or transitional expression. Can they both stand alone as sentences? If so, you have found a comma splice or a run-on sentence.

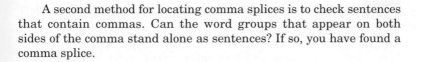

A second method for locating comma splices is to check sentences that contain commas. Can the word groups that appear on both sides of the comma stand alone as sentences? If so, you have found a comma splice.

Repair comma splices and run-on sentences in one of five ways.

1. Join the two clauses with a comma and a coordinating conjunction (*and, but, or, nor, for, so, yet*).

   ➤ **Dogs that compete in the annual Dog Show are already**
      for
      champions, they have each won at least one dog show
               ^

      before arriving at this competition.

2. Join the two clauses with a semicolon.

   ➤ **From time to time, new breeds enter the ring; the Border**
                                                ^

      Collie is a recent addition to the show.

   You can also add an appropriate conjunctive adverb or transitional expression, followed by a comma.

                                                    ; for instance,
   ➤ **From time to time, new breeds enter the ring the Border**
                                                  ^

      Collie is a recent addition to the show.

3. Separate the clauses into two sentences.

   ➤ **Salt is very bad for the body's absorption of calcium.**
      . Therefore,
      ~~**therefore**~~ **women in danger of developing osteoporosis**
                    ^

      should cut down on the amount they consume.

4. Turn one of the independent clauses into a dependent clause.

   ➤ **English majors should make sure to leave lots of reading**
                                    because
      time in their schedules, some of these novels are
                              ^

      extremely long.

5. Transform the two clauses into a single independent clause.

                                 or
   ➤ **Some engineers played with Lego/ ~~some even liked~~**
                                      ^

      meccano sets when they were young.

39a   REPAIRING WITH A COMMA AND A COORDINATING CONJUNCTION.

If you decide to correct a comma splice or run-on by joining the two clauses, be sure to choose the coordinating conjunction, such as *and, but, or, nor, for, so,* or *yet,* which most clearly expresses the logical relationship between the clauses. In the example below, the logical coordinating conjunction is *so.*

➤ Anika is a very stubborn person, *so* I had a hard time convincing

   her to let me do the dishes for her when she was sick.

39b   REPAIRING WITH A SEMICOLON.

Like a coordinating conjunction, a semicolon tells your reader that two clauses are logically connected. However, a semicolon does not spell out the logic of the connection.

➤ Most nurses complied with the new policy**;** a few refused

   to do so.

To make the logic of the connection clear, you can add an appropriate conjunctive adverb or transitional expression.

➤ Most nurses complied with the new policy **; however,** a few refused

   to do so.

Familiar Conjunctive Adverbs and Transitional Expressions

also	incidentally	now
as a result	indeed	nonetheless
besides	in fact	of course
certainly	in other words	on the contrary
consequently	instead	otherwise
finally	in the meantime	similarly
for example	likewise	still
for instance	meanwhile	then
furthermore	moreover	therefore
however	nevertheless	thus
in addition	next	undoubtedly

Note: The conjunctive adverb or transitional expression is usually followed by a comma when it appears at the beginning of the second clause. It can also appear in the middle of a clause, set off by two commas, or at the end, preceded by a comma.

➤ Most nurses complied with the new policy/; a few *, however,* refused

to do so.

➤ Most nurses complied with the new policy/; a few refused
      , however
to do so.

Often the first independent clause introduces the second one. In this situation, you can add a colon instead of a semicolon. A colon is also appropriate if the second clause expands on the first one in some way. (*See Tab 9: Editing for Correctness, pp. 362–364.*)

➤ Professor Jafarpour then revealed his most important point: the

paper would count for half of my grade.

39c REPAIRING BY SEPARATING INTO TWO SENTENCES.

The simplest way to correct comma splices and run-on sentences is to turn the clauses into separate sentences. This is not always the best solution, however, especially if the result is one short, simple sentence followed by another. The simplest solution works well in this example because the second sentence is a compound sentence.

➤ I realized that it was time to choose/ ~~either~~ I had pursue
           . Either

engineering, or I had to follow my life-long dream of becoming

an opera singer.

When the two independent clauses are part of a quote, with a phrase such as *he said* or *she noted* between them, each clause should be a separate sentence.

➤ "This was the longest day of my life," she said/ ~~"unfortunately,~~
          . "Unfortunately,

it's not over yet."

39d REPAIRING BY MAKING ONE CLAUSE DEPENDENT.

In the following sentence, the writer chose to make the clause about a *few* her main point and the clause about *most students* a subordinate idea. Because she made this choice, readers will expect subsequent sentences to tell them more about those few nurses who refused to comply.

➤ *Although most*
~~Most~~ nurses complied with the new policy, ~~however~~ a few

refused to do so.

39e REPAIRING BY REWORKING THE SENTENCE.

It is possible (but not easy) to transform the two clauses into one clear and correct independent clause. This kind of transformation is often worth the work, however.

➤ I realized that it was time ~~to choose~~, either ~~I had~~ to pursue

engineering or ~~I had~~ to follow my life-long dream of becoming

an opera singer.

Often you can change one of the clauses to a phrase and place it next to the word it modifies.

➤ *, first printed in the nineteenth century,*
Baseball cards are an obsession among some collectors~~/. the~~

~~cards were first printed in the nineteenth century.~~

40   Subject-Verb Agreement

All verbs must agree with their subjects in person (first, second, or third—*I, we; you; he, she, it, they*) and number (singular or plural).

➤ A *judge lives* around the corner from me.

Judge is a third-person singular noun, and *lives* is the third-person singular form of the verb.

➤ **Many North American *writers wish* that they had the "no income tax" plan that Irish writers enjoy.**

Writers is a third-person plural noun, and *wish* is the third-person plural form of the verb.

For a summary of standard verb forms as well as the forms of the irregular verbs *be, have,* and *do,* see below.

Problems with subject-verb agreement tend to occur when writers do the following:

- Lose sight of the subject (*40b, p. 310*)
- Use compound, collective, or indefinite subjects (*40c–e, pp. 311–312*)
- Have a subject that follows the verb (*40f, p. 314*)
- Confuse a subject complement with the subject (*40g, p. 314*)
- Use a relative pronoun as the subject of a dependent clause (*40h, p. 315*)
- Use a phrase beginning with an *-ing* verb as the subject (*40i, p. 315*)

40a STANDARD SUBJECT-VERB COMBINATIONS.

For regular verbs, the present tense *-s* or *-es* ending is added to the verb if its subject is third-person singular; otherwise, the verb has no ending.

Present Tense Forms of the Regular Verb *walk*

	SINGULAR	PLURAL
First Person	I *walk.*	We *walk.*
Second Person	You *walk.*	You *walk.*
Third Person	He, she, it *walks.*	They *walk.*

Note, however, that the verb *be* has irregular forms in both the present and the past tense.

Present tense and past tense forms of the irregular verb *be*

	SINGULAR	PLURAL
First Person	I *am/was* here.	We *are/were* here.
Second Person	You *are/were* here.	You *are/were* here.
Third Person	He, she, it *is/was* here.	They *are/were* here.

The verbs *have* and *do* have the following forms in the present tense.

Present Tense Forms of the Verb *have*

	SINGULAR	PLURAL
First Person	I *have.*	We *have.*
Second Person	You *have.*	You *have.*
Third Person	He, she, it *has.*	They *have.*

Present Tense Forms of the Verb *do* and its Negative *don't*

	SINGULAR	PLURAL
First Person	I *do/don't.*	We *do/don't.*
Second Person	You *do/don't.*	You *do/don't.*
Third Person	He, she, it *does/doesn't.*	They *do/don't.*

40b A WORD GROUP BETWEEN SUBJECT AND VERB.

When you are checking for subject-verb agreement, begin by locating the subject. A word group often separates the subject and the verb.

To locate the subject of a sentence, find the verb (for example, *is*), and then ask the *who* or *what* question about it ("Who is?" "What is?"). Does that subject match the verb in number?

➤ The New Democratic Party ~~oppose~~ *opposes* the back-to-work legislation.

The answer to the question "Who opposes?" is *New Democratic Party,* a singular noun, so the verb should be in the singular form: *opposes.*

Note: If a word group beginning with *as well as, along with,* or *in addition to* follows a singular subject, the subject does not become plural.

➤ My teacher, as well as other faculty members, ~~oppose~~ *opposes* the new

school policy.

40c COMPOUND SUBJECTS CONNECTED BY CONJUNCTIONS (*AND, OR, NOR, BOTH . . . AND, EITHER . . . OR, NEITHER . . . NOR*).

Compound subjects are made up of two or more parts joined by either a coordinating conjunction (*and, or, nor*) or a correlative conjunction (*both . . . and, either . . . or, neither . . . nor*).

1. Most compound subjects are plural. Most subjects that are joined by *and* should be treated as plural.

PLURAL   *The CEO and her advisors were* shocked by this

sharp downturn in business.

PLURAL   This poem's *first line and last word have* a powerful

effect on the reader.

2. Some compound subjects are singular. There are exceptions to the rule that subjects joined by *and* are plural. Compound subjects should be treated as singular in the following circumstances:

- When they refer to the same entity:

  ➤ *My best girlfriend and most dependable advisor is* my
  mother.

- When they are considered as a single unit:

  ➤ In some ways, *forty hectares and a tractor continues* to be
  what is needed.

- When they are preceded by the word *each* or *every:*

  ➤ *Each* student, professor, and member of the support staff
  deserves respect.

3. Some compound subjects can be either plural or singular. Compound subjects connected by *or, nor, either . . . or, or neither . . . nor* can take either a singular or a plural verb, depending on the subject that is closest to the verb.

SINGULAR   **Either the economy or *the government is* to blame.**

PLURAL   **Neither the experimenter nor *her subjects were***

aware of the takeover.

40d COLLECTIVE SUBJECTS (*AUDIENCE, FAMILY, COMMITTEE, JURY*).

A collective noun names a unit made up of many persons or things, treating it as an entity. Some familiar examples are *audience, family, group, committee, jury,* and *team.*

1. Most often, collective nouns are singular. Collective nouns such as *audience, family, group, crowd, team, committee, chorus, herd,* and *tribe* are usually treated as singular. *News* is usually singular as well, despite its *-s* ending, because it functions as a collective subject, representing a collective unit. Units of measurement used collectively, such as *six centimetres* or *20%,* are also treated as singular.

➤ The *audience is* restless.

➤ That *news leaves* me speechless.

➤ *One-fourth* of the liquid *was* poured into test tube 1.

Note: Titles of works or names of companies are singular.

➤ Timothy Findley's *The Wars is* a brutal account of one young

man's experiences during World War I.

2. Some collective subjects are plural. When the members of a group are acting as individuals, the collective subject can be considered plural.

➤ The *group were* passing around a bottle of beer.

You may want to add a modifying phrase that contains a plural noun to make the sentence clearer and avoid awkwardness.

➤ The *group of troublemakers were* passing around a bottle of beer.

The modifying phrase *of troublemakers* makes the sentence less awkward.

When units of measurement refer to people or things, they are plural.

➤ *Forty percent* of first marriages in Canada *end* in divorce.

40e INDEFINITE SUBJECTS (*EVERYBODY, NO ONE*).

Indefinite pronouns such as *everybody* and *no one* do not refer to a specific person or item.

1. Most indefinite pronouns are singular. The following indefinite pronouns are always singular: *all, anybody, anyone, anything, each, either, everybody, everyone, everything, neither, nobody, no one, none, nothing, one, somebody, someone,* and *something.*

➤ *Everyone* in my hiking club *is* an experienced climber.

None and *neither* are singular when they appear by themselves.

➤ Last spring we had five baby birds fly away from the nest on our

porch, but *none returned* this year.

➤ *Neither sees* a way out of this predicament.

If a prepositional phrase that includes a plural noun or pronoun follows *none* or *neither,* the indefinite pronoun seems to have a plural meaning. Although some writers treat *none* or *neither* as plural in such situations, other authorities on language maintain that these two pronouns are always singular. It is safe to consider them singular.

SINGULAR   Last spring we had five baby birds fly away from

the nest on our porch, but *none* of them *returned*

this year.

SINGULAR   *Neither* of the hikers *sees* a way out of this

predicament.

2. Some indefinite pronouns are always plural. A handful of indefinite pronouns (*both, few, many, several*) are always plural because they mean more than one by definition. *Both,* for example, always indicates two.

➤ *Both* of us *want* to go to the rally for the environment.

➤ *Several* of my friends *were* miserable about missing the last
episode of *Lost*.

3. Some indefinite pronouns can be either plural or singular.
Some indefinite pronouns (*some, any, all, most*) may be either plural
or singular. To decide, consider the context of the sentence, especially
noting any noun or pronoun that the indefinite pronoun refers to.

➤ *Some* of the *collection is* missing, but *all* of the Star Wars *figures are*
here.

40f SUBJECT FOLLOWING VERB.

In most English sentences, the verb comes after the subject. Sometimes, however, a writer will switch this order. In the following
sentence, you can locate the subject by asking, "Who or what stand?"
The answer is the sentence's subject: *an oak and a weeping willow.*
Because the subject is a compound subject (two subjects joined by
and), the verb must be plural.

➤ Out back behind the lean-to *stand an old oak tree and a weeping
willow.*

In sentences that begin with *there is* or *there are,* the subject
always follows the verb.

➤ There *is* a worn wooden *bench* in the shade of the two trees.

40g SUBJECT COMPLEMENTS.

A subject complement renames and specifies the sentence's subject.
It follows a **linking verb**—a verb, often a form of *be*, that joins the
subject to its description or definition. In the sentence below, the
singular noun *gift* is the subject. *Books* is the subject complement.
Therefore, *are* has been changed to *is* to agree in number with *gift*.

➤ One gift that gives her pleasure ~~are~~ books.
　　　　　　　　　　　　　　　　is

40h RELATIVE PRONOUNS (*WHO, WHICH, THAT*).

When a relative pronoun such as *who, which,* or *that* is the subject of a dependent clause, the pronoun is taking the place of a noun that appears earlier in the sentence—its **antecedent**. Therefore, the verb that goes with *who, which*, or *that* needs to agree with this antecedent. In the following sentence, the relative pronoun *that* is the subject of the dependent clause *that has dangerous side effects. Disease*, a singular noun, is the antecedent of that; therefore, the verb in the dependent clause is singular.

➤ Measles is a childhood *disease that has* dangerous side effects.

The phrases *one of the* and *only one of the* imply number. When *one of the* or *only one of the* precedes the antecedent in a sentence, writers can become confused about which form of the verb to use. The phrase *one of the* implies more than one and is, therefore, plural. *Only one of the* implies just one, however, and is singular. Generally, use the plural form of the verb when the phrase *one of the* comes before the antecedent. Use the singular form of the verb when *only one of the* comes before the antecedent.

PLURAL Tuberculosis is *one of the* diseases *that are*

developing resistance to antibiotics.

SINGULAR Barbara is the *only one of the* scientists *who has* a

degree in physics.

40i -*ING* PHRASES (GERUND PHRASES) AS SUBJECTS.

A **gerund phrase** is an -*ing* verb form followed by objects, complements, or modifiers. When a gerund phrase is the subject in a sentence, it is singular.

➤ *Canoeing* in the spring when the water is still very cold *is* a

dangerous practice.

41 Problems with Verbs

Verbs provide a great deal of information. They report action (*run, write*) and show time (*going, gone*). They change form to indicate person (first, second, or third—*I, we; you; he, she, it, they*) and number (singular or plural). They also change to indicate voice and mood.

41a PRINCIPAL FORMS OF REGULAR AND IRREGULAR VERBS.

All English verbs have five main forms, except for the *be* verb, which has eight.

- The **base form** is the form you find if you look up the verb in a dictionary. (*For irregular verbs, other forms are given as well. See pp. 317–318 for a list.*)
- The **present tense** form is used to indicate an action occurring at the moment or habitually, as well as to introduce quotations, literary events, and scientific facts (*41e, pp. 322–324 and 41g, p. 324*).
- The **past tense** is used to indicate an action completed at a specific time in the past (*41e, pp. 322–324*).
- The **past participle** is used with *have, has,* or *had* to form the perfect tenses (*41e, pp. 322–324*); with a form of the *be* verb to form the passive voice (*41k, pp. 328–329*); and as an adjective (the *polished* silver).
- The **present participle** is used with a form of the *be* verb to form the progressive tenses (*41e, pp. 322–324*). It can also be used as a noun (the *writing* is finished) and as an adjective (the *smiling* man).

Regular verbs always add *-d* or *-ed* to the base verb to form the past tense and past participle. **Irregular verbs**, by contrast, do not form the past tense or past participle in a consistent way. Here are the five principal forms of the regular verb *walk* and the irregular verb *begin* as well as the eight forms of the verb *be*.

Principal Forms of *walk* and *begin*

BASE	PRESENT TENSE (THIRD PERSON)	PAST TENSE	PAST PARTICIPLE	PRESENT PARTICIPLE
walk	walks	walked	walked	walking
begin	begins	began	begun	beginning

Principal Forms of *be*

BASE	PRESENT TENSE	PAST TENSE	PAST PARTICIPLE	PRESENT PARTICIPLE
be	I *am*.	I *was*.	I have *been*.	I am *being*.
	He, she, it *is*.	He, she, it *was*.		
	We, you, they *are*.	We, you, they *were*.		

1. Refer to the list of common irregular verbs. If you are not sure which form of an irregular verb is called for in a sentence, consult the list of common irregular verbs that follows. You can also find the past tense and past participle forms of irregular verbs by looking up the base form in a standard dictionary.

Forms of Common Irregular Verbs

BASE	PAST TENSE	PAST PARTICIPLE
awake	awoke	awoke/awakened
arise	arose	arisen
be	was/were	been
beat	beat	beaten
become	became	become
begin	began	begun
blow	blew	blown
break	broke	broken
bring	brought	brought
buy	bought	bought
catch	caught	caught
choose	chose	chosen
cling	clung	clung
come	came	come
do	did	done
draw	drew	drawn
drink	drank	drunk
drive	drove	driven
eat	ate	eaten
fall	fell	fallen
fight	fought	fought
fly	flew	flown
forget	forgot	forgotten/forgot

BASE	PAST TENSE	PAST PARTICIPLE
forgive	forgave	forgiven
freeze	froze	frozen
get	got	gotten/got
give	gave	given
go	went	gone
grow	grew	grown
hang	hung	hung (for things)
hang	hanged	hanged (for people)
have	had	had
hear	heard	heard
know	knew	known
lose	lost	lost
pay	paid	paid
raise	raised	raised
ride	rode	ridden
ring	rang	rung
rise	rose	risen
say	said	said
see	saw	seen
set	set	set
shake	shook	shaken
sit	sat	sat
spin	spun	spun
steal	stole	stolen
spend	spent	spent
strive	strove/strived	striven/strived
swear	swore	sworn
swim	swam	swum
swing	swung	swung
take	took	taken
tear	tore	torn
tread	trod	trod/trodden
wear	wore	worn
weave	wove	woven
wring	wrung	wrung
write	wrote	written

Find a verb's principal forms. If you are unsure of a verb's principal forms, check a dictionary. If the verb is regular, the dictionary will list only the present form and you will know that you should form the verb's past tense and past participle by adding *-ed* or *-d*. If the verb is irregular, the dictionary will give its principal forms.

Canadian Oxford Dictionary **entry for an irregular verb:**

Preferred past tense form given first

sing • *verb* (*past* **sang**; *past participle* **sung**) . . . **sing·able** *adjective* **sing·ing** *noun & adjective*. . .

2. Use the correct forms of irregular verbs that end in *-en* (*rode/ ridden*). The forms of irregular verbs with past tenses that end in *-e* and past participles that end in *-n* or *-en,* such as *ate / eaten, rode / ridden, wore / worn, stole / stolen,* and *swore / sworn,* are sometimes confused.

➤ He had ~~wore~~ the shirt to the job interview and then tried to

   worn

   return it to the store.

➤ They had ~~rode~~ from Moncton to Churchill on the train.

   ridden

➤ I could have ~~stole~~ a hundred chocolate bars if the cashier

   stolen

   hadn't already suspected me.

3. Use the correct forms of *went* and *gone, saw* and *seen.* *Went* and *saw* are the past tense forms of the irregular verbs *go* and *see. Gone* and *seen* are the past participle forms. These verb forms are commonly confused. Check carefully to make sure that you are using the correct form as you edit your writing.

➤ I had ~~went~~ to the store with the intention of buying a bunch

   gone

   of carrots.

➤ We ~~seen~~ the man fall into the ditch and called for help.

   saw

4. Use the correct forms of irregular verbs such as *drink* (*drank/ drunk*). For a few irregular verbs, such as *swim* (*swam / swum*), *drink* (*drank / drunk*), and *ring* (*rang / rung*), the difference between the past tense form and the past participle is only one letter. Be careful not to mix up these forms in your writing.

> *swum*
>
> ➤ I had ~~swam~~ all the way across Lake Ontario just like Marilyn
>   ^
>
> Bell in 1954.

41b *LAY* AND *LIE, SIT* AND *SET, RISE* AND *RAISE*.

Even the most experienced writers commonly confuse the verbs *lay* and
lie, *sit* and *set*, and *rise* and *raise*. The correct forms are given below.

Often-Confused Verb Pairs and Their Principal Forms

BASE	PAST	PAST PARTICIPLE	PRESENT PARTICIPLE
lay (to place)	laid	laid	laying
lie (to recline)	lay	lain	lying
sit (to be seated)	sat	sat	sitting
set (to put on a surface)	set	set	setting
rise (to go/get up)	rose	risen	rising
raise (to lift up)	raised	raised	raising

One verb in each of these pairs (*lay, set, raise*) is **transitive**, which
means that an object receives the action of the verb. The other verb
(*lie, sit, rise*) is **intransitive** and cannot take an object. You should
use a form of *lay, set,* or *raise* if you can replace the verb with *place*
or *put*. (*See Tab 10: Basic Grammar Review, pp. 435–438 for more on
transitive and intransitive verbs.*)

> direct object
> ➤ The dog *lays a bone* at your feet, then *lies* down and closes
>
> his eyes.

> direct object
> ➤ The technician *sits* down at the table and *sets the samples* in
>
> front of her.

> direct object
> ➤ As Fawkes, the phoenix *rises* from the ashes, Dumbledore *raises*
>
> his wand in anticipation.

Use *lay* and *lie* correctly. *Lay* (to place) and *lie* (to recline) are also
confusing because the past tense of the irregular verb *lie* is *lay* (*lie,
lay, lain*). To avoid using the wrong form, always double-check the
verb *lay* when it appears in your writing.

laid
➤ He washed the dishes carefully, then ~~lay~~ them on a clean towel.
 ⌃

41c -S OR -ES ENDINGS.

In the present tense, almost all verbs add an *-s* or *-es* ending if the subject is third-person singular. (*See pp. 309–310, for more on standard subject-verb combinations.*) Third-person singular subjects can be nouns (*woman, Benjamin, desk*), pronouns (*he, she, it*), or indefinite pronouns (*everyone*).

rises
➤ The crowd ~~rise~~ to its feet in a standing ovation when the concert
 ⌃

is especially good.

If the subject is in the first person (*I*), the second person (*you*), or the third-person plural (*people, they*), the verb does *not* add an *-s* or *-es* ending.

➤ You wants̸ to help, but you just don't have the time.

➤ People needs̸ to learn not to stick their fingers into electrical

outlets.

41d -D OR -ED ENDINGS.

When they are speaking, people sometimes leave the *-d* or *-ed* ending off certain verbs such as *asked, fixed, mixed, supposed to*, and *used to*, but in writing the endings should be included on all regular verbs in the past tense and all past participles of regular verbs.

asked
➤ The driving instructor ~~ask~~ the student driver to pull over to
 ⌃

the curb.

mixed
➤ After we had ~~mix~~ the formula, we let it cool.
 ⌃

Also check for missing *-d* or *-ed* endings on past participles used as adjectives.

concerned
➤ The ~~concern~~ doctor didn't want to have to relay such bad news.
 ⌃

41e   VERB TENSES.

Tenses show the time of a verb's action. English has three basic time frames, present, past, and future, and each tense has simple, perfect, and progressive verb forms to indicate the time span of the actions that are taking place. (*For a review of the present tense forms of a typical verb and of the verbs* be, have, *and* do, *see 40a, on standard subject-verb combinations, pp. 309–310; for a review of the principal forms of regular and irregular verbs, which are used to form tenses, see 41a, pp. 316–320.*)

1. The simple present and past tenses use only the verb itself, without a helping verb or verbs. The **simple present tense** is used for actions occurring at the moment or habitually. The **simple past tense** is used for actions completed at a specific time in the past.

SIMPLE PRESENT

Every May, she *plans* next year's convocation.

SIMPLE PAST

In the early morning hours before the office opened, she *planned* the convocation.

Check verb tenses. Is the time frame of your paper predominantly present, past, or future? Keep this time frame in mind as you edit, and you will be better able to see and solve problems with the accuracy and consistency of your verb tenses.

2. The simple future tense takes *will* plus the verb. The **simple future tense** is used for actions that have not yet begun.

SIMPLE FUTURE

In May, I *will plan* next year's convocation.

3. Perfect tenses take a form of *have* (*has, had*) plus the past participle. The **perfect tenses** are used to indicate actions that were or will be completed by the time of another action or a specific time.

PRESENT PERFECT

She *has* already *planned* next year's convocation.

PAST PERFECT

By the time she resigned, Mary *had* already *planned* next year's convocation.

FUTURE PERFECT

By the end of May, she *will have planned* next year's convocation.

When the verb in the past perfect is irregular, be sure to use the proper form of the past participle.

grown
➤ By the time the week was over, both plants had ~~grew~~ seven

centimetres.

4. Progressive tenses take a form of *be* (*am, are, were*) plus the present participle.
The progressive forms of the simple and perfect tenses are used to indicate ongoing action.

PRESENT PROGRESSIVE

She *is planning* next year's convocation now.

PAST PROGRESSIVE

She *was planning* next year's convocation when she started to look for another job.

FUTURE PROGRESSIVE

During the month of May, she *will be planning* next year's convocation.

CROSS-DISCIPLINE **WRITING**

Reporting Research Findings

Although a written work may be seen as always present, research findings are thought of as having been collected at one time in the past. Use the past or present perfect tense to report the results of research:

responded
➤ Three of the compounds (nos. 2, 3, and 6) ~~respond~~ positively

by turning purple.

have determined
➤ Magliaro and Ezeife (2007) ~~determine~~ that the type of

undergraduate degree obtained by pre-service teachers was

a factor in their computer self-efficacy status.

5. Perfect progressive tenses take *have* plus *be* plus the verb.
Perfect progressive tenses indicate an action that takes place over a specific period of time. The *present perfect progressive tense* is used for actions that start in the past and continue to the present; the *past and future perfect progressive tenses* are used for actions that ended or will end at a specified time or before another action.

PRESENT PERFECT PROGRESSIVE

She *has been planning* next year's convocation since the beginning of May.

PAST PERFECT PROGRESSIVE

She *had been planning* next year's convocation when she was offered another job.

FUTURE PERFECT PROGRESSIVE

By May 18, she *will have been planning* next year's convocation for more than two weeks.

41f PAST PERFECT TENSE.

When a past event was ongoing but ended before a particular time or another past event, use the past perfect rather than the simple past.

had
➤ Before the Riel Rebellion in 1885, the Métis expressed concerns
  ^
  about their treatment at the hands of the Canadian government.

People expressed their concern before the rebellion occurred.
    If two past events happened simultaneously, however, use the simple past, not the past perfect.

➤ When the Red River flooded, many farmers in the area ~~had~~ lost
  their livelihoods.

41g SPECIAL USES OF THE PRESENT TENSE.

If the conventions of a discipline require you to state what your paper does, do so in the present, not the future, tense.

➤ In this paper, I *describe* the effects of increasing NaCl
  concentrations on the germination of radish seeds.

Here are some other special uses of the present tense.

- By convention, events in a novel, short story, poem, or other literary work are described in the present tense.

  ➤ **Duddy Kravitz's determination to make a name for**
     is
     himself ~~was~~ his triumph as well as his downfall.
     ^

- Like events in a literary work, scientific facts are considered to be perpetually present, even though they were discovered in the past.

     have
  ➤ **Mendel discovered that genes ~~had~~ different forms, or**
     ^
     alleles.

- The present tense is also used to introduce a quote, paraphrase, or summary of someone else's writing.

     writes
  ➤ **Margaret Atwood ~~wrote~~ that "the central symbol for**
     ^
     Canada . . . is survival" (32).

41h TENSE WITH INFINITIVES AND PARTICIPLES.

Infinitives and participles are **verbals**, words formed from verbs that have various functions within a sentence. Because they are derived from verbs and can express time, verbals need to fit with the main verb in a sentence. Verbals can also form phrases by taking objects, modifiers, or complements.

1. Use the correct tense for infinitives. An **infinitive** is *to* plus the base verb (*to breathe, to sing, to dance*). The perfect form of the infinitive is *to have* plus the past participle (*to have breathed, to have sung, to have danced*). The tense of an infinitive needs to fit with the tense of the main verb. If the action of the infinitive happens at the same time as or after the action of the main verb, use the present tense (*to* plus the base form). If the action of the infinitive happened before the action of the main verb, use the perfect form.

➤ **I hope *to sing* with the Canadian Opera Company someday.**

The infinitive expresses an action (*to sing*) that will occur later than the action of the sentence (*hope*), so the infinitive needs to be in the present tense.

➤ **My talented mother would like *to have sung* with the Canadian**

Opera Company, but she never had the chance.

The action of the main verb (*would like*) is in the present, but the missed opportunity is in the past, so the infinitive needs to be in the perfect tense.

2. Use the correct tense for participles that are part of phrases.

Participial phrases can begin with the present participle (*breathing, dancing, singing*), the present perfect participle (*having breathed, having danced, having sung*), or the past participle (*breathed, danced, sung*). If the action of the participle happens simultaneously with the action of the sentence's verb, use the present participle. If the action of the participle happened before the action of the main verb, use the present perfect or past participle form.

➤ *Singing several hours a day together,* **the chorus developed**

perfect harmony.

The chorus developed harmony as they sang together, so the present participle (*singing*) is appropriate.

➤ *Having breathed* **the air of Toronto, I exulted in the possibilities**

for my life in the city but worried about the smog.

The breathing took place before the exulting and the worrying, so the present perfect (*having breathed*) is appropriate.

➤ *Tinted* **with a strange green light, the western sky looked**

threatening.

The green light had to appear before the sky started to look threatening, so the past participle (*tinted*) is the right choice.

41i COMPLETE VERBS.

With only a few exceptions, all English sentences must contain complete verbs. A **complete verb** consists of the main verb along with any helping verbs that are needed to express the tense (*see pp. 322–324*) or voice (*see pp. 328–329*). **Helping verbs** include forms of *be, have,* and *do* and the modal verbs *can, could, may, might, shall, should,* and *will.* Helping verbs can be part of contractions (*He's running, we'd better go*), but they cannot be left out of the sentence entirely.

will
➤ **They be going on clinical rotation next week.**
   ^

Linking verbs are another type of verb that writers sometimes accidentally omit. A **linking verb,** often a form of *be,* connects the subject to a description or definition of it. Linking verbs can be part of contractions *(She's a student),* but they should not be left out entirely.

is
➤ **Montreal a major Canadian city with a big jazz festival every**
   ^

summer.

41j MOOD.

The **mood** of a verb indicates the writer's attitude. Use the **indicative mood** to state or to question facts, acts, and opinions *(Our collection is on display. Did you see it?).* Use the **imperative mood** for commands, directions, and entreaties. The subject of an imperative sentence is always *you,* but the *you* is usually understood, not written out *(Shut the door!).* Use the **subjunctive mood** to express a wish or a demand or to make a statement contrary to fact *(I wish I were a millionaire).* The mood that writers have the most trouble with is the subjunctive.

Verbs in the subjunctive mood may be in the present tense, the past tense, or the perfect tense. Present tense subjunctive verbs do not change form to signal person or number. The only form used is the verb's base form: *accompany* or *be,* not *accompanies* or *am, are, is.* Also, the verb *be* has only one past tense form in the subjunctive mood: *were.*

1. Use the subjunctive mood to express a wish.

WISH

If only I *were* more prepared for this test!

Note: In everyday conversation, most speakers use the indicative rather than the subjunctive when expressing wishes *(If only I was more prepared for this test).*

2. Use the subjunctive mood for requests, recommendations, and demands. Because requests, recommendations, and demands have not yet happened, they—like wishes—are expressed in the subjunctive mood. Words such as *ask, insist, recommend, request,* and

suggest indicate the subjunctive mood; the verb in the following *that* clause should be in the subjunctive.

DEMAND

I insist that all applicants *find* their seats by 8 a.m.

3. Use the subjunctive in statements that are contrary to fact. Often such statements contain a subordinate clause that begins with *if*: the verb in the *if* clause should be in the subjunctive mood.

CONTRARY-TO-FACT STATEMENT

He would not be so irresponsible if his father *were* [not *was*] still alive.

Note: Some common expressions of conjecture are in the subjunctive mood, including *as it were, come rain or shine, far be it from me,* and *be that as it may.*

41k VOICE.

A verb is in the **active voice** when the subject of the sentence does the acting; it is in the **passive voice** when the subject is acted upon by an agent that is implied or expressed in a prepositional phrase. To make a verb passive, use the appropriate form of the *be* verb plus the past participle. Only transitive verbs—verbs that take objects—can be passive.

ACTIVE	Professor Therriault *solved* the problem.
PASSIVE	The problem *was solved.*
PASSIVE	The problem *was solved* by Professor Therriault.

CROSS-DISCIPLINE **WRITING**

Passive Voice in Scientific Writing

To keep the focus on objects and actions, scientists writing about the results of their research regularly use the passive voice in their laboratory reports.

PASSIVE   A sample of 20 radish seeds *was germinated* on filter paper soaked in a 10% sodium chloride solution.

Whenever possible, choose the active voice. The passive voice emphasizes the recipient rather than the doer of the action. Use it only when the doer is not known or is not important.

PASSIVE   My car *was stolen* last night.

Problems with Pronouns   42

A **pronoun** (*he / him, it / its, they / their*) takes the place of a noun. The noun that the pronoun replaces is called its **antecedent**. In the following sentence, *snow* is the antecedent of the pronoun *it*:

➤ The *snow* fell all day long, and by nightfall *it* was forty-five

centimetres deep.

Like nouns, pronouns are singular or plural.

SINGULAR

The *house* was dark and gloomy, and *it* sat in a grove of

tall cedars.

PLURAL

The *cars* swept by on the highway, all of *them* doing more

than one hundred kilometres per hour.

A pronoun needs a specific and explicit antecedent to refer to and agree with, and a pronoun must match its antecedent in number (*plural / singular*) and gender (*he / his, she / her, it / its*). A pronoun must also be in a form, or case, that matches its function in the sentence.

42a   PRONOUN-ANTECEDENT AGREEMENT.

Problems with pronoun-antecedent agreement tend to occur when a pronoun's antecedent is an indefinite pronoun, a collective noun, or a compound noun. Problems may also occur when writers are trying to avoid the generic use of *he*.

1. Avoid bias when you use indefinite pronouns. Indefinite pronouns such as *someone, anybody,* and *nothing* refer to non-specific people or things. They sometimes function as antecedents for other pronouns. Most indefinite pronouns are singular (*anybody, anyone, anything, each, either, everybody, everyone, everything, much, neither, nobody, none, no one, nothing, one, somebody, something*).

ALWAYS
SINGULAR
Did *either* of the boys lose *his* bicycle?

A few indefinite pronouns—*both, few, many,* and *several*—are plural.

ALWAYS
PLURAL
Both of the boys lost *their* bicycles.

The indefinite pronouns *all, any, more, most,* and *some* can be either singular or plural depending on the noun to which the pronoun refers.

PLURAL
The students debated, *some* arguing that *their* assumptions about the issue were more credible than the teacher's.

SINGULAR
The bread is on the counter, but *some* of *it* has already been eaten.

Problems arise when writers attempt to make indefinite pronouns agree with their antecedents without introducing gender bias. In the following sentence, for example, the writer chose to change the indefinite pronoun *none* to *all* instead of changing the plural pronoun *their* to a singular form. Why?

> ~~None~~ of the great Romantic writers believed that their
> All
> ^
> achievements ~~equalled~~ their aspirations.
> fell short of
> ^

Replacing *their* in the original sentence with *his* would have made the sentence both untrue and biased: many women—like Mary Shelley, the author of *Frankenstein*—were writing and publishing during the Romantic Age. The writer could have changed *their* to *his or her* to avoid bias but thought *his* or *her* sounded awkward. The writer solved the problem by choosing an indefinite pronoun that can have a plural meaning (*all*) and revising the sentence. An alternative would be to eliminate the indefinite pronoun altogether:

➤ **The great Romantic writers believed that their achievements**

fell short of their aspirations.

To summarize, here are the three ways to avoid gender bias when an indefinite pronoun is the antecedent in a sentence:

- If possible, change a singular indefinite pronoun to a plural pronoun.
- Reword the sentence to eliminate the indefinite pronoun.
- Substitute *he or she* or *his or her* (but never *his/her*) for the singular pronoun to maintain pronoun-antecedent agreement.

2. Avoid bias when you use generic nouns. A **generic noun** represents anyone and everyone in a group. Because most groups consist of both males and females, using male pronouns to refer to generic nouns is unacceptable. To fix agreement problems with generic nouns, use one of the three options suggested above.

INCORRECT

A college *student* should have a mind of *their* own.

CHANGE TO PLURAL

College *students* should have minds of *their* own.

REWORD TO AVOID PRONOUN

A college student should have an independent point of view.

USE *HIS OR HER*

A college *student* should have a mind of *his or her* own.

3. Treat most collective nouns as singular. Collective nouns such as *team, family, jury, committee,* and *crowd* are treated as singular unless the people in the group are acting as individuals.

➤ **All together, the crowd surged through the palace gates,**

its

trampling over everything in ~~their~~ path.

The phrase *all together* indicates that this writer does not see— and does not want readers to see—the crowd as a collection of distinct individuals. Therefore, the plural *their* has been changed to the singular *its*.

➤ The committee left the conference room and returned to ~~its~~ *their*
offices.

In this case, the writer sees—and wants readers to see—the members of the committee as individuals.

If you are using a collective noun that has a plural meaning, consider adding a plural noun to clarify the meaning.

➤ The *committee members* left the conference room and returned to *their* offices.

4. Choose the right pronoun for a compound antecedent. Compound antecedents joined by *and* are almost always plural.

➤ To remove all traces of the crime, James put the book and the *their*
magnifying glass back in ~~its~~ place.

When a compound antecedent is joined by *or* or *nor*, the pronoun should agree with the closest part of the compound antecedent. If one part is singular and the other is plural, the sentence will be more effective if the plural antecedent is closest to the pronoun.

PLURAL Neither *the professor nor the students* wanted to reschedule *their* exam.

Note: When the two parts of the compound antecedent refer to the same person, or when the word *each* or *every* precedes the compound antecedent, use a singular pronoun.

SINGULAR Being *a teacher and a mother* keeps *her* busy.

SINGULAR *Every* poem and letter by Keats has *its* own special power.

42b PRONOUN REFERENCE.

If a pronoun does not clearly refer to a specific antecedent, readers can become confused. Two common problems are ambiguous references and implied references.

1. Avoid ambiguous pronoun references. If a pronoun can refer to more than one noun in a sentence, the reference is ambiguous. In the following unedited sentence, who is the antecedent of *her*—Farnaz or Gabrielle?

VAGUE   The heated debate between Farnaz and Gabrielle provoked her to walk out of the room.

To clear up the ambiguity, the writer decided to eliminate the pronoun and use the appropriate noun.

CLEAR   The heated debate between Farnaz and Gabrielle provoked Farnaz to walk out of the room.

Sometimes the ambiguous reference can be cleared up by rewriting the sentence.

VAGUE   Jane Austen and Cassandra corresponded regularly when she was in London.

CLEAR   When Jane Austen was in London, she corresponded regularly with Cassandra.

2. Watch out for implied pronoun references. The antecedent that a pronoun refers to must be present in the sentence, and it must be a noun or another pronoun, not a word that modifies a noun. Possessives and verbs cannot be antecedents.

> In ~~Layton's~~ book "Homelessness," ~~he~~ argues for a national
> housing program, funded by the federal government.

(his ... Layton)

Replacing *he* with *Layton* gives the pronoun *his* an antecedent that is stated explicitly, not just implied. Note that in the revised sentence the antecedent follows the pronoun.

> Every weekday afternoon, my brothers skateboard home from
> school, and then they leave ~~them~~ in the driveway.

(their skateboards)

In the original sentence, *skateboard* is a verb, not a noun, and cannot act as a pronoun antecedent.

3. Use clear references for *this, that,* and *which*. The pronouns *this, that,* and *which* are often used to refer to ideas expressed in preceding sentences. To make the sentence containing the pronoun clearer, either change the pronoun to a specific noun or add a specific antecedent or clarifying noun.

VAGUE	As government funding for higher education decreases, tuition increases. Are we students supposed to accept *this* without protest?
CLEAR	As government funding for higher education decreases, tuition increases. Are we students supposed to accept *these higher costs* without protest?
CLEAR	As government funding for higher education decreases, tuition increases. Are we students supposed to accept *this situation* without protest?

4. Use clear references for *you, they,* and *it*. The pronouns *you, they,* and *it* should refer to definite, explicitly stated antecedents. If their antecedents are unclear, they should be replaced with appropriately specific nouns, or the sentence should be rewritten to eliminate the pronoun.

➤ In countries such as Canada, ~~they pay~~ *the government pays* for such medical

procedures.

➤ According to university policy, ~~you~~ *students* must have a permit to park

a car on campus.

➤ ~~In the~~ *The* textbook/ ~~it~~ states that borrowing to fund the purchase

of financial assets results in a double-counting of debt.

42c PRONOUN CASE (FOR EXAMPLE, *I* VS. *ME*).

When a pronoun's form, or **case**, does not match its function in a sentence, readers will feel that something is wrong. Most problems with pronoun case involve the subjective and objective forms.

- Pronouns in the subjective case are used as subjects or subject complements in sentences: *I, you, he, she, it, we, they, who, whoever.*

- Pronouns in the objective case are used as objects of verbs or prepositions: *me, you, him, her, it, us, them, whom, whomever.*

1. Use the correct pronouns in compound structures. Compound structures (words or phrases joined by *and, or,* or *nor*) can appear as subjects or objects. If you are not sure which form of a pronoun to use in a compound structure, treat the pronoun as the only subject or object, and note how the sentence sounds.

SUBJECT
I
Ameen and ~~me~~ were cleaning up the kitchen.

If you treat the pronoun as the only subject, the sentence is clearly wrong: *Me [was] cleaning up the kitchen.* The correct form is the subjective pronoun *I*.

OBJECT
My parents waited for an explanation from Anil
me
and ~~I~~.

If you treat the pronoun as the only object, the sentence is clearly wrong: *My parents waited for an explanation from I.* The correct form is the objective pronoun *me*.

2. Use the correct pronoun in subject complements.

A **subject complement** renames and specifies the sentence's subject. It follows a **linking verb**, which is a verb, often a form of *be,* that links the subject to its description or definition.

SUBJECT
COMPLEMENT
I
Mark's best friends are Tharini and ~~me~~.

If you think the edited sentence sounds too awkward or formal, try switching the order to make the pronoun into the subject: *Tharini and I are Mark's best friends.*

3. Use the correct pronoun in appositives.

Appositives are nouns or noun phrases that rename nouns or pronouns. They appear right after the word they rename and have the same function in the sentence that the word has.

➤ The two weary travellers, Ramon and ~~me~~, found shelter in an
I
old cabin.

The appositive renames the subject, *two weary travellers,* so the pronoun should be in the subjective case: *I*.

➤ The police arrested two protesters, Suki and ~~I~~.
me

The appositive renames the direct object, *protesters,* so the pronoun should be in the objective case: *me*.

4. Use either *we* or *us* before a noun, depending on the noun's function. When *we* or *us* comes before a noun, it has the same function in the sentence as the noun it precedes.

    We
➤ ~~Us~~ students never get to decide such things.

    We renames the subject: *students.*

                                    us
➤ Things were looking desperate for ~~we~~ campers.

    Us renames the object of the preposition *for: campers.*

5. Use the correct pronoun in comparisons with *than* or *as*. In comparisons, words are often left out of the sentence because the reader can guess what they would be. When a pronoun follows *than* or *as,* make sure you are using the correct form by mentally adding the missing word or words.

➤ Meg is quicker than she [is].

➤ I can't do Sudoku puzzles as quickly as you [do].

If a sentence with a comparison sounds too awkward or formal, add the missing words: *Meg is quicker than she is.*

6. Use the correct form when the pronoun is the subject or the object of an infinitive. An **infinitive** is *to* plus the base verb (*to breathe, to sing, to dance*). Whether a pronoun functions as the subject or the object of an infinitive, it should be in the objective case.

           Subject   Object
➤ We wanted *her* to defend *us* against this unfair charge.

    Both the subject of the infinitive (*her*) and its object (*us*) are in the objective case.

7. Use the possessive case in front of an *-ing* noun (a gerund). When a noun or pronoun appears before a **gerund** (an *-ing* verb form functioning as a noun), it should usually be treated as a possessive. Possessive nouns are formed by adding *'s* to singular nouns (*the teacher's desk*) or an apostrophe only (') to plural nouns (*three teachers' rooms*). (*See Tab 9: Editing for Correctness, pp. 364–368.*) The possessive pronouns are *my, your, his / her / its, our, their.*

    animals'
➤ The ~~animals~~ fighting disturbed the entire neighbourhood.

➤ *their*
   Because of ~~them~~ screeching, no one could get any sleep.
                ^

42d *WHO VS. WHOM.*

The relative pronouns *who, whom, whoever,* and *whomever* are used to introduce dependent clauses and in questions. Their case depends on their function in the dependent clause or question.

- **Subjective:** *who, whoever*
- **Objective:** *whom, whomever*

1. Determine how the pronoun functions in a dependent clause.
If the pronoun is functioning as a subject and is performing an action, use *who* or *whoever.* If the pronoun is the object of a verb or preposition, use *whom* or *whomever.*

➤ Joseph Seagram, *who* founded the Seagram Company, was a

   civic leader as well as an industrialist.

Who, which refers to *Joseph Seagram,* is performing an action in the dependent clause: founding a company.

➤ Seagram's early partners, *whom* the distiller bought out by 1883,

   were also successful merchants in the Waterloo area.

Whom, which refers to *partners,* is the object of the verb *bought out.* You can check the pronoun by changing the order within the clause: *The distiller bought out whom* [*them*].

2. Determine how the pronoun functions in a question.
To choose the correct form for the pronoun, answer the question with a personal pronoun.

➤ *Who* founded the Hudson's Bay Company?

The answer could be *He founded it. He* is in the subjective case, so *who* is correct.

➤ *Whom* did the Liberal Party turn to for leadership in the 1980s?

The answer could be *It turned to him. Him* is in the objective case, so *whom* is correct.

43 Problems with Adjectives and Adverbs

Adjectives and **adverbs** are words that describe. Because they qualify the meanings of other words—for example, telling which, how many, what kind, or where—we say that they *modify* them. Adjectives modify nouns and pronouns. Adverbs modify verbs, adjectives, and other adverbs. When used thoughtfully, they add flavour and precision to writing.

43a ADVERBS.

Adverbs modify verbs, adjectives, other adverbs, and even whole clauses. They tell where, when, why, how, how often, how much, or to what degree.

➤   The authenticity of the document is *hotly* contested.

➤   The water was *brilliant* blue and *icy* cold.

➤   Dickens mixed humour and pathos *better* than any other

English writer after Shakespeare.

➤   *Consequently,* Dickens is still read by millions.

Distinguish between *bad* and *badly*, *real* and *really*, *good* and *well*. In casual speech, the adjectives *bad, good,* and *real* sometimes substitute for the adverbs *badly, well,* and *really;* in formal writing, however, it is not acceptable to substitute an adjective for an adverb.

                      badly
➤   He plays the role so ~~bad~~ that it is an insult to Shakespeare.

              really ^
➤   At times, he gets ~~real~~ close to the edge of the stage.
              ^

                              well
➤   I've seen other actors play the role ~~good~~, but they were
                            ^

classically trained.

43b ADJECTIVES.

Adjectives modify nouns and pronouns; they do not modify any other kind of word. Adjectives tell what kind or how many and may come before or after the noun or pronoun they modify.

➤ *Ominous dark* clouds loomed over the lake.

➤ The *looming* clouds, *ominous* and *dark,* frightened the children.

Some proper nouns have adjective forms. Proper adjectives, like the proper nouns they are derived from, are capitalized: *Victoria/Victorian, Britain/British, Canada/Canadian, Shakespeare/Shakespearean.*

In some cases, a noun is used as an adjective without a change in form:

➤ *Cigarette* smoking causes cancer and is banned in all public

places.

Occasionally, descriptive adjectives function as if they were nouns:

➤ The *unemployed* should not be equated with the *lazy.*

1. Do not use an adjective when an adverb is needed. In common speech, we sometimes treat adjectives as adverbs. In writing, this informal usage should be avoided.

NON-STANDARD   He hit that ball *real good.*

REVISED   He hit that ball *really well.*

Both *real* and *good* are adjectives, but they are used here as adverbs, *real* modifying *good* and *good* modifying the verb *hit.*

NON-STANDARD   She *sure* made me work hard for my grade.

REVISED   She *certainly* made me work hard for my grade.

Here the adjective *sure* tries to do the work of an adverb modifying the verb *made.*

2. Use adjectives after linking verbs to describe the subject.
Linking verbs connect the subject of a sentence to its description. The most common linking verb is *be.* Descriptive adjectives that modify a sentence's subject but appear after a linking verb are called **subject complements**.

➤ During the movie, both Wallace and Gromit *were fooled* by the were-rabbit.

➤ The road *is long, winding,* and *dangerous.*

Other linking verbs are related to states of being and the five senses: *appear, become, feel, grow, look, smell, sound,* and *taste.* Verbs related to the senses can be either linking or action verbs, depending on the meaning of the sentence.

ADJECTIVE   The dog smelled *bad.*

Bad modifies the noun *dog,* which is connected to the adjective by the linking verb *smelled.* The sentence indicates that the dog needed a bath.

ADVERB   The dog smelled *badly.*

Badly modifies the verb *smelled,* an action verb in this sentence. The sentence indicates that the dog had lost its sense of smell and could not track anything.

3. Be aware that some adjectives and adverbs are spelled alike. In most instances, *-ly* endings indicate adverbs; however, words with *-ly* endings can sometimes be adjectives (*the lovely girl*). In standard English, many adverbs do not require the *-ly* ending, and some words are both adjectives and adverbs: *fast, only, hard, right,* and *straight.* Note that *right* also has an *-ly* form as an adverb: *rightly.* When you are in doubt, consult a dictionary.

43c POSITIVE, COMPARATIVE, AND SUPERLATIVE ADJECTIVES AND ADVERBS.

Most adjectives and adverbs have three forms: positive (*smart*), comparative (*smarter*), and superlative (*smartest*). The simplest form of the adjective is the positive form.

1. Distinguish between comparatives and superlatives. Use the comparative form to compare two things and the superlative form to compare three or more things.

➤ In total area, Ontario is a *larger* province than New Brunswick.

➤ Nunavut is the *largest* territory in the country.

2. Learn when to use -er/-est endings (*bigger/biggest*) and when to use *more/most* (*more dependable/most dependable*). To form comparatives and superlatives of short adjectives, add the suffixes *-er* and *-est* (*brighter/brightest*). With longer adjectives (three or more syllables), use *more* or *less* and *most* or *least* (*more dangerous/most dangerous*).

➤ Mercury is the ~~most near~~ planet to the sun.
   _{nearest} ^

A few short adverbs have *-er* and *-est* endings in their comparative and superlative forms (*harder/hardest*). Most adverbs, however, including all adverbs that end in *-ly*, use *more* and *most* in their comparative and superlative forms (*more loudly/most loudly*).

➤ She sings *more loudly* than we expected.

Two common adjectives—*good* and *bad*—form the comparative and superlative in an irregular way: *good, better, best* and *bad, worse, worst.*

➤ He felt ~~badder~~ as his illness progressed.
   _{worse} ^

3. Watch out for double comparatives and superlatives. Use either an *-er* or an *-est* ending or *more/most* to form the comparative or superlative, as appropriate; do not use both.

➤ Since World War II, Canada has been the ~~most~~ closest ally of the

United States.

4. Be aware of concepts that cannot be compared. Do not use comparative or superlative forms with adjectives such as *unique, infinite, impossible, perfect, round, square,* and *destroyed.* These concepts are *absolutes.* If something is unique, for example, it is the only one of its kind, making comparison impossible.

➤ You will never find ~~a more unique~~ restaurant ~~than~~ this one.
   _{another}   _{like}

43d DOUBLE NEGATIVES.

The words *no, not,* and *never* can modify the meaning of nouns and pronouns as well as other sentence elements.

NOUN   You are *no* friend of mine.

ADJECTIVE   The red house was *not* large.

VERB   He *never* ran in a marathon.

However, it takes only one negative word to change the meaning of a sentence from positive to negative. When two negatives are used together, they cancel each other out, resulting in a positive meaning. Unless you want your sentence to have a positive meaning (*I am not unaware of your feelings in this matter*), edit by changing or eliminating one of the negative words.

> *any*
> They don't have ~~no~~ reason to go there.

> *can*
> He ~~can't~~ hardly do that assignment.

Note that *hardly* has a negative meaning and cannot be used with *no*, *not*, or *never*.

9

EDITING FOR CORRECTNESS

9 Editing for Correctness

CROSS-DISCIPLINE WRITING

Styles within Disciplines

The rules for capitalizing, abbreviating, and italicizing terms, as well as conventions for using numbers and hyphens, vary across disciplines. If you are not sure about the conventions for a discipline, see what rules your course textbook follows. In particular, look for answers to these questions:

- Does the text use numerals or words for numbers under one hundred? Under ten?
- What abbreviations appear throughout the text?
- Does the book include a list of abbreviations for technical terms, as many books in the natural and applied sciences do?

If the style convention is not clear from your text, ask your instructor for help, or consult one of the following style manuals:

- *The Chicago Manual of Style*, sixteenth edition (used in history and in the humanities)
- *The Canadian Press Stylebook,* sixteenth edition (used in media studies)
- *Caps and Spelling*, eighteenth edition (used in journalism)
- *MLA Style Manual and Guide to Scholarly Publishing*, third edition or the *MLA Handbook for Writers of Research Papers*, seventh edition (used for literature, composition, and other humanities disciplines)
- *Publication Manual of the American Psychological Association*, sixth edition (used for the social sciences, such as psychology and sociology)
- *Scientific Style and Format: The CBE Manual for Authors, Editors, and Publishers*, sixth edition (used for the natural sciences, such as biology)

Punctuation is a set of signals intended to help readers make sense of written communication. Like physical gestures in spoken communication, correct punctuation helps to create and clarify meaning.

Dealing with Mechanics. It is a challenge to write a thoughtful, well-organized paper and at the same time make sure you are following every rule of punctuation, abbreviation, and spelling. To improve the accuracy of your paper, try going through an extra draft or two.

For the first draft, pay close attention to the content and organization of your paper, but do not focus on the mechanics. When you have revised your paper and are satisfied that the content is sound, the writing is clear (*see Tab 7*), and your sentences are grammatically correct (*see Tab 8*), edit the revised draft for correct punctuation, abbreviation, and spelling, keeping in mind the problem areas mentioned in this Tab.

Next, have a friend or peer review your draft, commenting on anything that does not seem right. When you get the paper back, try making the corrections yourself. If the comments are not clear, ask the reader to explain what is wrong and suggest possible solutions, or ask for help from a tutor at a writing centre. Then prepare the final copy, and review it one more time before handing it in.

Commas

44

COMMON USES OF THE COMMA.

To clarify meaning, commas are used in the following situations:

- Following introductory elements (*p. 348*)
- After each item in a series and between coordinate adjectives (*pp. 348–349 and 349–350*)
- Between coordinated independent clauses (*p. 349*)
- To set off non-essential elements and phrases that interrupt or interject something in a sentence (*pp. 350–352*)
- To set off direct quotations (*p. 353*)
- In dates, addresses, people's titles, and numbers (*pp. 354–355*)
- To take the place of an omitted word or phrase or to prevent misreading (*p. 355*)

44a INTRODUCTORY WORD GROUPS.

An introductory word group must be distinct from, yet clearly attached to, what follows. A comma both attaches an introductory word, phrase, or clause to and distinguishes it from the rest of the sentence.

➤ **Finally, the eagle banked to the right, narrowly avoiding the small plane.**

➤ **Reflecting on her life experiences, Montreuil attributed her successes to her own efforts.**

➤ **Until he noticed the handprint on the wall, the detective was frustrated by the lack of clues.**

Do not add a comma after a word group that functions as the subject of the sentence, however.

➤ **Being able to speak to the riding's constituents/ is one of the benefits of an all-candidates meeting.**

Note: When the introductory phrase is less than five words long and there is no danger of confusion without a comma, the comma can be omitted.

➤ **For several hours we rode on in silence.**

➤ **In 1991 Dr. Seuss died.**

44b ITEMS IN A SERIES.

A comma should appear after each item in a series, which generally consists of at least three items.

➤ **Three characteristics that help with schoolwork are perseverance, focus, and a capacity for hard work.**

Commas clarify which items are part of the series. In the following example, the third comma clarifies that the hikers are packing lunch *and* snacks, not chocolate and trail mix for lunch.

CONFUSING	For the hiking trip, we needed to pack lunch, chocolate and trail mix.
CLEAR	For the hiking trip, we needed to pack lunch, chocolate, and trail mix.

CROSS-DISCIPLINE **WRITING**

Commas in Journalism

If you are writing for a journalism course, you may be required to leave out the final comma that precedes *and* in a series, just as magazines and newspapers usually do. Follow the conventions of the *Canadian Press Stylebook* or the criteria determined by your professor.

44c INDEPENDENT CLAUSES JOINED BY A COORDINATING CONJUNCTION.

When a coordinating conjunction (*and, but, for, nor, or, so, yet*) is used to join clauses that could each stand alone as a sentence, put a comma before the coordinating conjunction.

➤ **Injuries were so frequent that he began to worry, and his style of play became more cautious.**

If the word groups you are joining are not independent clauses, do not add a comma. See 44m on page 356.

Note: If you are joining two short clauses, you may leave out the comma unless it is needed for clarity.

➤ **The doctor gave them the bad news and the family wept.**

44d SERIES OF ADJECTIVES.

When a series of adjectives comes before a noun or pronoun, each may modify the noun independently (*a brave, intelligent, persistent woman*), or each adjective may modify the ones that follow it (*the world-famous Canadian soprano*). Use a comma between adjectives only if they are the first type, or **coordinate adjectives**—that is, if they could be joined by *and* (brave *and* intelligent *and* persistent) or if their order could be changed (*a persistent, brave, intelligent woman*).

➤ **This brave, intelligent, persistent woman was the first female to earn a PhD in psychology.**

If you cannot add *and* between the adjectives or change their order, they are **cumulative adjectives** and should not be separated with a comma or commas.

➤ **Measha Brueggergosman, the world-famous Canadian soprano,**

was born in Fredericton, New Brunswick.

World-famous modifies *Canadian soprano,* not just the noun *soprano.* You could not add *and* between the adjectives (*world-famous* and *Canadian soprano*) or change their order (*Canadian world-famous soprano*).

44e NON-ESSENTIAL ADDITIONS TO A SENTENCE.

Non-essential, or **non-restrictive,** words, phrases, and clauses add information to a sentence but are not required for its basic meaning to be understood. Non-restrictive additions are set off with commas.

NON-RESTRICTIVE

Mary Shelley's best-known novel, *Frankenstein or the Modern*
^

***Prometheus,* was first published in 1818.**
^

The sentence would have the same basic meaning without the title (*Mary Shelley's best-known novel was first published in 1818*).

However, **restrictive** words, phrases, and clauses are essential to a sentence because they identify exactly who or what the writer is talking about. Restrictive additions are not set off with commas.

RESTRICTIVE

Mary Shelley's novel *Frankenstein or the Modern Prometheus*

was first published in 1818.

Without the title, the reader would not know which novel the sentence is referring to, so *Frankenstein or the Modern Prometheus* is restrictive.

Three types of additions to sentences often cause problems for writers: adjective clauses, adjective phrases, and appositives.

1. Adjective clauses. Adjective clauses include a subject and verb, but they do not function independently. They begin with a relative pronoun or an adverb—*who, whom, whose, which, that, where,* or *when*—and modify a noun or pronoun within the sentence by telling *how many, what kind,* or *which one.* The relative pronoun or adverb at the beginning of the clause connects it to the noun or pronoun it modifies and usually appears right after the modified word.

NON-RESTRICTIVE

With his tale of Odysseus, *whose journey can be traced on modern maps,* Homer brought accounts of alien and strange creatures to the ancient Greeks.

RESTRICTIVE

The Sudoku player *whom she most wanted to beat* was catlover79.

Note: Use *that* only with restrictive clauses. *Which* can introduce either restrictive or non-restrictive clauses. Some writers prefer to use *which* only with non-restrictive clauses.

2. Adjective phrases. Like an adjective clause, an adjective phrase also modifies a noun or pronoun in a sentence by answering the question *how many? what kind?* or *which one?* Adjective phrases begin with a preposition (for example, *with, by, at,* or *for*) or a verbal (a word formed from a verb that can have various functions within a sentence). Adjective phrases can be either restrictive or non-restrictive.

NON-RESTRICTIVE

Some people, *by their faith in human nature or their general good will,* bring out the best in others.

The phrase that begins with the preposition *by* is non-essential because it does not specify which people are being discussed. The sentence would have the same basic meaning without it (*Some people bring out the best in others*).

RESTRICTIVE

People *fighting passionately for their rights* can inspire others to join a cause.

The phrase *fighting passionately for their rights,* which begins with the verbal *fighting,* indicates which people the writer is talking about and therefore is restrictive. It is not set off with commas.

3. Appositives. Appositives are nouns or noun phrases that rename nouns or pronouns and appear right after the word they rename.

NON-RESTRICTIVE APPOSITIVE

One researcher, *the widely respected R. S. Smith,* has shown that a child's performance on IQ tests can be very inconsistent.

Because the word *one* already restricts the word *researcher,* the researcher's name is not essential to the meaning of the sentence, and the appositive phrase is non-restrictive.

RESTRICTIVE APPOSITIVE

The researcher *R. S. Smith* has shown that a child's performance on IQ tests is not reliable.

The name *R. S. Smith* tells readers which researcher is meant.

44f TRANSITIONAL AND PARENTHETICAL EXPRESSIONS, CONTRASTING COMMENTS, AND ABSOLUTE PHRASES.

1. Transitional expressions. Transitional expressions show the relationship between ideas in a sentence and make the sentence clearer. Conjunctive adverbs (*however, therefore, moreover*) and other transitional phrases (*for example, on the other hand*) are usually set off by commas when used at the beginning, in the middle, or at the end of a sentence. (*For a list of transitional expressions, see Tab 8: Editing for Grammar and Mechanics, p. 306*)

➤ The undergraduate students, for example, were given the option of doing a collaborative project rather than an individual activity for their final course assignment.

➤ However, none of the participants in the Fall 2011 term reported that they had participated in the collaborative project.

➤ Moreover, the analysis showed no significant correlation between participation in the collaborative project and increased community cohesion.

When a transitional expression connects two independent clauses, use a semicolon before and a comma after it.

➤ Michael Jackson became a star at the age of 8 performing with his brothers in the Jackson 5; certainly, his solo album *Thriller* became the best selling album of all time

Note: Short expressions such as *also, at least, certainly, instead, of course, then, perhaps,* and *therefore* do not always need to be set off with commas.

➤ I found my notes and *also* got my story in on time.

2. Parenthetical expressions. Parenthetical expressions are like whispered asides or a shrug in a conversation. The information they provide is relatively insignificant and could easily be left out. Therefore, they are set off with a comma or commas.

➤ **Human cloning, so they say, will be possible within a decade.**

➤ **The experiments would take a couple of weeks, more or less.**

3. Contrasting comments. Contrasting comments beginning with words such as *not*, *unlike*, or *in contrast to* should be set off with commas.

➤ **According to the Committee on the Status of Endangered Wildlife**

in Canada, the polar bear is in trouble, but not endangered.

4. Absolute phrases. Absolute phrases usually include a noun (*water*) followed by a participle (*sparkling*) and are used to modify whole sentences.

➤ **The canoe glided over the still lake, the water sparkling in**

the moonlight.

44g WORDS OF DIRECT ADDRESS, *YES* AND *NO*, MILD INTERJECTIONS, AND TAG QUESTIONS.

Like non-restrictive phrases and clauses, words that interrupt a sentence are set off by commas because they are not essential to the sentence's meaning.

➤ **We have finished this project, Mr. Danowski, without any help**

from your foundation.

➤ **Yes, I will vote in the next election.**

➤ **Of course, if you think that's what we should do, then we'll do it.**

➤ **We can do better, don't you think?**

44h DIRECT QUOTATIONS.

Commas are used with quotation marks to set off what the source of the quotation says from the words identifying the source, such as *she said* or *Robert Rubin maintains. (See Chapter 48, pp. 369–378, for more on quotation marks.)*

➤ In her journal, Lucy Maud Montgomery wrote, "How I love
‸

this old manse where my children were born and where I have

tasted such rapturous happiness and endured so much

hideous agony" (365).

➤ "How I love this old manse where my children were born and

where I have tasted such rapturous happiness and endured so

much hideous agony," Lucy Maud Montgomery wrote in her
‸

journal (365).

Note: A comma is not needed to separate an indirect quotation or a paraphrase from the words that identify its source.

➤ Lucy Maud Montgomery notes/ that she loved the old

manse (365).

44i PARTS OF DATES, ADDRESSES, PEOPLE'S TITLES, AND NUMBERS.

1. Dates. Use paired commas in dates when the month, day, and year are included. Do not use commas when the day of the month is omitted or when the day appears before the month.

➤ On March 4, 1952, she travelled to Montreal.

➤ She travelled to Montreal in March 1952.

➤ She travelled to Montreal on 4 March 1952.

2. Addresses. Use commas to set off the parts of an address or the name of a province, but do not use a comma preceding a postal code.

➤ He lived at 1400 Crabgrass Lane, Charlottetown, Prince

Edward Island.

➤ In Jasper, Alberta, hundreds of tourists are drawn to the

Athabasca Glacier.

➤ Here is my address for the summer: 63 Oceanside Drive, Apt. 2A,

Salisbury, New Brunswick E4J 2K7.

3. People's titles or degrees. Put a comma between the person's name and the title or degree when it comes after the name, followed by another comma.

➤ **Kara Singh, MD, gave her the green light to resume her exercise**

regimen.

4. Numbers. When a number has more than four digits, use commas to mark off the numerals by hundreds—that is, by groups of three beginning at the right.

➤ **Over 20,000 fans cheered on the Toronto Raptors.**

If the number is four digits long, the comma is not required.

➤ **The survey had 3065 [or 3,065] respondents.**

Exceptions: Street numbers, postal codes, telephone numbers, page numbers (p. 2304), and years (1828) do not include commas.

44j OMITTED WORDS OR PHRASES, CONFUSING COMBINATIONS.

When a writer omits one or more words from a sentence to create an effect, a comma is often needed to make the meaning of the sentence clear for readers.

➤ **Under the bushes he found a gas can, and under the car, a book**

of matches that might have been used to start the fire.

The second comma substitutes for the phrase *he found.*

Commas are also used to keep readers from misunderstanding a writer's meaning when words are repeated or might be misread.

➤ **Many birds that sing, sing first thing in the morning.**

➤ **Any electronic items that can be, are recycled for other uses.**

COMMON MISUSES OF THE COMMA.

Just as a comma used correctly can clarify the meaning of a sentence, a comma used incorrectly can confuse readers. Commas should *not* be used in the following situations:

- To separate major elements in an independent clause (*below*)

- In front of the first or following the last item in a series (*below*)
- To join compound word groups that are not independent clauses (*p. 356*)
- To set off restrictive modifiers or appositives (*p. 357*)
- To set off very slight asides (*p. 358*)

44k TO SEPARATE MAJOR ELEMENTS IN AN INDEPENDENT CLAUSE.

Do not use a comma to separate a subject from a verb or a verb from its object.

➤ **Reflecting on one's life/ is necessary for emotional growth.**

The subject, *reflecting*, should not be separated from the verb, *is*.

➤ **Rhonda decided/ *that her career as a doctor was being***

undermined by her male colleagues.

The verb *decided* should not be separated from its direct object, the subordinate clause *that her career as a doctor was being undermined by her male colleagues.*

44l IN FRONT OF THE FIRST OR FOLLOWING THE FINAL ITEM IN A SERIES.

Use commas to separate items in a series but never before or after the series.

➤ **Canadians work longer hours than/ German, French, or British**

workers/ are expected to work.

Note: Commas should never be used after *such as* or *like*. (*See p. 359.*)

44m TO SEPARATE COMPOUND WORD GROUPS THAT ARE NOT INDEPENDENT CLAUSES.

A comma should not be used between word groups joined with a coordinating conjunction such as *and* unless they are both full sentences.

➤ **Security was so lax at the park that he became worried/ and**

begged his daughter to quit her summer job.

Here, *and* joins two verbs (*became* and *begged*), not two independent clauses.

➤ **He was worried that breaches of security were becoming more frequent/ and that his daughter was actually in danger at work.**

Here, *and* joins two subordinate clauses—both beginning with the word *that*—not two independent clauses.

44n TO SET OFF RESTRICTIVE MODIFIERS, APPOSITIVES, OR SLIGHTLY PARENTHETICAL WORDS OR PHRASES.

If a word, phrase, or clause in a sentence is necessary to identify the noun or pronoun that precedes it, it is **restrictive** and should not be set off with commas. (*For more on restrictive and non-restrictive elements, see pp. 350–351.*)

➤ **The students *who had studied for the history test* were restless and eager for it to begin.**

Because only those students who had studied were eager for the test to begin, the clause *who had studied for the history test* is restrictive and should not be set off with commas.

1. Appositives identifying nouns and pronouns should not be set off with commas. An **appositive** is a noun or noun phrase that renames a noun or pronoun and appears right after the word it renames.

➤ **The director/ Michael Curtiz/ was responsible for many great films in the 1930s and 1940s, including *Casablanca*.**

The name *Michael Curtiz* identifies the director for readers.

2. Concluding adverb clauses that are necessary to the meaning of the sentence should not be set off with commas. Adverb clauses beginning with *after, as soon as, before, because, if, since, unless, until,* and *when* are usually essential to a sentence's meaning and therefore are not usually set off with commas when they appear at the end of a sentence.

RESTRICTIVE   I am eager to test the children's IQ again *because significant variations in a child's test score indicate that the test itself may be flawed.*

Clauses beginning with *although, even though, though,* and *whereas* present a contrasting thought and are usually non-restrictive.

> NON-RESTRICTIVE   IQ tests can be useful indicators of a child's abilities, *although they should not be taken as the definitive measurement of a child's intelligence.*

Note: An adverb clause that appears at the beginning of a sentence is an introductory element and is usually followed by a comma: *Until we meet, I'm continuing my work on the budget. (See p. 348.)*

3. Words and phrases that are slightly parenthetical should not be set off with commas. Commas should be used for most parenthetical expressions. (*See p. 353.*) However, if setting off a brief parenthetical remark with commas would draw too much attention to the remark and interrupt the flow of the sentence, the commas can be left out.

➤ Deep space is *basically* the final frontier.

44o OTHER COMMON ERRORS.

- **Between cumulative adjectives**: Do not use a comma with **cumulative adjectives,** adjectives that modify each other and therefore are dependent on each other for their meaning to be clear. (*For more on cumulative adjectives, see pp. 349-350.*)

  ➤ Three/ well-known/ Canadian writers visited the artist's studio.

  The three are well-known Canadian writers, not just well-known writers and not just Canadian writers; you would not write *three Canadian well-known writers.*

- **Between adjectives and nouns:** A comma should not separate a noun from the adjective or adjectives that modify it.

  ➤ An art review by a celebrated, powerful/ writer would be guaranteed publication.

- **Between adverbs and adjectives**: A comma should not separate an adjective from the adverb that modifies it.

  ➤ The artist's studio was a delightfully/ chaotic environment, with canvases on every surface and paints spilled out in a fiesta of colour.

- **After coordinating conjunctions** (*and, but, or, nor, for, so, yet*):

  ➤ The new library was still under construction, but/ the ribbon cutting ceremony went ahead anyway.

- **After** *although, such as,* **or** *like*:

  ➤ There are far better forms of transportation than airplanes for short distances, although/ trains and buses have their own challenges.

  ➤ The firefighter gave us many good safety tips such as/ changing the batteries in the smoke detectors every New Year's Day and not blocking windows needed for fire exits with furniture.

- **Before an opening parenthesis:**

  ➤ Whenever he sat in his cubicle/ (which reminded him of a closet), he tended to daydream about the wide open spaces of his home in Saskatchewan.

- **With a question mark or an exclamation point that ends a quotation** (*Also see Chapter 48, p. 374*):

  ➤ "Are there not enough champagne glasses?/" the bride asked in alarm.

Semicolons

45

Semicolons are used to join ideas that are closely related and grammatically equivalent. Usually, there must be a full sentence (independent clause) on each side of the semicolon.

45a INDEPENDENT CLAUSES.

A semicolon should be used to join closely related independent clauses when they are not joined by a comma and a coordinating conjunction (*and, but, or, nor, for, so, yet*). A semicolon is an effective way to link two clauses if readers are able to see the relationship between the two without the help of a coordinating conjunction.

➤ **Before 8000 B.C.E. wheat was not the luxuriant plant it is today;**

it was merely one of many wild grasses that spread throughout

the Middle East.

The writer could have separated the clauses with a period but chose a semicolon to mark the close relationship between the ideas in the two clauses.

Sometimes, the close relationship is a contrast.

➤ **Philip had completed the assignment; Andrew had not.**

Note: If a comma is used between two clauses without a coordinating conjunction, the sentence is a comma splice, a serious error. One way to correct a comma splice is by changing the comma to a semicolon.

➤ **Salam always wanted to study architecture/; other people's taxes**

is what he ended up doing instead.

If no punctuation appears between the two clauses, the sentence is a run-on. One way to correct a run-on sentence is to add a semicolon between the two clauses.

➤ **Tulips bloom in the early spring; daffodils blossom at the**

same time.

(*For more on comma splices and run-on sentences, see Tab 8: Editing for Grammar, pp. 304–308.*)

45b INDEPENDENT CLAUSES WITH TRANSITIONAL EXPRESSIONS.

Transitional expressions, including transitional phrases (*after all, even so, for example, in addition, on the contrary*) and conjunctive adverbs (*consequently, however, moreover, nevertheless, then, therefore*), indicate the way that two clauses are related to each other. When a transitional expression appears between two clauses, it is preceded by a semicolon and usually followed by a comma. (*For a list of transitional expressions, see Tab 8, Editing for Grammar, p. 306.*)

➤ **Monique had to wait until the plumber arrived; consequently,**

she was late for the exam.

Note: The semicolon always appears between the two clauses, even when the transitional expression appears in another position within the second clause. Wherever it appears, the transitional expression is usually set off with a comma or commas.

➤ **My friends are all taking golf lessons; my roommate and I,**

however, are more interested in tennis.

Coordinating conjunctions (*and, but, or, nor, for, so, yet*) also indicate the way clauses are related. Unlike transitional expressions, however, they are preceded by a comma, not a semicolon, when they join two independent clauses. (*For more on comma splices and run-on sentences, see Tab 8: Editing for Grammar, pp. 304–308.*)

45c ITEMS IN A SERIES THAT CONTAINS COMMAS.

Because the following sentence contains so many elements, the semicolons are needed for clarity.

➤ **The committee included Dr. Curtis Youngblood, the medical**

examiner; Roberta Collingwood, the director of the bureau's

criminal division; and Darcy Coolidge, the chief of police.

Note: This rule is an exception to the general principle that there should be a full sentence (independent clause) on each side of a semicolon.

45d COMMON ERRORS.

■ **To join a dependent clause to an independent clause:**
A semicolon can join two independent clauses because they are grammatically equivalent, but a dependent clause is never equivalent to an independent clause.

➤ **Professional writers need to devote time every day to**

their writing; because otherwise they can lose momentum.

➤ **Although housecats seem tame and lovable; they can be**

fierce hunters.

- **To join independent clauses linked by a coordinating conjunction (*and, but, or, nor, for, so, yet*):** A comma, not a semicolon, should precede the coordinating conjunction.

  ➤ **Lady Gaga wears outrageous costumes, so many people**

     think she is a lunatic.

- **To introduce a series or an explanation:** A colon should usually be used for this purpose.

  ➤ **My day was ruined: a broken-down washing machine, an**

     appointment with the principal, spilled cereal all over the

     kitchen floor, and a sick child. No wonder I wanted to

     run away from home sometimes!

  ➤ **The doctor finally diagnosed the problem: a severe sinus**

     infection.

46 Colons

A colon draws the reader's attention to what it is introducing. It also has other conventional uses.

46a WITH LISTS, APPOSITIVES, OR QUOTATIONS.

In sentences, colons are most often used to introduce lists, appositives (nouns or noun phrases that rename nouns or pronouns and appear right after the word they rename), and quotations. They are almost always preceded by complete sentences (independent clauses). (*For more on quotations, see Chapter 48, pp. 369–377.*)

LIST **The novel deals with three kinds of futility:**

     pervasive poverty, unrequited love, and

     inescapable aging.

APPOSITIVE   **In September 2003, the eastern shores of Nova**

Scotia were devastated by a ferocious storm:
                                                      ^
Hurricane Juan.

QUOTATION   **He took my hand and said the words I had been**

dreading: "I really want us to be just friends."
            ^

46b WITH A SECOND INDEPENDENT CLAUSE THAT ELABORATES ON THE FIRST ONE.

The colon can be used to link independent clauses when the second clause restates or elaborates on the first. Use it when you want to emphasize the second clause.

➤ **I can predict next term's sequence of events: I will pick courses**
                                                ^
that I will end up hating, I will catch the flu, and I will fall

hopelessly behind in my schoolwork.

Note: When a complete sentence follows a colon, the first word may begin with either a capital or a lowercase letter. Whatever you decide to do, though, you should use the same style throughout your document.

46c OTHER CONVENTIONAL USES.

Use colons in business letters, to indicate ratios, to indicate times of day, for city and publisher citations in bibliographies, and to separate titles and subtitles.

CROSS-DISCIPLINE **WRITING**

Biblical Citations

Colons are often used to separate biblical chapters and verses (John 3:16), but the Modern Language Association (MLA) recommends using a period instead (John 3.16).

➤ Dear Mr. Eystein:

➤ The ratio of armed to unarmed members of the gang was 3:1.

➤ He woke up at 6:30 in the morning.

➤ Toronto: McGraw-Hill Ryerson, 2004.

➤ *Cambodia: A Book for People Who Find Television Too Slow*

46d COMMON ERRORS.

■ Between a verb and its object or complement:

➤ The critical elements in a good smoothie are⁄ yogurt, fresh fruit, and honey.

■ Between a preposition and its object or objects:

➤ The novel deals with⁄ pervasive poverty.

➤ Many feel that cancer can be prevented by a diet of⁄ fruit, nuts, and vegetables.

■ After *such as, for example,* or *including:*

➤ I am ready for new challenge, such as⁄ skydiving or rock climbing.

47 Apostrophes

Apostrophes show possession (*the dog's bone*) and indicate omitted letters in contractions (*don't*). They are also used to express concepts of duration (*an hour's wait*) and of monetary value (*five dollars' worth*). Apostrophes are used in such a wide variety of ways that they can be confusing. The most common confusion is between plurals and possessives.

Note: If you are wondering whether a particular noun should be in the possessive form, reword the sentence using the word *of* (*the bone of the dog*) to make sure that the noun is not plural.

Hint: shared possession, shared apostrophe; individual ownership, individual apostrophes.

47a TO INDICATE POSSESSION.

For a noun to be possessive, two elements are usually required: someone or something is the possessor; and someone, something, or some attribute or quality is possessed.

POSSESSION	POSSESSOR	PERSON, THING, ATTRIBUTE, QUALITY, VALUE, OR FEATURE POSSESSED
the woman's son	woman	son
Juanita's shovel	Juanita	shovel
a child's bright smile	child	bright smile

Sometimes the thing possessed precedes the possessor.

➤ **The laptop is the student's.**

Sometimes the sentence may not name the thing possessed, but its identity (in this case, *house*) is clearly understood by the reader.

➤ **I saw your cousin at Janet's.**

1. Forming possessives with -'s. To form the possessive of all singular nouns, as well as plural nouns that do not end in -*s*, add an apostrophe plus -*s* to the noun.

NOUN/PRONOUN	NUMBER	AS A POSSESSIVE
baby	singular	a baby's smile
hour	singular	an hour's time
men	plural	the men's club
children	plural	the children's papers

Even singular nouns that end in -*s* form the possessive by adding -*'s*.

➤ **James's swim, Ross's flag, Alanis's songs**

Note: If a singular noun with more than two syllables ends in -*s* and adding -*'s* would make the word sound awkward, it is acceptable to use only an apostrophe to form the possessive.

➤ **Socrates' students remained loyal to him.**

2. Forming possessives with only an apostrophe. Plural nouns that end in -*s* take only an apostrophe to form the possessive.

NOUN/PRONOUN	NUMBER	AS A POSSESSIVE
babies	plural	the babies' smiles
companies	plural	the companies' employees
robbers	plural	the robbers' clever plan

3. Showing joint possession. To express joint ownership by two or more people, use the possessive form for the last name only; to express individual ownership, use the possessive form for each name.

➤ *Harold and Kumar's Adventure to White Castle*

➤ **The city's and the province's finances**

4. Forming the possessive of compound nouns. For compound words, add an apostrophe plus -*s* to the last word in the compound to form the possessive.

➤ **My father-in-law's job**

➤ **The editor-in-chief's responsibilities**

47b WITH INDEFINITE PRONOUNS.

Indefinite pronouns such as *no one, everyone, everything,* and *something* do not refer to a specific person or a specific item. They are generic references to people and things. (*See Tab 8: Editing for Grammar, pp. 313–314.*)

➤ **Well, it is *anybody's* guess.**

47c FOR MISSING LETTERS IN CONTRACTIONS AND FOR MISSING NUMBERS.

A contraction is a shortened word or group of words formed when some letters or sounds are omitted. In a contraction, the apostrophe serves as a substitute for the omitted letters.

it's	for *it is* or *it has*
weren't	for *were not*
here's	for *here is*

In informal writing, apostrophes can also substitute for omitted numbers in a decade. It is usually better to spell out the name of the decade in formal writing, however:

INFORMAL
In the twentieth century, the *'50s* were relatively calm; the *'60s* were much more turbulent.

MORE FORMAL
In the twentieth century, the *fifties* were relatively calm; the *sixties* were much more turbulent.

47d TO FORM PLURAL NUMBERS, LETTERS, ABBREVIATIONS, AND WORDS USED AS WORDS.

An apostrophe plus *-s* (*'s*) can be used to show the plural of a number, a letter, or an abbreviation. Underline or italicize single letters but not the apostrophe or the *-s*.

➤ **He makes his 2's look like 5's.**

➤ **Committee has two *m*'s, two *t*'s, and two *e*'s.**

➤ **Professor Jarinder has two PhD's.**

Exceptions: If an abbreviation does not have periods, the apostrophe is not necessary (*CD-ROMs*). The apostrophe is also not necessary to form the plural of dates (*1990s*).

If a word is used as a word rather than as a symbol of the meaning it conveys, it can be made plural by adding an apostrophe plus *-s*. The word should be italicized or underlined but not the *-s*.

➤ **There are twelve *no's* in the first paragraph.**

CROSS-DISCIPLINE **WRITING**

Plurals of Numbers, Letters, and Abbreviations

Style guides differ in their rules for making numbers, letters, and abbreviations plural. For example, the Modern Language Association (MLA) recommends adding an *s* without an apostrophe to form the plurals of abbreviations and numbers: *DVDs, 3s and 4s*.

47e INCORRECT USE WITH SOME PROPER NAMES.

If you are not sure whether to add an apostrophe to a place name or leave it out, look up the name in a dictionary or an atlas. If you need to verify the spelling of an organization's name, try searching for its Web site. For example, St. John's, Newfoundland, is not spelled the same way as St. John, New Brunswick.

➤ Kings Point

➤ St. Catharines

47f INCORRECT USE WITH SOME PLURAL NOUNS.

Most often, writers misuse the apostrophe by adding it to a plural noun that is not possessive. The plurals of most nouns are formed by adding -s: *boy/boys; girl/girls; teacher/teachers*. Possessives are formed by adding an apostrophe plus -s ('s): *boy/boy's; girl/girl's; teacher/teacher's*. The possessive form and the plural form are not interchangeable.

  teachers   *girls*   *boys*
➤ The ~~teacher's~~ asked the ~~girl's~~ and ~~boy's~~ for their attention.

47g DISTINGUISHING BETWEEN POSSESSIVE PRONOUNS AND CONTRACTIONS.

Be careful not to use a contraction when a possessive is called for, and vice versa. Personal pronouns and the relative pronoun *who* have special possessive forms, which never require apostrophes (*my/mine, your/yours, his, her/hers, it/its, our/ours, their/theirs, and whose*). When an apostrophe appears with a pronoun, the apostrophe usually marks omissions in a contraction, unless the pronoun is indefinite. (*See p. 366*.)

The following pairs or groups of words often cause problems for writers.

Its/it's: *Its* is a possessive pronoun. *It's* is a contraction for *it is* or *it has: It's* [*It + is*] too hot.

➤ The elephant at African Lion Safari held the paintbrush in its trunk to paint T-shirts for the tourists.

➤ *It's* often been said that English is a difficult language to learn.

Their/there/they're: *Their* is a possessive pronoun. *There* is an adverb of place. *They're* is a contraction of *they are.*

➤ They gave *their* lives in Afghanistan.

➤ I saw her standing *there.*

➤ *They're* reading more Michael Ondaatje this semester.

Whose/who's: *Whose* is the possessive form of *who; who's* is a contraction of *who is.*

➤ Harry, *whose* dream had always been to own a 1969 Camaro,

searched the used car lot in vain.

➤ *Who's* there?

Your/you're: *Your* is a possessive pronoun; *you're* is a contraction of *you are.*

➤ Is that *your* family over by the pool?

➤ *You're* going to have to work a lot harder than that if you want

to pass.

Quotation Marks

48

Quotation marks always appear in pairs (except when a quote is broken into paragraphs, as noted below). They are used to enclose words, phrases, and sentences that are quoted directly; titles of short works such as poems, articles, songs, and short stories; and words and phrases used in a special sense.

48a EXACT WORDS OF A SPEAKER OR WRITER.

Direct quotations from written material may include whole sentences or only a few words or phrases.

➤ In *Angela's Ashes,* Frank McCourt writes, "Worse than

the ordinary miserable childhood is the miserable Irish

childhood" (11).

➤ **Frank McCourt believes that being Irish worsens what is all too**

"ordinary"—a "miserable childhood" (11).

Use quotation marks to enclose everything a speaker says in written dialogue. If the quoted sentence is interrupted by a phrase like *he said,* enclose the rest of the quotation in quotation marks. When another person begins to speak, begin a new paragraph to indicate a change in speaker.

> "I don't know what you're talking about," he said. "I did listen to everything you told me."
> "If you had been listening, you would know what I was talking about."

If a speaker continues for more than a paragraph, begin each subsequent paragraph with quotation marks, but do not insert a closing quotation mark until the end of the quotation.

Note: Do not use quotation marks to set off an indirect quotation, which reports what a speaker said but does not use the exact words.

➤ **He said that ʺhe didn't want to do anything that might get him**

into trouble with the police.ʺ

Two or three lines of poetry may be run in to your text, much like any other *short* quotation. Line breaks are shown with a slash. Leave a space before and after the slash. (*For more on slashes, see Chapter 49, pp. 378–387.*)

➤ **In the nineteenth century, Wordsworth wrote of the weary**

acquisitiveness of our modern age: "The world is too much with

us; late and soon, / Getting and spending, we lay waste our

powers" (lines 1–2).

Note: In the style of the Modern Language Association (MLA), line numbers should appear in parentheses following the quotation. The word *lines* should precede the numbers the first time the poem is quoted.

48b LONG QUOTATIONS IN INDENTED BLOCKS.

If you are using a quotation longer than four typed lines, set it off from the text as a block quotation. Start a new line for the quotation, type it double-spaced, and indent every line of the quotation one inch (ten spaces) from the left margin. Double-space above and below the quotation. Be sure that you indent every line in a block quotation.

A block quotation is *not* surrounded by quotation marks. If the text you are quoting includes a direct quotation, however, use quotation marks to set that off. If your quotation is more than one paragraph long, indent the first line of each new paragraph an extra quarter-inch (0.25 cms or three spaces). A block quotation is usually introduced by a sentence that ends with a colon.

> Isabel Beaton Graham of Winnipeg was an advocate for homesteading rights, putting it this way for her audience of the National Council of Women:
>
>> Here and there over the Canadian West great tracts of fertile lands lie awaste, waiting an occupant. Here and there over the Dominion, and, indeed, over the Empire, numbers of us unattached women working for fathers, working for brothers—work and wait, work and wait—waiting for what—Eternity? . . . Why hasn't a Canadian woman a birthright in her country? In every economic distress that sweeps a land, in every epidemic of disease, in storm or stress of whatsoever sort woman bears a full burden. (202)

Longer verse quotations (four lines or more) are indented block-style, like long prose quotations. (*For short quotations of poetry, see pp. 370 and 385–386.*) If you cannot fit an entire line of poetry on a single line of your typescript, you may indent the turned line an extra quarter-inch (0.25 cm).

> In the following lines from "Crossing Brooklyn Ferry," Walt Whitman celebrates the beauty of the Manhattan skyline, and his love for that city:
>
>> Ah, what can ever be more stately and admirable to me
>>> than mast-hemm'd Manhattan?
>> River and sunset and scallop-edg'd waves of flood-tide?
>> The sea-gulls oscillating their bodies, the hay-boat in the
>>> twilight, and the belated lighter?
>> What gods can exceed these that clasp me by the hand,
>>> and with voices I love call me promptly and loudly
>>> by my nighest name as I approach? (lines 92–95)

Note: Because they interrupt your text and decrease its readability, you should use block quotations sparingly. (*For more on when to use quotations, see Tab 3: Researching, pp. 154–157.*)

48c A QUOTATION WITHIN A QUOTATION.

Unless you are using a block quotation, set off a quotation within a quotation with a pair of single quotation marks.

➤ **H. G. Wells' *The New Machiavelli* was "one of the literary**

'sensations' of the season."

48d TITLES OF SHORT WORKS.

The titles of long works, such as books, are usually underlined or put in italics. (*See Chapter 53, p. 398.*) The titles of book chapters, essays, most poems, and other short works are usually put in quotation marks. Quotation marks are also used for titles of unpublished works, including student papers, theses, and dissertations.

- **Book chapters or sections**
  "Kimociwinikewin: Raid" (a chapter in *Three Day Road* by Joseph Boyden)
  "Science and Technology" (Part 4 of *The Universal Almanac*)

- **Essays**
  "Radical Dreamer: Jane Jacobs on the streets of Toronto," by Robert Fulford
  "Law-abiding and Law-resisting: Baseland and hinterland tendencies in Canadian Poetry," by D. M. R. Bentley

- **Songs**
  "Wavin' Flag," sung by Young Artists for Haiti
  "The Suburbs" written and performed by Arcade Fire

- **Short poems**
  "Death of a Young Son by Drowning," by Margaret Atwood
  "Le vaisseau d'or," by Émile Nelligan

- **Articles in periodicals**
  "Ottawa cancels funding for Toronto theatre festival that presented terrorist play" (from the *Globe and Mail*)
  "Guardians of the North?" (from *Canadian Frontier*)

CROSS-DISCIPLINE **WRITING**

Documentation Styles

Providing the page number (without punctuation) in parentheses after the quotation is a convention of the Modern Language Association "English..." (Rubens 29). The American Psychological Association (APA), a system widely used in the social sciences, employs a different documentation convention: ". . . Rome" (Bieder, 2010, p. 273). The APA also has different rules for setting off long quotations. *(For more on the differences between documentation styles, see Tabs 4–6.)*

- **Short stories**

  "The Summer My Grandmother Was Supposed to Die," by Mordecai Richler

  "Cape Breton is the Thought Control Centre of Canada," by Ray Smith

- **Episodes of radio and television programs**

  "Hannah the Healer" (Episode 33 of *Afghanada* on CBC Radio)

  "Return of the Prairie Bandit" (on *The Nature of Things*)

Note: If quotation marks are needed within the title of a short work, use single quotation marks: "The 'Animal Rights' War on Medicine."

48e A WORD OR PHRASE USED IN A SPECIAL WAY.

Put quotation marks around a word or phrase that someone else has used in a way that you or your readers may not agree with. Quotation marks used in this way function as raised eyebrows do in conversation and should be used sparingly.

➤ The **"workers' paradise"** of Stalinist Russia included slave-labour camps.

Words cited as words can also be put in quotation marks, although the more common practice is to italicize them.

➤ The words **"compliment"** and **"complement"** sound alike but have different meanings.

48f OTHER PUNCTUATION MARKS WITH QUOTATION MARKS.

As you edit, check all closing quotation marks and the marks of punctuation that appear next to them to make sure that you have placed them in the right order.

- Periods (.) always belong inside quotation marks.
- Commas (,) always belong inside quotation marks.
- Semicolons (;) always belong outside quotation marks.
- Colons (:) always belong outside quotation marks.
- Exclamation points (!) belong inside quotation marks if they are part of the statement or title being quoted but outside quotation marks if they are the end mark for the entire sentence.
- Question marks (?) belong inside quotation marks if they are part of the question or title being quoted but outside quotation marks if they are the end mark for the entire sentence.
- Dashes (—) belong inside quotation marks if they are part of the quotation but outside quotations marks if they are part of the sentence that introduces or surrounds the quotation.

1. Periods and commas. Place the period or comma before the final quotation mark even when the quotation is only one or two words long.

➤ The publication of poetry was an especially benevolent activity, as Caswell estimated the entire Canadian market for a poetry book in 1901 to be "not more than 100 or 200."

➤ Caswell estimated the entire Canadian market for a poetry book in 1901 to be "not more than 100 or 200," so the publication of poetry was an especially benevolent activity.

Note: In British punctuation, the comma and period are placed outside the quotation mark; Canadian and American usage places these punctuation marks inside the quotation marks, except in some specific instances in documenting sources.

2. Colons and semicolons. Place colons and semicolons after the final quotation mark.

➤ **Dean Wilcox cited the items he called his "daily delights": a free parking space for his scooter at the faculty club, a special table in the club itself, and friends to laugh with after a day's work.**

3. Question marks and exclamation points. Place a question mark or an exclamation point after the final quotation mark if the quoted material is not itself a question or an exclamation.

➤ **Why did she name her cat "Tristan"?**

Place a question mark or an exclamation point inside the final quotation mark when it is part of the quotation. No additional punctuation is needed after the closing quotation.

➤ **He had many questions, such as "Can you really do unto others as you would have them do unto you?"**

4. Dashes. Place a dash outside either an opening or a closing quotation mark, or both, if it precedes or follows the quotation or if two dashes are used to set off the quotation.

➤ **One phrase—"time is running out"—haunted me throughout my dream.**

Place a dash inside either an opening or a closing quotation mark if it is part of the quotation.

➤ **"Where is the—" she called. "Oh, here it is. Never mind."**

48g INTEGRATING QUOTATIONS INTO SENTENCES.

1. Formal introductions. If you introduce a quotation with a complete sentence, you can use a colon before it.

➤ **He was better than anyone else at public speaking, but he didn't want to do it: "I actually don't believe in your cause," he said.**

2. *She said* and similar expressions. If you introduce a direct quotation with *he said, she noted,* or a similar expression, add a comma after the expression and use a capital letter to begin the quotation. If the expression follows the quotation, add a comma at the end of the quotation, before the closing quotation mark.

➤ **He said, "She believed I was lying."**

➤ **"She believed I was lying," he said.**

Note: Do not use a comma after such expressions as *he said* or *the researchers note* if an indirect quotation or a paraphrase follows.

➤ **He said/ that she believed he was lying.**

3. Quotations that are integrated into a sentence. When a quotation is integrated into a sentence's structure, treat the quotation as you would any other sentence element, adding a comma or not as appropriate.

➤ **Telling me that she wanted to "play hooky from her life," she set off on a three-week vacation.**

➤ **He said he had his "special reasons."**

4. Quotations that begin a sentence. If your quotation begins a sentence, capitalize the first letter after the quotation mark even if the first word does not begin a sentence in the original source.

➤ **"The only white people who came to our house were welfare workers and bill collectors," James Baldwin wrote.**

5. Interrupted quotations. If the sentence you are quoting is interrupted by an expression such as *she said,* begin the sentence with a quotation mark and a capital letter, end the first part of the quotation with a comma and a quotation mark, insert the interrupting words followed by another comma, and then resume the quotation with a lowercase letter.

➤ **"Were the Canadian market a larger one, and a better one for Canadian books" wrote Caswell to Catharine Parr Traill in 1894, "we would not think of mentioning such terms."**

If you end one quoted sentence and insert an expression such as *he said* before beginning the next quoted sentence, place a comma at the end of the first quoted sentence and a period after the interruption.

➤ **"There are at least four kinds of doublespeak," William Lutz observes. "The first is the euphemism, an inoffensive or positive word or phrase used to avoid a harsh, unpleasant, or distasteful reality."**

48h COMMON ERRORS.

- **To distance yourself from slang, clichés, or trite expressions:** It is best to avoid overused or slang expressions altogether in formal academic writing. If your writing situation permits slang, however, do not enclose it in quotation marks.

  WEAK   Vancouver is so "laid back."

  REVISED   Many Vancouver residents have a relaxed, carefree style.

- **For indirect quotations:** Do not use quotation marks for indirect quotations. Watch out for errors in pronoun reference as well. (*See Tab 8: Editing for Grammar, pp. 332–333.*)

  INCORRECT   He wanted to tell his boss that "he needed a vacation."

  CORRECT   He told his boss that his boss needed a vacation.

  CORRECT   He said to his boss, "You need a vacation."

- **In quotations that end with a question:** Only the question mark that ends the quoted sentence is needed, even when the entire sentence that includes the quotation is also a question.

  ➤ **What did Juliet mean when she cried, "O Romeo, Romeo!**

  Wherefore art thou Romeo?"?

  If a question is quoted before the end of a sentence that makes a statement, place a question mark before the last quotation mark and put a period at the end of the sentence.

  ➤ **"What was Pearson's greatest contribution as prime**

  minister?" he asked.

- **To enclose the title of your own paper:**

  ➤ **"Tristan, Intertextuality, and National Literatures"**

  If you use a quotation or a title of a short work in your title, though, put quotation marks around it.

  ➤ **"All Art is Collaboration": Tristan, Intertextuality, and**

  National Literatures

49 Other Punctuation Marks

49a PERIODS.

1. Use a period to end most statements. Most English sentences are statements.

➤ **Engineers usually make a good salary.**

Polite requests that do not ask a question also end in a period.

➤ **Will those not on the list please remain seated.**

Statements that ask questions indirectly end in a period.

➤ **She asked me where I had parked the car.**

2. Use periods in abbreviations when convention requires them. A period or periods are used with the following common abbreviations, which end in lowercase letters.

Mr.	Dr.	Jan.
Ms.	i.e.	e.g.
Mrs.		

If the abbreviation is made up of capital letters, however, the periods are optional.

RN (or R.N.)	BA (or B.A.)
MD (or M.D.)	PhD (or Ph.D.)

Periods are omitted in abbreviations for organizations, famous people, provinces in mailing addresses, and acronyms (words made up of initials).

CBC	ON	NATO
PET	QC	NAFTA
CSIS	NASA	HRDC

When in doubt, consult a dictionary.

When an abbreviation ends a sentence, the period at the end of the abbreviation serves as the period for the sentence. If a question mark or an exclamation point ends the sentence, place it *after* the period in the abbreviation.

➤ **When he was in the seventh grade, we called him "Willy," but**

 now he is William Percival Abernathy, Ph.D.!

49b   QUESTION MARKS.

Use a question mark after a direct question.

➤ **Who wrote *The Journals of Susanna Moodie*?**

Occasionally, a question mark changes a statement into a question.

➤ **You expect me to believe a story like that?**

When questions follow one another in a series, each one can be followed by a question mark even if the questions are not complete sentences, as long as the meaning is understood.

➤ **What will you contribute? Your time? Your talent? Your money?**

Use a question mark in parentheses to indicate a questionable date, number, or word, but do not use it to convey an ironic meaning.

➤ **Chaucer was born in 1340 (?) and lived until 1400.**

➤ **His cousin claimed to be an honest (?) lawyer even though he**

   defended members of the Hell's Angels biker gang.

Note: Do not use a question mark after an indirect quotation, even if the words being indirectly quoted were originally a question.

➤ **He asked her if she would be at home later?.**

49c   EXCLAMATION POINTS.

Use exclamation points sparingly to convey shock, surprise, or some other strong emotion.

➤ **Stolen! The bike was stolen! Who would steal a bike from a little**

   boy at the park?

Note: Using numerous exclamation points throughout a document actually weakens their force. As much as possible, try to convey emotion with your choice of words and your sentence structure instead of with an exclamation point.

49d   A DASH OR DASHES.

Think of the dash as a very strong pause intended to emphasize what follows—and sometimes to emphasize what comes immediately before. A typeset dash, sometimes called an *em dash,* is a single, unbroken line. Most word-processing programs provide the em dash as a special character. Otherwise, the dash can be made on the keyboard with two hyphens in a row. Do not put a space before or after the dash.

1. Use a dash or dashes to set off parenthetical material.

➤ All finite creations—including humans—are incomplete and contradictory.

➤ I think the Leafs have a chance to win the cup—if they can just get through this next series with the Senators.

2. Use a dash or dashes to set off a series or an explanation. Sometimes a dash will set off a series of nouns placed for special emphasis at the beginning of a sentence and then summarized by a pronoun after the dash.

➤ Cola, potato chips, and cheeseburgers—this is a recipe for heart disease.

A dash can also be used to set off a series or an explanation that appears at the end of a sentence.

➤ A surprising number of people have taken up birdwatching—a peaceful, relatively inexpensive hobby.

3. Use a dash or dashes to add, and emphasize, a non-essential independent clause. Sometimes a dash is used to set off an independent clause within a sentence. In such sentences, the set-off clause provides interesting information but is not essential to the main assertion.

➤ The first rotary gasoline engine—it was made by Mazda—burned 15% more fuel than conventional engines.

4. Use a dash or dashes to indicate a sudden change in tone or idea.

➤ Breathing heavily, the archaeologist opened the old chest in wild anticipation and found—an old pair of socks and an empty soda can.

5. Do not overuse dashes. Used sparingly, the dash can be an effective mark of punctuation, but if it is overused, it can make your writing disjointed.

CHOPPY | After I phoned the park—which I had meant to do all morning—I apologized for the confusion—although I'm pretty sure it was their fault, actually—and tried to work out my schedule—to patch things up with my boss.

SMOOTHER | After I phoned the park, which I had meant to do all morning, I apologized for the confusion—although I'm pretty sure it was their fault, actually—and tried to work out my schedule to patch things up with my boss.

49e PARENTHESES.

Parentheses are used to set off relatively unimportant or supplementary information, a digression, or a comment that interrupts the flow of thought within a sentence or paragraph. Parentheses enclose material that is useful or interesting but not important enough to receive any emphasis, unlike material set off by commas or dashes.

➤ **The new Winnipeg hockey team's season tickets (which sold out in just 17 minutes) were certainly popular.**

When parentheses enclose a whole sentence by itself, the sentence begins with a capital letter and ends with a period before the final parenthesis. A sentence that appears inside parentheses *within a sentence* should neither begin with a capital letter nor end with a period.

➤ **Folktales and urban legends often reflect the concerns of a particular era. (The familiar tale of a cat accidentally caught in a microwave oven is an example of this phenomenon.)**

➤ **John Henry (he was the man with the twelve-pound hammer) was a hero to miners fearing the loss of their jobs to machines.**

If the material in parentheses is at the end of an introductory or non-essential word group followed by a comma, the comma should be placed after the closing parenthesis. A comma should never appear before the opening parenthesis.

➤ **As he walked past/ (dressed, as always, in his hockey jacket), I got ready to ask for his autograph.**

Parentheses are used to enclose numbers or letters that label items in a list.

➤ **He says he wants to switch schools because (1) the other school has the program he wants to take, (2) the school is close enough that he could live at home, and (3) his new girlfriend goes to that school.**

Parentheses also enclose in-text citations in many systems of documenting sources. (*For more on documenting sources, see Tabs 4–6.*)

Note: Too many parentheses are distracting to readers. If you find that you have used a large number of parentheses in a draft, revise carefully to see if any of the material within parentheses really deserves more emphasis.

49f   BRACKETS.

Brackets set off information you add to a quotation that is not part of the quotation itself. Use brackets to add significant information that is needed to make the quote clear.

➤ **Allan writes, "This process of falling out of fashion and having to be resurrected is one that she [Lazarus] shares with many other (often women) writers, such as Harriet Beecher Stowe, who fell, for a time, out of the gaze of academic study."**

In this sentence, the writer is quoting Allan, but Allan's sentence does not include the name of the woman writer being discussed. The writer places the name—Lazarus—in brackets so that readers will know the identity of the writer Allan is talking about.

Information that explains or corrects something in a quotation is also bracketed.

➤ **Vasco da Gama's man wrote in 1487, "The body of the church [it was not a church but a Hindu shrine] is as large as a monastery."**

Brackets are also used around words that you insert within a quotation to make it fit the grammar or style of your own sentence. If you replace a word with your own word in brackets, ellipses are not needed.

➤ **At the end of *Pygmalion,* Henry Higgins confesses to Eliza**

Doolittle that he has "grown accustomed to [her] voice and

appearance."

To make the quote fit properly into the sentence, the bracketed word *her* is inserted in place of *your.*

If you are adding ellipses to a passage that already contains ellipses, distinguish them from the ellipses that appear in the original by using brackets. (*See the following section on ellipses.*)

Note: Brackets may be used to enclose the word *sic* (Latin for "thus") after a word in a quotation that was incorrect or uses an archaic spelling in the original. The word *sic* should not be underlined or italicized when it appears in brackets.

➤ **We are going to publish a new edition of Lewis Carroll's *Alice's***

***Adventures in Wonderland* since "this celebrated masterpiece of**

phantasy (sic) seems to increase in value year by year."

Sic should be used sparingly, because it can appear pretentious and condescending, and it should not be used to ridicule what someone has written.

49g ELLIPSES.

If you wish to shorten a quotation, you may omit words, phrases, or even entire sentences. To show readers that you have done so, use three spaced periods, called ellipses or an ellipsis mark. Some instructors suggest that you use brackets to enclose any ellipses that you add, as shown in the second and fourth examples below. Other punctuation either precedes or follows the brackets, depending on what you have left out.

FULL QUOTATION FROM A WORK BY NELLIE MCCLUNG

I mean the cases of dependent women now living with unwilling relatives. Everyone can cite cases. Some of them have seen Mrs. G. wheeling her daughter's baby in the park at the dinner hour so she will be out of the way when her son-in-law comes home all tired out after a hard day at the office. Mrs. G.'s insurance money was all lost in his oil company in 1927 and so, of course, she looks like a bit of bad news to him. If Mrs. G. had an annuity of $100 a month she and her son-in-law would be good friends. It is surprising how even a smaller sum than that, when it is sure to come each month, adds to any woman's charm, improves her conversation and gives weight to her opinions. It makes her a welcome guest at any of her children's houses, and that is no slam on her children either, for young people have their own burdens.

EDITED QUOTATION

In her 1937 essay, "Women and Their Money," McClung argues that "$100 a month . . . adds to any woman's charm, improves her conversation and gives weight to her opinions."

EDITED QUOTATION (ALTERNATIVE STYLE, WITH BRACKETS)

In her 1937 essay, "Women and Their Money," McClung argues that "$100 a month [. . .] adds to any woman's charm, improves her conversation and gives weight to her opinions."

If you are leaving out the end of a quoted sentence, the three ellipsis points are preceded by a period to end the sentence. If you are using the alternative style, however, the ellipsis points, enclosed in brackets, precede the period.

EDITED QUOTATION

In describing the sad "cases of dependent women now living with unwilling relatives," McClung paints a picture of "Mrs. G. wheeling her daughter's baby in the park . . . so she will be out of the way when her son-in-law comes home all tired out after a hard day at the office. . . ."

EDITED QUOTATION (ALTERNATIVE STYLE, WITH BRACKETS)

In describing the sad "cases of dependent women now living with unwilling relatives," McClung paints a picture of "Mrs. G. wheeling her daughter's baby in the park [. . .] so she will be out of the way when her son-in-law comes home all tired out after a hard day at the office[. . .]."

When you need to add a parenthetical reference after the ellipses at the end of a sentence, place it after the quotation mark but before the final period: . . ." (253). or [. . .]" (253).

Ellipses are usually not needed to indicate an omission when only a word or phrase is being quoted.

➤ Money makes a woman "a welcome guest at any of her children's houses," according to McClung.

To indicate the omission of an entire line or more from the middle of a poem, insert a line of spaced periods. Enclose the line of periods with brackets if you have been using brackets with other ellipsis points.

In his most famous poem, "Tantramar Revisited," Charles

G. D. Roberts seems to be describing nature, but the real

issue is change and loss:

> Summers and summers have come, and gone with
>
> > the flight of the swallow;
>
> Sunshine and thunder have been, storm, and winter,
>
> > and frost;
>
> Many and many a sorrow has all but died from
>
> > remembrance,
>
> Many a dream of joy fall'n in the shadow of pain.
>
> [. . .]
>
> Even the bosom of Earth is strewn with heavier
>
> > shadows, —
>
> Only in these green hills, aslant to the sea, no change!
>
> > (1–4, 7–8)

Ellipses should be used only as a means of shortening a quotation, never as a device for changing its fundamental meaning or for creating emphasis where none exists in the original.

Ellipses may be used at the end of a sentence if you mean to leave a thought hanging. In the following passage, Dick Gregory uses an ellipsis to suggest that there was no end to his worries.

➤ **Oh God, I'm scared. I wish I could die right now with the feeling I have because I know Momma's gonna make me mad and I'm going to make her mad, and me and Presley's gonna fight . . . "Richard, you get in here and put your coat on. Get in here or I'll whip you."**

49h SLASHES.

The slash has only a few uses. As a rule, use the slash to show divisions between lines of poetry when you quote more than one line of a poem as part of a sentence. Add a space on either side of the slash.

When you are quoting four or more lines of poetry, use a block quotation instead. (*See pp. 370–371.*)

➤   **In "The Tower," Yeats makes his peace with "All those things**

whereof / Man makes a superhuman / Mirror-resembling

dream" (163–65).

The slash is sometimes used between two words that represent choices or combinations. Do not add a space on either side of the slash when it is used in this way.

➤   **The cafeteria offers three vegetarian/kosher meals per day.**

➤   **She is the owner/manager of that store.**

Slashes are also used to mark divisions in online addresses (URLs): *http://www.senecac.on.ca/ce.*

Some writers use the slash as a marker between the words *and* and *or* or between *he* and *she* or *his* and *her* to avoid sexism. Most writers, however, consider such usage awkward. It is usually better to rephrase the sentence. (*See also Tab 8: Editing for Grammar, pp. 332–333.*)

➤   **A health and safety order can originate with management,**
      with   *, or both*   ^
   ~~**and/or**~~ **the workers.**
      ^   ^

                                 his or her
➤   **Everyone should be acquainted with** ~~**his/her**~~ **neighbours.**
                                             ^

Note: Occasionally, the slash is used to show that an event happened over a span of two calendar years.

➤   **The book sold well in 2010/11.**

It is usually better to use *and* or to show inclusive dates with an *en dash* (–) or a hyphen, however.

➤   **The book sold well in 2010 and 2011.**

➤   **The book sold well in 2010–11.**

Capitalization

50

Many rules for the use of capital letters have been fixed by custom, such as the convention of beginning each sentence with a capital letter, but the rules change all the time. A recent dictionary is a good guide to capitalization. As you revise your drafts, check to make sure you are using capital letters appropriately in the following types of words:

- Proper nouns (names), words derived from proper nouns, brand names, and certain abbreviations (*below*)
- People's titles (*p. 389*)
- Titles of works of literature, art, and music; documents; and courses (*p. 389*)
- Names of areas and regions (*p. 390*)
- Names of races, ethnic groups, and sacred things (*p. 390*)
- The first word of a quotation (*p. 391*)
- The first word of a sentence (*p. 392*)
- The first word of an independent clause after a colon (*p. 392*)

50a NAMES OF PEOPLE AND DERIVED NAMES, INCLUDING BRAND NAMES, CERTAIN ABBREVIATIONS, AND CALL LETTERS.

Proper nouns are the names of specific people, places, or things, names that set off the individual from the group, such as the name *Jane* instead of the common noun *person*. Capitalize proper nouns, words derived from proper nouns, brand names, abbreviations of capitalized words, and call letters at radio and television stations.

PROPER NOUNS

Jack Layton

The CN Tower

WORDS DERIVED FROM PROPER NOUNS

Siamese cat

Trudeaumania

BRAND NAMES

an Apple computer

Kleenex

ABBREVIATIONS

CSIS (government agency)

A&E (cable television station)

CALL LETTERS

CITY (television)

CKCU (radio)

Note: Although holidays and the names of months and days of the week are capitalized, seasons, such as *summer,* are not. Neither are the days of the month when they are spelled out.

➤ Why would *Valentine's Day,* the day representing love and romance, fall in *winter*—and in the coldest month of the year at that?

➤ She'll be available to meet with you on Sunday, the *seventh* of March.

Types and Examples of Proper Nouns

1. **People:** Gilles Duceppe, Roberta Bondar, Bob Hunter
2. **Nationalities, ethnic groups, and languages:** English, Swiss, Arabs, Chinese, Turkish
3. **Places:** Canada, Yukon Territory, the Irunia Restaurant, the Great Lakes
4. **Organizations and institutions:** Phi Beta Kappa, Liberal Party, Department of Justice, Woodsworth College, Toronto Varsity Blues
5. **Religious bodies, books, and figures:** Jews, Christians, Baptists, Hindus, Roman Catholic Church, the Bible, the Koran, the Torah, God, Holy Spirit, Allah
6. **The genus in scientific names:** *Homo sapiens, H. sapiens, Acer rubrum, A. rubrum*
7. **Days and months:** Monday, Remembrance Day, August, Canada Day
8. **Historical events, movements, and periods:** World War II, Impressionism, the Renaissance, the Jazz Age

50b TITLES OF PERSONS.

Capitalize titles when they come before a proper name, but do not capitalize them when they appear alone or after the name.

TITLE USED BEFORE A NAME

Every Sunday, *Aunt Lou* tells fantastic stories.

TITLE USED BEFORE A NAME

Everyone knew that *Senator Maria Chaput* of Manitoba chairs the Standing Committee on Official Languages.

TITLE USED ALONE

My *aunt* is arriving this afternoon.

TITLE USED AFTER A NAME

The Chair of the Standing Committee on Official Languages is Maria Chaput, *senator* from Manitoba.

Exceptions: If the name for a family relationship is used alone (without a possessive such as *my* before it), it should be capitalized.

➤ **I saw *Father* hiding at the back of the auditorium.**

Most writers do not capitalize the title *president* unless they are referring to the President of the United States: "The *president* of this university has seventeen honorary degrees." Although usage varies, you should be consistent. If you write "the President of the University," you should also write "the Chair of the History Department."

50c TITLES OF CREATIVE WORKS, DOCUMENTS, AND COURSES.

Capitalize the important words in titles and subtitles. Do not capitalize articles (*a, an,* and *the*), the *to* in infinitives, or prepositions and conjunctions unless they begin or end the title or subtitle. Capitalize both words in a hyphenated word. Capitalize the first word after a colon or semicolon in a title.

Book: *The Backwoods of Canada* by Catherine Parr Traill

Play: *Les Belles-Sœurs* by Michel Tremblay

Building: the CN Tower

Ship or aircraft: the *Titanic* or the *Concorde*

Painting: *The West Wind* by Tom Thompson

Article or essay: "On Old Age" by Cicero

Poem: "Tantramar Revisited" by Charles G. D. Roberts

Music: "O Canada"

Document: the *Canadian Charter of Rights and Freedoms*

Course: Police Fundamentals PFP.101: Criminal Justice System in Canada

50d NAMES OF AREAS AND REGIONS.

Names of geographical regions are generally capitalized if they are well established, like *the Midwest* and *Central Europe.* Names of directions, as in the sentence *Turn south,* are not capitalized.

> CORRECT   *East* meets *West* at the summit.

> CORRECT   You will need to *go west* on Bloor.

Note: The word *western,* when used as a general direction or the name of a genre, is not capitalized. It is capitalized when it is part of the name of a specific region.

> western
> ➤ The ~~Western~~ *High Noon* is one of my favourite movies.
>   ^

> Western
> ➤ I visited ~~western~~ Europe last year.
>   ^

50e NAMES OF RACES, ETHNIC GROUPS, AND SACRED THINGS.

The words *black* and *white* are usually not capitalized when they are used to refer to members of racial groups because they are adjectives that substitute for the implied common nouns *black person* and *white person.* However, names of ethnic groups and races are capitalized: *Italians, Asians,* and *Caucasians.*

Note: In accordance with current APA guidelines, most social scientists capitalize the terms *Black* and *White,* treating them as proper nouns.

Many religious terms, such as *sacrament, altar,* and *rabbi,* are not capitalized. The words *Bible* and *Koran* are capitalized (though *biblical* is not), but it is never capitalized when it is used as a metaphor for an essential book.

➤ His book *Winning at Stud Poker* used to be the *bible* of gamblers.

50f FIRST WORD OF A QUOTED SENTENCE.

Capitalize the first word of a quoted sentence but not the first word of an indirect quotation.

➤ She cried, "Help!"

➤ He said that hockey is Canada's national sport.

The first word of a quotation from a printed source is capitalized if the quotation is introduced with a phrase such as *she notes* or *he concludes.*

➤ Ralph Connor notes, "The solid forests of Glengarry have

vanished, and with the forests the men who conquered them"

in the opening line of his book *The Man from Glengarry* (iv).

When a quotation from a printed source is treated as an element in your sentence, not a sentence on its own, the first word is not capitalized.

➤ *The Man from Glengarry* was written to celebrate the Ottawa

Valley forests and "the men who conquered them" (iv).

If you need to change the first letter of a quotation to fit your sentence, enclose the letter in brackets.

➤ The lawyer noted that "[t]he man seen leaving the area after

the blast was not the same height as the defendant."

If you interrupt the sentence you are quoting with an expression such as *he said,* the first word of the rest of the quotation should not be capitalized.

➤ "When I come home an hour later," she explained, "the trains

are usually less crowded."

Many authors in earlier centuries and some writers today—especially poets—use capital letters in outdated or eccentric ways. When quoting a text directly, reproduce the capitalization used in the original source, whether or not it is correct by today's standards.

➤ Blake's marginalia include the following comment: "Paine is

either a Devil or an Inspired Man" (603).

50g FIRST WORD OF A SENTENCE.

A capital letter is used to signal the beginning of a new sentence.

➤ **Robots reduce human error, so they produce uniform products.**

Sentences in parentheses also begin with a capital letter unless they are embedded within another sentence:

➤ **The poor man lost his cat and his dog within a month of each other. (He never wants to go through that again.)**

➤ **The poor man lost his cat and his dog within a month of each other (and he never wants to go through that again.)**

50h FIRST WORD OF AN INDEPENDENT CLAUSE AFTER A COLON.

If the word group that follows a colon is not a complete sentence, do not capitalize it. If it is a complete sentence, you can capitalize it or not, but be consistent throughout your document.

➤ **The question is serious: do you think the peace process has a chance?**

or

➤ **The question is serious: Do you think the peace process has a chance?**

50i EMPHASIS IN E-MAIL.

When you are writing an e-mail message, you may be tempted to use all capital letters for emphasis when italics are not available. Although capital letters are sometimes used this way in print documents, they are not always welcome in online chat rooms and electronic mailing list postings, where participants may feel that they are equivalent to shouting. Also, strings of words or sentences in capital letters can be difficult to read. If you want to emphasize a word or phrase in an online communication, put an asterisk before and after it instead:

➤ *I *totally* disagree with what you just wrote.*

Abbreviations and Symbols

Unless you are writing a scientific or technical report, spell out most terms and titles, except in the following cases.

51a TITLES THAT ALWAYS PRECEDE OR FOLLOW A PERSON'S NAME.

Some abbreviations appear before a person's name (*Mr., Mrs., Dr.*) and some follow a proper name (*Jr., Sr., MD, Esq., PhD*). Abbreviations that follow a person's name often indicate academic or professional degrees or honours. When an abbreviation follows a person's name, a comma is placed between the name and the abbreviation.

TITLES BEFORE NAMES

Ms. Jean Bascom

Dr. Epstein

TITLES AFTER NAMES

Robert Robinson, Jr.

Elaine Less, CA, LL.D.

Do not use two abbreviations that represent the same thing: *Dr. Peter Joyce, MD*. Use either *Dr. Peter Joyce* or *Peter Joyce, MD*.

Spell out titles used without proper names.

➤ Mr. Carew asked if she had seen the ~~dr.~~
                                        doctor.
                                        ^

CROSS-DISCIPLINE **WRITING**

Scientific Abbreviations

Most abbreviations used in scientific or technical writing, such as those related to measurement, should be given without periods: *mph, kg, dc, rpm*. If an abbreviation looks like an actual word, however, you can use a period to prevent confusion: *in., Fig.*

CROSS-DISCIPLINE **WRITING**

Latin Abbreviations

In some types of scholarly writing, the use of Latin abbreviations is acceptable. When Latin abbreviations are used in scholarly work, they generally appear in parenthetical statements and are usually italicized.

51b FAMILIAR VS. UNFAMILIAR ABBREVIATIONS.

If you use a technical term or the name of an organization in a report, you may abbreviate it as long as your readers are likely to be familiar with the abbreviation. Abbreviations of three or more capital letters generally do not use periods: *CTV, GTA, CUPE, HRDC, CNE, CBC, YMCA.*

> **FAMILIAR ABBREVIATION** The CRTC regulates broadcasting, among other things.

> **UNFAMILIAR ABBREVIATION** **After you have completed them, take these** *the Human Resources and Education Centre.* **forms to HREC.**
> ^

Write out an unfamiliar term or name the first time you use it, and give the abbreviation in parentheses.

➤ **The National Anti-Poverty Organization (NAPO) is**

strongly advocating a youth poverty initiative, where it

will investigate the causes and consequences of youth

poverty in Canada.

51c WORDS TYPICALLY USED WITH TIMES, DATES, AND NUMERALS; UNITS OF MEASUREMENT IN CHARTS AND GRAPHS.

Abbreviations or symbols associated with numbers should be used only when accompanying a number: *3 p.m.*, not *in the p.m.; $500*, not *How many $ do you have?* The abbreviation B.C. ("Before Christ") follows a date; A.D. (the Latin *Anno Domini* or "in the year of our Lord") precedes the date. The alternative abbreviations B.C.E. ("Before the

Common Era") and *c.e.* ("Common Era") can be used instead of *b.c.* or *a.d.*, respectively.

6 p.m. or 6 P.M.

9:45 a.m. or 9:45 A.M.

498 b.c. (or 498 b.c.e.)

a.d. 275 (or 275 c.e.)

6000 rpm

271 cm

Note: Be consistent. If you use *a.m.* in one sentence, do not switch to *A.M.* in the next sentence. If an abbreviation is made up of capital letters, the periods are optional: *b.c. or bc. (For more on using periods with abbreviations, see Chapter 49, p. 378.)*

In charts and graphs, abbreviations and symbols such as = for *equals, cm* for *centimetres, %* for *percent,* and *$* with numbers are acceptable because they save space.

51d LATIN ABBREVIATIONS.

Latin abbreviations can be used in notes or works-cited lists, but in formal writing it is usually a good idea to avoid even common Latin abbreviations (*e.g., et al., etc.,* and *i.e.*). Instead of *e.g.,* use *such as* or *for example.*

cf.	compare (*confer*)
e.g.	for example, such as (*exempli gratia*)
et al.	and others (*et alia*)
etc.	and so forth, and so on (*et cetera*)
i.e.	that is (*id est*)
N.B.	note well (*nota bene*)
viz.	namely (*videlicet*)

CROSS-DISCIPLINE **WRITING**

Abbreviations and Symbols

Some abbreviations and symbols may be acceptable in certain contexts, as long as readers will know what they stand for. For example, a medical writer might use *PT (physical therapy)* in a medical report or professional newsletter.

51e INAPPROPRIATE ABBREVIATIONS AND SYMBOLS.

Days of the week (*Sat.*), places (*ON* or *Ont.*), the word *company* (*Co.*), people's names (*Wm.*), disciplines and professions (*econ.*), parts of speech (*v.*), parts of written works (*ch., p.*), symbols (@), and units of measurement (*kg*) are all spelled out in formal writing.

➤ **The *environmental* (not *env.*) engineers from the Paramus Water**

Company (not *Co.*) are arriving in *Toronto* (not *T.O.*) this *Thursday*

(not *Thurs.*) to correct the problems in the *physical education*

(not *phys. ed.*) building in time for *Christmas* (not *Xmas*).

Exceptions: If an abbreviation such as *Inc., Co.,* or *Corp.* is part of a company's official name, then it can be included in formal writing: *Time Inc. announced these changes in late December.* The ampersand symbol (&) can also be used but only if it is part of an official name as it often is in company names (publishers, law firms, accounting firms, and so on) made up of surnames: *Church & Dwight.*

52 Numbers

52a NUMBERS UP TO ONE HUNDRED AND ROUND NUMBERS OVER ONE HUNDRED IN NON-TECHNICAL WRITING.

In non-technical writing, spell out numbers up to one hundred and round numbers greater than one hundred.

➤ **Approximately *twenty-five* students failed the exam, but more**

than *two hundred and fifty* passed.

When you are using a great many numbers or when a spelled-out number would require more than three or four words, use numerals.

➤ **This regulation affects nearly *10,500* taxpayers, substantially**

more than the *200* originally projected. Of those affected,

***2325* filled out the papers incorrectly and another *743* called**

the office for help.

52b NUMBERS THAT BEGIN A SENTENCE.

If a numeral begins a sentence, reword the sentence or spell out the numeral.

➤ *Twenty-two* years ago a lone gunman killed 14 women at École Polytechnique in Montreal.

52c NUMBERS IN TECHNICAL AND BUSINESS WRITING.

In technical and business writing, use numerals for exact measurements and all numbers greater than ten.

➤ Five endosperm halves were placed in each of 14 small glass test tubes.

➤ A solution with a GA_3 concentration ranging from 0 g/ml to 10^5 g/ml was added to each test tube.

➤ With its $1.9 trillion economy, Germany has an important trade role to play.

52d DATES, TIMES OF DAY, ADDRESSES, AND OTHER QUANTITATIVE INFORMATION.

Use numerals for dates, times of day, addresses, and similar kinds of conventional quantitative information.

Dates: October 9, 2012; A.D. 1066 (*or* AD 1066)

Time of day: 6 A.M. (*or* AM *or* a.m.), a quarter past eight in the evening, three o'clock in the morning

Addresses: 21 Meadow Road, Apt. 6J

Percentages: 73 percent, 73%

Fractions and decimals: 21.84, 6½

Measurements: 60 km/h, 100 mph, 9 kg

Volume, page, chapter: volume 4, chapter 8, page 44

Scenes in a play: *Hamlet,* act 2, scene 1

Scores and statistics: 0 to 3, 98–92, an average age of 35

Amounts of money: $125, $2.25, $2.8 million

53 Italics (Underlining)

To set off certain words and phrases, printers have traditionally used *italics,* a typeface in which the characters slant to the right. Now any word-processor program can produce italics. If italics are not available, however, you can <u>underline</u> words that would be typeset in italics.

➤ Paul Gross gives one of his best performances in *Passchendaele.*

➤ Paul Gross gives one of his best performances in <u>Passchendaele.</u>

53a TITLES OF LENGTHY WORKS OR SEPARATE PUBLICATIONS.

Italicize (or underline) titles of books, magazines, journals, newspapers, comic strips, plays, films, musical compositions, choreographic works, artworks, Web sites, software, long poems, pamphlets, and other long works. In titles of lengthy works, *a, an,* or *the* is capitalized and italicized (underlined) if it is the first word, but *the* is not generally treated as part of the title in names of newspapers and periodicals: the *New York Times.*

➤ Picasso's *Guernica* captures the anguish and despair of violence.

➤ Plays by Shakespeare provide details and story lines for Verdi's opera *Falstaff,* Cole Porter's musical comedy *Kiss Me, Kate,* and Franco Zeffirelli's film *Romeo and Juliet.*

TECH TIPS

Italics and Underlining

Depending on the software you are using, italics or underlining may not be available for your e-mail messages. To indicate underlining, put an underscore mark or an asterisk before and after what you would italicize or underline in a manuscript: Paul Gross gives one of his best performances in _Passchendaele_.

➤ *The Seed Catalogue* by Robert Kroetsch is my favourite

long poem.

Court cases may also be italicized or underlined.

Exceptions: Do not use italics or underlining when referring to the Bible and other sacred books.

Quotation marks are used for the titles of short works—essays, newspaper and magazine articles and columns, short stories, individual episodes of television and radio programs, short poems, songs, and chapters or other book subdivisions. Quotation marks are also used for titles of unpublished works, including student papers, theses, and dissertations. (*See Chapter 48, pp. 372–373, for more on quotation marks with titles.*)

53b NAMES OF SHIPS, TRAINS, AIRCRAFT, AND SPACESHIPS.

Italicize (or underline) the names of ships, trains, aircraft, and spaceships.

➤ The commentators were stunned into silence when the space

shuttle *Challenger* exploded.

53c FOREIGN TERMS.

Italicize (or underline) foreign terms.

➤ In the Paris airport, we recognized the familiar no smoking sign:

Défense de fumer.

Many foreign words have become so common in English that everyone accepts them as part of the language and they require no italics or underlining: rigor mortis, pasta, and sombrero, for example.

53d SCIENTIFIC NAMES.

The scientific (Latin) names of organisms are always italicized (or underlined).

➤ Most chicks are infected with *Cryptosporidium baileyi,* a

parasite typical of young animals.

Note: Although the whole name is italicized, only the genus part of the name is capitalized.

53e WORDS, LETTERS, AND NUMBERS REFERRED TO AS THEMSELVES.

For clarity, italicize (or underline) words or phrases used as words rather than for the meaning they convey. (You may also use quotation marks for this purpose.)

➤ **The term *romantic* does not mean the same thing to the Shelley scholar as it does to the fan of Danielle Steele novels.**

Letters and numbers used alone should also be italicized (or underlined).

➤ **The word *bookkeeper* has three sets of double letters: double *o*, double *k*, and double *e*.**

➤ **Add a *3* to that column.**

53f OVERUSE.

Sometimes writers are tempted to italicize (or underline) words to show the kind of emphasis they would give the word in speaking. An occasional word in italics (or underlining) helps you make a point. Too much emphasis, however, may mean no emphasis at all.

> WEAK *Where* have you *been*, *what* have you *been doing,* and *who* have you been *doing it with,* young man?

> REVISED Where have you been, what have you been doing, and who have you been doing it *with,* young man?

Note: If you add italics or underlining to a quotation, indicate the change in parentheses following the quotation.

➤ **Instead of promising that no harm will come to us, Blake only assures us that we "need not *fear* harm" (emphasis added).**

Hyphens

54

54a COMPOUND WORDS.

A hyphen joins two nouns to make one compound word. Scientists speak of a *kilogram-metre* as a measure of force, and professors of literature talk about the *scholar-poet*. The hyphen lets us know that the two nouns work together as one. As compound nouns come into general use, the hyphens between them tend to disappear: *firefighter, thundershower.*

A dictionary is the best resource when you are unsure about whether to use a hyphen. The dictionary sometimes gives writers several options, however. If you cannot find a compound word in the dictionary, spell it as two separate words. Whatever spelling you choose, be consistent throughout your document.

54b COMPOUND ADJECTIVES OR NOUN FORMS.

A noun can also be linked with an adjective, an adverb, or another part of speech to form a compound adjective.

    accident-prone

    quick-witted

Hyphens are also used in nouns designating family relationships and compounds of more than two words:

    brother-in-law

    stay-at-home

    stick-in-the-mud

Note: Compound nouns with hyphens generally form plurals by adding *-s* or *-es* to the most important word.

    attorney general/attorneys general

    mother-in-law/mothers-in-law

    court-martial/courts-martial

Some proper nouns that are joined to make an adjective are hyphenated.

    the Franco-Prussian war

    the Sino-Japanese agreement

Hyphens often help clarify adjectives that come before the word they modify. If you say "She was a quick thinking person," you might mean that she was quick and that she was also a thinking person. If you say "She was a quick-thinking person," though, your meaning is unmistakable: she thought rapidly. Modifiers that are hyphenated when they are placed *before* the word they modify are usually not hyphenated when they are placed *after* the word they modify.

➤ It was a *bad-mannered* reply.

➤ The reply was *bad mannered.*

Do not use a hyphen to connect *-ly* adverbs to the words they modify.

➤ They explored the newly/discovered territories.

In a pair or series of compound nouns or adjectives, add *suspended hyphens* after the first word of each item.

➤ The childcare centre accepted three-, four-, and five-year-olds.

54c FRACTIONS AND COMPOUND NUMBERS.

Use a hyphen when writing out fractions or compound numbers from twenty-one to ninety-nine.

three-fourths of a litre

thirty-two

twenty-five thousand

Note: Use a hyphen to show inclusive numbers: *pages 100-140.*

54d WITH SOME PREFIXES AND SUFFIXES.

Use a hyphen to join a prefix and a capitalized word.

➤ In the pre-Confederation period, Sir John A. Macdonald lobbied

hard for Canadian unity.

A hyphen is sometimes used to join a capital letter and a word: *T-shirt, V-six engine.*

The prefixes *ex-, non- self-,* and *all-* and the suffixes *-elect* and *-odd* (or *-something*) generally take hyphens; however, many prefixes are not attached by hyphens. Sometimes a hyphen is needed to show pronunciation or to reveal a special meaning that distinguishes the

TECH **TIPS**

Dividing Internet Addresses

If you need to divide an Internet address between lines, divide it after the backslash. Do not divide a word within the address with a hyphen; readers might assume the hyphen is part of the address.

word from the same word without a hyphen: *recreate* vs. *re-create.* Check the *Canadian Oxford Dictionary* to be certain you are using the standard Canadian spelling.

➤ **Because he was an *ex-convict,* he was a *non-judgmental co-worker.***

➤ **The *president-elect* of the *extracurricular* support group suffers from *post-traumatic* stress syndrome.**

➤ **They were *self-sufficient, anti-social* neighbours.**

54e TO DIVIDE WORDS AT THE ENDS OF LINES.

When you must divide words, do so between syllables, but pronunciation alone cannot always tell you where to divide a word. If you are unsure about how to break a word into syllables, consult your dictionary.

➤ **My writing group had a very fruitful *collab-oration.* [not *colla-boration*]**

Never leave just one or two letters on a line.

➤ **He seemed so sad and vulnerable and so *discon-nected* from his family. [not *disconnect-ed*]**

Compound words such as *hardworking, rattlesnake,* and *book-case* should be broken only between the words that form them: *hard-working, rattle-snake, book-case.* Compound words that already have hyphens, like *brother-in-law,* are broken after the hyphens only.

Note: Never hyphenate an acronym (*CSIS*) or a one-syllable word.

55 Spelling

Frequent or even occasional misspellings can make people believe that you are careless, and you will then have to work hard to convince them to take your ideas seriously. Proofread your writing carefully. Misspellings creep into the prose of even the best writers. Here are some suggestions to help you improve your spelling.

- Use your computer software's spell checker. Remember, though, that a spell checker cannot tell how you are using a particular word. If you write *their* when you should write *there,* the spell checker cannot point out your mistake. Keep a dictionary nearby to check words you are unsure of.

- Become familiar with major spelling rules and commonly misspelled words, and use your *Canadian Oxford Dictionary* whenever you are unsure about the spelling of a specific word.

- Learn to distinguish *homophones*—words pronounced alike but with different meanings and spellings. *(See Tab 7: Editing for Clarity, pp. 286–295.)*

55a SPELLING RULES AND THEIR EXCEPTIONS.

Learn the rules that generally hold for spelling, as well as their exceptions.

1. *i* before *e*. Use *i* before *e* except after *c* or when sounded like *a,* as in *neighbour* and *weigh.*

I BEFORE *E*	believe, relieve, chief, grief, wield, yield
EXCEPT AFTER *C*	receive, deceive, ceiling, conceit
EXCEPTIONS	seize, caffeine, codeine, weird, height

2. Adding suffixes.

- **Final silent -*e*:** When adding a suffix that begins with a vowel, drop the final silent -*e* from the root word. Keep the final -*e* if the suffix begins with a consonant.

   force/forcing

   surprise/surprising

   remove/removable

care/careful

achieve/achievement

Exceptions: argue/argument, true/truly, change/changeable, judge/judgment, acknowledge/acknowledgment

Exception: Keep the silent -e if it is needed to clarify the pronunciation or if the word would be confused with another word without the -e.

dye/dyeing (to avoid confusion with *dying*)

hoe/hoeing (to avoid mispronunciation)

- **Final -y:** When adding the suffix -ing to a word ending in -y, retain the -y.

enjoy/enjoying

cry/crying

Change the y to i or ie when the final y follows a consonant but not when it follows a vowel.

happy/happier

defray/defrayed

- **Final consonants:** When adding a suffix to a word that ends in a consonant preceded by a vowel, double the final consonant if the root word has only one syllable or an accent on the last syllable.

grip/gripping	refer/referred
stun/stunning	transmit/transmitted

Exceptions: bus/busing, focus/focused

3. Forming plurals.

- **-s or -es:** Add a final -s to make most nouns plural. Add a final -es to form a plural when the singular form of a noun ends in -s, -x, -ch, or -sh.

cobra/cobras	kiss/kisses
scientist/scientists	box/boxes

Exception: The plural of a few nouns ending in -is is formed by changing -is to -es.

analysis/analyses	basis/bases
crisis/crises	thesis/theses

- **Other plurals:** If a noun ends in -*y* preceded by a consonant, change the -*y* to -*i* and add -*es* to form the plural; if the final -*y* is preceded by a vowel, keep the -*y* and add -*s* to make the plural.

  beauty/beauties   boy/boys

  city/cities   bay/bays

Exceptions: Always keep the final -*y* when forming the plural of a person's name.

  Joe and Mary Kirby/the Kirbys

When a noun ends in a consonant and an -*o* in the singular, form the plural by adding -*es*. If the -*o* is preceded by a vowel, add an -*s*.

  hero/heroes   potato/potatoes

  tomato/tomatoes

Exception: solo/solos

- **Irregular plurals:** Most plurals follow standard rules, but some have irregular forms (*child / children, tooth / teeth*), and some words with foreign roots create plurals in the pattern of the original language, as do these words derived from Latin and Greek.

  addendum/addenda   datum/data

  alumna/alumnae   medium/media

  alumnus/alumni   phenomenon/phenomena

  criterion/criteria   stimulus/stimuli

Note: Some writers now treat *data* as though it were singular, but the preferred practice is still to recognize that *data* is plural and takes a plural verb.

➤ **The *data* that Statistics Canada collects *are* used to**

   produce reports on everything from divorce rates to

   average salaries to mother tongue.

4. American, British, and Canadian spelling. Standard British spelling differs from American spelling for some words—among them, *color / colour, canceled / cancelled, theater / theatre, realize / realise,* and *judgment / judgement*. It also differs in some instances from Canadian spelling: *tire / tyre, analyze / analyse,* and *aluminum / aluminium*.

55b WORDS PRONOUNCED ALIKE BUT SPELLED DIFFERENTLY.

Homophones are words that sound alike but have different meanings and different spellings. Many are commonly confused. (*See Tab 7: Editing for Clarity, pp. 286–295.*)

55c COMMONLY MISSPELLED WORDS.

Words that are exceptions to standard spelling rules are commonly misspelled. In a list or spelling log, write down words you often misspell. Try to group your errors. Misspellings often fall into patterns—errors with suffixes or plurals, for example. (*See below for a sampling of commonly misspelled words.*)

A SAMPLING OF COMMONLY MISSPELLED WORDS

accommodate	kindergarten	questionnaire
already		quizzes
	licence	
conscience	lieutenant	recommend
conscious	livelihood	reminisce
	luxury	restaurant
eighth		rhyme
embarrass	meant	rhythm
exaggerate	misspelled	
exercise	mortgage	sacrilegious
	muscle	separate
fascinate		sophomore
February	nuclear	supersede
foreign	nuisance	
fulfill		tomatoes
	occasion	tomorrow
gauge	occurrence	twelfth
guard	omission	
		vacuum
innocuous	parliament	vengeance
inoculate	personnel	
irrelevant	playwright	wholly
	practice	
jealousy	pronunciation	
judgment		

10

BASIC
GRAMMAR
REVIEW

10 Basic Grammar Review

Written Language. Written language, although based on the grammar of spoken language, has a logic and set of rules of its own. The chapters that follow explain the basic rules of standard written English. Also, take note of the Language Tips feature in this section for more information on language differences.

Recognizing language differences. The standard structures of sentences in languages other than English can be very different from those in English. In other languages, the way verbs are conjugated can indicate their grammatical function more powerfully than can their placement in the sentence. In addition, in languages other than English, adjectives may take on the function that articles (*a, an,* or *the*) perform, or articles can be absent entirely.

Parts of Speech

56

Grammar gives us a way of talking about how sentences are put together to make sense. Although *the slithy toves / Did gyre and gimble in the wabe*—from Lewis Carroll's poem "Jabberwocky"—is a group of words that in and of themselves do not make sense, the sentence does make grammatical sense. Because what makes a sentence meaningful is not just the individual words but also the pattern or ordering of its parts, you can answer questions like *What gimbled in the wabe?* (*the toves*), *What did the toves do in the wabe?* (*they gimbled*), and *Where did the toves gimble?* (*in the wabe*).

English has eight primary grammatical categories, or parts of speech: *verbs, nouns, pronouns, adjectives, adverbs, prepositions, conjunctions,* and *interjections.* All English words belong to one or more of these categories. Particular words can belong in different categories, depending on the role they play in a sentence.

56a VERBS.

Verbs report action (*run, write*), condition (*bloom, sit*), or state of being (*be, seem*). Verbs also change form to indicate person, number, tense, voice, and mood. To do all this, a **main verb** is sometimes accompanied by one or more **helping verbs**, thereby becoming a **verb phrase**. Helping verbs precede the main verb in a verb phrase.

mv
➤ The play *begins* at eight.

hv   mv   hv   mv
➤ I *may change* seats after the play *has begun.*

1. Main verbs. Main verbs change form (**tense**) to indicate when something has happened. If a word does not indicate tense, it is not a main verb. All main verbs have five forms, except for *be,* which has eight.

BASE FORM	(*talk, sing*)
PAST TENSE	Yesterday I (*talked, sang*).
PAST PARTICIPLE	In the past, I have (*talked, sung*).
PRESENT PARTICIPLE	Right now I am (*talking, singing*).
-*S* FORM	Usually he/she/it (*talks, sings*).

Verb forms—especially irregular verb forms—can be troublesome. (*For more on subject-verb agreement and verb tense, see Tab 8: Editing for Grammar, pp. 308–315 and 322–325, and the list of common irregular verbs on pp. 317–318.*)

Language Tip: *Using verbs followed by gerunds or infinitives*

When verbs are followed by other verbs to make a verb chain, some can be followed only by a gerund (the -*ing* form of the verb used as a noun) and some are usually followed by an infinitive (*to* plus the base form of the verb).

Gerunds. The following verbs can only be followed by a gerund. The gerund usually names an action occurring before the action of the main verb: *admit, appreciate, avoid, complete, deny, discuss, dislike, enjoy, finish, imagine, keep, miss, postpone, practice, put off, quit, recall, recommend, resist, risk, suggest, tolerate.*

VERB + GERUND

She *recommends reading Life of Pi* by Yann Martel.

The *recommendation* occurs before the *reading* by the other person.

Infinitives. Some verbs are typically followed by an infinitive that names an action occurring after the action of the main verb. Verbs that are followed by an infinitive include the following: *afford, agree, arrange, ask, beg, choose, claim, decide, deserve, expect, fail, hope, manage, need, offer, plan, pretend, promise, refuse, want, wish.*

VERB + INFINITIVE

She wants *to win.*

The winning would happen after the wanting.

Sometimes a noun or pronoun comes between the verb and the infinitive. Verbs that are followed by a noun or pronoun plus an infinitive include the following: *advise, allow, ask, cause, command, convince, encourage, expect, force, need, order, persuade, remind, require, tell, urge, want, warn.*

VERB + NOUN/PRONOUN + INFINITIVE

She wants *her friend* to win.

Note: *Make, let,* and *have* are followed by a noun or pronoun plus the base form without *to: Make that boy come home on time.*

2. Helping verbs that show time. Some helping verbs—mostly forms of *be, have,* and *do*—function to signify time (*will have been playing, has played*) or emphasis (*does play*). Forms of *do* are also used to ask questions (*Do you play?*). Here is a fuller list of such helping (or **auxiliary**) verbs.

be, am, is	being, been	do, does, did
are, was, were	have, has, had	

Matching helping verbs (*do, have, be*) with the appropriate form of the main verb.

Do, Does, Did. The helping verb *do* and its forms *does* and *did* combine with the base form of a verb to ask a question or to emphasize something. It can also combine with the word *not* to create an emphatic negative statement.

QUESTION	*Do* you want a piece of pie?
EMPHATIC STATEMENT	I *do* want a piece of pie.
EMPHATIC NEGATIVE	I *do not* want to have to eat the pie all by myself.

Have, Has, Had. The helping verb *have* and its forms *has* and *had* combine with a past participle (usually ending in *-d, -t,* or *-n*) to form the *perfect tenses.* Do not confuse the simple past tense with the present perfect tense (formed with *have* or *has*), which is distinct from the simple past because the action can continue in the present. (*For a review of perfect tense forms, see Tab 8: Editing for Grammar, pp. 322–325.*)

SIMPLE PAST	Emilie *played* video games all day
PRESENT PERFECT	Emilie *has played* video games all day
PAST PERFECT	Emilie *had played* video games all day.

Be. Forms of *be* combine with a present participle (ending in *-ing*) to form the *progressive tenses,* which express continuing action. Do not confuse the simple present tense or the present perfect with these progressive forms. Unlike the simple present, the present progressive form indicates an action that is going on right now. In its past form, the progressive tense indicates actions that are going on simultaneously. (*For a review of progressive tense forms, see Tab 8: Editing for Grammar, pp. 323–324.*)

SIMPLE PRESENT	Emilie *plays* video games all the time.
PRESENT PROGRESSIVE	Emilie *is playing* video games right now
PAST PROGRESSIVE	Emilie *was playing* video games while her brother *was trying* to study for an exam.

Forms of *be* combine with the past participle (which usually ends in *-d, -t,* or *-n*) to form the passive voice, which is often used to express a state of being instead of an action.

BE + PAST PARTICIPLE

PASSIVE	Emilie *was criticized* for her constant game playing.
PASSIVE	I *was satisfied* by her answer.

3. Modals. Other helping verbs, called **modals**, signify the manner, or mode, of an action. Unlike the auxiliaries *be, have,* and *do,* one-word modals such as *may, must,* and *will* are almost never used alone as main verbs, nor do they change form to show person or number. Modals do not add *-s* endings, two modals are never used together (such as *might could*), and modals are always followed by the base form of the verb without *to* (*He could be nicer*).

The one-word modals are *can, could, may, might, will, would, shall, should, must.*

➤ **Contrary to press reports, she *will* not *run* for political office.**

hv   mv

Note that a negative word such as *not* may come between the helping and the main verb.

Phrasal modals, however, do change form to show time, person, and number. Here are some phrasal modals: *have to, have got to, used to, be supposed to, be going to, be allowed to, be able to.*

➤ **Yesterday, I *was going to* study for three hours.**

hv   mv

➤ **Next week, *I am going to* study three hours a day.**

hv   mv

Understanding the form and meaning of modals.

To indicate intention: *will, shall*; *would* + *have* + past participle

I *will* (*shall*) go today. I *would have gone* yesterday.

To indicate ability: *can, am / is / are able to*; *would, was / were able to*

I *can* (*am able to*) take one child to the doctor at a time.

I *would have taken* (*was able to take*) both children to the doctor if I had to.

To ask for permission: *may, might, can, could*

May (*Might / Can / Could*) I come at five o'clock?

To pose a polite question: *would*

Would you please open the door?

To speculate: *would* (*could, might*) or *would* (*could, might*) + *have* + past participle

She *would* be there if the weather were nice.

She *could* (*might*) still come.

He *would have been* pleased by this outcome.

He *could* (*might*) *have known* yesterday.

To indicate advisability: *should* or *should* + *have* + past participle

You *should* wear a coat.

You *should have worn* a coat.

To indicate necessity: *must (have to)*; *had to*

> I *must (have to)* pass this test.
>
> I *had to* find a new apartment.

To prohibit: *must + not*

> You *must not* go there.

To indicate expectation: *should* or *should + have* + past participle

> I *should* finish my project today.
>
> I *should have finished* my project yesterday.

To indicate possibility: *may (might)* or *might + have +* past participle

> She *may (might)* return this afternoon.
>
> She *might have been* delayed.

To indicate logical assumption: *must* or *must + have* + past participle

> He *must* be there by now.
>
> He *must have been* pleased with your success.

To indicate repeated past action: *would (used to)* + base form

> I *would (used to)* always take the early train.

56b NOUNS.

Nouns name people (*Shakespeare, actors, Englishman*), places (*Vancouver, city, island*), things (*Kleenex, handkerchief, sneeze, cats*), and ideas (*Marxism, justice, democracy, clarity*).

➤ **Shakespeare lived in *England* and wrote *plays* about the human condition.**

1. Proper and common nouns. Proper nouns name specific people, places, and things and are always capitalized: *Céline Dion, Regina, Hinduism, Microsoft.* All other nouns are **common nouns:** *singer, capital, religion, corporation.*

2. Count and non-count nouns. A common noun that refers to something specific that can be counted is a **count noun.** Count nouns can be singular or plural, like *cup* or *suggestion* (*four cups, several suggestions*). **Non-count nouns** are non-specific; these common nouns refer to categories of people, places, or things and cannot be counted. They do not have a plural form. (*The pottery is beautiful. His advice was useful.*)

Count and Non-count Nouns

COUNT NOUNS	NON-COUNT NOUNS
cars	transportation
computers	Internet
facts	information
clouds	rain
stars	sunshine
tools	equipment
machines	machinery
suggestions	advice
earrings	jewellery
tables	furniture
smiles	happiness

Using quantifiers with count and non-count nouns. Ideas about what is countable vary across cultures. *Furniture* might be a count noun in some languages, but in English, it is a non-count noun. Consult a dictionary to determine whether a word is a count or non-count noun. If a word is a non-count noun, it will not have a plural form.

Count and non-count nouns are often preceded by **quantifiers**, words that tell how much or how many. Use the following quantifiers:

- **With count nouns only:** *several, many, a couple of, a few*
- **With non-count nouns only:** *a good deal of, not much, a little, less*
- **With either count or non-count nouns:** *some, a lot of, plenty of, a lack of, most of the*

(*For help using articles with count and non-count nouns, see the section below.*)

3. Concrete and abstract nouns. Nouns that name things that can be perceived by the senses are called **concrete nouns**: *boy, wind, book, song.* **Abstract nouns** name qualities and concepts that do not have physical properties: *charity, patience, beauty, hope.* (*For more* *on using concrete and abstract nouns, see Tab 7: Editing for Clarity, p. 261.)*

4. Singular and plural nouns. Most nouns name things that can be counted and are **singular** or **plural.** Singular nouns typically become plural by adding -*s* or -*es*: *boy / boys, ocean / oceans, church / churches, agency / agencies.* Some have irregular plurals, such as *man / men, child / children,* and *tooth / teeth.* Non-count nouns like *intelligence* and *electricity* do not form plurals.

5. Collective nouns. Collective nouns such as *team, family, herd,* and *orchestra* are treated as singular. They are not non-count nouns, however, because collective nouns can be counted and can be made plural: *teams, families. (Also see Tab 8: Editing for Grammar, pp. 312 and 329–332.)*

6. Possessive nouns. When nouns are used in the **possessive case** to indicate ownership, they change their form. To form the possessive case, singular nouns add apostrophe plus -*s* ('*s*), whereas plural nouns ending in -*s* just add an apostrophe ('). (*Also see Tab 9: Editing for Mechanics, pp. 365–366.*)

| SINGULAR | doctor | doctor's stethoscope |
| PLURAL | engineers | engineers' slide rule |

Using articles (a, an, the) appropriately. Some languages such as Russian, Chinese, Japanese, Farsi, and Swahili do not use articles at all, and most languages do not use articles in the same way as English. In English, there are only three articles: *a, an,* and *the.* When an article identifies a noun, it functions as an adjective. (*For more on adjectives, see pp. 422–424.*)

A or *an* refers to one non-specific person, place, or thing. Count nouns that are singular and refer to a non-specific person, place, or thing take *a* or *an* (*A girl is here; I have an apple*). Non-count nouns and plural nouns do not take *a* or *an.*

Note that *a* is used before words that begin with consonant sounds, whether or not the first letter is a vowel (*a European vacation, a country*), and *an* is used before words that begin with vowel sounds, whether or not the first letter is a consonant (*an hour, an opener*).

The, on the other hand, refers to a specific person, place, or thing and can be used with singular or plural nouns. It means "this (these) and no other (none others)." (*The girl you have been waiting for is here; the girls you have been waiting for are here.*)

Common nouns that refer to a specific person, place, or thing take the article *the*. Most proper nouns do not use articles unless they are plural, in which case they take the article *the*. There are some exceptions, however:

- Proper nouns that include a common noun and *of* as part of the title (*the Art Gallery of Ontario, the United Church of Canada*)
- Names of highways (*the Trans-Canada Highway*)
- Landmark buildings (*the Hotel Frontenac*)
- Hotels (*the Marriott Hotel*)
- Cultural and political institutions (*the Canadian Opera Company, the Houses of Parliament*)
- Parts of the globe, names of oceans and seas, deserts, land and water formations (*the West, the Equator, the North Pole, the Mediterranean, the Sahara, the Bering Strait*)
- Countries with more than one word in their names (*the Dominican Republic*)

56c PRONOUNS.

A pronoun takes the place of a noun. The noun that the pronoun replaces is called its **antecedent**. (*For more on pronoun-antecedent agreement, see Tab 8: Editing for Grammar, pp. 329–334.*)

➤   The *snow* fell all day long, and by nightfall, *it* was fifty

centimetres deep.

The box on pages 420–421 summarizes the different kinds of pronouns.

1. Personal pronouns. The personal pronouns *I, me, you, he, his, she, her, it, we, us, they,* and *them* refer to specific people or things and vary in form to indicate person, number, gender, and case. (*For more on pronoun reference and case, such as distinguishing between* I *and* me, *see Tab 8: Editing for Grammar, pp. 332–337.*)

➤   *You* told *us* that *she* gave the registrar an envelope from *her* bag.

2. Possessive pronouns. Like possessive nouns, possessive pronouns indicate ownership. However, unlike possessive nouns, possessive pronouns do not add apostrophes: *my / mine, your / yours, her / hers, his, its, our / ours, their / theirs.*

➤   Brunch is at *her* place this Saturday.

Pronouns

PERSONAL (INCLUDING POSSESSIVE)

SINGULAR	PLURAL
I, me, my, mine	we, us, our, ours
you, your, yours	you, your, yours
he, him, his	they, them, their, theirs
she, her, hers	
it, its	

REFLEXIVE AND INTENSIVE

SINGULAR	PLURAL
myself	ourselves
yourself	yourselves
himself, herself, itself	themselves
oneself	

RELATIVE

who	whoever	what	whatever	that
whom	whomever	whose	whichever	which

DEMONSTRATIVE

this, that, these, those

3. Reflexive and intensive pronouns. Pronouns ending in *-self* or *-selves* are either reflexive or intensive. **Reflexive pronouns** refer back to the subject and are necessary for sentence sense.

➤ Many of the neighbours blamed *themselves* for not reporting the unfenced swimming pool.

Intensive pronouns add emphasis to the nouns or pronouns they follow and are grammatically optional.

➤ Prime Minister Mackenzie King *himself* went to séances.

INTERROGATIVE

who	what	which
whoever	whatever	whichever
whom	whomever	whose

INDEFINITE

SINGULAR		PLURAL	SINGULAR/PLURAL
anybody	nobody	both	all
anyone	no one	few	any
anything	none	many	either
each	nothing	several	more
everybody	one		most
everyone	somebody		some
everything	someone		
much	something		
neither			

RECIPROCAL

each other

any other

4. Relative pronouns. *Who, whom, whose, that,* and *which* are relative pronouns. A **relative pronoun** relates a dependent clause—a word group containing a subject and verb and a subordinating word—to an antecedent noun or pronoun in the sentence.

dependent clause

➤ **In Kipling's story, Dravot is the man *who* would be king.**

The form of a relative pronoun varies according to its case—the grammatical role it plays in the sentence. (*For more on pronoun case, particularly distinguishing between* who *and* whom, *see Tab 8: Editing for Grammar, pp. 337–338.*)

5. Demonstrative pronouns. The **demonstrative pronouns** *this, that, these,* and *those* point out nouns and pronouns that come later.

➤ *This* **is the book literary critics have been waiting for.**

Sometimes these pronouns function as adjectives: *This book won the Pulitzer.* Sometimes they are noun equivalents: *This is my book.*

6. Interrogative pronouns. Interrogative pronouns such as *who, whatever,* and *whom* are used to ask questions.

➤ *Whatever* **happened to Baby Jane?**

The form of the interrogative pronouns *who, whom, whoever,* and *whomever* indicates the grammatical role they play in a sentence. (*See Tab 8: Editing for Grammar, pp. 337–338.*)

7. Indefinite pronouns. Indefinite pronouns such as *someone, anybody, nothing,* and *few* refer to a non-specific person or thing and do not change form to indicate person, number, or gender.

➤ *Anybody* **who wants to come and make grape jelly with me may**

take *some* **home.**

Most indefinite pronouns are always singular (*anybody, everyone*). Some are always plural (*many, few*), and a handful can be singular or plural (*any, most*). (*See Tab 8, pp. 313–314 and Tab 9, p. 366.*)

8. Reciprocal pronouns. Reciprocal pronouns such as *each other* and *one another* refer to the separate parts of their plural antecedent.

➤ **My sister and I are close because we live near** *each other.*

56d ADJECTIVES.

Adjectives modify nouns and pronouns by answering questions like *Which one? What kind? How many? What size? What colour? What condition?* and *Whose?* They can describe, enumerate, identify, define, and limit (*one person, that person*). When articles (*a, an,* and *the*) identify nouns, they function as adjectives.

Sometimes proper nouns are treated as adjectives; the proper adjectives that result are capitalized: *Britain / British.* Pronouns can also function as adjectives (*his green car*), and adjectives often have forms that allow you to make comparisons (*great, greater, greatest*).

➤ **The** *supportive* **and** *diligent* **mayor regularly attended council**

meetings. [What kind of mayor?]

➤ *These four artistic* qualities affect how an advertisement is received. [Which, how many, what kind of qualities?]

➤ *My little blue* Volkswagen died *one icy winter* morning. [Whose, what size, what colour car? Which, what kind of morning?]

Like all modifiers, adjectives should be close to the words they modify. Most often, adjectives appear before the noun they modify, but **descriptive adjectives**—adjectives that designate qualities or attributes—may come before or after the noun or pronoun they modify for stylistic reasons. Adjectives that describe the subject and follow linking verbs (*be, am, is, are, was, being, been, appear, become, feel, grow, look, make, prove, taste*) are called **subject complements**.

BEFORE THE SUBJECT

The *sick* and *destitute* poet no longer believed that love would save him.

AFTER THE SUBJECT

The poet, *sick* and *destitute,* no longer believed that love would save him.

AFTER A LINKING VERB

No longer believing that love would save him, the poet was *sick* and *destitute.*

Language Tip: *Putting adjectives in the correct order*

When several single-word adjectives precede a noun, each modifying the words that follow (*the beautiful new baby*), they are **cumulative adjectives** and do not have commas between them. Cumulative adjectives usually appear in the following order:

➤ *Two priceless small old round handmade blue Swedish wine* glasses were displayed in the cabinet.

Order of Cumulative Adjectives

1. **Limiting adjective:** *Two*
2. **Quality:** *priceless*
3. **Size:** *small*
4. **Age:** *old*

5. **Shape:** *round*
6. **Participle:** *handmade*
7. **Colour:** *blue*
8. **Origin:** *Swedish*
9. **Type:** *wine*
10. **Noun:** *glasses*

Using present and past participles as adjectives to describe feelings. The present and past participle forms of verbs that refer to feelings can also be used as adjectives. Use the past participle to describe having a feeling:

➤ *The <u>confused</u> man felt let down by the Google Maps directions.*

Use the present participle to describe what is causing the feeling:

➤ *The <u>confusing</u> Google Maps directions let the man down.*

Other past and present participle forms that often cause problems include the following:

bored / boring	*interested / interesting*
confused / confusing	*pleased / pleasing*
excited / exciting	*satisfied / satisfying*
frightened / frightening	*surprised / surprising*

56e ADVERBS.

Adverbs often end in *-ly* (*beautifully, gracefully, quietly*) and usually answer such questions as *When? Where? How? How often? How much? To what degree?* and *Why?*

Say No Only Once

In English, it only takes one negator (*no / not / never*) to change the meaning of a sentence from positive to negative. In fact, when two negatives are used together, they may seem to cancel each other out.

any
➤ **They don't have ~~no~~ reason to go there.**

➤ **The authenticity of the document is** *hotly* **contested. [How is**

it contested?]

Adverbs modify verbs, other adverbs, and adjectives. Like adjectives, adverbs can be used to compare (*less, lesser, least*). In addition to modifying individual words, they can be used to modify whole clauses. Adverbs can be placed at the beginning or end of a sentence or before the verb they modify, but they should not be placed between the verb and its direct object.

➤ **The water was** *brilliant* **blue and** *icy* **cold. [The adverbs intensify**

the adjectives *blue* **and** *cold.*]

➤ **Dickens mixed humour and pathos** *better* **than any other English**

writer after Shakespeare. [The adverb compares Dickens with

other writers.]

➤ *Consequently,* **he is still read by millions.**

Consequently is a conjunctive adverb that modifies the independent clause that follows it and shows how the sentence is related to the preceding sentence. (*For more on conjunctive adverbs, see the material on conjunctions, p. 432.*)

The negators *no, not,* and *never* are among the most common adverbs.

56f PREPOSITIONS.

Prepositions (*on, in, at, by*) usually appear as part of a **prepositional phrase**. Their main function is to allow the noun or pronoun in the phrase to modify another word in the sentence. Prepositional phrases always begin with a preposition and end with a noun, pronoun, or other word group that functions as the **object of the preposition** (in *time,* on the *table*).

A preposition can be one word (*about, despite, on*) or a word group (*according to, as well as, in spite of*). Place prepositional phrases as close as possible to the words they modify. Adjectival prepositional phrases usually appear right after the noun or pronoun they modify and answer questions like *Which one?* and *What kind of?* Adverbial phrases can appear anywhere in a sentence and answer questions like *When? Where? How?* and *Why?*

AS **ADJECTIVE**	Many types *of careers* can follow from a degree in health sciences.
AS **ADVERB**	The fire truck raced *out the door.*

Common Prepositions

about	by	near
above	by means of	of
according to	by way of	on
across	down	on account of
after	during	over
against	except	since
along	except for	through
along with	excluding	to
among	following	toward
apart from	from	under
as	in	underneath
as to	in addition to	until
as well as	in case of	up
at	in front of	up to
because of	in place of	upon
before	in regard to	via
behind	including	with
below	inside	with reference to
beside	instead of	with respect to
between	into	within
beyond	like	without

Language Tip: *Using prepositions*

Every language uses prepositions idiomatically in ways that do not match their literal meaning, which is why prepositional phrases can be difficult for many writers. In English, prepositions combine with other words in such a variety of ways that the combinations can only be learned with repetition and over time (*see pp. 428–429*).

Idiomatic uses of prepositions indicating time and location. The prepositions that indicate time and location are often the most idiosyncratic in a language. In English, the prepositions *at, by, in,* and *on* all have different uses, depending on context. The following are some common ways in which these words are used.

Time

AT   The convocation ceremony starts *at two o'clock.*
[a specific clock time]

BY   Our project plans should be ready *by next week.*
[a particular time]

IN   The concert will start *in the evening.* [a portion of the day]

ON   The job interview will take place *on May 1.* The convocation is *on Tuesday.* [a particular date or day of the week]

Location

AT   I will meet you *at the zoo.* [a particular place]
You need to turn right *at the light.* [a corner or an intersection]
We took a seat *at the table.* [near a piece of furniture]

BY   Meet me *by the fountain.* [a familiar place]

IN   Park your car *in the parking lot* and give the money to the attendant *in the booth.* [on a space of some kind or inside a structure]
I enjoyed the bratwurst *in Kitchener* at Oktoberfest. [a city, province, or other geographic location]
I found that article *in this book.* [a print medium]

ON   An excellent restaurant is located *on Temperance Street.* [a street, avenue, or other thoroughfare]
I spilled milk *on the floor.* [a surface]
I watched the report *online.* [an electronic medium]

Prepositions plus gerunds (-ing). A gerund is the *-ing* form of a verb acting as a noun. A gerund can occur after a preposition (*thanks for coming*), but when the preposition is *to,* be careful not to confuse it with the infinitive form of a verb.

INFINITIVE	I want to win at poker
	I used to win at poker.
PREPOSITION + GERUND	I look forward to winning at poker again.
	I am used to winning at poker.

Common Idiomatic Expressions in English

COMMON ADJECTIVE + PREPOSITION COMBINATIONS

afraid of: fearing someone or something
anxious about: worried
ashamed of: embarrassed by someone or something
aware of: know about
content with: having no complaints about; happy about
fond of: having positive feelings for
full of: filled with
grateful to (someone) (for something): thankful; appreciative
interested in: curious; wanting to know more about
jealous of: feeling envy toward
proud / suspicious of: pleased about/distrustful of
tired of: had enough of; bored with
responsible to (someone) (for something): accountable; in charge
satisfied with: having no complaints about

COMMON VERB + PREPOSITION COMBINATIONS

apologize to: express regret for actions
arrive in (a place): come to a city/country (*I arrived in Vancouver.*)
arrive at (an event at a specific location): come to a building or a house (*I arrived at the National Gallery at ten.*)
blame for: hold responsible; accuse
complain about: find fault; criticize
concentrate on: focus; pay attention
consist of: contain; be made of
congratulate on: offer good wishes for success
depend on: trust
explain to: make something clear to someone
insist on: be firm
laugh at: express amusement
look up: visit
rely on: trust
smile at: act friendly toward
take care of: look after; tend
thank for: express appreciation
throw to: toss something to someone to catch

throw at: toss an object toward someone or something without the intention that the object will be caught

throw (something) away: discard

throw (something) out: discard; present an idea for consideration

worry about: feel concern; fear for someone's safety or well-being

COMMON PARTICLES (verb + preposition combinations that create *verb phrasals,* expressions with meanings different from the meaning of the verb itself)

break down: stop functioning

bring up: mention in conversation; raise a child

call off: cancel

call up: contact by telephone

catch up with: reach the same place as

catch up on: get up-to-date information on

drop in on: visit unexpectedly

drop off: deliver

fill out: complete

find out: discover

get away with: avoid discovery

get off (your chest): tell a long-concealed secret or problem

get off (the couch): stand up

get over: recover

give up: surrender; stop work on

leave out: omit

look down on: despise

look forward to: anticipate

look into: research

look up: check a fact

look up to: admire

put up with: endure

run across: meet unexpectedly

run out: use up

send off: say goodbye to

stand up for: defend

take after: resemble

take off: leave the airport (a plane); miss time from work

turn down: reject

56g CONJUNCTIONS.

Conjunctions join words, phrases, or clauses and indicate their relation to each other.

1. Coordinating conjunctions. The common **coordinating conjunctions** (or **coordinators**) are *and, but, or, for, nor, yet,* and *so.* Coordinating conjunctions join elements of equal weight or function.

➤ She was strong *and* healthy.

➤ I'm free *but* I'm focused

I'm green *but* I'm wise.

[from "Hand in my Pocket," Alanis Morissette]

➤ They must have been tired, *for* they had been fighting the forest fire all day long.

2. Correlative conjunctions. The **correlative conjunctions** also link sentence elements of equal value, but they always come in pairs: *both . . . and, either . . . or, neither . . . nor,* and *not only . . . but also.*

➤ *Neither* the doctor *nor* the police believe his story.

3. Subordinating conjunctions. Common **subordinating conjunctions** (or **subordinators**) link sentence elements that are not of equal importance. They include the following words and phrases:

Subordinating Words

after	once	until
although	since	when
as	that	whenever
because	though	where
before	till	wherever
if	unless	while

Subordinating Phrases

as if	even though	in that
as soon as	even when	rather than
as though	for as much as	so that
even after	in order that	sooner than
even if	in order to	

Because subordinating conjunctions join unequal sentence parts, they are used to introduce dependent, or subordinate, clauses in a sentence.

➤ **The software will not run properly *if* the computer lacks sufficient memory.**

Using coordination and subordination appropriately. Some languages (such as Arabic, for example) favour coordination over the inclusion of subordinate clauses. In English, however, writers who rely too much on coordination tend to use *and* and *so* excessively, which becomes tiresome for readers. In other languages (such as Chinese), conjunctions occur in pairs. Be careful not to include double conjunctions, such as *although . . . but* or *because . . . so* or *even . . . also,* in the same sentence, unless you are using a standard correlative conjunction such as *either . . . or.*

INCORRECT

Although I was devastated, *but* I could not cry.

CORRECT

Although I was devastated, I could not cry.

When you use a coordinating conjunction (*and, but, or, for, nor, yet,* and *so*), make sure that you use the conjunction that expresses the relationship between the two clauses that you want to show.

NOT PRECISE

My college is close to my house, and my summer job is far away.

PRECISE

My college is close to my house, but my summer job is far away.

In the revised version, *but* shows the contrast the writer is describing.

When you use a subordinating conjunction, make sure you attach it to the clause that you want to subordinate and not to the main idea in the sentence. For example, if the main point is that commuting to school takes too much time, then the following sentence is unclear.

MAIN POINT OBSCURED	Although commuting to school takes two hours out of every day, I use the time to catch up on my reading.
MAIN POINT CLEAR	Commuting to school takes two hours out of every day, although I use the time to catch up on my reading.

(For help in punctuating sentences with conjunctions, see Tab 9: Editing for Mechanics, pp. 349 and 356.)

4. Conjunctive adverbs. Conjunctive adverbs indicate the relation between one clause and another, but unlike conjunctions (*and, but*), they are not grammatically strong enough on their own to hold the two clauses together. A period or semicolon is also needed.

➤ **Pocket calculators were in wide circulation by the 1970s;**

  ***however*, many engineers still preferred to use the slide rule.**

The most common conjunctive adverbs include the following:

accordingly	however	now
also	incidentally	otherwise
anyway	indeed	similarly
as a result	instead	specifically
besides	likewise	still
certainly	meanwhile	subsequently
consequently	moreover	suddenly
finally	nevertheless	then
furthermore	next	therefore
hence	nonetheless	thus

56h INTERJECTIONS.

Interjections are forceful expressions, usually written with an exclamation point. They are not often used in academic writing except in quotations of dialogue.

➤ **"*Wow!*" Davis said. "Are you telling me that there's a former**

  prime minister who hasn't written a book?"

➤ **Autobiographies are, *alas*, the biggest sellers.**

Parts of Sentences

57

Every complete sentence contains at least one **subject** (a noun and its modifiers) and one **predicate** (a verb and its objects, complements, and modifiers) that fit together to make a statement, ask a question, or give a command.

　　　　subject　　　　　predicate
➤ The *children solved* the puzzle.

> **Language Tip:** *Putting sentence parts in the correct order for English*
>
> In some languages (such as Spanish), it is acceptable to omit subjects; in others (such as Arabic), to omit certain kinds of verbs. Other languages (such as Japanese) place verbs last; and still others (such as Hebrew) allow verbs to precede the subject. English, however, has its own distinct order for sentence parts that most sentences follow.
>
> MODIFIERS + SUBJECT → VERB + OBJECTS, COMPLEMENTS, MODIFIERS
>
> 　　mod　　subj　　v　　　mod　　obj　　obj comp
> **The playful kitten batted the crystal glasses on the shelf.**

57a SUBJECTS.

The **simple subject** is the word or words that name the topic of the sentence; it is always a noun or pronoun. To find the subject, ask who or what the sentence is about. The **complete subject** is the simple subject plus its modifiers.

　　　　　　simple subject
➤ Did *Johnny Fairplay* give Jeff Probst the requisite respect on

　Survivor Micronesia? [Who gave Jeff Probst respect?]

　　　　　complete subject
　　　　　　　　　　simple subject
➤ *The Survivor team of Zapatera* solved the puzzle in less than five

　minutes. [Who solved the puzzle?]

A **compound subject** contains two or more simple subjects connected with a conjunction such as *and, but, or,* or *neither . . . nor.*

```
                  compound
         ┌─────────────────────────────┐
         simple            simple
```
➤ *Original thinking* and *bold design* **are characteristic of her**

work.

In **imperative sentences**, which give directions or commands, the subject *you* is usually implied, not stated. A helping verb is needed to transform an imperative sentence into a question.

➤ **[*You*] Keep this advice in mind.**

➤ ***Would* you keep this advice in mind?**

In sentences beginning with *there* or *here* followed by some form of *be,* the subject comes after the verb.

```
              simple subject
```
➤ **Here are the *remnants* of the fabric I used for my new quilt.**

Language Tip: *Including a subject (but not two)*

Every clause in English has a subject, even if it is only a stand-in subject like *there* or *it.* Check your clauses to make sure that each one has a subject.

it

NO SUBJECT   **No one thought the party could end, but**
                                                          ^

ended abruptly when the stock market

crashed.

However, do not repeat your subject.

TOO MANY   **The celebrity ~~he~~ signed my playbill.**
SUBJECTS

57b VERBS AND THEIR OBJECTS OR COMPLEMENTS.

In a sentence, the **predicate** says something about the subject. The verb constitutes the **simple predicate**. All the words (the verb plus its object or complement) in a predicate make up the **complete predicate**.

Including a complete verb. Verb structure, as well as where the verb is placed within a sentence, varies dramatically across languages, but in English each sentence needs to include at least one complete verb. *(See Chapter 56, pp. 411–416.)* The verb cannot be an infinitive—the *to* form of the verb—or an *-ing* form without a helping verb.

NOT COMPLETE	The veterinarian *to bring* the cat back from surgery.
COMPLETE VERBS	The veterinarian *brings* the cat back from surgery.
	The veterinarian *will bring* the cat back from surgery.
	The veterinarian *is bringing* the cat back from surgery.
NOT COMPLETE	Children *running* in the park.
COMPLETE VERBS	Children *are running* in the park.
	Children *have been running* in the park.
	Children *will be running* in the park.

Verb functions in sentences. According to how they function in sentences, verbs are *linking, transitive,* or *intransitive.* The kind of verb determines what elements the complete predicate must include and therefore determines the correct order of sentence parts. Most meaningful English sentences use one of five basic sentence patterns.

1. SUBJECT + LINKING VERB + SUBJECT COMPLEMENT

   Canadians are friendly people.

2. SUBJECT + TRANSITIVE VERB + DIRECT OBJECT

   The police officer caught the jaywalker.

3. SUBJECT + TRANSITIVE VERB + INDIRECT OBJECT + DIRECT OBJECT

   The officer gave the jaywalker a ticket.

4. SUBJECT + TRANSITIVE VERB + DIRECT OBJECT + OBJECT COMPLEMENT

   The ticket made the jaywalker unhappy.

5. SUBJECT + INTRANSITIVE VERB

   She sighed.

1. Linking verbs and subject complements. A **linking verb** joins a subject to a piece of further information about the subject that is located on the other side of the verb. That piece of information is called the **subject complement.** The subject complement may be a noun, a pronoun, or an adjective.

>   subj   lv   comp
> **Ann Yearsley was** *a farmer.*

The most frequently used linking verb is the *be* verb (*is, are, was, were*), but verbs such as *seem, look, appear, feel, become, smell, sound,* and *taste* can also function as links between a sentence's subject and its complement.

>   subj   lv   comp
> **That hot blueberry pie** *smells* **wonderful.**

2. Transitive verbs and direct objects. A **transitive verb** identifies an action that the subject performs or does to somebody or something else—the receiver of the action, or **direct object**. To complete its meaning, a transitive verb needs a direct object in the predicate. Direct objects are usually nouns, pronouns, or word groups that act like nouns or pronouns.

NOUN	I threw *the ball.*
PRONOUN	I threw *it* over a fence.
WORD GROUP	I put *what I needed* into my backpack.

Most often, the subject is doing the action, the direct object is being acted upon, and the transitive verb is in the **active voice.**

>   subj   tv   dir obj
> ACTIVE   **Writers sometimes consider their** *readers*
>   **essential to the writing process.**

If the verb in a sentence can be in the active voice, it can be in the **passive voice** as well. In the following revised sentence, the direct object (*children*) has become the subject; the original subject (*parents*) is introduced with the preposition *by* and is now part of a prepositional phrase.

> PASSIVE   Readers are considered essential by writers.

Language Tip: *Including only one direct object*

In English, a transitive verb takes a direct object, which must be explicit. For example, *Take it!* is a complete sentence but *Take!* is not, even if *it* is clearly implied. Be careful not to repeat the object, especially if the object includes a relative adverb (*where, when, how*) or a relative pronoun (*which, who, what*), even if the relative pronoun does not appear in the sentence but is only implied.

➤ **I won't care if I can be here on the street** *where* **you**

live ~~there.~~

3. Transitive verbs, indirect objects, and direct objects. **Indirect objects** name to whom an action was done or for whom it was completed and are most commonly used with verbs such as *give, ask, tell, sing,* and *write.*

<pre>   subj   v   ind obj   dir obj</pre>
➤ **Jursson wrote *Anika* a heartrending letter.**

Note that indirect objects appear after the verb but before the direct object.

4. Transitive verbs, direct objects, and object complements. In addition to a direct object and an indirect object, a transitive verb can take another element in its predicate: an **object complement**. An object complement describes or renames the direct object it follows.

<pre>   dir obj   obj comp</pre>
➤ **His investment in Research in Motion made Johnson *a rich man.***

5. Intransitive verbs. An **intransitive verb** describes an action by a subject, but it is not an action that is done directly to anything or anyone else. Therefore, an intransitive verb cannot take an object or a complement. However, adverbs and adverb phrases often appear in predicates built around intransitive verbs. In the sentence that follows, the complete predicate is in italics and the intransitive verb is underlined.

➤ **As a ballet school student, I *complied with the dress code***

mandating long hair.

Some verbs, such as *cooperate, assent, disappear,* and *insist,* are always intransitive. Others, such as *increase, grow, roll,* and *work,* can be either transitive or intransitive.

	tv
TRANSITIVE	I *grow* carrots and celery in my victory garden.
	iv
INTRANSITIVE	My son *grows* taller every week.

Using the dictionary to determine prepositions and transitive and intransitive verbs. Your dictionary will note if a verb is *v.i.* (intransitive), *v.t.* (transitive), or both. It will also tell you—or show by example—the appropriate preposition to use when you are modifying an intransitive verb with an adverbial phrase. For example, we may *accede* to a rule, but if and when we *comply,* it has to be *with* something or someone.

58 Phrases and Dependent Clauses

A **phrase** is a group of related words that lacks either a subject or a predicate or both. Phrases function within sentences but not on their own. A **dependent clause** has a subject and a predicate but cannot function as a complete sentence because it begins with a subordinating word.

58a NOUN PHRASES.

A **noun phrase** consists of a noun or noun substitute plus all of its modifiers. Noun phrases can function as a sentence's subject, object, or subject complement.

SUBJECT	It was *a dark and stormy night.*
OBJECT	Greg cooked *an authentic, delicious haggis* for the Robbie Burns dinner.
SUBJECT COMPLEMENT	Tom became *an accomplished and well-known cook.*

58b VERB PHRASES AND VERBALS.

A **verb phrase** is a verb plus its helping verbs. It functions as the predicate in a sentence. **Verbals** are words derived from verbs. They function as nouns, adjectives, or adverbs, not as verbs.

VERBAL AS NOUN	*Debating* is a key job requirement for lawyers.
VERBAL AS ADJECTIVE	Aida enjoyed watching the *talking* heads who commented on the news.
VERBAL AS ADVERB	The professor began *to talk.*

Verbals may take modifiers, objects, and complements to form **verbal phrases**. There are three kinds of verbal phrases: participial, gerund, and infinitive.

1. Participial phrases. A **participial phrase** begins with either a present participle (the *-ing* form of a verb) or a past participle (the *-ed* or *-en* form of a verb). Participial phrases always function as adjectives.

➤ *Working in groups,* **the engineers solved the problem of how to get Apollo 13 back to Earth.**

➤ *Inspired by his lecture,* **Elisabeth decided that she needed to work with Dr. Suzuki.**

➤ **His favourite mug,** *broken into two pieces,* **could be glued but would never be the same again.**

2. Gerund phrases. A **gerund phrase** uses the *-ing* form of the verb, just as some participial phrases do. But gerund phrases always function as nouns, not adjectives.

subj
➤ *Walking one hour a day* **will keep you fit.**

dir obj
➤ **The instructor praised** *my acting in both scenes.*

3. Infinitive phrases. An **infinitive phrase** is formed using the infinitive, or *to* form, of a verb: *to be, to do, to live.* It can function as an adverb, an adjective, or a noun and can be the subject, subject or object complement, or direct object in a sentence.

noun/subj
➤ *To finish his novel* **was his greatest ambition.**

adj/obj comp
➤ **He made many efforts *to finish his novel* for his publisher.**

adv/dir obj
➤ **He needed *to finish his novel.***

58c APPOSITIVE PHRASES.

Appositives rename nouns or pronouns and appear right after the word they rename.

noun ┌─────── appositive ───────┐
➤ **One researcher, *the widely respected R. S. Smith,* has shown that**

a child's performance on such tests can be very inconsistent.

58d ABSOLUTE PHRASES.

Absolute phrases modify an entire sentence. They include a noun or pronoun, a participle, and their related modifiers, objects, or complements.

➤ **The sheriff strode into the bar, *his hands hovering over his***

pistols.

58e DEPENDENT CLAUSES.

Although **dependent clauses** (also known as **subordinate clauses**) have a subject and predicate, they cannot stand alone as complete sentences. They are introduced by subordinators—either by a subordinating conjunction such as *after, in order to, since (for a more complete listing, see p. 432)* or by a relative pronoun such as *who, which,* or *that (for more, see box on pp. 420–421)*. They function in sentences as adjectives, adverbs, or nouns.

1. Adjective clauses. An **adjective clause** modifies a noun or pronoun. Relative pronouns (*who, whom, whose, which,* or *that*) or relative adverbs (*where, when*) are used to connect adjective clauses to the nouns or pronouns they modify. The relative pronoun usually follows the word that is being modified and also serves to point back to the noun or pronoun. *(For help with punctuating restrictive and non-restrictive clauses, see Tab 9, pp. 350–351 and 357–358.)*

➤ Odysseus' journey, *which can be traced on modern maps*, has

inspired many works of literature.

In adjective clauses, the direct object sometimes comes before rather than after the verb.

dir obj   subj   v

➤ The Sudoku player *whom she most wanted to beat* was

catlover79.

2. Adverb clauses.

An **adverb clause** modifies a verb, an adjective, or an adverb and answers the questions adverbs answer: *When? Where? What? Why?* and *How?* Adverb clauses are often introduced by subordinators (*after, when, before, because, although, if, though, whenever, where, wherever*).

➤ *After we had talked for an hour*, he began to get nervous.

➤ He reacted *as if he already knew.*

3. Noun clauses.

A **noun clause** is a dependent clause that functions as a noun. Often the noun clause is so essential that without it, the independent clause would be incomplete. In a sentence, a noun clause may serve as the subject, object, or complement and is usually introduced by a relative pronoun (*who, which, that*) or a relative adverb (*how, what, where, when, why*).

SUBJECT	*What he saw* shocked him.
OBJECT	The instructor found out *who had skipped class.*
COMPLEMENT	The book was *where I had left it.*

As in an adjective clause, in a noun clause the direct object or subject complement can come first, violating the typical sentence order.

dir obj   subj

➤ The veterinarian wondered *to whom he* should address his

remarks.

Understanding the purposes and constructions of *if* clauses.

If clauses (also called **conditional clauses**) state facts, make predictions, and speculate about unlikely or impossible events. These conditional constructions most often employ *if,* but *when, unless,* or other words can introduce conditional constructions as well.

- Use the present tense for facts. When the relationship you are describing is usually true, the verbs in both clauses should have the same tense.

  STATES FACTS

  If people *practise* doing good consistently, they *have* a sense of satisfaction.

  Whenever Deepika *found* a new Bollywood film, she always *talked* about it incessantly.

- In a sentence that predicts, the verb in the *if* clause is in the present tense. The verb in the independent clause is a modal plus the base form of the verb.

  PREDICTS POSSIBILITIES

  If you *practise* doing good through politics, you *will have* a greater effect on your community.

- If you are speculating about something that is unlikely to happen, use the past tense in the *if* clause and *could, should,* or *would* plus the base verb in the independent clause.

  SPECULATES ON THE UNLIKELY

  If you *were* a better person, you *would practise* doing good every day.

- Use the past perfect tense in the *if* clause if you are speculating about an event that did not happen. In the independent clause, use *could have, might have,* or *would have* plus the past participle.

  SPECULATES ON SOMETHING THAT DID NOT HAPPEN

  If you *had practised* doing good when you were young, you *would have been* a different person today.

- Use *were* in the *if* clause and *could, might,* or *would* plus the base form in the main clause if you are speculating about something that could never happen.

  SPECULATES ABOUT THE IMPOSSIBLE

  If Riel were alive today, he would continue to fight for the rights of indigenous peoples.

Types of Sentences

Sentences can be classified by the number of clauses they contain and how those clauses are joined. This method of classification results in four types of sentences: simple, compound, complex, and compound-complex. Sentences can also be classified by the purpose they fulfill: declarative, interrogative, imperative, and exclamatory.

59a SENTENCE STRUCTURES.

A clause is a group of related words that includes a subject and a predicate. Some clauses are independent; others are dependent, or subordinate. **Independent clauses** can stand on their own as complete sentences. **Dependent**, or **subordinate**, **clauses** cannot stand alone. They function in sentences as adjectives, adverbs, or nouns. The presence of one or both of these two types of clauses, and their relation to each other, determines whether the sentence is simple, compound, complex, or compound-complex.

1. Simple sentences. A simple sentence is composed of only one independent clause. Simple does not necessarily mean short, however. Although a simple sentence does not include any dependent clauses, it may have several embedded phrases, a compound subject, and a compound predicate. No matter how long it is, however, a sentence that has only one independent clause is, grammatically speaking, a simple sentence.

INDEPENDENT CLAUSE

The bloodhound is the oldest known breed of dog.

INDEPENDENT CLAUSE: COMPOUND SUBJ + COMPOUND PRED

Historians, novelists, short-story writers, and playwrights write about characters, design plots, and usually seek the dramatic resolution of a problem.

2. Compound sentences. A compound sentence contains two or more coordinated independent clauses but no dependent clause. The independent clauses may be joined by a comma and a coordinating conjunction or by a semicolon with or without a conjunctive adverb.

➤ **The police arrested him for drunk driving,** *so* **he lost his car.**

➤ The sand blasts the pyramids on a regular basis; *therefore*, they have eroded over time.

3. Complex sentences. A complex sentence contains one independent clause and one or more dependent clauses.

independent clause   dependent clause

➤ He consulted the dictionary *because he did not know how to pronounce the word.*

4. Compound-complex sentences. A compound-complex sentence contains two or more coordinated independent clauses and at least one dependent clause (italicized in the example).

➤ She believed that the movie was too violent, but her son, *who likes to watch action movies*, thought she was wrong.

59b SENTENCE PURPOSES.

When you write a sentence, your purpose helps you decide which sentence type to use. If you want to provide information, you usually use a declarative sentence. If you want to ask a question, you usually use an interrogative sentence. To make a request or give an order (a command), you use the imperative. An exclamatory sentence emphasizes a point or expresses strong emotion.

DECLARATIVE	He watches *Corner Gas* reruns.
INTERROGATIVE	Does he watch *Corner Gas* reruns?
IMPERATIVE	You must watch reruns of *Corner Gas*.
EXCLAMATORY	I'm really looking forward to watching *Corner Gas* reruns with you!

CREDITS

Text credits

Page 24 Concept Map for honeybees. Innovations, 2007: Tim FisherPoff/Office of Communications and Marketing, Virginia Tech College of Agriculture and Life Sciences.

Page 26 Sketch of three babies under a blanket, The McGraw-Hill Companies, Inc.

Page 50 Synonyms for "influence." Entry for the word "influence" from ROGET'S THESAURUS, 4TH EDITION, REVISED by ROBERT L. CHAPMAN. Copyright © 1977 by Harper & Row, Publishers, Inc. Reprinted by permission of HarperCollins Publishers; Definition of "charisma." From *Canadian Oxford Dictionary 2nd edition.* © Oxford University Press Canada 2004. Reprinted By Permission of the Publisher.

Page 54 Rolling Around In My Head blog available at <http://www.davehingsburger.blogspot.com/>.

Page 60 June 18 article from *AviationNow.com Insider.* Used by permission of the publisher.

Page 63 "Canadian provincial labour markets—April 2010," adapted from Statistics Canada website <http://www40.statcan.gc.ca/l01/cst01/lfss01a-eng.htm> (September 2010).

Page 65 "Structure of the Ontario Economy, 2009 percent share of GDP," based on Statistics Canada data and retrieved on Ontario Ministry of Finance, 2011 at this address: <http://www.fin.gov.on.ca/en/economy/ecaccts/eca.pdf>; © Queen's Printer for Ontario, 2011. Reproduced with permission; "Exports and Imports of Processed Coffee, 1999-2009," based on Statistics Canada data and retrieved on Agriculture Canada Website <http://www4.agr.gc.ca/AAFC-AAC/display-afficher.do?id=1172237152079&lang=eng>.

Page 66 Chart 12.2: "Greenhouse gas emissions, 1990 to 2004" adapted from Government of Canada, 2006, Canadian Environmental Sustainability Indicators, Catalogue 16-251-XIE2006000; Diagram of the Supreme Court of Canada's appeal process. Source: <www.scc-csc.gc.ca/stat/html/proc-eng.asp> Statistics 2000 to 2010 (Ottawa: Supreme Court of Canada, 2010), p. 3. Reproduced with the permission of the Supreme Court of Canada, 2011.

INDEX

FOCUS ON LANGUAGE INDEX